My Vermonters
The Northeast Kingdom
1800-1940

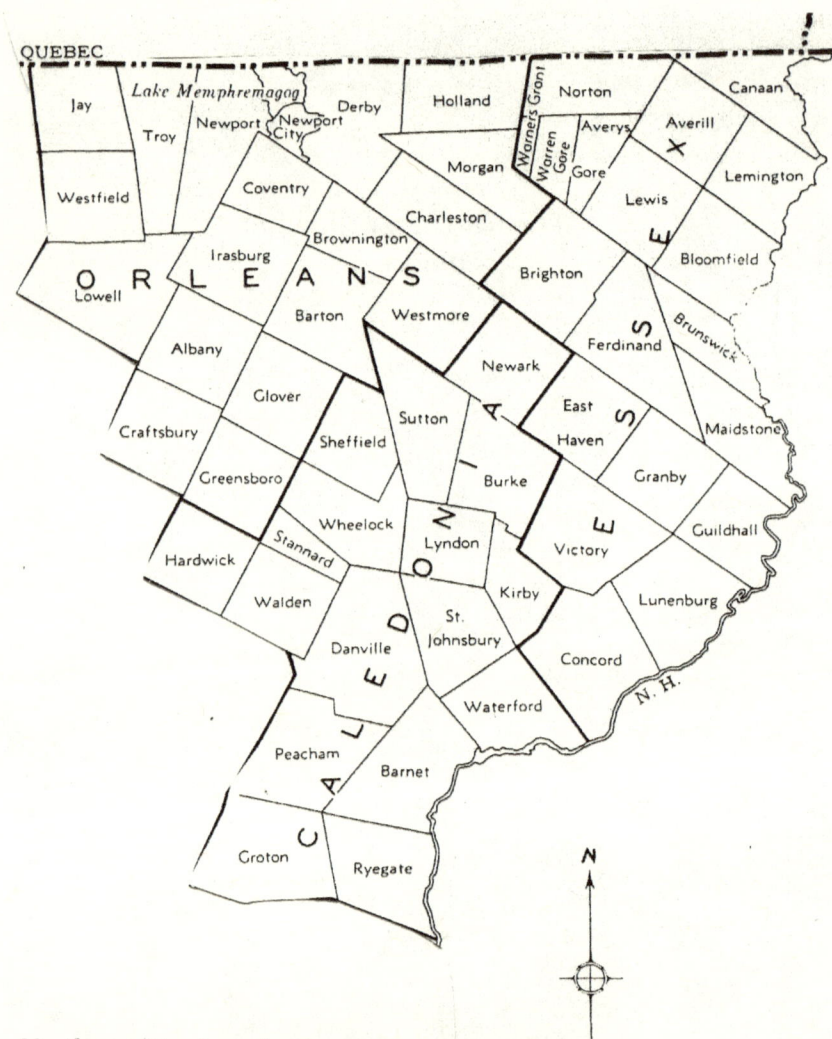

The Northeast Kingdom showing its counties and towns.
Source: The original county and township map was produced by The Vermont Almanach. *It has been widely distributed over the years with this version deriving from* Vermont: A Bibliography of its History: Volume Four of Bibliographies of New England, *edited by D. Seymour (G. K. Hall, Boston, 1981.)*

My Vermonters
The Northeast Kingdom
1800-1940

Roger Lee Emerson
of
Barton, Vermont
and London, Ontario

The Grimsay Press
2016

Published by:

The Grimsay Press
An imprint of Zeticula Ltd
Unit 13
196 Rose Street
Edinburgh, EH2 4AT
Scotland

http://www.thegrimsaypress.co.uk

First published in 2016

Text © Roger L. Emerson 2016
Cover photograph: What the Emersons thought was the nicest view in the Northeast Kingdom. *The picture was taken in the late 1930s by a family member but coloured by Max Derrick of Orleans.*
© Roger L. Emerson 2016

Paperback ISBN 978-1-84530-157-6

Hardback ISBN 978-1-84530-159-0

All rights reserved.   No reproduction, copy or transmission of this publication may be made without prior written permission.

For Lois and the late Charles Barrows
with fond memories and thanks for so much.

Orleans County.
Source: *F. W. Beers, Atlas of Lamoile and Orleans Counties, Vt. (F. W. Beers & Co., New York, 1878).*

Acknowledgements

No book like this can be written without the help of others. To the Town Clerks of Albany, Craftsbury, Sutton, and Burke - Debra Ann Geoffrey, Yvette Brown, Debora Gutteriez Ogden, and Priscilla Aldrich - I am grateful for their help and generosity. Others at Craftsbury Academy and Lyndon Institute, in Lyndonville, have graciously answered questions. I am also indebted to Enoch Rowell of Albany for allowing me to read an account book which he owns which once belonged to Jabez Page. Paul Patrick Daniels and James Oliver of Albany and Joan Alexander of Glover have kindly made available papers in their possession or keeping. Without the gift of manuscripts by the late Rosemary Rogers of Lantana, Florida, it would not have been possible to write this book. I am also in debt to my cousins, Cynthia Emerson Washer of Barton, and the late Eldon Sanders of East Hartford, Connecticut, for genealogical and other information. I regret that neither Rosemary nor Eldon have lived to read it. Other sources are noted below. Images, postcards, and maps are mostly from my collections; those belonging to others have been acknowledged in the captions.

I owe rather different debts to others. Among them are former colleagues at the Department of History in The University of Western Ontario. The late Frederick A. Dreyer read early drafts of three essays and, with good-humored sarcasm, acerbically corrected my errors - as he did for nearly forty years. Jean Matthews, Thomas Guinsburg, J. Neville Thompson, and Donald Hair have read all or parts of the manuscript and provided insights or criticisms. Arthur and Eugenia Kaledin of Cambridge and Lexington, Massachusetts, have constantly goaded me to get these essays written. In Vermont, Lois and the late Charles Barrows of Glover; Darlene Young of Barton, and Breck Viets, Charles Morrissey, Allen Davis, and Elizabeth Dow of Hardwick, have been helpful in many ways. So too have other friends such as Ronald Black, Neil Hultin, Frits van Holthoon, Esther Mijers, Nina Reid-Maroney, Jerry Mulcahy, and Mark Spencer. They, too, have made suggestions which have improved my book. To the living, I express my thanks; the dead, I remember with affection and thanks.

I am indebted, for permission to quote from their manuscripts or to use images, to the Albany Historical Society, Albany, Vermont; to the Old Stone House, Brownington, Vermont; to the Hardwick Historical Museum, Hardwick, Vermont; to the University Press of New England, to the Map Libraries of the University of Western Ontario and the Bailey/Howe Library, and the University of Vermont. Credits appear with the items used.

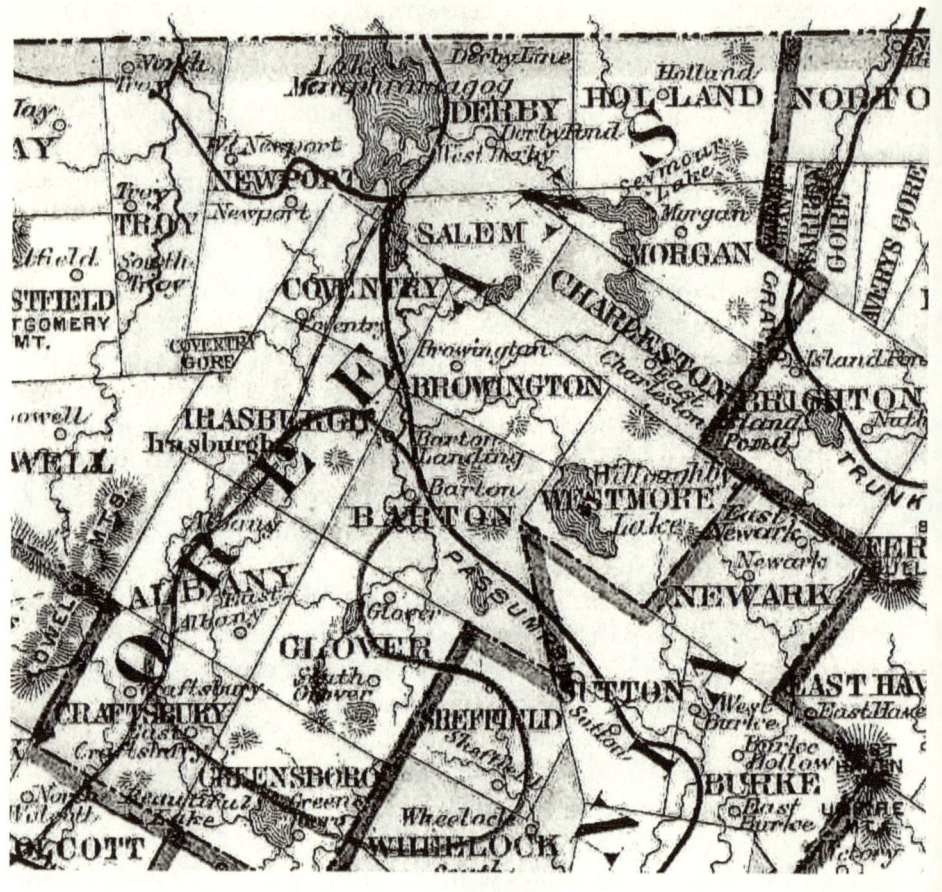

Barton and its neighbours
Source: Beers, 1878.

Contents

Acknowledgements		vii
Maps		xi
Illustrations		xiii
Preface		xxi
Notes on this Text		xxvii
I	Family Stories	1
II	Other Lines, Other Tales	29
III	Getting Gear, Accumulating Objects	53
	Appendix to Chapter III	90
IV	What's in a Name?	95
	Appendix to Chapter IV: Vermont Names	106
V	Jabez Page: 8 October 1793-25 November 1876	114
VI	Leonard Watson (c. 1835-1912): Rail-hand, Farmer, and Jack-of-all-trades	135
VII	The Education of a Vermont girl: Mary Abby Tenney (1847-1914)	166
VIII	A Few of Mary Abby's friends: Teenage Life, 1862-1868	180
IX	Robbie Rogers (1870-1896)	198
X	The Courtship of Jennie Rogers (1868-1963)	221
XI	Campfires and Other Matters: The Civil War and the Glover, Vermont, Grand Army of the Republic (GAR) Post No. 16, the Mason Post	236
	Appendix I: Memorial Day in Albany, Vermont	248
	Appendix II: The Talks Given in the Post and at Campfires, 1894-1915	250
XII	Another Farmer's Life: Arthur Frank Emerson (1896-1939)	254

Epilogue	329
Select Bibliography	340
Notes	348
Indices	379
Selected Names	379
Selected Subjects	383

Maps

The Northeast Kingdom showing its counties and towns.	ii
Orleans County.	vi
Barton and its neighbours.	viii
Albany in 1878.	7
West Albany in 1878. Isaac Sanders's store is shown on the map as is his house. Just off it, to the northwest, was the mill of Alden Darling which drew power from the Mill Brook as did the starch factory. Other enterprises used the Black River.	8
Craftsbury in 1878. The Ira Sanders farm, then held by G. D. Bagley, is in the top northeast section. Being a taxpayer in Craftsbury meant his children could go free to Craftsbury Academy in North Craftsbury, now called Craftsbury Common.	9
Craftsbury Village and its watercourse. Source: Beers, 1878.	10
East Craftsbury in 1878. Craftsbury Common was the site of the Academy and of the best stores. East Craftsbury had the Presbyterian Church.	12
North Craftsbury.	13
Mill Village in 1878. Craftsbury had water to power shops and mills as did Mill Village.	13
Irasburg in 1859. This town, built around a common, was small but a shire town in the centre of the county. It was named for Ira Allen, to whom its land had been sold and who helped to develop it. In 1859, it had the county court, three resident lawyers, a printer and newspaper, two physicians, a bank, and several mills and shops. Unlike Albany and Craftsbury, but like Danville, also a shire town, there was little in its hinterland but farms.	16

Irasburg, 1878. 17

Barton Landing [now the village of Orleans]. This was the second village in the township and was called 'the Landing' because it was the southern point to which boats could come from Lake Memphremagog. Its railhead was as important to the area as the one in Barton village. 30

Brownington, 1878. 51

Barton in 1859. The shops and manufacturers follow the course of the outlet from Crystal Lake. The Railroad had reached the town but not gone beyond it. 56

Township of Barton. The Emerson farm is in the northeast corner of the map. 57

The riverside by 1878 now had about a dozen mills and shops. Many operated into the 1920s and several were reopened during World War II. 58

Coventry Falls. These villages are examples of two kinds of developments in the Northeast Kingdom. Where there was water power, tanneries, fulling and other mills followed stream courses. Villages about a common tended to be at the intersections of roads and their shops made things from wood, cloth, and leather which required skills but little power. 119

Troy Village. 120

Sutton. Leonard Watson's house is shown between the two roads on the lower right. His uncle Henry Esterbrooks's house is the last on the road to Lyndonville. 139

Illustrations

Lottie Harriman (1870–1960) and her cousin, Jennie Rogers Sanders (1868- 1963), story-tellers.   xxviii

Lottie Harriman c. 1890.   4

Craftesbury Business Directory   11

Hayden House c. 1915.   20

Hayden House and Grounds c. 1918.   21

The family of William Henry Hayden (c. 1890).   23

Craftsbury's 'laird', Miss Jean Simpson.   27

Business Directory for selected Orleans County towns, 1859.   28

Amanda Sanders c. 1920.   31

Amanda's Methodist Church in Albany, c. 1900.   32

Amanda's Sanders flow-blue china and stoneware   33-34

Statue of Hannah Duston in Haverhill, Massachusetts.   36

Jonathan Emerson (1829-1908) and his second wife, Betsy(?-?) and the Emerson pewter charger (c. 1720).   38

Margaret Russell's Phillips Academy paper of 1849.   40

John Russell's teacups with deep saucers, English, c. 1810.   41

Benjamin Emerson about the time he went to war in 1862.   42

Benjamin Emerson's letters home, 1863 showing some of the horrors endured by men on both sides.   44-47

Regular Meeting of Mason Post 16, GAR.   48

Benjamin Emerson's Boss and Buckle.	49
Views of the Columbian Exposition.	50
Business Directory for Barton, 1878.	59-60
The still-standing Rogers house.	61
A Rogers house bedroom, c. 1900.	62
Kerosene lamps such as this were used in the Rogers house.	63
Elizabeth [Lizzie] Darling Rogers.	64
Mary Abby Rogers (c. 1888).	65
Napkin rings of the Rogers Family.	66
Some Rogers silver.	67
View of a party at the Rogers farm in c. 1910.	68
An 1889 bill from Jordan, Marsh & Co., Boston, for cloth.	69
Day Book page for Christmas Day 1867.	70
This Aladdin house was built in Newport in 1912.	72
A page from the extensive Aladdin House catalog.	73
This cover of the facsimile of the 1897 Sears Catalogue.	74
The highchair shown dates from c. 1890.	75
This toy cannon was said to be made in the South c. 1860-65.	76
These objects belonged mostly to Jennie Rogers.	77
Silhouettes of Jennie Rogers Sanders and Cornelius Rogers.	77

Bible Characters, A Question and Answer Game.	78
Nature cards for children, c. 1900.	79
Rebus cards dating from the 1870s.	80
This shows a Barton Band member, H. B. Orcutt.	81
The Albany Town Band in 1905.	82
A book mostly about clothes and adornments.	83
Songs in this collection included twelve Scottish, several German and some English.	83
This album was purchased to hold 94 postcards and brochures.	84
The photograph album belonged to the Emerson family.	84
Colourful trade cards advertised the shops at which Mary Abby bought souvenirs in 1906.	85
Mary Abby visited another oriental curio shop in Los Angeles.	85
Gold filled watch chain purchased by Alden H. Darling.	87
Jennie Rogers's jewellery.	87
The Rogers family 'road wagon'.	88
This postcard shows the Barton Fair Grounds.	89
A quarterly telephone bill from 1901.	89
This note, probably issued by Jabez Page and his wife.	114
Bill drawn on Jabez Page for $5.50 which was owed by Asa Glines.	116
Jabez Page's 1854 Commission to be a County Justice of the Peace.	125

Jabez Page (1793-1876).	126
Orphenia Page (1806-1860).	127
Lyman P. Tenney, J. P., c. 1870s.	131
This thin mid-nineteenth century glass holds 3.5 ounces.	134
Sugaring.	141
Sugaring.	142
A snow roller used on highways.	144
Unpacked snow could be very deep and a problem to horses.	148
'Camp Meeting' in Lyndonville.	151
The diary pages which give the account of Bradbury Watson's death and funeral.	153
The Watson family monument in Sutton showing the face dedicated to Bradbury Watson.	154
The Bennington Monument from a postcard sent in 1908.	160
The Old Stone house in the late 19th century.	161
One of the electric trains running along the Maine coast c. 1900.	162
One of Newport's two ports.	163
The American Sunday School Union published books and periodicals for children and adults.	167
Memoir of Florence Kidder.	168
The Question Book.	169
J. N. Pine, Mary Pine's father.	172

Mary Abby's Musical Association ticket from before 1875	173
Delia Darling Honey c. 1869.	176
Mary Pine's 'beau' come a courting with his dog.	185-186
Greek antiquity vied with that of Romans and the Hebrews in academic settings.	193
Robbie and Jennie Rogers, c. 1872.	199
Robbie's toy gun.	201
The three foot long yoke, painted with red lead paint.	201
Craftsbury Academy as it was rebuilt after the 1879 fire.	204
An illustration from Fish's *Arithmetic*.	205
The contents pages of Fish's *Arithmetic*.	206
Ribbon worn by supporters of Benjamin Harrison.	211
This Singing School ticket dates from c. 1890.	213
Albany, c. 1918. The view of the town had not much changed for many years.	215
The Rogers store, c. 1900.	216
This programme is typical of the events at which Ira enjoyed appearing throughout his life.	224
Three Academy girls: Grace Gibbs, Jennie Rogers, and Clara Reed.	227
One of the rooms at the Darling Inn.	228
Amanda Sanders' wedding gift to her son and his wife.	230
The wedding photographs of Jennie and Ira Sanders.	231

The Sanders farmhouse c. 1910.	233
Ira Sanders' round barn finished in 1907.	234
The Sanders family in their parlor, c. 1910.	235
Major Murray Clement of Waltham, Massachusetts.	238
Mason Post GAR Minutes of 17 May 1894.	240
The Union House was an old posting hotel.	241
Christmas card mailed by Arthur's Barton relatives in Barton on December 24 and received that day or the next.	257
Arthur Emerson's report cards for the third, fifth, and ninth grades.	258
Attendance card, Hardwick Elementary School, c. 1906.	259
The Ninth Grade Graduates at Hardwick Graded School in 1912.	260
Arthur Emerson's Ninth Grade Graduation Certificate	261
Academies published annual guides. This is one from Hardwick Academy c. 1915.	262
Arthur's Women's Christian Temperance Union medal for 'Declamation', c. 1914.	263
Frank Emerson's Granite Shed in 1909 and 1910	265-266
Frank Emerson's badge and work crew, date unknown.	267
The Emerson Farm c. 1915.	268
Four views of Lyndonville in 1912.	270-271
The smaller park and Depot Street, Lyndonville, c. 1910.	272
Lyndon Center.	273

The Vail Mansion was built almost haphazardly by continuous additions.	273
Milk room friends. Arthur is on the right.	274
This is one of a set of fifteen or so pictures of the team taken in front of their dormitory in 1916.	276
The Lyndon Aggie.	277
Arthur with his friend Lyman Morrill.	278
Vermont Agricultural School dorm rooms, 1916.	280
It looks as if Arthur was the 'M. C.' for this Phoney musical group.	281
Matheson Hall, the girls' dormitory at Lyndon Institute.	282
One of Arthur's surviving dance programs.	285
Menu and Toasts for the Alumni Banquet.	288
Watch Fob purchased by men graduating in 1916 from The Vail Agricultural School.	290
Dan and Daisy hitched to pull logs or draw a machine.	292
The sugar label used by Frank A. Emerson (c. 1922).	293
Arthur's sugar labels from 1938 and 1934.	294
Top House. Mount Moosilaukee is now known for its skiing.	296
Grange Badge of Arthur Emerson or his father, Frank.	297
Arthur's Masonic Penny.	301
Induction Notice.	302
Courting Couple, c. 1931.	305

Anxious new father, 1934.   306

Portrait photograph by Max Derick, 1937/38.   308

Barton Farmers' Day 1934.   314-315

Barton Farmers' Day 1937.   316-318

One of the organizers of the Farm Day, Mr Nute, in his general store.
                                                                 319

Some of the items in Arthur's billfold when he died.   325-7

Centennial moulded-glass goblets.   339

Preface

I am a Vermonter in spirit but I have not lived year-round in the State since 1946. My mother, Doris Sanders Brennan Emerson (1894-1994), continued to make her home there so I returned frequently until her death. For a while, I owned a property in Albany, and a building site and summer place in Barton, which is still my US voting address.[1] I go back each year to see a few old friends, visit the local bookstores, the Old Stone House in Brownington, and to buy my maple syrup. Then, I drive south to Hanover, New Hampshire, for a look at the town where I went to school from 1946 until I graduated from Dartmouth College in 1956. After that, I generally drive to Boston, where I was a graduate student and a teacher for several years. I cherish my long roots in New England but I know a good deal about two other societies – Canada, where I have lived and worked since 1964, and Scotland, on whose history I have written five books. I am a social and intellectual historian who began college teaching in 1961. My beat was, is, the European Enlightenment, particularly its Scottish versions (c. 1680-1830), and, secondarily, British intellectual and social history c. 1660-1830. Most of my teaching career was spent in the History Department of The University of Western Ontario, from which I retired in 1999.

Through the years, I have read some New England and Vermont history. Being at the end of two family lines, I have also inherited many boxes of family papers, pictures, and books which I have been sorting through before they go into an archive in Vermont. It seemed to me that I needed to make something of that material before it was deposited somewhere. Having an archive in my spare room means that a fellow who has done so much archival research will not lack for work in retirement when there are no travel grants and age makes travel increasingly difficult. I have enough materials to keep me busy as long as I can work.

In 2002, I was given two boxes of family papers which had belonged to my maternal grandmother's Scots-Irish family named Rogers. Among the items was a small box full of receipts and letters dealing with Jabez Page (1796-1876), the grandfather of Mary Abby Tenney Rogers (1847-1914). Mary Abby became the second wife of Cornelius Rogers (1841-1919) and thus my maternal grandmother's step-mother. Mary Abby was a diarist who kept daily reminder diaries from 1862-1914. I have a run of her diaries which covers forty-seven, years, most

xxi

of which are complete. Day by day, her diary entries are not impressive (*e.g.*, 'rained, Cornelius took in sap buckets today. Mother and father Rogers here for supper. We all went to the social in the evening – good time') but, *in toto*, they are interesting because they show patterns of life and changes to them during the period she kept them. From time to time, they contain moments of drama and excitement. That is true of eight others kept by her father, son, husband, and another relative. Those are augmented by scrap books made by Mary Abby and by others kept by my grandmother, Jennie Lena Rogers Sanders (1868-1963). In addition, there are more letters from this grandmother to her children and to me. That material is supplemented by items from grandmother's cousin, Lottie Rogers Harriman (1870-1960). Those include a small packet of papers which she wrote in the 1950s. I wish she had given me the much larger collection of old deeds and documents, letters and papers which she threw out and others which she sent to the Vermont Historical Society in Barre, Vermont. What survives there, I have read and used. I also have a few books collected by the Rogers family which range from chapbooks, to textbooks, reference works, poetry, and a few novels. My maternal grandfather, Ira D. Sanders (1863-1946) left a few items as did other members of his family.

Another body of family materials was provided by my mother. Until she went to a nursing home (1988), she never threw anything out. Like her mother, she had room to store papers, including most of her checks and checkbooks from 1913 to 1992. From her, I have eleven legal-sized document boxes of old papers, photographs, postcards and letters – and the oddments of a long and often unhappy life. To keep her as sane as it was possible to do in her paranoiac old age, I tried to get her to write an autobiography. That was a task which she resisted but on which she worked for years. The result was a number of short autobiographical pieces. Some were published, principally in the *Vermont Folklore Magazine.* In the end, my mother wrote a good deal about her life and left a small horde which documents her youth, schooling, times as a young teacher, as a wife, as a hairdresser, and as an employee in various schools and summer camps. She wrote verses all her life beginning at age eleven and, finally, wrote, somewhat humourously, about herself as an elderly person living in a nursing home. Her writing is parallelled, in part, by another manuscript left by her brother, Leslie Ward Sanders (1891-1980). He started to write his 'memoirs' but stopped when he discovered that his family was not much interested in what he had to say about himself or the times in which he had grown up.

One of my cousins, Eldon Sanders (1927-1998), did a great deal of careful genealogical research on our family tracing some of the Rogers, Sanders, Wylie, Bosworth and other lines back to Britain and — in the case of the first two families — back to Northern Ireland and England c. 1700. I have copies of some of his work.

On the Emerson side of my family, the pickings are scarcer because they probably were more private people. They were also seem to have been more selective about what was saved and passed on. I have a few documents from my great-grandparents and many unidentified pictures c. 1860-1940. Still, there are several legal-size boxes of records, pictures and such things as report cards for some of the children from c. 1870 through the 1920s. There are University of Vermont [UVM] course notes taken by my Uncle Karl (1893-1919). He attended UVM between 1912-1916, graduating with distinction. My father, Arthur Emerson (1896-1939), kept several diaries for at least parts of the year – usually from the first of the year until 'sugaring' in the spring made life too hectic and tiring. Those have interesting things about his school years and the final year of his life in which he worked himself to death. One of his sisters, Flora (1899-1985), took a trip to Europe in 1927 and made a scrap book which describes her travels. She too was a genealogist but was selective about what she recorded about the family. The family heroine, Hannah Dustin, had her exploits recorded but her sister, Elizabeth Emerson, who was hanged on Boston Common, did not. Flora knew about both of them.

Finally, there are my own recollections. I know memory is fallible. I have tried to check what I can; I have treated with some scepticism much that I cannot check.

My manuscripts include a few that I purchased in the early 1970s. There are forty-seven daily reminder diaries kept by Leonard Watson (c. 1835-1912). Watson was a farmer in Sutton, Vermont. There are nine more diaries kept by members of his family. I was given or picked up in junk-antique stores several account books. One, very incomplete, was kept by the Hayden family in Albany during the years in which William Hayden II erected one of the most expensive houses in Orleans County (1849-1861). Another is a Day Book, kept for several months in 1866-67, by an unknown merchant in Barton. I bought the minutes of the Mason Post of the Grand Army of the Republic (Glover) for the years 1893-1914. I have also spent time looking at pertinent records in the Towns of Albany, Craftsbury, Sutton, Burke and Lyndonville.

My first effort at using this material was to write an unfinished autobiography/biography of my mother. I used what she wrote and tied it together with bridging sections to which I added some sections wholly written by me. Small pieces of this were published by my mother and one by me. My second effort to use my materials is this present work which has proven to be a very satisfying retirement project. It was mostly written in the years 2012 to 2015.

This book, then, is a collection of essays about members of my own family, their friends, and a few others who lived between c. 1800 and 1940 in the Northeast Kingdom of Vermont – the three counties in northeastern Vermont: Caledonia, Orleans, and Essex. Those hard-working, God-fearing, and often clever people, were literate, respectable, and fairly well-off. They came from the yeomanry of the region, if that is not too archaic a term. Possessed of some knowledge of the world, they were, also, all too human. To explore some of their lives and to put them in a wider perspective is my object in this book. Doing so, I hope, will paint a less glamorized picture of their times, show us 'the world we have lost', and perhaps, prompt reflections on the values and problems of our times. Popular historical works are often marked by an insistence on the innocence of people in the past, on their goodness, and, sometimes, on their relative un-sophistication and quaintness. American pioneers were brave and hardy; their successors were pious and hard-working. They were always independent and, after 1776, patriotic and self-sacrificing. They were brave and fought well. Their successors, battered by political and economic forces which they could neither control nor always understand, were also admirable. Once we get to the late nineteenth and twentieth century, equally good people struggle with rural decline, wars, and depressions – often doing so with something resembling heroism. Some of that is true but it is not the whole story.

Lacking in so many accounts, is the grime, grit, and irritants of life, its quiet, untold miseries and disappointments, its violence – what one is tempted to call the reality of evil, as real among Yankees as among others elsewhere. Many accounts also lack the humdrum details of ordinary lives or a sense of the parlous condition of all societies and of the people who live in them. This is a shortcoming which the following essays have tried to avoid. The Vermonters with whom I deal we should not envy in most respects. They lived shorter lives in a world of fewer social safety nets, with fewer opportunities for women, and without the conveniences we enjoy or the technologies on which they rest. My Vermonters often suffered, or reveled in, things we can hardly imagine, such as building their own houses, not being overly honest or always peaceful, butchering their own meat, driving away Gypsies camped on their land and attending Ku Klux Klan meetings in the 1920s. There is often a certain smugness about the virtues of the North in the years leading to the Civil War and in its aftermath. Not all my folks were nice. Not all were admirable. Few lives described here were notable.

I have also tried to put local material in more than local contexts. The Vermonters about whom I write lived mostly in towns in Orleans and Caledonia Counties, but they often knew they were affected by non-local events, forces, trends and circumstances. From time to time, I have tried to make that clear. And, I think my people were typical of many others living in the Northeast Kingdom and elsewhere in small-town rural New England.

In writing these pieces, I have had in mind the very fine book of Lynn Bonfield and Mary Morrison called *Roxana's Children: The Biography of a Nineteenth-Century Vermont Family* (1995). Like their book, mine is a personal statement of sorts, a reflection upon people and, in my case, what I would like remembered and thought about. My Vermonters are not everyone's, but they helped make the Northeast Kingdom what it was and cannot be again.

Notes on this Text

Quotations from manuscripts usually have not changed spellings, grammar or punctuation – which is often merely a space left in the line. Where changes have been made, they are noted. A few *sics* have been inserted for clarity. Images and illustrations are noted by including in brackets the relevant page number for the illustration or maps, *e.g.* (p.202). Efforts have been made to trace all copyright holders but two have not been found and two never responded. All the towns mentioned are in Vermont unless otherwise noted.

My Vermonters: The Northeast Kingdom 1800-1940

Lottie Rogers Harriman (1870–1960) and her cousin, Jennie Rogers Sanders (1868- 1963), story-tellers, in 1958.

I

Family Stories

1. Foreword

Every family has its myths and tales. What follows are some of the ones with which I grew up in the 1940s and glimpses of the society from which they came. Such stories form some of our conceptions of whom we are and of our society. Illusions and reality mix in many ways.

The stories of the Rogers family, first told to me by my grandmother, Jennie Rogers Sanders (1868-1963) *(opposite)*, are the ones I was most familiar with as a child and were certainly the ones which struck me as being the most exciting. That side of my family had one historic figure, Major Robert Rogers (1731-1795), remembered for his exploits in the French and Indian War (1754-1763) and for books which included accounts of his exploits as a ranger/soldier, a geography of sorts, and a play on Chief Pontiac, with whom he had had some dealings.[2] His forebears had been well-off West of Scotland settlers in Ulster and, later, in New England. Some of their descendants became new settlers in the American West. Such memories resonated with a boy whose first grade classroom had a picture of Puritans, religious exiles, on their way to church guarded by brave (if bashful) Myles Standish.[3] Godly and heroic pioneers had made the country great and left it a legacy of hardiness, thrift, and the ability to do almost anything. All that was interesting. And, I suppose, it made me proud. What small boy used to playing 'cowboys and Indians' in 1940 would not have wanted to be related to Major Robert Rogers, leader of a famous company of Rangers?

Later Rogerses thought the family came to America c. 1720 with a parish group from Northern Ireland which was led by the Presbyterian minister of the community they had left. They emigrated for religious and political reason and fetched up in Derry, New Hampshire, where other Ulster Scots had settled in 1717/18.[4] Not all the Rogerses stayed there. Some moved west or north, speculated in frontier lands, and fought Indians. Others moved southwest to Connecticut. In the aftermath of the Revolutionary War, as the northern New England frontier opened to settlers availing themselves of cheap land granted to Revolutionary War officers, a son of a Rogers family settled in mid- or southern New Hampshire, moved to Lutterloh, now Albany, Vermont. There, land, granted to a Revolutionary War Colonel and one of Washington's Quartermasters as payment for his services, was to be had. Colonel Lutterloh sold it on and one of the buyers of good bottom land on the Black River was Jesse Rogers I. He did not come alone but was joined by William Hayden I, a man from Connecticut, whose family is said to have maintained contact with the Rogers family from c. 1720 on. Their descendants remained friendly neighbors until the Haydens died out in 1927 – just as a curse they were under said they would.

Before going to Vermont, these two enterprising and entrepreneurial pioneer-families generally, but not always, did well with their business ventures. They cleared land, then sold it, and moved again. They bought and sold cattle and were not riveted to the places where they settled. When Jesse Roger and William Hayden I finally settled permanently as farmers in Albany, they started taverns, built dams and mills, opened small shops, and traded in wood, wool, grain, and livestock. They and their children tended to be somewhat rootless. Some of their descendants joined the mid-nineteenth-century exodus of Vermonters to the West and to urban areas. Those who stayed in Vermont had relatives everywhere – Philadelphia, New York City, Brooklyn, New Hampshire, Massachusetts, even in Iowa, Missouri, California, and Oklahoma. Large families encouraged migration but also travels and visits.

For a time, those stories faded away and meant little to me. Then, about forty years ago, I began to find them interesting again and reflected on the part they had played in my early conception of myself and my family. This was partly because my cousin, Eldon Sanders, had become a serious genealogist and had awakened interest in family matters among my mother and her three brothers. As bicentennial projects proliferated in the early 1970s, they set out to reconstruct the family tree and to fill in what details they could about the experience of their forebears. But, for me, the stories also changed. The Rogerses might have gone to Ireland for religious reasons but they had probably come to America for economic, political and religious ones. The family proudly remembered the Major's exploits as a Ranger, particularly the bloody raid on the St. Francis Indians and his arduous trek back through Vermont and New Hampshire to southern New England, but not his early involvement with counterfeiters or his Revolutionary War record as a Tory officer or his later years in England as a penniless debtor and drunk. The family history was not quite as it was remembered.

The Rogerses married others like themselves – or maybe not. I am sure that most of my Rogers ancestors thought they were descended from Adam and Eve but they did not, like some Scottish aristocrats of the eighteenth century, have pedigrees to prove it. The closest they came to a remarkable and noble pedigree was claiming 'the Bosworth line', into which they had married, was descended 'on the wrong side of the blanket' from a Duke of Buccleuch, a Scottish Borders magnate. As one might expect, there is no evidence that this was the case.[5] My grandmother liked to tell this story – but not out of the family. Every family has to start somewhere and my mother's maternal-line had a nicer story of itself with the Duke included.

The interactions between the Rogers and Hayden families also became the stuff of family legend known to a few and passed on to me in the early 1950s by Aunt Lottie Harriman (1870-1960), my grandmother's cousin. As motherless children, Aunt Lottie and her sister and my grandmother and her brother had lived together for two years when they were cared for by their grandparents while their sibling fathers looked for new wives to replace the ones who had recently died of consumption.

2. Aunt Lottie's Tales of Two Families

Aunt Lottie was a formidable woman. Tall and elegant in early life, she became in old age, gaunt, neatly but, usually, rather drably dressed. She smelled of Pond's face cream which Gramma also used. As a little boy, I rather feared Aunt Lottie. She too often told me, 'Little pitchers have big ears', or, 'Children are to be seen and not heard!' She was something of a trial to people who crossed her. When I was older, I liked her very much. She was a bright, self-possessed old lady with a sense of humor and a twinkling eye. I now recall with pleasure her conversations and story-telling, which always made my grandmother so happy. Aunt Lottie's gossipy, well-told tales were interesting. Many of them dealt with human foibles – stories of Craftsbury or Albany folks who drank too much, cheated on their wives, shot deer out of season, or had marriages going awry – but many showed deep interest in kin and ancestry, both legitimate and illegitimate. In that, she was like many of the Scots-Irish from whom she and others in region descended. She was curious enough to have read histories of early New England, to have 'written away for information' about the family, and to have checked some local records for herself. Neither she nor my grandmother was sufficiently skeptical to dismiss outright the story of murder behind the Hayden Curse – or, perhaps, the efficacy of the Curse it had brought on that family. That may tell us that not all their spiritual realities were to be found in the Bible. Aunt Lottie's story of the Rogers and Hayden families follows with a few bracketed additions to make a somewhat smoother narrative.[6] It shows how difficult it is to reconcile family stories with the surviving public records when they exist. In Albany, the earliest records are missing. The case is not much better in some of the near-by towns. Some of the story must remain unproven; some of it is simply wrong. Aunt Lottie's prose is often good but sometimes one remembers that she had but two or three years of grammar school and did not take the Latin course offered at Craftsbury Academy. She made the most of her seven or eight years of formal schooling and later read a great deal and wrote occasional verses. She liked to argue and was good on her feet.

Lottie Harriman c. 1890.

Aunt Lottie and my grandmother thought the Rogers and Hayden families differed in many ways. The more adventurous, risk-taking Haydens prospered beyond the expectations of simple farmers thanks, mainly, to the efforts of William Hayden II. He became a railroad contractor in New Hampshire, Maine and, 'out West'.[7] He spent much of his money emulating the wealthy in other places. After shining for a generation, the extravagant Haydens went broke. They were also peculiar people – Spiritualists who were odd in other ways. Albany's Rogers family was less spectacular in its success but did not die out in the direct male line until 1991. The following account of those families comes in three parts: Lottie Harriman's story in her own words of the relations between two families; her story of Mercie Dale's 'Curse' upon the Hayden family; and, my own recollections of conversations between Aunt Lottie and my grandmother. The first two parts take up thirty-two pages of small foolscap. The last I heard as a child in the 1940s. Aunt Lottie might not approve of this retelling (or of my recollecting her gossip) but she was, in her own way, an historian. By giving me the story of the Curse, she must have expected it to be passed on in some fashion. When she told it, it had more certainties than does her written version, some of which is clearly erroneous – as family traditions often are.

Aunt Lottie's Story

The first Rogers family [we] know about was [that of] Robert Rogers, born about 1730 who came from Wales about 1760-61.[8] On the same ship was a man by the name of Hayden who came from England. They became acquainted on ship board. It was the beginning of a friendship between the two families which had continued for three generations [really from the 1720s to the 1920s].

Both men settled first in Connecticut. [There,] Robert Rogers married Sally Alexander. Three sons were born to them.[9] About the year 1763-64, Rogers moved to New Hampshire. About the same time Hayden moved to Massachusetts. They continued to keep in touch with each other. Rogers's son Jesse I was born in 1769; Hayden's son William was born in 1777. [Jesse I married Sarah Wylie (1770-1861) of Hancock, New Hampshire in 1793; William Hayden I married Silence Dale of Bridgewater, Massachusetts in 1798.[10]]

Following the Revolutionary War and Shays Rebellion, men came from Connecticut, Massachusetts and New Hampshire to settle in the wilderness along the Hazen Road. These two young men [Jesse Rogers I and William Hayden I.] came together to look at the prospect. Rogers bought a lot and in 1798 built a log cabin. Hayden did not buy at that time.[11] Both went back home that winter and returned to Lutterloh in the spring of 1799. Hayden then bought a lot and built a log cabin. He brought his family there in September 1799. Jesse Rogers stayed in his cabin alone [through] the winter of 1799-1800. His wife stayed through the winter with her family in Derry, New Hampshire but [probably] came to Lutterloh in the spring of 1800, in time to be with Silence Hayden when her first child William [II] was born.

No record has been found so far of the purchase of the first lot by Jesse Rogers, No. 75. An old Gazeteer in speaking of Rogers land bought in 1805 says 'his title to this land was good'.[12] I have [a] deed record of that land bought in 1805 [and] recorded in Greensboro.[13] It may not have been [good] for the first land he is said to have bought. [The family lived on the second lot] until c. 1918.[14]

That may have been the reason for returning to New Hampshire in 1802 [which he seems to have done]. I found a deed to Jesse Rogers of a farm in Greenfield, New Hampshire in 1802-3. An old Gazeteer says that the family came to Lutterloh from Greenfield in 1806. It may be that Jesse Rogers returned to New Hampshire, coming back to Vermont in 1806. I found a record of the birth of two sons to the Rogers family in 1796-99 in New Hampshire but no record of a daughter born in 1801 [possibly] in Vermont. Among the old papers in my possession, some were recorded in Greensboro [where] the town records were burned in 1830 [31 August 1831]. So, I may never find the record of the purchase of the first [Rogers] home. No town records [exist] in Albany [formerly Lutterloh] until 1806 when the town was organized. [Jesse I] may in fact have returned [to New Hampshire] but a record was found in Albany [town] clerk's office of the sale of [lot No. 75] in 1815, [it] shows that he did own it at one time but not the date of purchase.

[Whenever they came], they had three children, Robert, James and Sally. The fourth child, Jesse, was born in December but died at the age of three years. A son born four months later was given the same name.[15] [Whatever the year was,] Jesse and his wife came by oxteam over the Hazen Road bringing their household goods and provisions to last for a time. [While this sounds like a difficult journey, it was one made by people who were not poor. They had some capital, perhaps realized by the sale of land in New Hampshire. For their possessions see below pp.53.] When they got out of grain, as they did before harvest, Mr Rogers[16] had to go to Newbury [about forty or fifty miles away] for more. He stopped at Hardwick to get it ground.

William Hayden's lot bordered the Craftsbury line (See Map, p.7). Jesse Rogers's first lot [was] 1½ miles north. The lots bought by these two men did not join. Not being too familiar with the lines between the towns, [the Hayden's] first home was built over the line in Craftsbury and here William [Hayden] II was born in July 1800 but most of the lot was in Lutterloh. Later, both men bought more land and then the farms joined as they do today [c. 1950]. An elm tree (by the side of the road [c. 1950) a few rods south of the drive way into the Rogers yard marks the line between the two

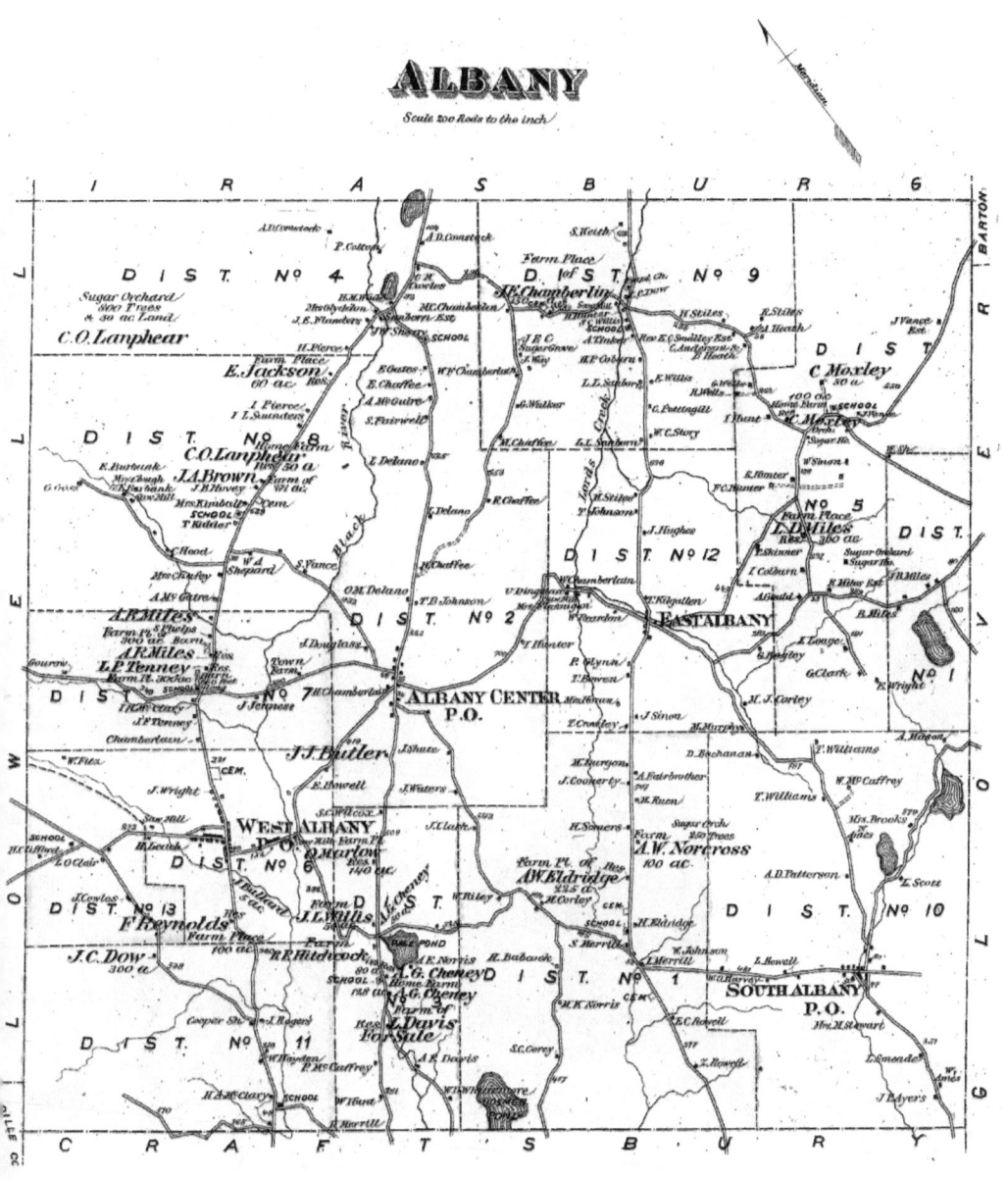

Albany in 1878.

Many of the family homes noticed in the text are on this map. The Rogers and Hayden farms are in the southwest corner on the Black River. Jabez Page's farm is somewhat north of them, in District 1, toward the Lowell border; his fulling mill was in West Albany, the principal village which had two streams powering its mills. The Tenney farm is a bit north of Page's. Beers charged people more to have their names in larger type and probably to be included on the very skimpy list of businessmen and farmers.

Source: Beers, 1878.

My Vermonters: The Northeast Kingdom 1800-1940

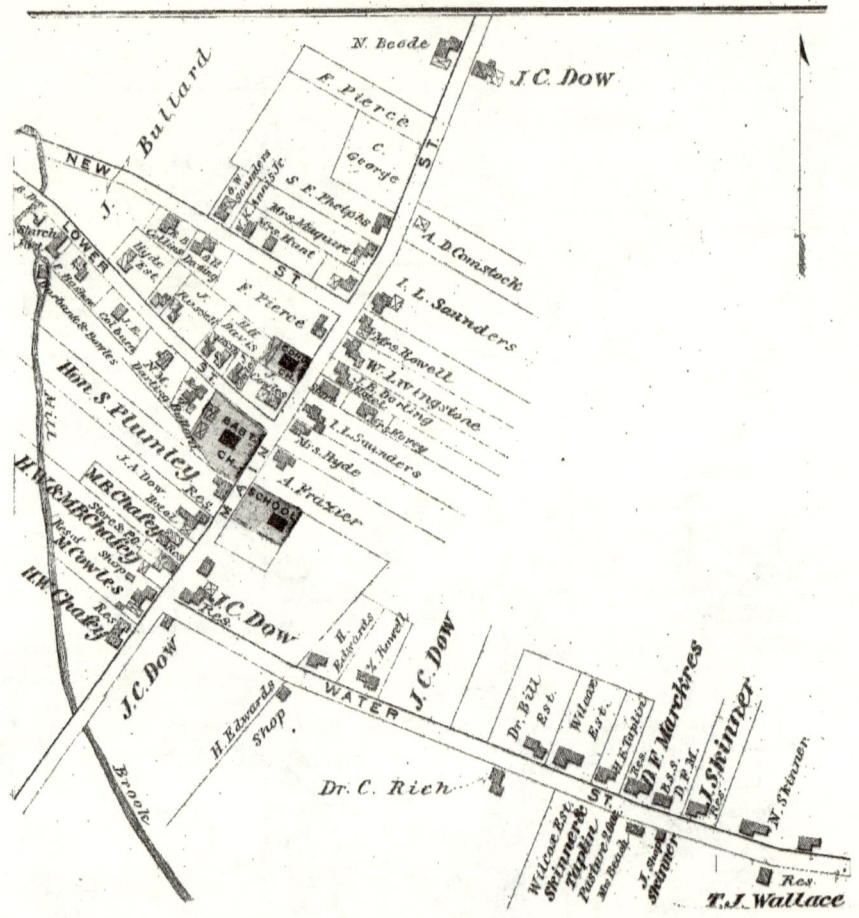

West Albany in 1878. Isaac Sanders's store is shown on the map as is his house. Just off it, to the northwest, was the mill of Alden Darling which drew power from the Mill Brook as did the starch factory. Other enterprises used the Black River.
Source: Beers, 1878.

Craftsbury in 1878. The Ira Sanders farm, then held by G. D. Bagley, is in the top northeast section. Being a taxpayer in Craftsbury meant his children could go free to Craftsbury Academy in North Craftsbury, now called Craftsbury Common.
Source: Beers, 1878.

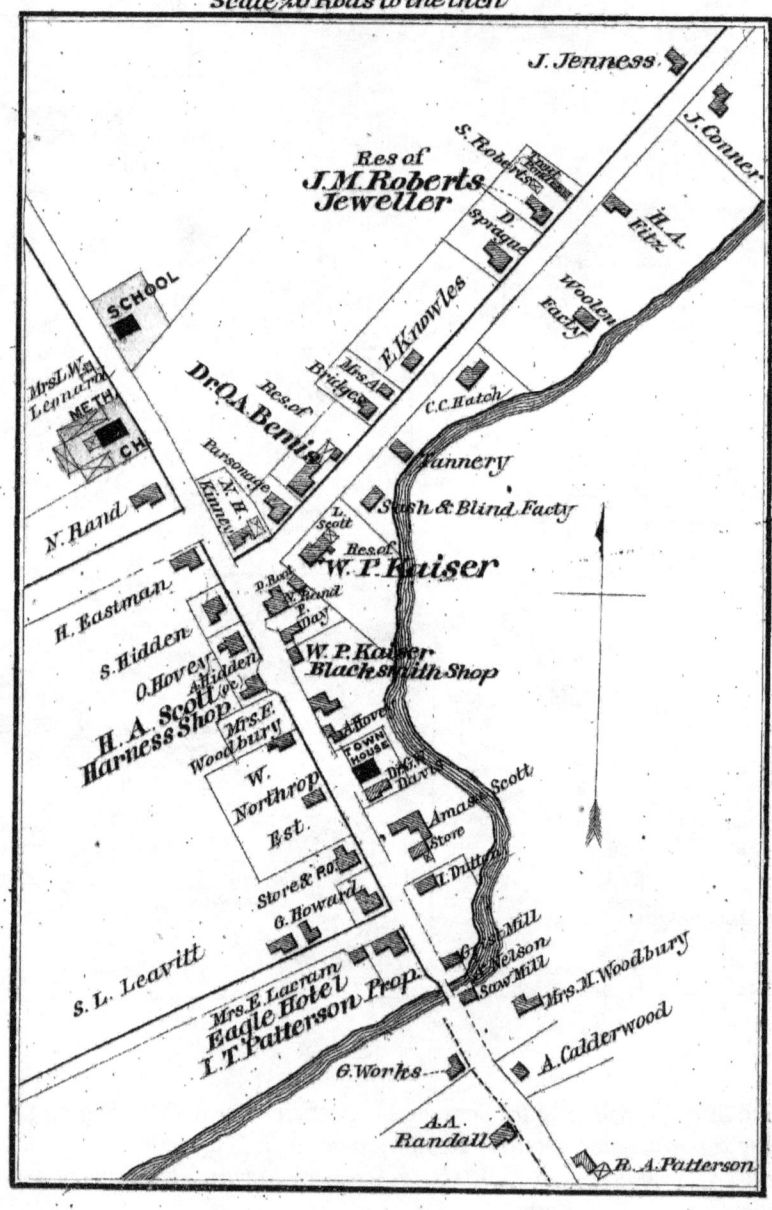

Craftsbury Village and its watercourse. Source: Beers, 1878.

Craftsbury.

BLACKSMITH.

W. P. KAISER, Blacksmithing and all kinds of Job work done in a workmanlike manner. Carriages and Sleighs repaired, &c

HOTEL.

EAGLE HOTEL. I. T. Patterson, Propr. Travelers will here find the best of accommodations at prices to suit the times. Board by the day or week. Livery connected with Hotel

HARNESS MAKER.

H. A. SCOTT, Harnesses of all kinds constantly on hand and made to order. Prices reasonable and the best of workmanship. I would invite people of this and neighboring towns to give me a call, and examine my work and prices. Satisfaction guaranteed. Repairing done

JEWELER.

J M. ROBERTS, Dealer in American and Foreign Watches of every description. Fine Gold and Plated Jewelry, Spectacles, Silver Ware, Clocks and Fancy Goods

PHYSICIAN.

O. A. BEMIS, Homeopathic Physician and Surgeon

North Craftsbury.

LAWYER.

W. W. MILES ... Atty and Counselor at Law

MERCHANTS AND DEALERS.

A PADDOCK. Customers will at all times find a good assortment of Teas and first-class goods of every description of general merchandise, as is usually found in a first-class Country Store, and at prices that defy competition. All kinds of Country Produce taken in exchange for goods. Clothing, Boots and Shoes a specialty

H. N. STEVENS, Manufr and Dealer in all kinds of Sitting Room Dining Room, Kitchen, and Chamber Furniture, Mattresses, Spring Beds and Lounges. All kinds of Oval and Square Picture Frames, Black Walnut and Gilt Mouldings, Glass, Cord, Knobs, Bronzes of all descriptions, Brackets, &c. A large assortment of Coffins and nice Caskets always on hand, and trimmed at short notice, and in the best style. Also Ladies and Gent's Burial Robes at low rates. North Craftsbury, Vt.

L. P. WHITNEY I will sell my large stock of Wares, consisting of Stove Pipes. Tin and Hollow Ware, Hardware, Cookery, Glassware, Wooden-ware, Plated Ware and Pedler's Furnishing Goods. Also a large assortment of Teas, Tobacco and Groceries, at the lowest price for cash or ready pay. And I invite all persons desiring goods in my line to bring their Oats, Corn, Rags, Old Iron Feathers, Scrip, &c., and give me a call, an I exchange for goods, as I shall not be undersold in Orleans Co.

RESIDENT.

HENRY DOUGLASS .... Farmer

East Craftsbury.

MERCHANT.

J. W. SIMPSON, Dealer in Staple and Fancy Dry Goods, Boots and Shoes, Hats and Caps, Groceries, Queensware, Hardware, Nails and Glass, Drugs and Medicines, Stationery, School Books, Collars and Cuffs, Crockery and Glassware, Knitting Cotton, Wool Yarn, Hosiery and Gloves, Table Covers, Suspenders, Laces and Edgings. Paints Oils, Dye Stuffs, Family Medicines, Perfumery and Notions generally. Goods sold cheap for cash. Call and examine my goods

RESIDENT.

W. ANDERSON .... Farmer

Mill Village.

DEALERS.

GEO. H. KENISTON, Dealer in Flour, Salt Fish, Teas, Coffees, Spices, Nuts, Tobacco, Coffee Berry, Prints, Toilet and Laundry Soaps, Dress Goods Prints, Cottons, Small Wares, Stationery, School Books, Collars and Cuffs, Crockery and Glassware. Surpenders, Laces and Edgings, Ready-made Clothing, &c

I S. PARKER. I keep on hand constantly the choicest brands of Flour, which I shall sell cheap for Cash. Also Corn and Meal, Buckwheat Flour, Graham Meal and all the different kinds of grain commonly kept in a grist mill. I am also prepared to do all kinds of grinding in a workmanlike manner, and shall make Wheat Grinding a specialty. Sawing of Dimension Lumber, Boards, Shingles, and Planing and Jointing of Boards, Sawing of Eaves, Spouts &c. &c, done in a manner to please and satisfy all. Come all who wish for anything in my line, and I will endeavor to do for you as I would be done by. A L STREETER, Agent.

MRS. A. L. STREETER, Dealer in Millinery and Small Wares

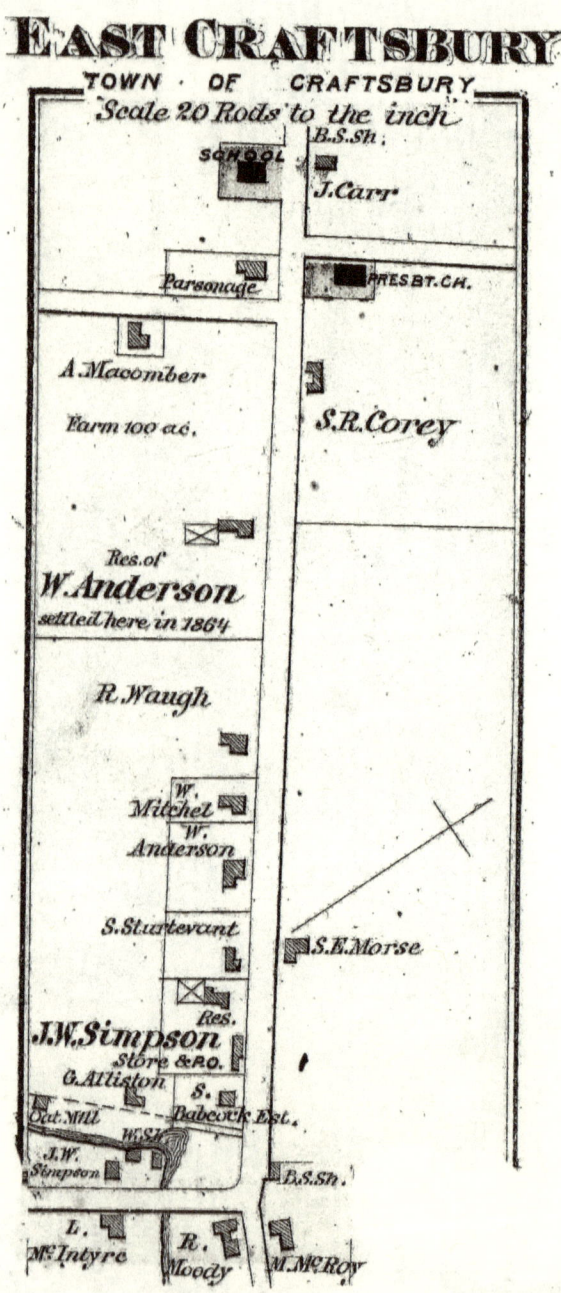

East Craftsbury in 1878. Craftsbury Common was the site of the Academy and of the best stores. East Craftsbury had the Presbyterian Church. Source:. Beers, 1878.

Family Stories

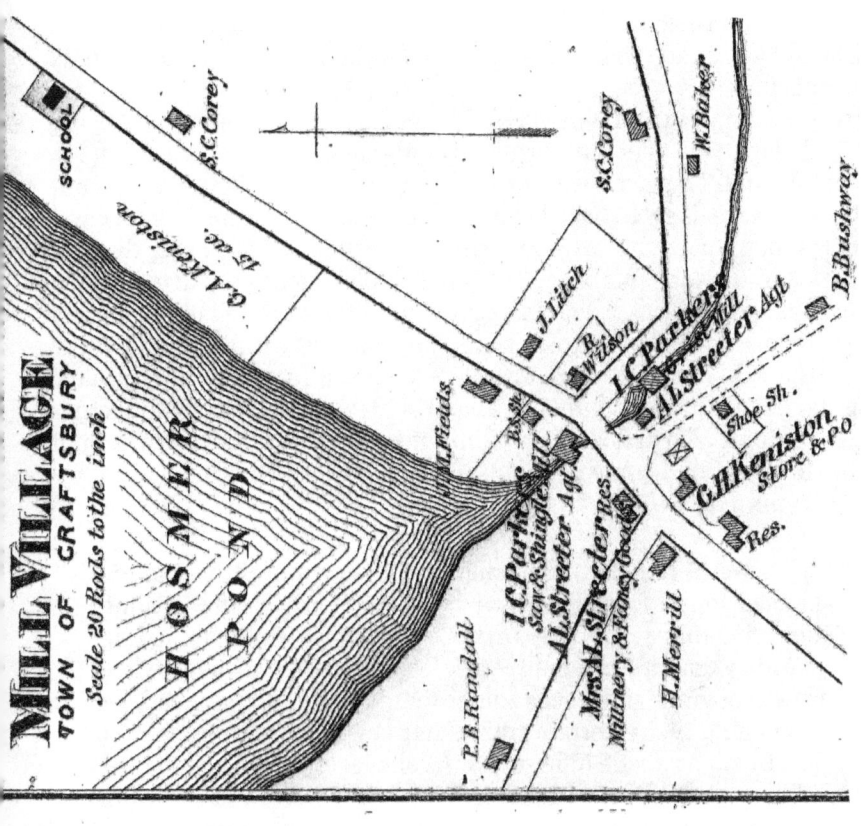

North Craftsbury and Mill Village in 1878. Craftsbury had water to power shops and mills as did Mill Village. Source: Beers, 1878.

farms. A line of bushes to the Black River shows where the line fence was once. The Hazen Road crossed Black River on the Rogers' land a few rods north of this line.

[Both Jesse Rogers I and William Hayden I (1777-1846), were enterprising men.] Their land was good and productive and Jesse was successful in his efforts of farming. The farm was like most producing a variety of things but its cash crops were likely to have been wool and wheat.[17] [Jesse Rogers I and William Hayden I used the surplus of their labors to invest in other things.] Mr Rogers and his sons put in the first grist mill in Albany [c. 1810]. It was in Albany Village on Black River. I believe the mill right is still in the Rogers name. [It seems to have been sold earlier, perhaps by 1812.] About the year 1838 [c. 1830-?], Jesse Rogers I also kept a tavern for some time. I have the original license granted him. [William Hayden had a cloth manufactory and at some point also had a tavern. Both men had wives who were helpful to them. Hayden's had some capital but Sarah Wylie was notable in other ways.] *Hemminway's Gazeteer* says:

> Mrs Rogers was a remarkable woman, tough and sprightly. She said she was used to go down the River meadow nearly to the Irasburg line [about five miles] for cows that strayed away. Her route led her through unbroken forest of many varieties of trees interwoven with a thick growth of vines and weeds sometimes higher than her head, her only guide being the uncertain trail of her cows. Sometimes she was overtaken by night, made hideous by the shrill repeated cries of birds and wild beasts as they reverberated from hill to hill. In her youthful days she was somewhat poetical and her smuggling and Patriotic songs were both pointed and cutting. I have specimens.

[The mention of 'smuggling songs' refers, in part, to an incident in the war of 1812.] About 1812, Sally, [while looking for her own cattle] discovered a herd of cattle being smuggled [through Albany] to Canada to feed the British Army. [She reported them to the local authorities, who, Aunt Lottie thought, arrested, tried, and convicted the smugglers.[18]]

William Hayden II [1800-1883] [19] and Jesse Rogers II continued to live on adjoining farms where their fathers had settled. William II had business interests besides his farm and became a wealthy man.[20] Jesse Rogers II lived the quiet life of a successful farmer [and cooper]. The two men were associated in business over a long period and were fast friends as long as they both lived. Two men more unlike, it would be hard to find. William II, wealthy, arrogant, turbulent and somewhat profane; Jesse II, not wealthy although in comfortable circumstances, the quiet type, 'Uncle Jess' to every body and a Christian man. In spite of these differences, they remained fast friends [until] William died in 1883. Jesse died in 1896.[21]

3 . "The Legend of the Dale Curse"

The fortunes of the two families diverged after the 1820s which brings us to Aunt Lottie's stories about 'the Dale Curse'. She first heard of it from her grandparents when she, her sister, and her cousins, Jennie and Robert, lived some time with their grandparents in the mid-1870s. The story was written out in a number of manuscripts when Lottie returned to her grandparents' home in the 1880s as a teenager with TB. It then seemed that she might die and, in dying at home, infect her sisters. As an old lady, she believed the story of the Dale Curse was a true tale told to amuse a sick child who would not live to pass it on. She wrote two copies of her account of the Curse in the mid-1880s. Other parts of Lottie's story of the Curse, came to her after the 1880s and seem to have been added as a result of her curiosity. In the 1940s and 1950s, Aunt Lottie added to her surviving copy and wrote an account of the two families over the time they knew each other. Those accounts she gave to me prior to her death in 1960. It was then not a story which either she or my grandmother thought was widely known.

The Dale Curse

The story of the Curse was first told by Sally Wylie Rogers to her daughter[-in-law] Mary [Bosworth] six years after Mary came into the family as the wife of the youngest son of Jesse II [c. 1846]. The occasion for her being told at this time was [that] word [had been] received of the death of William Hayden I. Mary had supposed their neighbor, Silence Hayden, to be a widow, as no mention of a husband living, had ever been made before her. In telling this story to Mary, Sally said, "Silence has been my friend for many years, Mary, and this must never be spoken of out of the family". Many years later, Mary, my grand mother told the story to me. I was at home, with my grandparents that year recovering from a tubercular condition and I suppose the story was told to me to give me something to think about besides myself. I was told by her that I <u>must not talk about it to any one</u>. I amused my self by writing a story about it, using fictitious names, as Grandfather objected to the story "being put on paper". I overheard Grandmother tell him she would see that it was "taken care of when I was through with it". She did. One day I found the light stand drawer empty but I had a copy she did not know about. It was put away and forgotten until a few years ago when in looking over old papers in an old desk, I came across my story written long ago.

The Dale Curse was not talked about in the Rogers family. If at times some visitor in the home mentioned "the Curse," they were hushed up at once. If later the children asked what they had meant, no explanation was given but the fact that there <u>was</u> something called a "Curse" in the Hayden family was not denied to them.

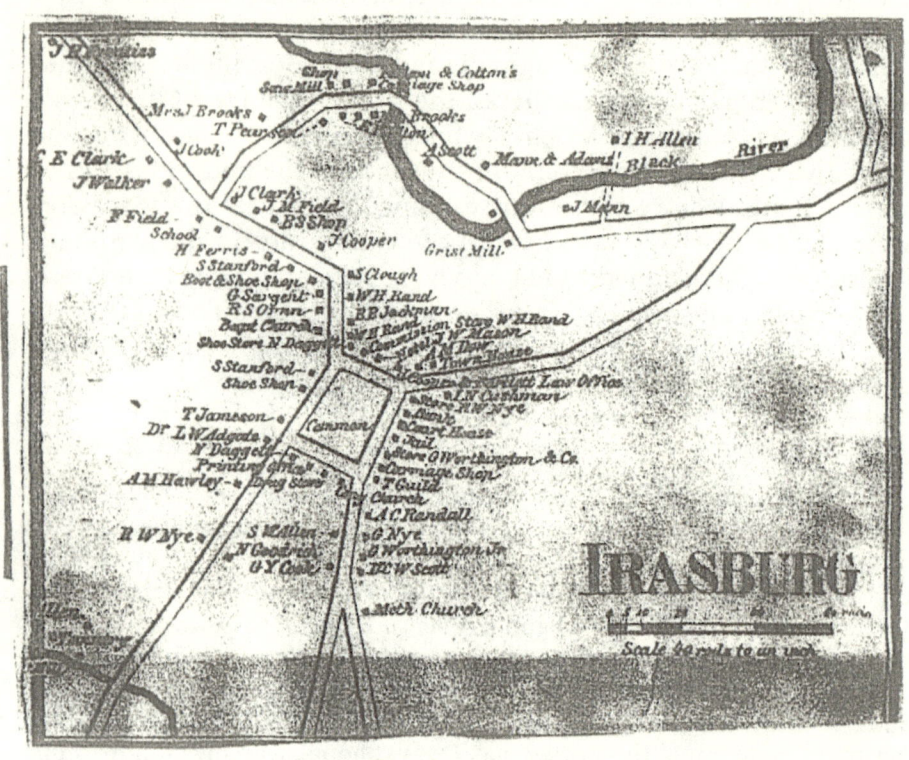

Irasburg in 1859. This town, built around a common, was small but a shire town in the centre of the county. It was named for Ira Allen, to whom its land had been sold and who helped to develop it. In 1859, it had the county court, three resident lawyers, a printer and newspaper, two physicians, a bank, and several mills and shops. Unlike Albany and Craftsbury, but like Danville, also a shire town, there was little in its hinterland but farms.
Source: H. E. Walling, Orleans, Lamoille and Essex Vermont (New York, 1859).

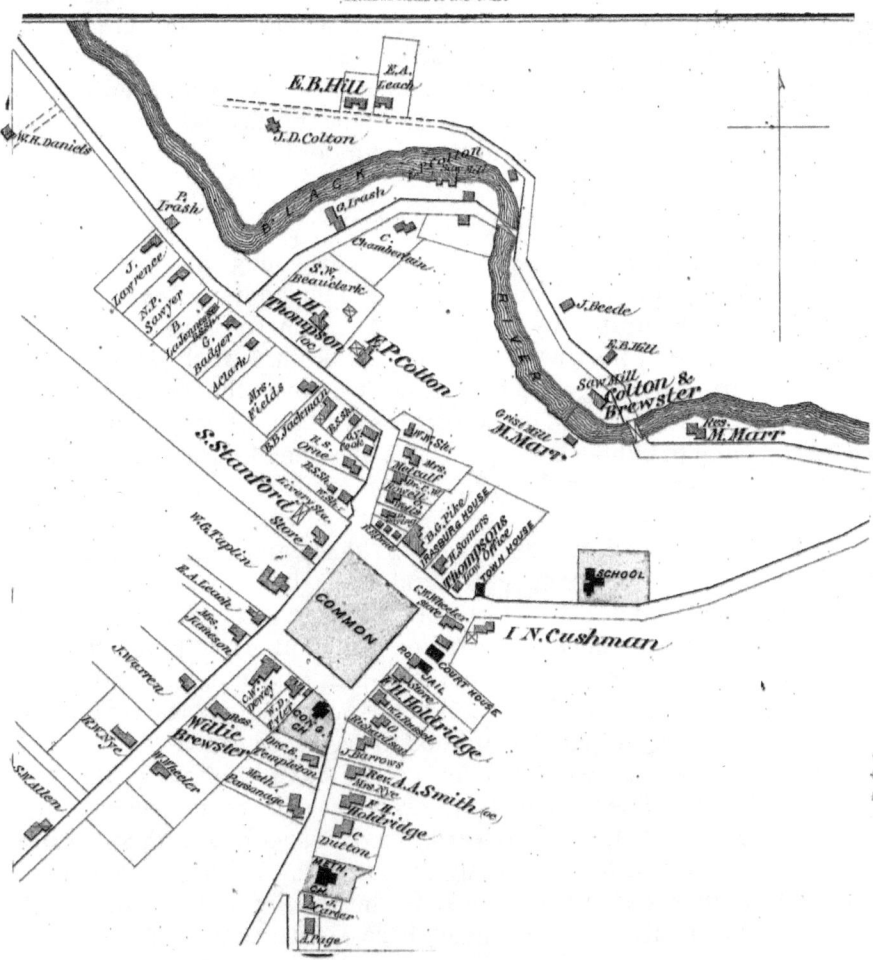

Irasburg, 1878.
Source: Beers, 1878.

The story told me was carried on to about the year 1883. From there on the story is from things told me by members of my family who were neighbors of the Haydens and some things told me by Armenia [Mamie] Hayden. Much of it [comes] from my personal knowledge of the family. What I have written I believe to be true. Some of the grandchildren of William Hayden I believed in the Curse, especially the last one of the name, Armenia M. Hayden, who died in Maine in 1927. Whether it was true or not that William Hayden I poisoned his mother in law, we will never know at this late date. But the mother in law believed that he did and, shortly before she died, she accused him of it and cursed him for it.

***

About the year 1799 William Hayden with his young wife, Silence Dale, and her widowed mother, Mercie Dale, left their home in Massachusetts and made the long journey by ox team to the northern part of Vermont to make a new home in the township called Lutterloh. It took several weeks to make the trip, stopping with friends several times; the last 20-25 miles there was only a trail through the wilderness. The going [was] so rough they had to stop often to tighten the ropes which held their household goods and they camped by the trail on the crude ox cart at night. At last they reached the site of their new home.

William put his stock, the oxen, a cow, 2 sheep and a pig into the crude shelter he had prepared for them. He unloaded the household goods and carried them into the log house he had built just before he went for his family, and the two women, Silence and her mother, prepared the first meal in the new home. It was then the month of September and before snow came William had made the buildings snug and tight against the cold winter ahead, and cut a high pile of wood to keep them warm.

In the early summer, with only her mother and a neighbor's wife [Sally Rogers] to help her, Silence's first son was born, William the second.

They all worked hard, William clearing land to raise food for them, Silence often helping him and Mercie, taking care of young William and spinning the wool from their own sheep to make warm clothing for them all. Shortly after young William's second birthday, little Mercie came to brighten the home, but she was a frail little thing, living only a few weeks. They laid her to rest in the wilderness. Frantic with grief, Silence spent most of the time out doors with her husband, helping him all her frail strength would allow.

William was [a] progressive man and [an] ambitious man; he built the first frame building in the township [a 'plank house'] and a store building stocked with goods. He opened the first licensed public house in the township. In the course of time he built a cloth manufacturing plant where he employed several women to spin and weave.[22]

About this time the lot of land adjacent to his was offered for sale and he wanted to buy it. He tried to persuade his mother in law to loan him money but she refused. But, with the help of a good neighbor [Jesse Rogers], he succeeded in raising the money and bought the coveted land.

The years drifted by. William's business ventures prospered and he wanted to increase his stock of goods, make improvements in his manufacturing plant, buy more land, etc. He tried again to persuade his mother in law (a fairly wealthy woman, for those times) to loan him money but she not only refused [?1823] but told him he would never get a cent of her money as long as she lived.

Not long after this [c. 1828], her health began to fail; she grew weaker until she could no longer assist her daughter about the work in [the] home. At last she was confined to her bed, much of the time lying in a semi-stupor. In these stupors, she had vivid dreams in which she thought she saw her son in law drop something in a glass of water on her bedside stand. Once, awakening suddenly from one of these dreams, she saw the door of her room closing and a man's hand on the latch as it closed. In the morning when her daughter brought her a fresh glass of water, she asked her to come back to her room with her husband. She told him she believed he was slowly poisoning her to get her money, and she cursed him for it, saying: "The Hayden name and race shall become extinct in the third generation and the last of the name shall die alone in poverty". She passed away that night [1830].

When the mother in law was ill, Sally Rogers, the neighbor's wife, often went to help care for her. [Mercie] confided her fears of poison to Sally and asked her to promise her that she would see that she was not buried on Hayden soil. In those days, there [were] no established cemeteries, each family buried their dead on their own land. When Mercie passed away, Sally Rogers kept her promise. She was placed in a small plot of ground on the Rogers farm where two Rogers children were buried. Some years later, a cemetery was established at Craftsbury Common and the bodies of the children were moved there and placed in the lot of Sally Rogers' parents. At Mrs. Hayden's request, the body of her mother was placed there also. The lot is in the front part of the cemetery, near the flat top monument. Three small stones mark the spot. The stones were for James Wylie and his wife and daughter, Molly. [There were] no stones for the [Rogers] children. There was a stone for Mrs. Dale but none there now [c. 1950], probably broken and thrown away. If there was a crime in connection with Mrs. Dale's death, the Rogers family must have known about it and kept still so [they] were not entirely blameless. They kept their secrets in those days.

Following her death it was found, by her will, that her property was entailed to the third generation of her direct descendants.[23] William was deeply involved financially, and he was so disappointed by this will that he took the "Poor-debtors" oath and left town to try to better his financial condition [in New York State where he had relatives]. His family heard from him from time to time in various ways and at last received notice of his death in New York State [in 1846].

William's interest in the farm home had previously been deeded by him to the oldest son, William II. For the protection of the family they continued to live [on the farm]. Time passed swiftly. The other children married and went to homes of their own until only William and his mother remained on the farm. William was much like his father, ambitious and progressive. With [his] family growing larger, he longed for more money than the farm supplied, so, leaving a man and his wife to carry on the work of the farm, he and his wife, Ajubah,[24] went to New Hampshire leaving four children with his mother. He got a job working on the railroad being built through New Hampshire to Canada. He showed much ability and soon was given a job as overseer over a gang of men at quite an increase of pay. About that time, the company building the road, were asking for bids on a contract to build a certain piece of road. I have been told it was from Nashua, New Hampshire to St. Hyacinth, Canada. William took time off to look of (*sic.*) the ground where the road was to go, [and] made a bid on the contract to get the job. It took several years to complete the work, but at last it was finished. He told different people that on that job, he made $60,000.[25]

He built had an impressive Brick house on his farm of now 900 acres in Albany but the land the brick house stands on was paid for by Jesse Rogers.[26]

Hayden House c. 1915.

Family Stories

Hayden House and Grounds c. 1918. Ira Sanders is in the foreground behind the wheel of his first car, a Model T. The estate's pond is on the left.

He signed the note when William Hayden [I] bought the lot. When William deserted his family and left town, Jesse Rogers paid the note. Some interesting things come to light when you look up old records. [The house] was elaborately and very expensively furnished, nothing to compare with it was to be found for many miles around. He told people that it cost him $40,000.00. While he was building the house, he was asked why he was building such a large house, and he replied, "I want to show the fools in Albany what money will do." The grounds around the house were landscaped and enclosed by a granite curbing, with tall ornamental posts at openings into the grounds. At one side of the grounds was a small pond. At great expense this was enlarged. Rustic seats were placed near it and added much to the beauty of the surroundings. When all was finished, William and his family moved to the new house. For a time they were happy there. Then, William, grew restless and wanted to again be making money. So he went back to railroad work, this time in the Western States, Michigan, I believe.[27] He now had a business partner to whom he eventually sold his interest in the contracting business.

Before he left [late 1850s], he hired a man, in whom he had great confidence, as general manager of everything on the farm. He lived at the new house to [care for] the carriages and carriage horses and took the two ladies (Mrs Hayden and her youngest daughter) wherever they wanted to go. William went off to his new work well satisfied to leave everything in his hands [but] coming home from time to time to see that all was as he wanted it.

In their middle years there was an estrangement between William and his wife over a personal matter and they lived for many years under the same roof without speaking to each other. At the table, at meal time, the conversation went something like this:

"Henry, ask your mother if she would like another helping of potato?"
"No, thank you Henry; ask your father if he is ready for his pie?"

Thus they lived for many years.

Ajubah was always a gracious Lady, managing the home in the same efficient way, looking after William's comfort in every way, always speaking of one another with respect [but] never speaking to each other. William provided well for her.

Nothing definite is was known as the cause of the estrangement. It was known that William came home unexpectedly [c. 1862]. What he found on reaching there, or what happened there that night, has never been known, but the estrangement seemed to date from that time. The morning after William's unexpected return, it was noticed that the manager was absent. When after several days, he was still absent, a search was started for the missing man. After several days, he was found in the home of a brother. He looked as though he had taken a bad beating and was still in bed after six days. He would make no statement whatever about the matter. The brother said, 'He fell down the stairs'. Nothing more was ever known about it. Not many weeks after this, William retired from Railroad work and spent the rest of his life on the farm. He made extensive improvements here in the dairy equipment, built new and very modern barns and bought registered Jersey cattle and blooded horses, and kept a man to take care of them. He was considered to be one of the wealthiest men in the county if not in the state. He lived to be 83 years old.

Other misfortunes in the family followed this estrangement. One of the daughters, in the delirium of a serious illness, became violently insane and never recovered. She [Mary (1830-1867)] was confined and cared for in the house until death came for *(sic.)* to release her. William Henry's only son, a boy of five and the only one to carry on the name, died after only a short illness.

After Mr. [William II] Hayden's death [1883], Mrs. Hayden lived on in the home with a woman servant who had been with her many years. She [Mrs. Hayden] died at the age of 91-92 years. Following her death [in 1892], the house was closed just as she had kept it. A key was left with her son [William] Henry, who lived nearby that he might go in from time to time to see that all was well. William's estate had not been settled and following the death of Mrs. Hayden, the heirs demanded a settlement. It was decided to sell and dispose of the personal property first. A few days before the date of the sale, the ones in charge went to the house to make arrangements. On going into the house, it was discovered that of the beautiful and valuable old furniture not much was left. The Duncan Fyfe tables, Chippendale chairs, the beautiful mahogany dining set, the tall highboy with its claw feet and the steeple clock were all gone. All that was left was ordinary furniture common to all the houses at that time.[28]

Not long after Mrs Hayden's death, the house was being spoken of as "The Haunted House." Anyone passing in the small hours of the night, might sometimes see a flicker of light through the shutters, hear sounds that seemed to come from inside the house and people were heard to say,

> Does Ajubah's restless spirit walk at night, weeping over her vanished treasures and sighing for the lost year of happiness that might have been? Does the spirit of the unfortunate daughter also walk at night in the empty rooms of the home?

Who can say? People living along the "River Road" recalled hearing loaded wagons pass in the night at about the time the house was first spoken of as "The Haunted House" but what became of the beautiful furnishings there that William bought for Agubah nobody knows.

The family of William Henry Hayden (c. 1890).
Front row: Lydia (1832-1904), William Henry (1833-1910), Mamie (1873-1927); Back row; Unknown, Carrie (1859-1910).

William Hayden's son, William Henry,[29] lived on the next farm adjoining his father's. Besides carrying on the farm, he was interested in the breeding of Jersey cattle and at one time owned the finest herd in the county. He married and four children came to the family, three daughters and the son [who] died at an early age. [Henry, as he was known,] did not seem to be the capable businessman that his father had been and many of his ventures were unsuccessful. During his father's life, these things were taken care of.

Following his father's death, there were several law suits connected with the settlement of his estate in which William Henry was involved. Illnesses and deaths in the family contributed to expenses until by the time he died, about 1910, he was a poor man, deeply in debt. The farm and personal property was sold at auction a few weeks after William Henry's death. When all the debts were settled, not much was left for the remaining daughter to live on and no home. She was not strong herself and not capable of supporting herself by working. She drifted from one old friend to another, from one relative to another for several years. Then, perhaps feeling that she had worn out her welcome, among her friends, she made other plans. Her mother had come from Maine and there was a home there that she still had an interest in, so she moved to Maine with a few household goods she had kept from her home (if she ever had another) and went to live among strangers. Perhaps she preferred to die among strangers than to have her old friends see her in poverty. What her life was like after she went to Maine, her Vermont friends had no way of knowing for to the few who heard from her, she gave no information about herself. After a few years, she was ill and taken to a local hospital where she died. She was brought back to the Vermont town where she was born and placed in the family lot in the small cemetery in the valley, the last of the name and race. It would be easy to believe that after more than 100 years the Dale Curse was fulfilled. Believe it or not, as we may, Armenia Hayden [when she] died in 1927 was [of] the third generation, the last of her name, and she died in poverty.

4. Recollections from the 1940s and 1950s

Aunt Lottie's written account leaves out things which she and my grandmother used to mull over on long Sunday afternoons when their religion prevented them from doing much but reading and talking – and my doing much but listening. Talk, even gossip, on the Sabbath was not sinful. When they spoke of the Haydens, other things got added to the foregoing version. Most of them concerned William Hayden I and II or recollections of times with the Hayden girls.

Both Hayden men liked their liquor – but this was the opinion of ladies who belonged to the Women's Christian Temperance Union.[30] Aunt Lottie, like my grandmother, probably 'took the pledge' as a teenager. Both the Hayden men had a temper and neither seems to have been quite as good at business as Aunt Lottie's story suggests. I think neither of the cousins really believed in 'the Curse' but they were tantalized by the fact that it really seemed to have come true and both believed that William Hayden I killed his mother-in-law. If 'the Curse' was not real, it ought to have been. It lent an aura of mystery to the House where locals sometimes picnicked around the pond and stood for photos on the granite piers which never supported the fence they were designed to carry.

Like others, Aunt Lottie and my grandmother pondered the cause of the 'estrangement' between William II and his wife. Aunt Lottie would generally work around to her theory, which was stated with euphemisms but amounted to William II having found his wife in bed with the manager. This led not only to the man's beating but possibly to the death of a child. I do not remember if this was a little Hayden boy, whom William II took to be not his own child but that of the manager, or, if it was another child who looked too much like William Hayden. Aunt Lottie claimed several children in the area looked very like Mr. Hayden. She would hint that the name died out but 'perhaps not the race'. Her story was that Henry Hayden's child 'died after a short illness' but I distinctly remember talk of a little boy who was coshed and died of the blow. The boy died when he was 'kicked by a horse' when only Mr. Hayden was around. Aunt Lottie said the print of a horse shoe was visible. Later, someone found a stout stick in the stable to which had been nailed a horse shoe. If William I was a murderer, William II may have been one also – or Aunt Lottie's memory was as wrong here as in many other places.

There were other things about which Aunt Lottie and my grandmother spoke. The Haydens were Spiritualists and were notable for the strength of their beliefs.[31] My mother swore she had been shown a photograph of one of the Hayden women with the spirit of her deceased son or brother, in faint-outline, holding out from the body of the woman a watch on a chain. As a child, I found that very eerie but the old ladies thought it was unlikely to be what my mother claimed it was – a real dead but embodied spirit. Neither Jennie nor Lottie had seen it but both knew of the picture and also knew that seances had been held in the great house. Spirits were said to have been raised to converse with the living. The Haydens were hardly good Congregationalists although they gave money to that Church and attended its donation suppers.

Gramma and Aunt Lottie also wondered if it were true that somewhere in the large house there was a place in which runaway slaves had been secreted. The story was that the Haydens had strongly opposed the South in the Civil War and earlier had provided shelter for slaves fleeing to Canada about twenty-five miles away. When portions of the big house burned in the 1940s or 1950s, both women asked the neighbors if there had been found a passage out of the house into the field behind. As far as could be learned, none was found but they still thought such a passage had been there.[32] For both, the Civil War and its stories were not old history but lived on thanks to the 'Campfires' they had attended (see below pp.244, 250-253).

They also remembered with fondness the parties which had been held in the big house, where the attic had a 'sprung floor' which allowed for dancing and the promenades in which the pious of their generation had been permitted to indulge.[33] They recalled the central heating arrangements and the fancy furniture and fitments which had disappeared. Both thought William Henry had sold them off on the sly. Sometimes, they recalled the fine herd of Jersey cattle which Henry Hayden bought and sold, kept and bred, and the blooded horses which he trained and drove. They spoke from experience since their own fathers, both cattle traders, had done about as well with their animals. And, they remembered the Hayden girls whom they had known well, especially Mamie who had stayed with each of them before her departure for Maine. Armenia or Mamie, was the last of the four Hayden girls, three of whom predeceased her: Carrie Azuba in 1910, and Willimina May in 1891; Mamie's twin sister, died as a young woman.

The Haydens were good for other kinds of speculation. Where had all the money gone? It seemed improbable to Gramma and Aunt Lottie that it had dribbled away. To both it seemed much more likely to have gone into some big project which had failed. They probably were correct as the settlement of the estates finally showed. They also thought that their grandparents and Cornelius Rogers, Gramma's father, had paid more Hayden bills than they ever were willing to admit.

All in all, even into the 1960s, the Haydens were the stuff of wonder and gossip among those who had known and remembered them. And, it was not only among my relatives that this was so. Aunt Lottie lived within sight of a wealthy woman in Craftsbury who fancied herself the 'laird of the village' – as Aunt Lottie and others sometimes called her. This was Jean Simpson (opposite), the town's largest landowner and its somewhat resented benefactor. 'Miss Jean', as she was known, was intensely curious about the Hayden story which she knew Aunt Lottie had written out. Lottie believed Miss Jean entered her house through a window and took the manuscript recounting the Hayden Curse. It certainly went missing, was searched for both by Aunt Lottie and her son, Neil, and eventually was found in the very place both of them said it had not been a day or so before. Lottie was not a paranoid old lady. It is not unlikely that Miss Jean had, indeed, gone into a house seldom locked and had carried the story away and copied it. Not all New Englanders are quite what they seem to be. That too offered a lot of topics for a Sunday afternoon and for speculations which today cannot be confirmed.[34]

My grandmother and her cousin had good memories but they were wrong about much they said and speculated on. That is a perennial problem with family histories.

Craftsbury's 'laird', Miss Jean Simpson.
Source: Vermont: Its Government 1945-46, *compiled and edited by Mari Tomasi (Modern Printing Co., Barre, Vt. 1945).*

My Vermonters: The Northeast Kingdom 1800-1940

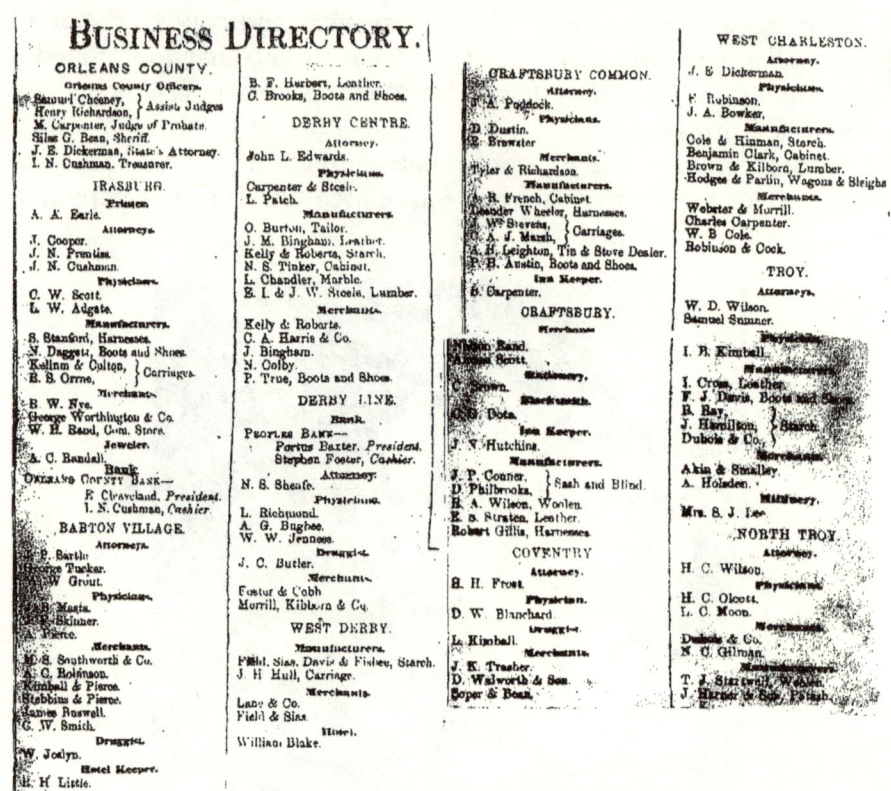

Business Directory for selected Orleans County towns. Walling's maps were accompanied by the list of businesses operating in the 1850s. The railway put towns it did not go through out of the way and began their decline.
Source: Walling, 1859.

II

Other Lines, Other Tales

1. A Bigamist and an Indian

My mother's father's family seems less interesting – but far less is known about them. They seem ordinary but, in a world where records were less well kept, they may have been more interesting than surviving papers suggest. Their name was Sanders and they probably came to New England sometime in the early or mid-eighteenth century and settled in Massachusetts and Connecticut. Most of them appear to have farmed and were not notable. In the mid-nineteenth century, the family produced a probable bigamist in the person of Isaac Levingston Sanders (1808-1890), one of my great-grandfathers.

Isaac Sanders was born in Cavendish in southern Vermont and lived there until about 1836. In 1831, he married Louisa Seward Wilder. Ten children were born to them before they parted. Since no divorce seems to have been recorded, he probably abandoned that family. Eventually, he moved north to Westfield, and, in 1850, to Lowell. Probably in Lowell, he met and married, in 1856, Amanda, the daughter of John Sawyer [35] and Mary Shortsleeves [Courtemanche?].[36] Six children were born to them: Alberta, Samuel, Elzada [or Elzade], Ira, Arthur, and Lottie [perhaps formally Charlotte, informally Tot]. In about 1980, someone showed up at my mother's door and announced that she was a cousin of sorts. The woman claimed to be the great-grand-daughter of Isaac. She believed he had never gotten a divorce from her ancestor, his first wife. She had searched State and County records for a divorce decree but had found nothing. Mother contacted my genealogist cousin, Eldon Sanders, who also sought it but could find no evidence of a divorce. It is likely that Isaac was a bigamist and that the Sanders family in Albany were not legitimate. It was not so hard to move on in the nineteenth century.

Family tradition has it that Isaac started life as a blacksmith but he did not follow that occupation in Albany. Instead, he farmed, kept a store and, after the late 1850s, ran a haulage business from Albany to Barton Landing (now the village of Orleans in Barton township).[37] He kept store from c. 1865 until 3 March 1889 when the store burned along with two adjoining properties. Great-grandfather never rebuilt

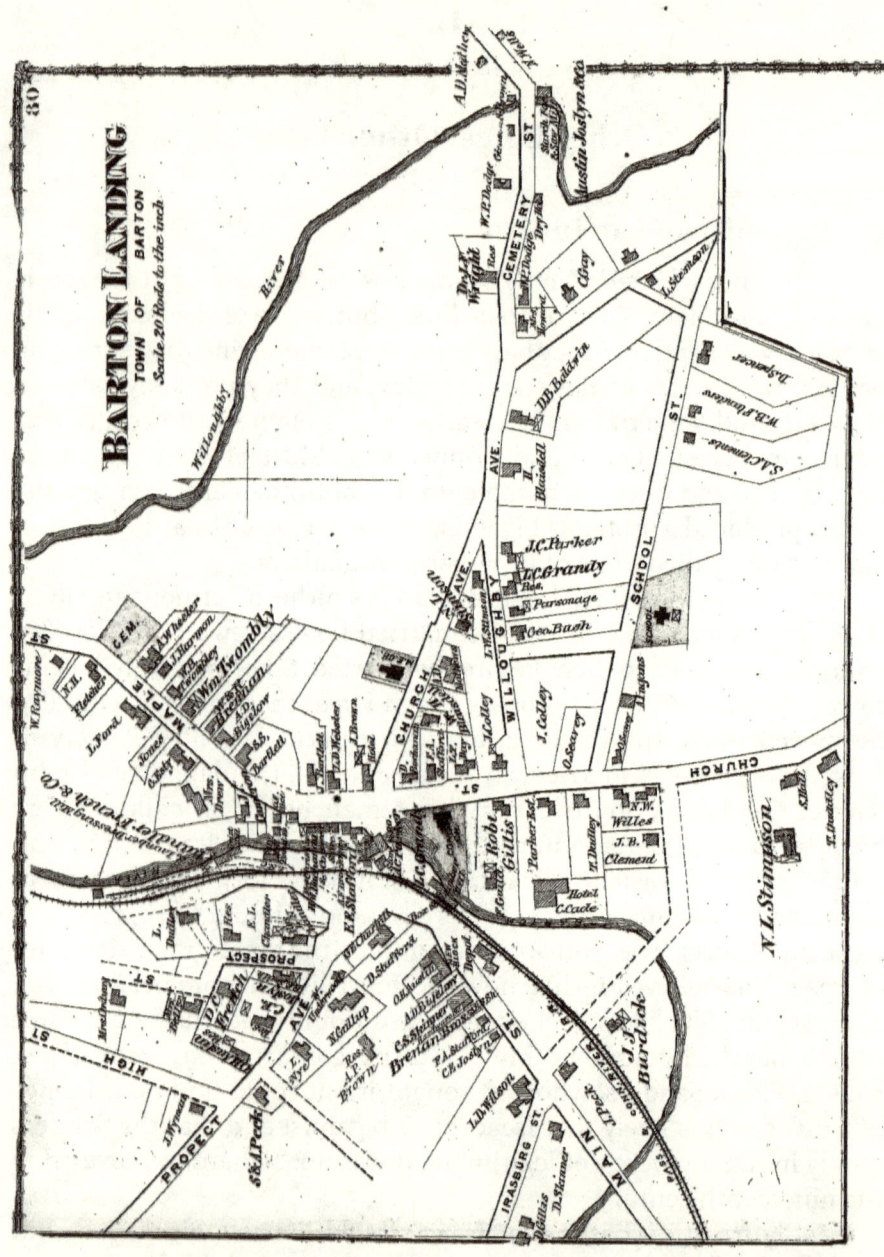

Barton Landing [now the village of Orleans]. This was the second village in the township and was called 'the Landing' because it was the southern point to which boats could come from Lake Memphremagog. Its railhead was as important to the area as the one in Barton village.
Source: Beers, 1878.

and died about a year later. His wife, Amanda, lived on until 1925; she died as a result of a suicide attempt. She probably did not die from strangling herself with a cord tied to the bed-post, but from the shock and exertion of the effort to do so – or so her doctor told her grieving family.

Amanda Sanders c. 1920.

Amanda spoke French with her sisters who lived in Albany and the nearby towns of Lowell and Morrisville – but only when no one else was around. She was ashamed of being French in a community which stigmatized foreigners, most of whom were Roman Catholics. She became a Wesleyan Methodist early in life and was fervent in her piety. She smoked a pipe now and then and was probably part Indian. This was cast up to my grandfather by Gramma whenever she was very angry with him. I remember her railing at him once when they thought I was not there: 'That is the Indian in you showing again!', she shouted – to which he replied, 'Shit a Goddam!'[38] Efforts to prove an Indian lineage have failed but marriages or liaisons to or with, Indians were not so uncommon as many think among eighteenth- and nineteenth-

My Vermonters: The Northeast Kingdom 1800-1940

Amanda's Methodist Church in Albany, c. 1900. It is now the Albany United Church, famous for its Church suppers.

century Canadians and New Englanders of lower social status. Still, it was not much talked about. Amanda seems to have been a nice old lady and a handsome one even in old age judging from a now lost portrait photograph made of her in her coffin.[39] She also liked showy things such as her flow-blue dishes *(below and overleaf)*.

Amanda's Sanders flow-blue china and stoneware in the Scinde pattern was made by J. and G. Alcock and Co., Cobleigh, Staffordshire, England, c. 1850. It was probably not bought as a set but she had many pieces which were dispersed among her children and their children. She also liked sparkly dishes made of moulded Sandwich-glass.

2. Another Family: 'The Unco Guid'

What I know about my father's family comes from published Emerson genealogies,[40] a few surviving papers, records, and photographs, and from what I was told about my forebears by my Emerson relatives and their friends, from my own memories, and from stirring accounts of one of them. Like most fairly long-established New England families, my Emerson forebears included people who can be traced back to the Mayflower. Those who married them were of course 'Puritans' who fled religious persecution in England and braved the terrors of the howling wilderness in order to be free. The family's real history was a bit different.

Massachusetts records show that my Emerson family can trace its antecedents in New England back to at least 1651 when Michael Emerson (1627-c. 1715) was cited to give evidence in a court in Essex County, Massachusetts.[41] He had emigrated from near Boston in Lincolnshire, England, and settled in Rowley and then in Haverhill, Massachusetts. There, he worked at his trade as a cordwainer or shoemaker. My Aunt Flora, a very amateur genealogist not given to saying anything bad about the family, thought he 'must have been a Puritan'. But, anyone who left England around 1650 was probably seeking to improve himself economically and not leaving a state where freedom of religion for those not Anglicans or Roman Catholics was a reality and where there were plans on foot to make the place 'truly godly'. One did not need to emigrate to build a city on the hill – unless one had become disillusioned with the too numerous schemes to create Zion in England. Perhaps he did not want to live in such a place. In any event, his reputation was not all that good. He is known to have severely beaten one of his children. And, Michael Emerson was not admitted to church membership for many years after he arrived in New England. That suggests that he was either something of a non-conformist, not very religious, or was disreputable in other ways – perhaps all three. Family tradition has it that the family were Baptists – but, it is likely they became Baptists in the Second Awakening in the early nineteenth century (in the 1820s).[42] Earlier, they were not noted as being particularly religious. Michael held various civic posts of the onerous sort. By 1700, the family had had two memorable members, only one of whom Aunt Flora Emerson wanted to recall.

The child of Michael (1627 - c. 1715) and Hannah Webster Emerson (?-?) whom Flora admired was their eldest daughter and first child, Hannah (23 December 1657 - after 1729) who married Thomas Dustin or Duston. Hannah was a heroine to early New Englanders because she avenged the killing of her new-born baby in 1697 by killing and scalping ten Indians – two men, two women and six children. She had been 'captivated' in an Indian raid on settlers near Haverhill, during the Second Indian War, often called King William's War (variously dated, 1688-1697). The Indians had killed her new-born child before her eyes and burned her house. They intended to take her north into what is now New Hampshire or, perhaps, even to Canada. Narratives say, a bit implausibly, that she, her nursemaid, and a captive boy had been told they might have to 'run the gauntlet'. They rose in the night, knocked the Indians on the head, and then scalped them so that they could collect the bounty on Indian scalps offered by the Great and General Court of Massachusetts. Having hurriedly taken the scalps, they paddled a canoe from roughly Penacook, New Hampshire, down the Merrimack River to safety. Their reward was fourteen shillings a scalp.[43] That story made it into all the early histories of New England and was a tale my Aunt Flora was pleased to recall. Hannah is said to have been the first woman to whom statues were publicly erected in the United States. They have been standing in Haverhill, Massachusetts *(below)* and Penacook, New Hampshire, since 1874. Local Indians would like them removed.[44] Why not just erect another showing Hannah's child being smacked against the tree with a house on fire in the background? One act of brutality had engendered another as both sides defended in war what they saw as right.

This statue of Hannah Duston was erected in Haverhill, Massachusetts, in 1879 and is said to have been the first erected with public money in memory of a woman.

The child Aunt Flora did not want to recall was Elizabeth Emerson (26 January 1665 - 8 June 1693), the sixth surviving child of Michael and Hannah. Elizabeth, in 1686, produced an illegitimate child named Dorothy. The brat was said by the Emersons to have been fathered by a neighbor, Timothy Swan. Swan's father, Robert, denied that his son had gone 'into that wicked house'. Nothing came of this affair but reprimands. In May 1691, Elizabeth was charged with the murder of two new bastard children born in the same room in which her parents were allegedly sleeping. They swore they had heard nothing. She confessed that the infants' bodies, found in a shallow grave in the backyard, were those of the children she had borne. She had no husband but her father named, as the children's father, a man who was known to have sired five other illegitimate children in and around Haverhill. Elizabeth confirmed that the children were his. She was arrested, sent to Boston, tried, and found guilty of murder in September 1691. While in jail awaiting execution or a pardon for concealing the death of a child presumed to have been killed – the other had been stillborn – she confessed to the Rev. Cotton Mather that she had killed one of the children before she buried it. Mather preached her hanging sermon and later published her confession in *Magnalia Christi Americana* (London, 1702). He preached on the text, 'They die in youth and their life is among the unclean'.[45] Elizabeth seems to have made a good end but she may not have written the confession below, pp.354/5.[46]

My Aunt Flora knew this story and its famous source. When reminded of it, she said it was not good to recall and should not be spoken of. The Emersons continued to engender children out of wedlock but they are not known to have murdered more of them.

The Emerson family produced no other memorable people for a very long time. Michael's son Jonathan had a 'garrison house' c. 1704. One of his children, Timothy, was an officer in a militia company during part of the French and Indian War (1755-1763). Timothy's son, Amos, also served in the Seven Years War and is said to have been at Bunker Hill. He died in receipt of a pension earned as a Captain in the Continental Army. Most of the later Emersons farmed, traded, and went North or West as did so many others who are un-remembered. Ones who were a bit out of the ordinary were Benjamin Folsom Emerson (13 February 1831-1 May 1902) and his son Albert (1859-1914).

Benjamin Emerson was born in Danville to Jonathan Emerson and Mary his wife. He grew up there and married a local girl in 1856, Margaret Russell (12 March 1831 - 7 September 1898). Danville,

Jonathan Emerson (1829-1908) and his second wife, Betsy, were photographed about 1880. He was the great-grandson of Mary Chase Morse (1726-?), from whom he inherited a pewter charger shown below.

which today is a sleepy little hill town, was not so sleepy in the early nineteenth century. It was then a shire town in Caledonia County which had been partly settled by people brought over by the Scotch American Company whose stockholders came mainly from the Glasgow and West of Scotland region. The Company was founded before the Revolutionary War and settled Scots from Newbury to the towns north of it, including many in Caledonia County. The settlers brought their cultural institutions.[47] Danville was on the circuit of the itinerant minister for the Presbyterian Church – one which took him also to Greensboro, Craftsbury, and to other towns down to Newbury. Danville had for some years a printer and shared an annual agricultural fair with other nearby towns. That annual event probably had some connection with an Agricultural Association which ran a library for its members in the 1860s.[48] Phillips Academy, a school whose models were to be found in Scotland and in the Dissenting Academies in England, provided educations for the children of the Danville area. Academies taught all the usual grammar school subjects but also practical ones, such as book-keeping, surveying and sometimes chemistry. Some offered equivalents to a few university courses. Both Benjamin and his wife attended Phillips Academy. Both probably shared the outlook expressed in a surviving paper of hers, written in 1849, when Margaret was seventeen:

> How pleasant is the thought that we can always be gaining knowledge, adding new stores to our mind, and drinking of those intellectual pleasures which never die. Yet how many there are who think when their school days are over that all is done, that there is no more need of study, when, indeed, it is only begun; they have received the kind instructions of their teachers, the sympathy of class-mates, and the anxious solicitude of parents, and are now prepared to go forth, to impart these instructions to others, yet while in this world they should never consider themselves to old to learn but constantly strive to improve and elevate their character. The vast book of Nature is open to all who choose to read from its pages, and affords to the contemplative mind rich stores of knowledge. Thus we find that while in this world we may be constantly improving and if we spend our time well while here, we shall ere long throw off the fetters of this frail body, and the mind [,] freed from this earthly tenement[,] will soar to brighter regions, where troubles are unknown, and where we shall be constantly improving and growing better.[49]

How pleasant is the thought that we can always be gaining knowledge, adding new ~~sotes~~ stores to our own mind, and drinking of those intellectual pleasures which never die. Yet how many there are who think when their school days are over that all is done, that there is no more need of study, when indeed, it is only begun; they have received the kind instructions of their teachers, the sympathy of class-mates, and the anxious solicitude of parents, and are now prepared to go forth, to impart these instructions to others; yet while in this world they should never consider themselves to old to learn but constantly strive to improve, and elevate, their character. The vast book of nature is open to all who choose to read from its pages, and affords to the contemplative mind rich stores of knowledge. Thus we find that while in this world, we may be costantly improving and if we spend our time well while here, we shall ere long throw off the fetters of this frail body, and the mind, freed of this earthly tenement shall soar to brighter regions, where troubles are unknown, and we shall be constantly improving and growing better.

                                    Margaret. C. Rupel.

Phillip's Academy.
April 7th 1849.

Margaret Russell's Phillips Academy paper of 1849.

This, probably unconsciously, echoes sentiments held by, among others, the Edinburgh philosopher, Adam Ferguson, who expressed similar thoughts in essays written fifty years earlier. It was the general view which the next three generations of Emerson's adopted. Study. Work to improve your lot. Expect your reward in Heaven – part of which will be a pleasant and continual improvement in the hereafter. That was also the message of a poem written and sung by the students at the end of the fall term in 1846 which Benjamin and his wife saved among their papers.

John Russell's teacups with deep saucers, English, c. 1810.

That is not all that is known of the couple's intellectual outlook. Margaret Russell's family had come to America around 1813 (probably from the somewhere in the Scottish Borders) with a bit more money and culture than many brought with them. John Russell, the first to come, was a shoemaker. His family was wealthy enough to have had a porcelain tea set of which four pieces survive – two cups made without handles and with deep saucers. They were made in England c. 1800. The Russells probably also brought a four-volume set of the poems of Robert Burns published in 1813, one volume of which survives. That book was well-read. The family continued to read poetry and plays since it had two volumes of those by Oliver Goldsmith (?, Dublin, 1777; ?, London, 1820). Margaret Russell's copy of Edward Young's *Night Thoughts*, also

Benjamin Emerson about the time he went to war in 1862. Note the fashionable Paisley waistcoat and the almost matching cravat.
This photograph appears with the permission of the Old Stone House Museum, Brownington, Vermont.

survives from her school days (Griffith & Simon, Philadelphia, 1847). Margaret's husband, Benjamin, by the 1870s subscribed to the *North American Review* and to similar publications over many years. They were still in the Emerson farmhouse in the 1970s. He was *au fait* with much which was happening in his world. When Frank, his oldest son, married, he gave him a great and expensive nineteenth-century Bible. That, too, sheds light on what interested Deacon Benjamin Emerson. It contained not only the biblical texts but a history and geography of the Holy Land, a chronological index of biblical history, charts of ancient weights and measures, and many pictures. In addition to those study aids, it had a concordance. That gift reflected the giver's many years of teaching Sunday School and the expectation that his son would do so too. Benjamin may have been a carpenter[50] and farmer but he was also a studious reader.

Benjamin and Margaret bought part what became the Emerson farm in Barton in 1858 and built or lived in a log house on a rise somewhat north of the present farmhouse.[51] The cabin's remains were still visible when I was a child and I sleep in a bed which my mother salvaged from the furniture remaining in that house in 1932 – a small cannon ball bed which once had ropes to hold up the bedding. Later, Benjamin and Margaret acquired more land and built a larger house. Part he built but most of it was made by putting together a small house from the eastern side of the road and a larger one from the opposite side. Those were rolled into place by oxen drawing the buildings on rounded logs. The same beasts had been used to drag foundation stones from a quarry three miles away and, later, to clear some of the land. In the end, the farm had maybe seventy acres of tillable land and hayfields and about 100 acres of pasture. Another 400 acres or so constituted the sugar-place and wood-lots. After 1882, Benjamin and Margaret were joint owners of the farm which he had purchased earlier but took years to pay off.

The Emersons had hardly established themselves in Barton before Benjamin enlisted or was drafted into Co. H. of the 15th Vermont Volunteer Infantry Regiment. That unit was raised in the summer of 1862. It trained a bit in Vermont and was then sent to guard Washington, D. C., in a Brigade composed of Vermont Regiments, the 12th through the 16th, under the command of Brigadier Edwin W. Stoughton,[52]. Benjamin and the 15th were stationed in Virginia, at Camp Vermont. We know this from several Grand Army of the Republic dues receipts and because Benjamin later wrote for a comrade who was seeking compensation for piles contracted while on service there.

Manassas Junction, June 16th /63
My Dear Margret

I will write you a few lines to let you know that I am alive and well when I wrote to you last we were on the point of moving we went to Bristoe Station and stoped one night and then came back here Co A was left one company not being a sufficient force to guards this place our Reg was sationed at thre diferent places on this railroad two companys here five at Bristoe and three at Catletts but we are expecting to move back towards Union Mills every hour there is Considerable excitement here now in consequence of the moveing of Hookers army they haveing evacuated all their fortifications on the Raphannock and are falling back they have been passing here ever since Sunday it is said that they going to interce[pt]

General Lee who is moving on towards Maryland the 5th 3rd army corps are encamped here now they will move tomorow I expect it is reported here to day that General McClellan is again in Command of the army of the Potomac the Regiment that John belonged to passed here sunday it belonged to the 11th army corps but I did not know that he belonged to that army corps so I was not on the lookout and did not see him although he passed right in site I have seen Frank Robbins Levie Robbins brother I have not seen but few that I know as the Vermont boys did not pass by here there has five army corps passed here and all or a greater part of Stonmans Cavelry there is so many rumors here in regard to the movement of the rebels that it would be useless for me to write any of them as the truth will not be not known untill there has been a battle fought somewhere write soon B H E

My Vermonters: The Northeast Kingdom 1800-1940

The Monitor and Merrimack.

Air—Landlady of France.

Way down at Fort Monroe
 The Rebels struck a blow
Which made a great commotion through the land,
  we know ;
 But they wish they'd stayed at home,
 And let the Yankee boys alone—
For they've got enough of Yankee Doodle Dandy,
  oh.

 Their iron Merrimack,
 With others at her back,
Commanded by Buchanan, the old granny, oh,
 From Norfolk started out,
 And tried to put to rout
And capture little Yankee Doodle Dandy, oh.

 The noble little band
 On board the Cumberland,
All disabled, was asked to surrender, oh ;
 "You may sink us, if you like,
 But my flag I will not strike,"
Says brave Morris, "to the last we will defend
  her, oh."

 The Congress soon went down,
 The Minnesota fast aground,
Which made our Yankee sailors feel abandoned,
  oh—
 But see, with hearthy cheers,
 The Monitor appears,
While the music struck up *Yankee Doodle Dandy*,
  oh !

 The rebel shot flew hot,
 But the Yankee answered not,
Till they got within a distance they called
  handy, oh—
 "Now," says Worden to his crew,
 "Boys, let's see what you can do—
If you take this iron rebel you're the dandy oh."

 Then the little Monitor
 Her iron hail did pour,
Which made the Merrimack squeal like a
  gander, oh—
 Then the rebels shook their heads,
 And to one another said :
Lord! they've got an IRON Yankee Doodle Dandy,
  oh."

 Says the rebels, "We're undone,
 Boys. I guess we'd better run,
For the bottom of the river is quite sandy, oh—
 We're sinking fast, I swear,
 So for Norfolk we will steer,
And DAMN that iron Yankee Doodle Dandy, oh.'

 Raise your voices, every one—
 Give three cheers for *Ericsson*,
Who gave us such a vessel, neat and handy, oh—
 And now we'll give three more
 For the gallant Monitor ;
And three we'll give for Yankee Doodle Dandy,
  oh.

 And now the Merrimack
 Has been blown to Bally Hack,
We'll give three rousing cheers,, so neat and
  handy, oh.
 Next John Bull will get his fill—
 For let the world say what they will,
The Yankee Boys for fighting are the dandy, oh.

Published by Charles Magnus, 12 Frankfort Street, N. Y.

Benjamin attested that his fellow soldier had had 'Chronic Diarrhoes' contracted in Camp Vermont which then had turned into chronic piles. Benjamin served somewhat over a year and saw a bit of action. The 15th had a memorable encounter with 1,800 of J. E. B. Stuart's cavalry in late December 1862 and guarded the baggage train at Gettysburg in July 1863.[53] Benjamin was luckier than many since he came home without wounds, illnesses, or piles. As a child, I remember seeing what I believed were his gun and bayonet at the Emerson farm house.[54] He was later active in the Grand Army of the Republic (G.A.R.). A certificate and mementos of his membership are now at the Old Stone House Museum in Brownington, Vermont.[55]

Benjamin Emerson's letter home (shown on the previous pages) as he marched towards Gettysburg in 1863. He bought fancy stationery with more than one engraving and poem/song in the package. The picture on his first letter (page 46) shows the Monitor *driving off the Confederate ironclad, the* Merrimack, *which had been victorious over several Union warships.*
Like many soldiers' letters, this second letter was written to reassure folks at home that Benjamin Emerson was alive and well – a sentiment belied by the image (above) which shows some of the horrors endured by men on both sides.

Regular Meeting of Mason Post No 16
G.A.R held at Gloves April 19 1894
Number Members Present 13
Opened in due form
Adjt report read and accepted
Q.M. Made the following report
Bal on hand Feb 22— 1894 $24 08
Received Cap tax   1 50
March 22— bal on hand   44 83
April 19. Paid out Paper Postage   75
~~Paper and postage~~   1 50
C.W Cook to Printing and Postage 1 50
Delegates Expences   4 00
Book for Adjt   50
Balance on hand to date (675) 38 04
report accepted
Gen orders No 5 and 6 read
Application of Josiah Gernett read
Balloted for and accted
he was Presented and was Mustered
in by Mustering officer Nye
Post closed in due form
        E H Nye Adjt pro tem
                Thomas Marnall Adj

Regular Meeting of Mason Post 16, GAR.

Boss, with his Regiment and Company scratched into the lead backing, and his belt buckle. The boss was sometimes called 'the Rebel snipers bull's eye'.

For many years Benjamin Emerson served as a school director and as the Senior Deacon at the Congregational Church in the village of Barton, to which he sometimes walked on the Sabbath. His wife is unlikely to have made the walk of six miles. In old age, they attended services at Westmore, two or three miles from the Emerson farm. He was buried in the family plot in the Westmore Cemetery overlooking Willoughby Lake. One of his sons, Albert, and his daughter Alice, inherited the farm.

Albert, according to the family, became friendly with Robert Frost, who spent time at Willoughby Lake during the summer of 1909. They shared an interest in botany. Albert is thought to have written something on the Lady Slippers which grew on the Emerson farm but no article of his has been found. He, but not Alice who kept house for him, visited the Columbian Exposition in 1893. There his first visits were to the horticultural and agricultural exhibits and then to the Vermont building. He probably stayed for about a week and saw old Vermont friends living in the area.

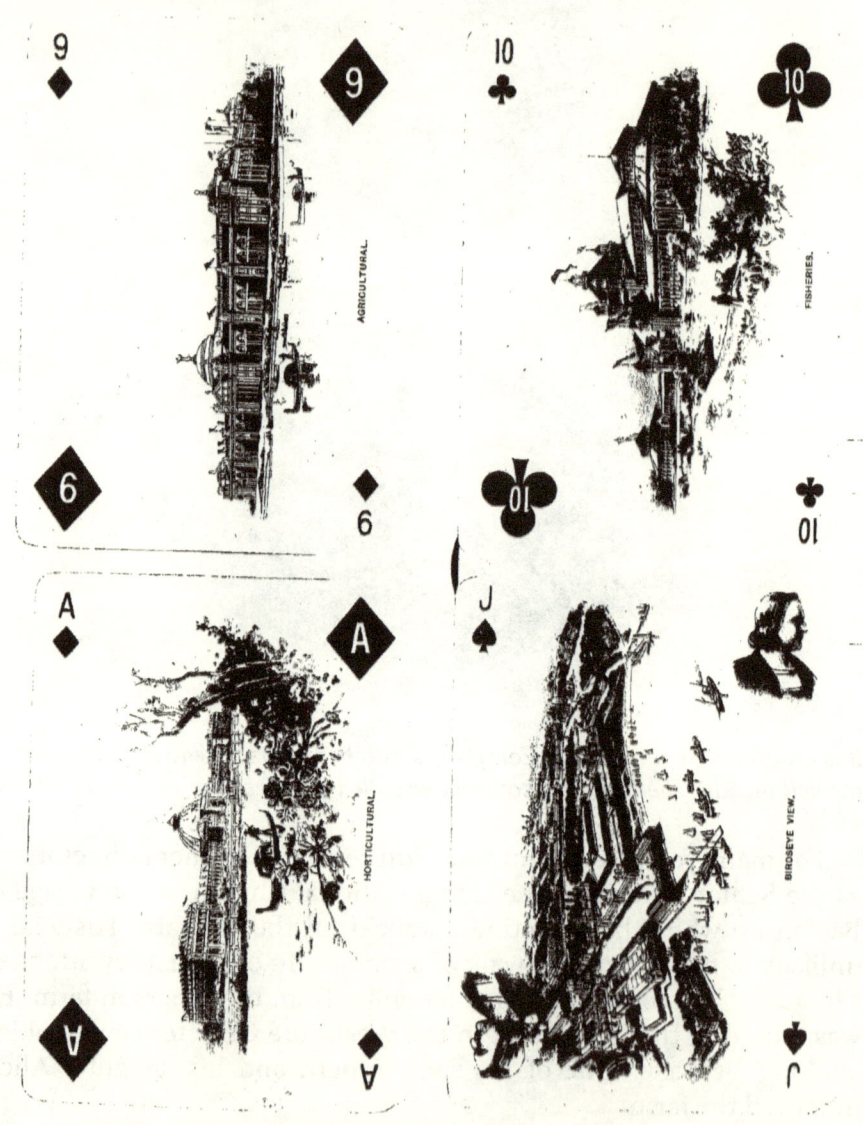

These views of the Columbian Exposition come from a souvenir deck of cards which Albert assuredly did not buy. He was tea-total and the cards were printed by the Hayner Distilling Co. Albert did visit the buildings shown.

Benjamin's second son, my grandfather Frank (1861-1923), was a granite-cutter and ran a granite business in Hardwick (see below., pp 265-267).[56] After Albert died in 1914, Frank inherited a share of the farm in Barton. Alice stayed on for a while but then went to Barton Village to look after her nieces who were in high school there. Later, she went to Burlington to keep house for her nieces while they attended the University of Vermont. She remained there, probably continuing to board other co-eds as did many spinster ladies.

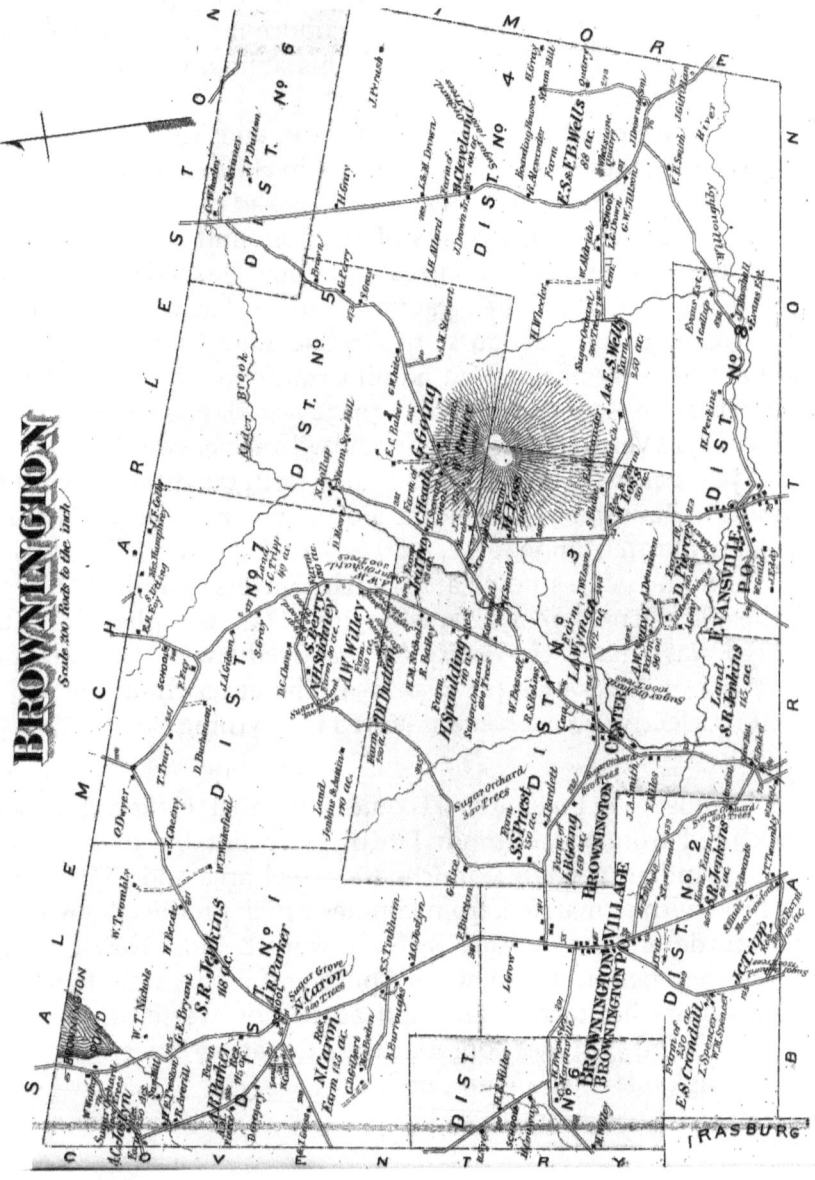

Brownington. Source: Beers, 1878.

My father's forebears were industrious and hard-working people who meant to get ahead. They had a large cousinage of similar people scattered around New England and the Midwest. Among them by the 1880s were, a musician in Hanover, New Hampshire, a Professor of English at the University of Vermont, a watchmaker at Waltham, Massachusetts, ministers in southern New Hampshire and Massachusetts, and many farmers and small businessmen. Others in the family went West where land was better. Such people intended to improve themselves and to do well in life. They prayed and worked for that success. They expected their children to do so too. My father's generation was little different. He and his siblings were better educated but only he remained a farmer.

Of the five children of Frank Emerson and Rosa Carr – Karl, and Arthur (my father) finished high school in Hardwick, while Lee, Flora, and Dorothy attended Barton Academy as had their father. Karl was an honor student at the University of Vermont and became a promising young business man in a Montreal company. He died of pneumonia or the flu in 1919. Arthur, after graduating from Hardwick Academy, took a two-year agricultural course run by the State University in Lyndon. He became a farmer and an administrator for the Farm Relief and Rehabilitation Agency (see below, pp.307-308). His sisters went to the University of Vermont. Flora graduated with a science B. A. Dorothy took a two year course to qualify as a teacher. Both taught in Massachusetts schools in Taunton and Agawam. Both took early retirement and ran the family farm from 1940 - c. 1980 — half that time selling real estate and "antiques". Lee studied at Syracuse University and, while working in the War Department in Washington, D.C., completed an LL.B. at George Washington University. He practiced law in Vermont and was Governor of the State from 1950-1954. The other child, Russell, was a mental defective who never amounted to anything.

***

Like most New Englanders, I could, if put to it, make a case for being descended from some minor Lincolnshire notable of around 1400, from an Indian woman from the Montreal area and the Frenchman she lived with or married, from families which produced bush-fighters and murderers and another with a bigamist. Most New Englanders, unless they belong to a few very pure and aristocratic families, can claim similar heritages – and find no end of Mayflower people who married them. I am now content to be a Canadian citizen but, in spirit, a New Englander and a Vermonter.

III

Getting Gear, Accumulating Objects

1. Stage One: Getting Started

Most of my Albany and Craftsbury forebears were Scottish or Scots-Irish folks who came to Vermont with relatively few goods. The fairly well off Rogers family is said to have gone to Albany with what they could load onto an oxen-drawn-cart to which was tied a cow and perhaps a horse. The family story was that they brought a well-wrapped tall-case clock with wooden works, a New Hampshire-made highboy (c. 1770) full of linens and clothing, also wrapped with quilts and blankets, a chair or two, a spinning wheel and the requisite other furnishings – pots, pans, kettles, dishes, knives and cutlery, and not much else for the house. Somewhere, there would have been axes, knives, a gun and powder horn, hoes, and other tools. Wooden shovels, forks, and rakes they could whittle in Albany. There would have been some seeds and certainly flour enough to see them through their first winter. Wrapped against the weather were a book or two and their Bible. There was probably not much else to put in a cabin lit with rush lights but which had a fireplace which many did not.

When Jesse Roger I, the original settler, died in 1838, his estate was appraised and valued and the return on his and his family's investment and hard work becomes clear.[57] The farm he had cleared, and for which he had provided a 'plank house' to replace the log cabin in which they first lived, now included a barn and sheds. It was valued at $1,700 – up from $400 in 1821.[58] The Rogers family lived not opulently but comfortably and most of their ten children lived to grow up – a testimony to their being well-fed and not living in squalor. Indeed, their family home, by 1838, probably had six or seven-rooms in a one and a half or two story house – kitchen, dining room, living-room, three or four bedrooms, one or more store-rooms and, perhaps, a partially unfinished upper storey used for storage and to sleep in. They seem still to have lacked a stove and there were no curtains listed but the place was probably homey enough and contained more than was listed. The inventory mentions as household items: three bed steads ($1.50), four beds [? feather beds] and bedding, flannel blankets, sheets and other covers ($50.00),[59] two tables, a stand ($4.75), the highboy

($5.00), the 'Woodden clock' ($5.00), an unspecified number of chairs, ($5.00), '2 small dish Ashets', and a 'Tea Kettle' ($2.00), 'Small pot [60] small Brass Kettle' ($2.00), a 'Set [of] tin ware' ($12.00),[61] 'Croakery Ware' ($ 8.00), three 'wash tubs' ($1.50), three 'meat tubs'[62] ($3.00), eight 'Pails and Churn' ($3.00). There is no mention of cutlery and glassware which may have belonged to his wife. Jesse, like his son, was probably a cooper but there is no mention of tools or a cooperage. He was likely to have given or sold them to his son prior to his own death. Other signs of prosperity are the value of the old man's clothes ($20.00) and two buffalo robes ($6.00). His gun was valued at $6.00. What is surprising, given his piety, is that there are no books listed and no personal objects, such as a watch. The home does not seem full of objects and what is known of the local stores suggests that there was not a lot to buy locally other than necessities – grain, cloth, some household furnishings, and sundries.

Still, the Rogers farm was not a subsistence enterprise but one producing for a market which was not only local. The appraisal shows Jesse had waiting to go to market 940 pounds of butter and 150 pounds of cheese – valued at $197.00. To feed their animals and themselves, there were twenty-five tons of hay (worth $100.00), ten bushels of wheat ($15.00), half as much rye ($5.00), 200 bushels of oats ($50.00), seventy bushels of 'indian Wheat' or buckwheat ($29.40), and twenty-five bushels of corn ($25.00) – for a total of $421.40. The family herd was comprised of a year-old bull ($10.00), eight milking cows ($184.00), one beef creature ($25.00), and eight calves ($48.00). There were presumably parts of other animals curing in their meat tubs. In addition, there were fourteen sheep ($23.34) which would have yielded wool and some meat, and three hogs ($72.00) and five shoats or weaned piglets ($40.00). The unspecified poultry was worth $7.00 – which points to many hens, turkeys and geese. Rounding out the livestock were two horses ($100.00) and two oxen ($80.00). Altogether the animals were worth $564.34. Any farm family of this sort would be eating well.

To work the place, Jesse Rogers had two plows ($5.00) and a harrow ($2.00), two chains for skidding logs ($4.00), two harnesses ($5.00), and two ox yokes ($3.00). Among the miscellany of other things listed were two scythes and snaths, three pitchforks, and two rakes, a barn shovel and two hoes – collectively worth $6.50. There was a one-horse wagon ($6.00) and a cart ($3.00), and 250 sap buckets and spouts ($10.00). Perhaps to boil the sap, and certainly to make soap, he had 'a Potash Kettle' and 'Caldren'. Both would have been large cast-iron pots ($15.00).

Many of their things would have been locally produced. Excluding the highboy and clock, chairs and tables were not beyond the skills of local carpenters; and, while the plows may have had shares and coulters made elsewhere, they too were not beyond the competence of local blacksmiths. In Vermont, they also made carts and wagons and fitted their wheels – as I well remember from the 1940s. Only the metal had to be bought elsewhere. The farm might make butter for those in distant places but local craftsmen made many of the things the family needed. Other things, they found in nearby stores or in the carts of the occasional peddlers who often sold tinware, pins and needles, and what in a growing consumer society came to be called 'notions'. That would change but it had not yet done so.

2. Stage Two: The Beginnings of the Consumer Society

By 1850 the US Census returns show that Jesse Rogers II had improved the value of the property and goods he inherited in 1838 by about 50%. It was now listed at $2,500.00. Ten years later he is listed as worth $1,000.00 and his property valued at $4,000. That increase was the product of farming, logging, dealing in cattle, and making cooperage items – buckets, tubs, kegs, and barrels. They were in ever greater demand because the railroads, by the 1860s, enabled farmers like Rogers to ship products with greater ease and lower costs. William Hayden II, by contrast, had seen his personal-worth increase in 1860 to $2,000 and then to $6,500 but his property valuation rose to be worth $50,000 – $40,000 of that sunk in his new house. The remainder points to the opulence in which the family lived. What could one buy with that sort of money? What did one buy? And where? The Haydens' Account Book entries for the 1850s and 1860s, and descriptions of their house offer a few hints about consumption beyond mere needs.

William Hayden II bought a lot he could not get locally. Lead pipes arrived by wagon via Greensboro – which probably meant from its rail head, first at Wells River and then at St. Johnsbury. Neither the central furnace and hot-air heating system nor the cast-iron heat vents resembling fire-place surrounds were locally available, just as there was little local demand for the fancy door knobs, faucets, and other fixtures Hayden put in. All those had to come from some distance but whence is not clear although his accounts show dealings with firms in Boston, Toronto, and the Eastern Townships of Quebec. Timbers, boards, and shingles for his new brick house seem to have been bought locally as were stones for foundations, steps, lintels, and decorations. Bricks for the house were made on the farm or in a kiln near the property.⁶³ Masons and stone-workers are likely to have come from other towns. Paint, and pigments, like Paris Green, could have been bought in Vermont but fancy rugs and ornate lamps came from some distance. It is hardly surprising that his house cost so much. What it represented was the possibility of high consumption of quality goods, even in the hinterlands – if one could pay for both the cost of the goods and the transport costs. A lot was available to those who could afford it – including fancy furniture, large pictures, fine glassware and much more. The Haydens had it all.

Barton in 1859. The shops and manufacturers follow the course of the outlet from Crystal Lake. The Railroad had reached the town but not gone beyond it. Source: Walling, Orleans, Lamoille and Essex Vermont (1859).

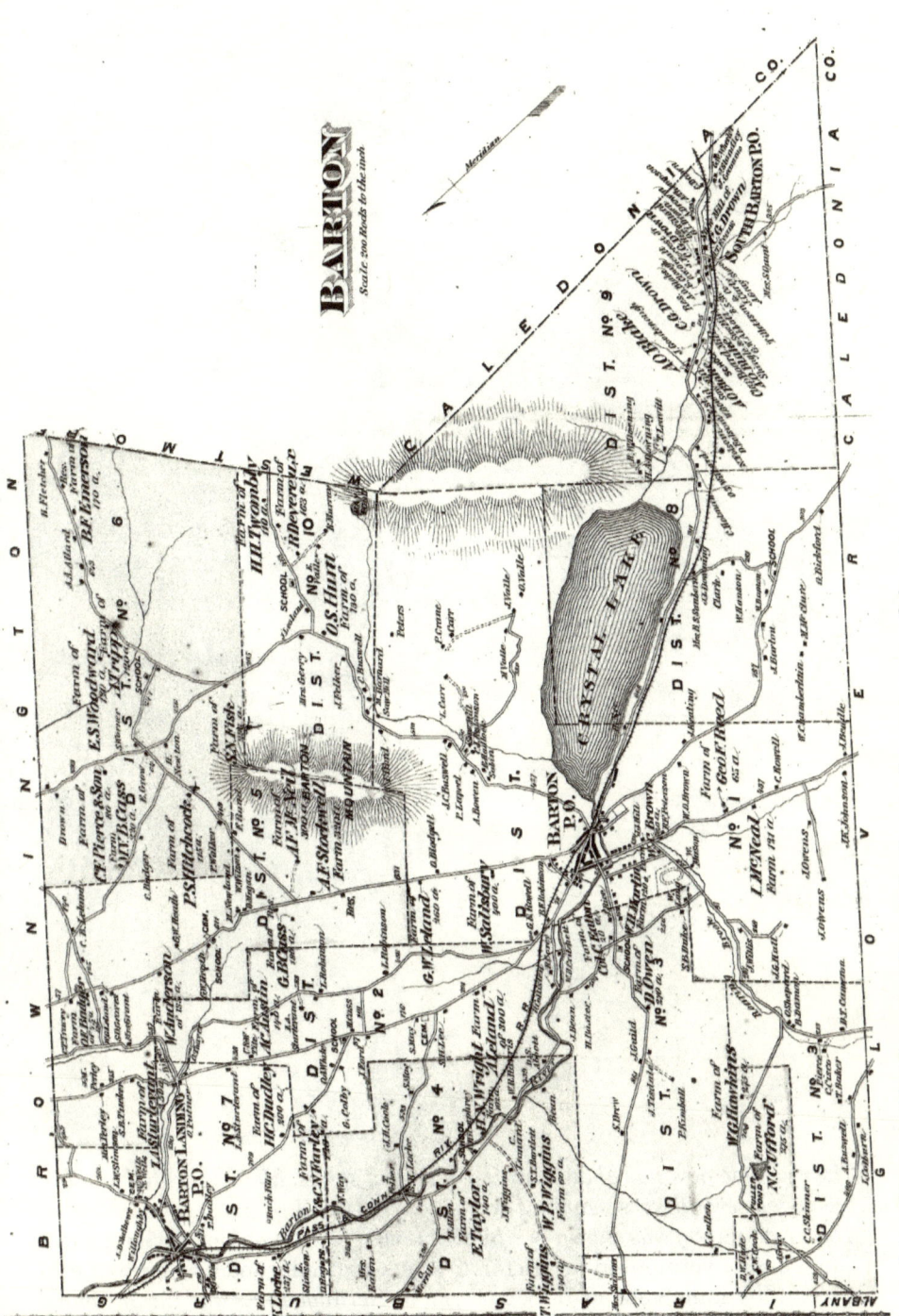

Township of Barton. The Emerson farm is in the northeast corner of the map. Source: Beers, Atlas of Lamoille & Orleans Vermont (1878).

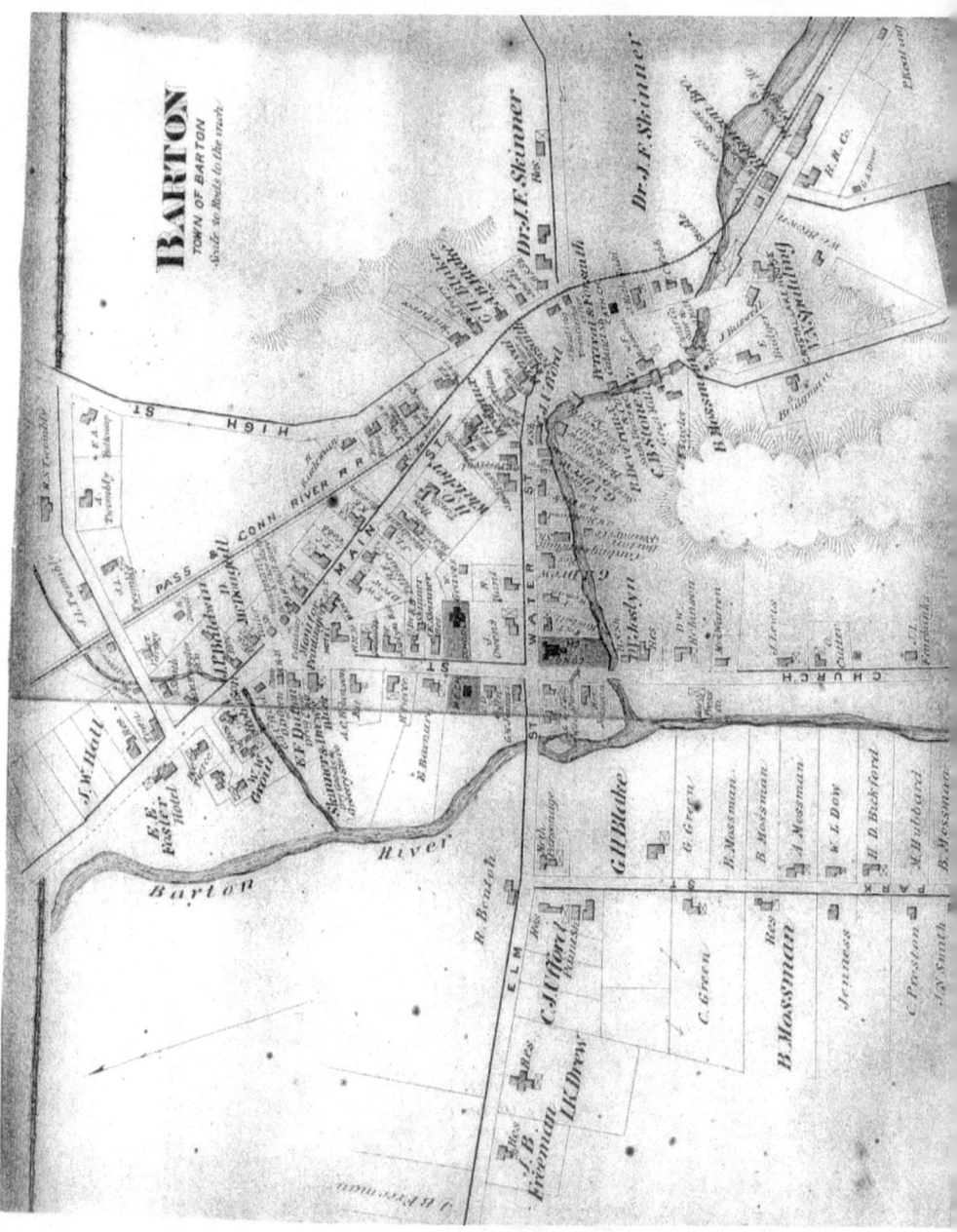

The riverside now had about a dozen mills and shops. Many operated into the 1920s and several were reopened during World War II.
The town in 1889 was shown in a bird's eye view by George Norris; See J. Kevin Graffagnino, Vermont in the Victorian Age: Continuity and Change in the Green Mountain State, 1850-1900 *(Vermont Heritage Press and the Shelburne Museum, Bennington and Shelburne, Vt.,1985, Plate xxiv).*

Barton.

MISCELLANEOUS.

F. W. BALDWIN, Attorney and Counselor at Law
Wm. W. GROUT, Attorney and Counselor at Law
O. V. JOSLYN, Blacksmith; Blacksmithing in all its branches
E. F. DUTTON, Successor to Wm. Joslyn & Sons, Druggist and Apothecary, Dealer in Paints, Oils, and Varnishes, Books, Stationery and Fancy Goods
I. K. DREW .... Resident
J. W. HALL & CO., Dealers in Dry and West India Goods, Hats, Caps, Ready-made Clothing, Flour Salt Fish, Nails, &c., Teas, Coffees Spices, Sugar and Molasses. Country produce of all kinds take in exchange for Merchandise

J. E. SKINNER
E. E. FOSTER, Propr of Foster's Hotel, lower part of Village. Free Carriage to and from Depot to every train
V. N. SPALDING, Propr of Crystal Lake Hotel, near Depot. First-Class Livery connected with the house.
D. McDOUGALL, Merchant Tailor. All the Latest Styles and Patterns on hand
J. F. SKINNER ..... Physician and Surgeon
A B BLAKE .... Resident
GEO. H. BLAKE, Publisher of Orleans County Monitor

MANUFACTURERS & DEALERS.

CHAS. J. UFFORD Manufr of all kinds of Carriages and Sleighs. Dealer in all kinds of Carriage Goods. New patterns for Sleighs this year. Particular attention given to repairing. Job and Blacksmith work of every description. I also keep the best Painter in this part of the State. All wishing good work are respectfully invited to call and see my stock. Barton Vt
WHITCHER & ELLIOTT, Manufrs of Tin-Sheet Iron, and Copper Ware; Dealers in Stoves, Pumps, Lead Pipes, Sinks, Hollow Ware, Wooden Ware Brooms, Glass Japanned and Britannia Ware. All kinds of Country Produce, Paper Stock, and Pedler's Barter bought and sold
J. P. BALDWIN, and G. A. DREW, Firm of Baldwin & Drew, Manufrs and Dealers in all kinds of Lumber. Saw Mill Water St. Manufrs of Doors, Sashes, Blinds and Mouldings; also Contractors and Builders. Dealers in Glass, and Putty, &c. Plans and specifications furnished, and General Jobbing done to order

DEVEREUX, REUBEN & CO., Manufrs and Dealers in Sashes, Doors, Blinds, Mouldings, Lumber of all kinds, Glass, Putty, &c. Also, Wheels, Hubs, Spokes and Rims. Specifications furnished and General Jobbing done to order
B. MOSSMAN ... Manufacturer of Chair Stock
PERCIVAL & FORSAITH, Manufrs and Dealers in all kinds of Parlor, Dining Room and Kitchen Furniture, Chamber Suits, Mirrors, Lounges, Spring Beds, Mattrasses, &c., also, Coffins and Caskets
C. B. STONE, Jr & CO, Manufrs and Dealers in Flour, Feed, Corn Meal, and all kinds of Grain. Mills in Barton and Glover
J. B. FREEMAN, Dealer in Butter, Cheese, Eggs, Poultry, Pressed Hay, &c. At home every Saturday.
C. A. ROBINSON, (Firm of Robinson Bros.), Wholesale Dealers in Corn, Four Meal, Shorts, Middlings, Iron, Nails, Salt Oils, Lime, &c. C. A. Robinson, W. T Robinson. Depot Store

FARMERS and DAIRYMEN.

A. C. AUSTIN, Dairy Stock, Hay, Grain Pork, Poultry and Sugar, Dist No. 2
W. ANDERSON, Dairy, Stock, Hay, Grain, Poultry, Pork and Sugar, Dist No 5
W. C. BROWN, Dairy, Stock, Hay, Grain, Poultry, Pork and Sugar, Dist No 1
O. F. BADGER, Dairy, Stock, Grain and Hay, Dist No 5
G. B CASS Dairy, Stock, Hay, Grain, Pork, Horse raiser, Sheep and Wool, Dist No 5
M. V. B CASS, Dairy, Stock, Hay, Grain Pork, Horse raiser, Sheep and Wool, Dist No 6
H. C. DUDLEY, Dairy, Stock, Hay, Grain, Poultry and Sugar, Dist No 7
RICHARD DEVEREUX, Dairy, Stock, Hay, Grain, Pork, Poultry and Sugar, Dist No 10
B. F. EMERSON, Dairy, Stock, Hay, Grain, Pork, Poultry and Sugar, Dist No 6
Col. C. EATON, Dairy, Stock, Hay, &c., Dist No 3
F. FARLEY, Dairy, Stock, Hay, Grain, Poultry and Sugar, Dist No 2
S. N. FISK, Dairy, Stock, Hay, Grain, Horses Poultry, Pork, Hops, Cheese Sheep, Wool, General Produce Saw Mill. Dist No 6
O. S. HUNT, Dairy, Stock, Hay, Grain, Poultry, Pork, Horses Hops, Sheep, Wool and general produce, Dis No 10
W. G. HAWKINS, Dairy, Stock, Hay, Grain, Poultry, Sheep, Wool, Horses, Sugar, &c. Dist No 3
P. S HITCHCOCK, Dairy, Stock, Hay, Grain, Sugar &c., Dist No 6
A. LELAND, Dairy, Stock, Hay, Grain, Sheep, Wool Poultry, Pork and Sugar, Dist No 2
G. W LELAND, Dairy, Stock, Hay, Grain, Wool, Sheep, Horses, Poultry, Pork, Sugar &c., Dist No 11
S. K. LOCKE, Dairy, Stock, Hay, Grain, Sugar Pork, Poultry, Potatoes, Sugar, Sheep and Wool, Dist No 7
I McNEAL, Dairy, Stock, Hay, Grain, Pork, Poultry, Sugar Sheep and Wool, Dist No 1
W. H. MARTIN, Dairy, Stock, Grain, Hay, &c, Dist 1

A. F. McNEAL, Dairy, Stock, Hay, Grain, Pork, Poultry, Potatoes, Sheep and Wool, Dist No 5
D. OWEN, Dairy, Stock, Hay, Grain, Pork, Poultry, Sugar, Sheep and Wool, Dist 3
C. F. PIERCE, Dairy, Stock, Hops, Grain, Pork and Poultry, Dist 6
GEO. F. REED, Dairy, Stock, Hay, Grain, Poultry, general Produce, Dist. 1
W. SALISBURY, Dairy, Stock, Hops, Grain, Poultry, &c, Dist 1
I. A. STURTEVANT, Dairy, Stock, Hops, Grain, Poultry, Pork &c, Dist 7
A. F STOCKWELL, Dairy, Stock, Sheep, Wool, Hay, Grain, Pork, Dist 5
E. TAYLOR, Dairy, Stock, Hay, Grain, Sheep, Wool, Pork, Sugar, Poultry, Dist 4
A. TRIPP, Dairy, Stock, Hay Grain, Poultry, Pork, Sugar, Sheep and Wool, Dist. 6
H. H. TWOMBLY, Dairy, Stock, Hay Grain, Poultry, Pork, Sugar, Sheep and Wool, Dist 10
N. C. UFFORD, Dairy, Stock, Hay, Grain, Sheep, Wool, Sugar, and general produce, Dist 3
W T. WIGGINS, Dairy, Stock, Hops, Hay, Grain, Poultry, Pork, Sheep, Wool, Sugar and general produce, Dist 4
H N. WRIGHT, Dairy, Stock, Hay, Grain, Sheep, Sugar, Wool and general produce, Dist 4
E. S. WOODWARD, Dairy, Stock, Hay, Grain, Sheep, Wool, Potatoes, Sugar, Poultry, Pork, and general produce, Dist 6

Barton Landing.

Attorney

C. J. ROWEL, Attorney and Counselor at Law

Insurance Agent

A. C. PARKER, Agent for Vermont Mutual, Union Mutual, Champlain Mutual. Sub-Agent for all principal Stock Insurance Co's doing business in the New England States

Merchants and Manufacturers

AUSTIN, JOSLYN & Co
J. CAMERON & Co, Dealers in Corn, Flour, Shorts, Graham, Corn and Oat Meal, Pearl, Barley, and Feed of all kinds   Custom grinding done to order
H. W. BUCHANAN & Co, Dealers in Dry Goods, Groceries, Boots, Shoes, &c.   H. W. Buchanan   Daniel Buchanan
C. H. GREEN, Dealer in Furniture, Carpetings, Window Shades and Fixtures, Children's Carriages, Coffins and Caskets, and the Ordway Spring Chair.   Austin & Joslyn's Block
L. C. GRANDY, Propr Barton Landing Steam Dressing Mills.   Manufr and Dealer in Hard and Soft Wood Lumber, Spruce Flooring and Sheathing, and Dressed Clapboards.   Packing Boxes a specialty

South Barton.

Manufacturers

A. O. BLAKE, Manufr and Wholesale Dealer in Lumber of every description.   Dimension bills sawed and shipped at short notice.   Chair Stock, Frill Boards, &c, sawed to order   Also, Packing Boxes of all kinds.   Orders by mail promptly attended to
C. G DROWN, Manufr and Wholesale Dealer in Lumber of every description.   Dimension bills sawed at short notice, &c

Business Directory for selected Orleans County towns.

ALMON PECK & SON, Dealers in Cook and Parlor Stoves, Glass, Wooden, Japanned, Brittania and Hollow Ware   Iron and Lead Pipe, Copper and Iron Pumps   Also Manufrs and Dealers in Tin, Sheet Iron, Copper and Brass Ware
C. S SKINNER (of the firm Skinner & Guild) Dealers in Hardware, Cutlery, Flour and Grain, Oils, Varnishes, Doors, Sash, Iron, Lime, Nails, Joiners' Tools and Agricultural Implements.   C. S. Skinner.   P. Guild
CHANDLER, FRENCH & Co, Manufrs and Wholesale Dealers in Dressed Lumber, Spruce and Hard Wood Flooring, Spruce and Ash Sheathing, Packing Boxes of every description, Barton Landing.   L. N. Chandler.   D. C. French.   E. L. Chandler
E. E. STAFFORD, Dealer in Flour, Produce, W. I. Goods, Groceries, Paints, Brushes, Medicines, Confectionery, Yank e Notions, &c.
N. L. STIMPSON............Lumberman
ROBT. GILLIS.............Harness Maker
JUD J BURDICK, House and Sign Painter, Carriage and Ornamental Painting and Paper Hanging
JUD J. BURDICK, Musician.   Burdick's Quadrille Band, Barton Landing   Half Fare on Rail Road.   Any number of pieces furnished and satisfaction guaranteed.   Terms reasonable.   Address Jud. J. Burdick, Barton Landing.
BRENAN BROS..............Blacksmiths
W. H. BLASDELL,......Resident, Church st

Physician and Surgeon

J. F. WRIGHT...... Physician and Surgeon

By the 1820s, one could buy ready-made clothing, furniture, shoes and much else in cities and large towns.[64] With the railways, which reached towns in northern Vermont in the 1850s and 1860s, the distribution system for such items was extended. Barton had a rail connection by 1857, Barton Landing (now Orleans) in the following year. Both had stations with sidings by 1863. Greensboro Bend had a station by 1869. Craftsbury and Albany were less than twenty miles from stations, a day's round trip for a freight wagon – but they were on no rail line and suffered as a result. The cornucopia of goods now available can be seen in the Day Book kept by a Barton merchant from July 1867 to January 1868. Since Barton was then nearly the same size as Albany, this store served a market about the same size as did the stores in Albany and neighboring Craftsbury.[65] It is likely to be indicative of what the Hayden and Rogers families now had available to them, not only in Barton, but closer to home at somewhat higher costs. Barton lacked little, in the way of dry goods, small tools, and even luxury items like bespoke suits, fine Balmorals, nice scarves or parasols. The industrial revolution and cheaper transport costs offered by railways transformed the lives of those in rural communities by giving them more to buy and by enlarging their marketing areas. By the time Jesse Rogers II died (1896), he left a much larger estate and many more objects.

This still-standing Rogers house probably had twelve rooms and storage space in the attic. Today it lacks the porch and the barn has been rebuilt to the right of the house.

Jesse II and his wife had a few books, more and better chairs and had enough spare cash to build a cooperage and the large new house across the road from it. The house (previous page), had, in the end, a large kitchen, dining room, parlor, and a bedroom on the ground floor and four bedrooms on the second floor, plus more space in the attic to store things, including summer guests. It was well-appointed with whale oil and later kerosene lamps. Eventually, it had an Argon lamp to read by. That house still stands but has lost its rather elegant porch which went half way round the building and accommodated many guests at parties. It was leased by Jesse's eldest son, Cornelius (1841-1919) from about the time of his first marriage in 1867 to Elizabeth Darling (1848-1873). Jesse and his wife moved to another property that he owned, the Bagley farm (see page 233).

A picture survives of the owners' bedroom from c. 1900. Cornelius Rogers' interest in travel and machines is recognized by a picture of a railway station and a port scene; his wife's concerns with fashions are acknowledged as is her piety and their regard for friends and family members. Mary Abby hung the wall paper herself.

Getting Gear, Accumulating Objects

Kerosene lamps such as this were used in the Rogers house.

During his marriages to Lizzie Darling (overleaf) and his to second wife, Mary Abby Tenney (1847-1914) (on following page), whom he married in 1875, the family's goods expanded greatly. That testified to Cornelius's success as a farmer and cooper and to his wives' eagerness for nice things.[66] Lizzie's kitchen sink had running water and there was a big range, replaced in 1876 by an even bigger stove with a large woodbox. There were enough pots and pans to cook a Thanksgiving feast for thirty or more people, and plates, cutlery, and glasses of varying quality, to serve them all at once on tables in the kitchen, dining room and probably the parlor. The normal dining room table seated eight comfortably and, with all its extra leaves inserted, at least twice that number. No one seems to have lacked a china plate although some of the serving dishes were stoneware. No pewter dishes seem to have been in use. There were table covers and napkins for everyone and individual silver or silver plate napkin rings for the family. By the 1880s, they had accumulated some coin silver pieces –mostly ice cream spoons– and a number of good silverplate serving pieces. Others came as thank-you gifts after summer visits by friends and relatives, including a berry spoon and fruit knife. There was now a kitchen clock as well as the tall-case wooden clock in the living room.[67]

Elizabeth [Lizzie] Darling Rogers. This locket, 2½ by 2 inches, has an unused space for a bit of hair on its reverse. The locket is gold-washed silver and meant to be worn as a pendant. It was probably made before 1867, before she was married, since she seems not to be wearing a wedding ring. The image has been finely coloured; the dress is a light tan with stripes of brown, white, and gold.

This picture of Mary Abby Rogers (c. 1888) is 22 by 16 inches and nicely coloured. It was probably done on a trip to Boston or New York.

The living room or the parlor, by the 1870s, had Mary Abby's flute, short-necked cello, and a small organ. A piano was added later. Somewhere, there was a sewing machine and a bookcase with probably about sixty books ranging from Bibles and religious works to a few novels, volumes of history, self-help works, and school books left behind by grown-up children (See Bibliography, pp. 345-347). There was probably a magazine rack to accommodate the papers and magazines to which the family subscribed. Mary Abby followed the fashions; her husband read political pieces, technical articles, and farmers' magazines. The living room eventually housed, a card table with a folding-top and some overstuffed pieces. The papered walls had pictures hanging on them and photographs of children, and, after 1906, views of Niagara Fall and other sights they had seen on their trips to Boston, New York and California. More such views were contained in photograph albums full of tintypes, cyanotypes and photographs. In the corner of the room, by 1906, was a fancy piece of wood painted with a California view of a road going through a redwood tree and elsewhere a souvenir 'sword' made of Chinese money held together with red string. There were other curios on shelves and tables which created a satisfying Victorian clutter.

Napkin rings of the Rogers Family. Left to right, back row: Jennie's, Robbie's, Cornelius's (engraved with a thistle); front row: Mary Abby's and Lizzie's (hallmarked with a London mark).

Each of the bedrooms was papered and festooned with bric-a-brac and mementos. There were prints and pictures in the bedrooms too – Mrs O'Leary's mythical cow kicking over the lantern to start the Great Chicago Fire, the 'Cotter's Saturday Night' by an unknown artist,[68] and a picture of the Madonna were among those my grandmother saved. Others reflected Cornelius's interest in great engineering works and machines. Every bedroom had a wooden or iron bedstead with springs (not ropes) on which lay a mattress and bedding. Next to each bed was a night stand. Probably each room had a pot or slop jar. There was a chair or two in each room and some had trunks or storage boxes made by Cornelius and covered by his wife with bright padded cloth (roughly 2' x 4' x 2' or 18" high). Those held stored items but also could be sat upon. They brightened rooms and back halls. I saw the last of them in the 1980s. There were lots of kerosene lights. The family no longer used candles although the memory of rush lights, used by Jesse I, had not died out. In the bedroom of Cornelius and his wife stood the highboy.

Some Rogers silver: The six coin-silver spoons on the left were made c. 1840-1860 and are engraved with the initials of Cornelius Rogers' aunt. The spoons below were gifts from 'E to CC' – members of a related Clifford family. The fruit knife and ladle were gifts to Cornelius and Mary Abby Rogers sometime in the 1880s by summer visitors named Etta and Hattie.

Outside the house on special Sunday summer afternoons, Cornelius, who liked company, served lemonade and metheglin made with his own honey taken from hives whose bees buzzed the porch. Beyond the porch were the sheds in which he kept wood, his 'road wagon' (see page 88) and surrey, maybe a horse and whatever. Behind the house was the barn in which he had stanchions for about twenty cows, a tie-up for his bull, stalls for at least three horses and a colt, pigpens, and a henhouse. By 1900, they raised sheep only for their meat, not wool. Since he cut ice in the winter, there was an icehouse somewhere in or near the barn. There, the blocks of ice, taken from the Black River, would be insulated with a covering of sawdust drawn from a local mill. The ice was used in the milk-room to cool the stored but un-churned cream and the butter waiting to be sold. Cornelius had the plows and implements he and his hired man needed to farm. He hired an extra hand during haying but he relied on outsiders for threshing. Since he spent part of each winter logging, there were chains and skids, peavies and poles to guide his logs down the Black River to the mill in Irasburg. Across the road was his cooperage in which he made such things as sledges, sleds, and sleigh bodies as well as sap-pails and tubs. His lathe was powered by a calf on a treadmill. The shop had some sort of a small forge.

View of a party at the Rogers farm in c. 1910.

When Cornelius and Mary Abby shopped c. 1880, they had at their disposal stores in Albany, Craftsbury, and more distant towns like Newport and Barton. There they could find many different items. Mary Abby regularly bought cloth in the closest stores and made her own dresses with patterns she bought elsewhere or cut out herself using designs and pictures in magazines. She was a skilled seamstress and made some of her own hats, decorated with plumes, ribbons, and lace from local and more distant stores such as Jordan, Marsh & Co. of Boston. A few years earlier, her father, another well off farmer,[69] had bought her a very nice dress costing $20.00 in which to play music before an audience. That perhaps came from Montpelier. By 1868, Barton was almost competitive with the capital of the State as can be seen from the Day Book of a Barton store covering the period from July 1867 to February 1868. That store was one of two serving the village, which, in 1870, had a population of 944. The people in the surrounding area probably about doubled the number of potential buyers.

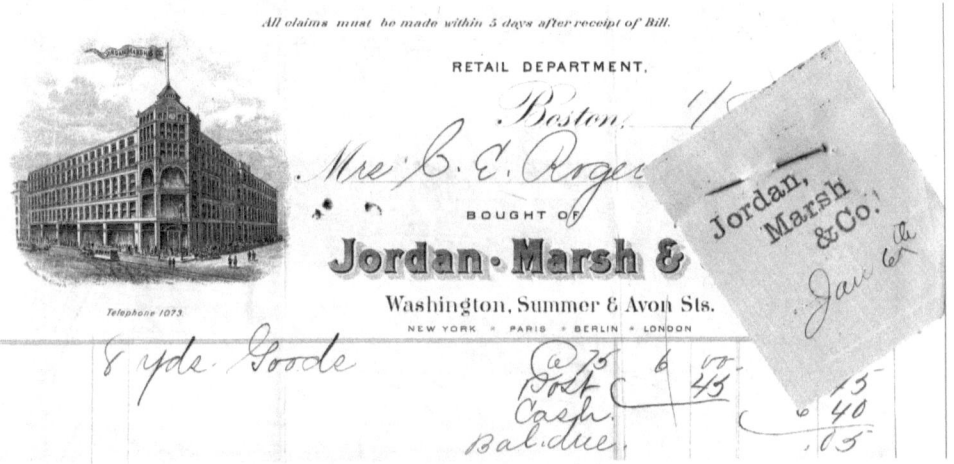

An 1889 bill from Jordan, Marsh & Co., Boston, for cloth. Note the low telephone number and the horse drawn street cars.

I do not know who kept the Day Book, illustrated overleaf, but I think it was probably kept by or for Amos C. Robinson who by 1878 owned the Depot Store in Barton and dealt wholesale in some things, like grain. Robinson was a successful merchant who became one of the largest shareholders and a Director of the Barton National Bank in 1875. The store did not lack capital since it was well-stocked with general merchandise. It served many families living on the Westmore Road for whom it would have been the first store they came to when they went

This is the Day Book's page for Christmas Day 1867.

to Barton. All the Robinsons in town seem to appear in its accounts. Still, the Day Book has charges made to Amos and his wife which, if he owned the store, might suggest that someone else was running it. The other likely general store was the one kept by Mason or R. M. Kimball which was down the street. About Kimball, who also bought at the first store, I have been able to find nothing. At some point, the Day Book came into the possession of Benjamin Emerson and was passed down in the Emerson family. I doubt the records are Benjamin's since he was then farming and before that had been a carpenter. Whoever owned it, the store was a place where one could buy most things needed in a household. (See the Appendix to this chapter.)

The store sold a lot of basic food – eggs by the dozen, butter by the tub (two, ten, twenty pound tubs), flour by the barrel or half-barrel, salt, spices and so on but very little fruit or green vegetables. One suspects that most of his customers had gardens. Much of the food was locally bought and seasonal so there were no berries until summer and no apples until the fall. Hog's-heads and feet were available in the autumn when pigs were traditionally butchered. Turkeys only appeared around Thanksgiving. Christmas, not yet much celebrated, created no bulge in the sales of anything, and was just another working day – as it would have been in Scotland. There seem to have been no canned goods, no candy, no toys, and not much that was exotic other than teas.

There was, however, an extensive line of dry goods, which points to a lot of home-made clothing. While men's suits and other things could be bought off the racks, as could most items women wore, what was exceptional was the store's ability to make clothes to order for both men and women. The owner or his tailors sometimes cut garments which the store seems not always to have sown up. The owner presumably had a lady to do the female tailoring and fittings. There were not a lot of children's clothes but some. One could also buy expensive things like a 'fur sett' – a matching fur hat, collar and cuffs, and, possibly, a muff.

In the housewares section, one could buy luxury items, like a $12.00 piano cover, and dishes or gadgets like a washing machine. Two washers were sold in the six months covered by the book. This section could have fitted out a house while the hardware section sold things with which to do minor repairs – and shingles to re-roof a dwelling. In a society using lots of horses, it is not surprising to find that the store dealt in stirrups, horse blankets, curry combs, and whips. Oddly, it does not seem to have carried horse-liniments, bag-balms or other medicines for animals.

The list of sundries is perhaps most interesting for what is missing. There were no toys sold during the half year, not even before Christmas. No personal hygiene items were sold other than soap and combs, not even shaving brushes and razors. The store seems not to have sold patent medicines. There were card tables but no cards; no skates, books, or pictures to hang on the wall, and no intoxicating drink. This increasingly affluent society was not yet a very self-indulgent one.

After 1872, those at the socio-economic level of the Rogers family and their friends could find in the pages of the annual *Montgomery Ward Catalogue* even more goods with a sort of guarantee of their quality.[70] They might also be cheaper. Cornelius's daughter bought a lot from catalogues after her marriage in 1888. Her furniture, bustles, and kitchen wares often came from catalogues. Those catalogues, year after year, when outdated, supplied bum-wad other than the corn cobs the family usually used – and which some members thought were better because they were softer and less abrasive – the best toilet paper of their times. By c. 1906, one could even buy a house from a catalogue, as did Cornelius Rogers' son Andrew. Such prefabricated houses were sold not only by the Aladdin House Co. but also by Montgomery, Ward & Co, Sears and Roebuck & Co., and by others in the United States and Canada, including T. Eaton Co. of Toronto. Their houses, school houses, and barns came in various styles and sizes. All were precut, boxed or bundled, and came with instructions about assembling them.

This Aladdin house was built in Newport in 1912 by Andrew Rogers. It had four rooms on the main floor and two glassed-in porches, added by Andrew. Upstairs were three bedrooms and a bath. The front porch came with the kit but Andrew may have added the back porch, one supported by cement filled iron pipes since the house was built on a hill.

THE ROLAND

A HOUSE with good lines outside and well arranged inside. Notice style of porch roof. This type hails from Kansas City. The gable placed broadside gives it an arch effect. First story in siding, second story shingles, or all siding, or all shingles can be furnished. One bed room across front of second floor with two corner bed rooms at rear — bath room just off the hall between them. Living room, dining room and kitchen with pantry on first floor. The Roland has a number of admirers and satisfied owners.

SPECIFICATIONS

Size, 20 x 26 ft. Price, $876. Cash Discount, 5%. Net Price, $832.20. See Terms on Page 2.

All lumber selected Yellow Pine, Red Cedar, and Huron Pine. Height of ceilings, 9 ft.; second floor, 8 ft. Sill, 6 x 8 in. Joists, 2 x 8 in. first floor, 2 x 6 in. second floor. Studding, rafters, and ceiling joists, 2 x 4 in. Joists, ceiling joist and studding placed every 16 in. Flooring, 1-in. clear and knotless. Sub-floor. Building paper. Side walls, sheathing lumber, 1-in., siding and shingles. Roof, 1-in. lumber, overlaid with shingles. Lath and plaster or patent plaster board. Base board, stairs and all interior trim and finish clear and knotless Oregon Fir. Windows, two sliding sash, glass double strength. Doors, outside, 2 ft. 8 in. x 6 ft. 8 in.; inside, 2 ft. 8 in. x 6 ft. 8 in.; front door, special design. Porch columns square, with railing. Front steps. Hardware, locks, hinges, knobs, nails, stains and paint for two coats outside; oils, stains, and varnishes inside.

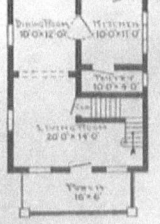

First Floor Plan, The Roland

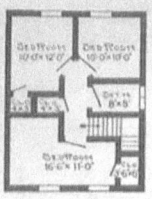

Second Floor Plan, The Roland

THE VERA

A COMPACT and comfortable little home. Every bit of space utilized to best advantage. Designed for rather small lot. Steps are placed at end of porch. Has open stairway, wide arch between living room and dining room, two bed rooms, and bath. The dormer shown on one side is balanced by similar dormer on opposite side. A comfortable home at an attractive price.

SPECIFICATIONS

Size, 18 x 24 ft. Price, $761. Cash Discount, 5%. Net Price, $722.95. See Terms on Page 2.

All lumber selected Yellow Pine, Red Cedar, and Huron Pine. Height of ceilings, 9 ft. first floor; 8 ft. second floor. Sill, 6 x 6 in.

Joists, first and second floors, 2 x 6 in., studding, rafters, and ceiling joists, 2 x 4 in.
Joists and studding placed on 16-in. centers.
Sheathing lumber, 1 in. Flooring, clear and knotless. Sub-floor. Building paper. Bevel siding or shingles.
Roof, inch lumber, overlaid with best prepared roofing or shingles.
Lath and plaster or patent plaster board.
Base board, stairs and all interior trim and finish clear and knotless Oregon Fir.
Windows, two sliding sash, double-strength glass.
Doors, outside, 2 ft. 8 in. x 6 ft. 8 in., inside, 2 ft. 8 in. x 6 ft. 8 in.; front door, upper half glass.
Turned porch columns.
Front steps.
Hardware, locks, hinges, knobs, nails, stain, and paint for two coats outside; oils, stains, and varnishes inside.

First Floor Plan, The Vera

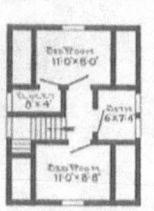

Second Floor Plan, The Vera

| ALADDIN | Read carefully pages 2-10, 101, and 127 of this catalog | READI-CUT |

A page from the extensive Aladdin House catalog.

My Vermonters: The Northeast Kingdom 1800-1940

This cover of the facsimile of the 1897 Sears Catalogue gives a good indication of the range of items offered in its 786 pages.

Getting Gear, Accumulating Objects

The highchair shown dates from c. 1890 and was used by a friend of my father. Similar chairs were advertised in the Sears, Roebuck and Montgomery Ward catalogues during the 1890s. They sold for between $1.00 and $2.00. The silver-plated cup was given to Elwood Sanders by his grandparents, Cornelius and Mary Abby Rogers c. 1890. The silver-plated baby-spoon belonged to one of the Sanders children and comes from about the same time.

Beginning in the 1860s, the families whose papers supply the database for these essays began to show much more varied purchases, particularly for their children. Some were utilitarian items, like highchairs and baby-cups, others were toys. A surviving cast-iron toy cannon said, improbably, to be a Civil War factory model or replica of a Confederate gun, joined hoops and tops.[71] For girls there were items to dress a doll's tea party table (opposite). A bit later came card games. Those were not only to play hearts or such like games but to learn with. The educational cards generally had, on one side, pictures, and on the other side facts to be learned about the Bible (page 78), nature (page 79)[72], history, or literature. Sometimes there were questions with answers included elsewhere in the decks. Some decks contained brain-teasers such as the rebuses my grandmother had as a child (page 80). Jennie Rogers in c. 1884 had roller skates which she used somewhere in Albany. That there was a 'rink' of some sort says something about changing community attitudes toward children and their need for fun.

This toy cannon was said to be made in the South c. 1860-65.

There were a few more things for adult diversion and amusement. Books and magazines appeared in greater variety, ranging from *The North American Review*, taken by Benjamin Emerson for many years, to Cornelius Rogers' *Thrice A Week New York World* – a Democratic paper started in the 1880s – with views very different from those of his local Republican papers. There were popular song books containing music played in the Rogers household and women's magazines (page 83). Collections of family silhouettes (opposite) and photos often begin in the 1860s with postcards coming a generation later (page 84).[73] There were pictures of boys going off to war, such as the portrait picture taken of Benjamin Emerson (page 42) – and girls' photos to take with them. On more formal occasions, expensive portraits were

Getting Gear, Accumulating Objects

These objects belonged mostly to Jennie Rogers in the 1870s and descended to her daughter, Doris Sanders, whose grandfather Darling made a dollies' table for her to set. They are, left to right: spelter knives and forks, a tiny wooden bucket, two butter stamps, a tin chest, a cast iron candlestick, a bisque pitcher, an iron frypan, and a flat iron.

The silhouette of Jennie Rogers Sanders was cut in 1895 in a Westfield, Massachusetts, dry goods store while she was visiting her friend Clara Reed. The silhouette of Cornelius Rogers was, as it says on the reverse, 'cut from life by the Great Dudley', in Boston in 1882. Dana Dudley published a history of the silhouette in 1881 and had other publications.

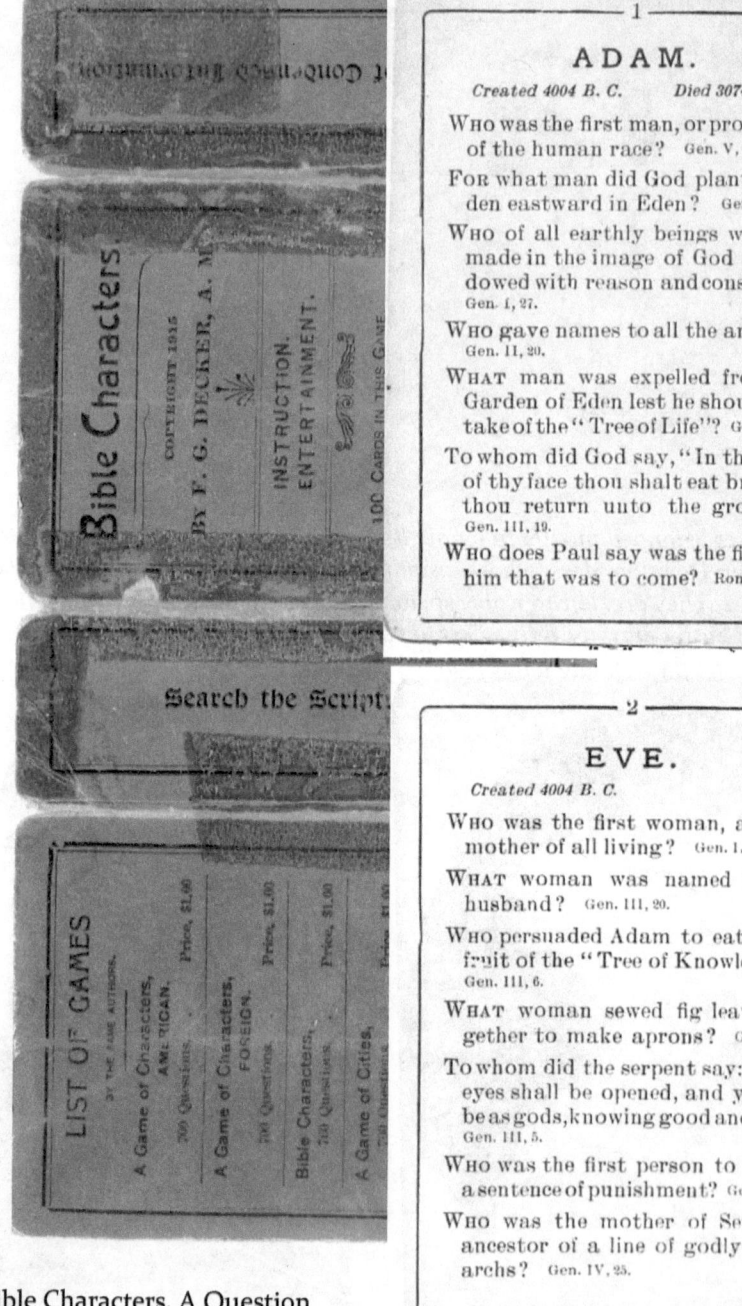

Bible Characters, A Question and Answer Game, 'Issued by O. F and F. G. Decker, Buffalo, N. Y., 1915'. This set begins with Adam and Eve and ends with Paul, card 100. The object was to give significant facts about each person named. The pious frowned on ordinary card-playing; this was a substitute.

"NEW SERIES OF BIRDS."
SET OF 30 DESIGNS.

A set of these cards (30 in all) accumulated in the ordinary course of buying housekeeping supplies, will form an interesting collection. Should all the cards be desired immediately, (six two-cent stamps) will about pay the cost and postage, and upon its receipt with your name and Post Office address (State and County must be plainly written), we shall be pleased to mail a complete set of the cards.

IMPORTANT REASONS

Why housekeepers should buy PACKAGE SODA or SALERATUS in preference to bulk Soda weighed and wrapped by the dealer. The retail price of the ARM AND HAMMER SODA in packages is the same as for inferior package Soda. Consumers gain nothing by buying unknown and inferior Soda; they simply put more money into the merchants' pockets. PACKAGE SODA like CHURCH & CO.'S ARM AND HAMMER has the guarantee of a responsible manufacturer.
Bulk Soda may be of anybody's manufacture, and generally of a poor quality

CHURCH & CO.,
Route 4, Wall St. Station, New York

6. MAGPIE.
(Pica pica hudsonica).

This handsome bird, a relative of the crows and jays, is found in varied species, in Western North America. It is a rare occasion when one is seen east of the Mississippi. The Magpie is omnivorous and its crafty disposition is exhibited in an aptitude for kleptomania and mimicry.

By 1900, nature cards for children were being used to advertise baking products. The predecessor of Arm and Hammer Baking Soda gave away bird cards by the early 1900s.

These are from a set of rebus cards dating from the late 1870s. It was bought by Cornelius Rogers for his children. The answer sheet has been lost.

made for Northeast Kingdom purchasers in St Johnsbury, Hardwick, or Newport, or purchased on trips to larger cities such as Springfield and Boston, Massachusetts, or New York City. Portraits, once an aristocratic item, were now within the reach of those in the middle and lower classes. With photos came the tinting of the best ones, buckram-, plush-, or leather-covered photo albums, and some large expensively framed pictures (pp.65, 199).

This shows a young Barton man, H. B. Orcutt, wearing the uniform of the Barton Band c. 1900. The medal he wears identifies him as the son of a Union Soldier of the Civil War. He is dressed as he would have looked on a Memorial Day Parade.

Another of the things which many families bought were musical instruments. Most of the small towns now had a flourishing local musical scene featuring a band (overleaf), church choirs, and home sing-songs – all needing instruments of some sort and in many cases uniforms. Musical instruments were now available in the larger Vermont towns such as Newport, Lyndonville, or St Johnsbury and from mail order catalogues.[74]

Shown is the Albany Town Band in 1905. Its twenty-two members included the town's doctor, storekeepers, a carpenter, the town tinkerer, a creamery worker and farmers. They played twelve instruments.

Getting Gear, Accumulating Objects

This book was mostly about clothes and adornments but there were selections of prose and poetry and a bit of music.

The songs in this collection included twelve Scottish, several German and some English. The American songs came from the pre-Civil War period but also included some patriotic Union songs and others sung by Confederate soldiers.

This album was purchased to hold 94 postcards and brochures showing places visited by Cornelius and Mary Abby Rogers on a trip to the West Coast in 1905-06. They sent about 25 more cards to relatives (which also survive) and came back with a collection of about 40 photographs.

The more ornate photograph album belonged to the Emerson family and has some studio pictures of soldiers serving in Vermont Regiments during the Civil War. The last photograph was probably added in the 1890s. The other album comes from the Rogers family and has similar materials. Both were probably bought sometime in the period 1870-1890.

Getting Gear, Accumulating Objects

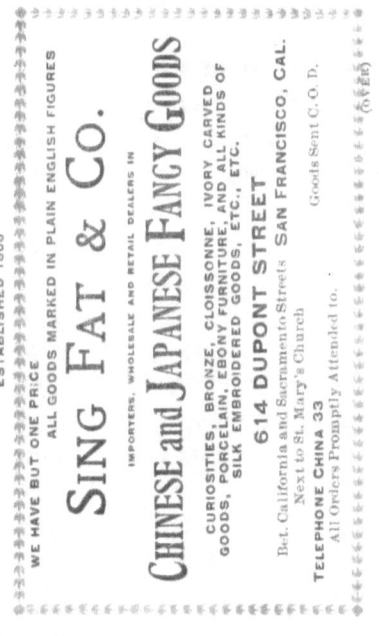

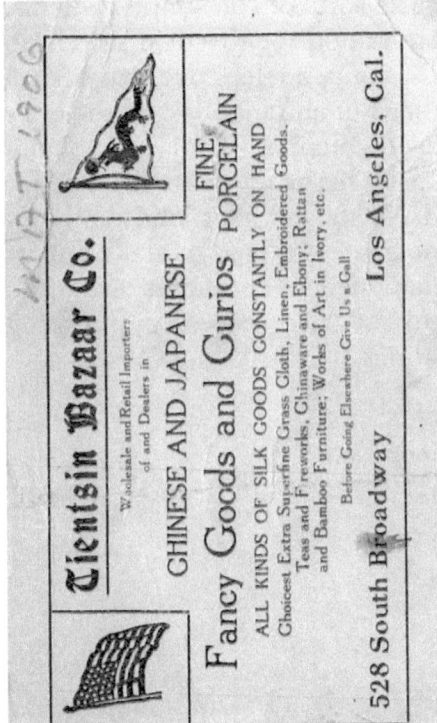

(Top) This colourful trade card advertised the shop at which Mary Abby bought souvenirs in 1906. The dragon, an imperial beast, is set against a yellow background which also had imperial connotations. (Left and above) Mary Abby visited another oriental curio shop in Los Angeles and may have bought there the ivory pill box.

There were more luxury items like muffs, watches, and jewellery. The Rogers men had had watches since at least the 1830s but the ones bought by them and other of my forebears later in the century grew larger and more complex and were fastened to chains of silver or gold or gold-filled links which ended with fobs. Some were now for their wives and daughters. Women accumulated other ornaments as well. By c. 1910 most of the women of my grandmother's generation had the sort of things shown opposite. Families accumulated fancy porcelain hair receivers, pictures to hang on walls, and trinkets purchased on trips, such as the carved ivory or bone pill-box bought in California by Mary Abby Rogers in 1906 at the Sing Fat Chinese and Japanese Fancy Goods Bazaar (previous page). At some point, Jesse Rogers' 1790s muzzle-loader was, replaced by one or more modern rifles. There were also better buggies and 'road wagons' (page 88), and, by c. 1890, surreys with fringes on the top, like the one Mary Abby drove to Church, and Cornelius Rogers and his wife drove to visit friends or to the Barton Fair (page 89). The consumer revolution did not stop with such items but went on almost endlessly. By the 1890s, the Montgomery Ward Catalogue was over 600 pages in length and the *Sears and Roebuck Catalogue* had reached nearly 800 pages.

Not all new spending went on those sorts of consumption items. Anyone born in the 1840s and dying around 1915 lived to see cheap travel on railroads, to send telegrams, to use a telephone (page 89) [75] or gasoline driven motors powering saws or automobiles. By the early 1900s, they could have seen 'Mr Edison's pictures', as Mary Abby did at the Congregational Church in Albany in 1902,[76] or an airplane [or perhaps it was a balloon] as Leonard Watson did in St Johnsbury (see n.155, p.363). By the early 1900s, some had crystal radio sets. Walmart and e-Bay are but present stages in an ongoing consumer revolution whose inevitable end is not yet in sight but will come with diminishing resources and greater income inequalities.

Getting Gear, Accumulating Objects

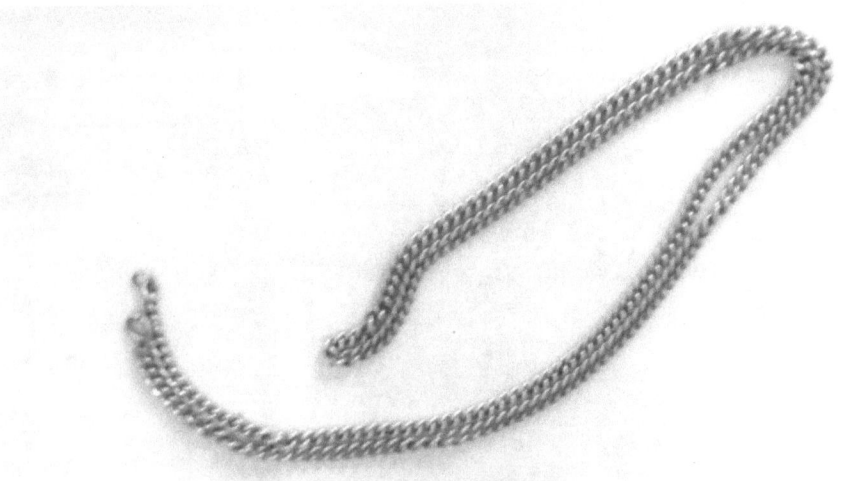

This gold filled watch chain was purchased by Alden H. Darling, grandfather to Jennie Rogers.

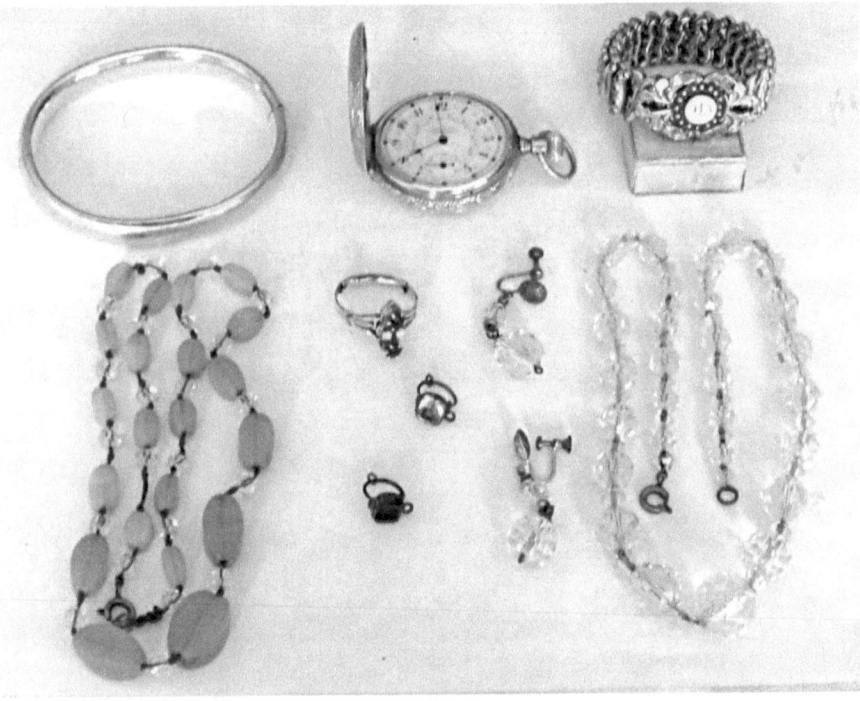

Left to right and top down: Jennie Rogers's gold filled bracelet c. 1890, a nice gold watch, an expansion bracelet with an initial plate set within a circle of tiny brilliants, necklaces and ear-rings and, in the centre, her 'engagement ring' (c. 1888) – two garnets and two opals set in red gold. Jennie also had a nice coral necklace which is not shown and an imitation coral one which is. Most of her other jewellery, save for several cameo pins, was glass and not valuable.

The Rogers family 'road wagon'. The Montgomery Ward Catalogue *for 1895 advertised such wagons for $28.00 to $53.00 depending the accessories one purchased.*

Getting Gear, Accumulating Objects

This postcard shows the Barton Fair Grounds in the late 19th Century before the Floral Hall Exhibition Building was constructed. The barns housed race horses over the winter months. The Fair Ground is where Ku Klux Klan meetings were held in the early 1920s.

A quarterly telephone bill from 1901. The company lasted until about 1910 when it was squeezed out of business by larger companies which denied it connexions to distant callers.

Appendix to Chapter III

The Barton General Store sold one or more of the following items, 31 July 1867 through 23 January 1868.

Presumably it stocked other items not sold in this period.

Food

Eggs
Butter (by the pound or tub)
Lard   "
Flour (white, graham, rye, buckwheat)
Corn meal
Sugar (white, dark, hard or granulated, Maple)
Honey
Molasses
Salt
Spices: allspice, cassia, cinnamon, ginger, nutmeg, pepper
Raising agents: Cremor tartara, soda, saleratus
Raisins
'Basic Soup' [probably stock cubes or cakes – 'Portable soup' was made by the 1720s in London, England, and probably earlier for the French and British Armies fighting in the Low Countries, c. 1708.]
Rice (probably by the pound)
Potatoes
Crackers [but no bread or even yeast]
Beans
Onions
Squash and gourds
Fish: (Fresh Pollock?), salted cod, salted salmon
Pork: whole pigs; pigs' heads, pigs' feet [in season]; pork cuts and organs
Beef :   "
Lamb: whole [1 sold] and in pieces
Chickens: sold as live chicks or whole grown birds; sold also as meat
Geese [2 sold]
Duck [1 sold]
Turkeys: sold as chicks or as whole birds in November
Condiments: Ketchup, Gherkins by the jar or keg, Pickles by the jar or keg
Johnny Cake [listed once]
'Berries' [in season], probably strawberries, raspberries, currants and maybe gooseberries. All were available from local sources in Barton during summers in the 1930s - 1950s
Apples
Cheese
Nuts: 'cashay', beechnuts by the quart, butternuts by the bushel [walnuts were not mentioned and were not as common locally]
Teas: Indian, Black, Jafa [Java], 'Jap'
Coffee

Clothing: Women's

Blummers
Undershirt [or underskirt?]
Corsets and 'corset springs' ('Whale Bones' or stays)
Girdles
Underskirts
Hosiery and stockings
Hoop skirts
Ready made dresses
Handkerchiefs
Coats
Kerchiefs
Hoods
Shawls (woolen, Cashmere, Paisley)
'Tibbet', (tippets)
Coats: '1 sett fur' [$12.00], cloth coats
Hats
Gloves
Mittens
Scarves and mufflers
Veils
'Ladies Boots' and shoes

Clothing: Men's

Underware [? union suits or 'long johns'], vest or flannel pants
Shirts
Collars
Stocks
Cuffs
Suspenders
Pants
Overalls
Vests [ready-made and bespoke]
3 piece suits [ready-made and bespoke, up to $73.00 in cost]
Coats [ready-made and bespoke]
Spencers (a kind of short jacket)
Overcoats [ready-made and bespoke]
'Balmorals' (a caped overcoat)
Slippers and moccasins ($2.25)
Shoes, walking shoes [these may have been for women; about $1.50]
'Gaiters' and 'rain gaiters'
Boots
'1 Pair Arctics' [boots], ($2.66)
Gloves (work and dress)
Mittens
Caps
Hats: straw hats, an 'Election Hat'

Clothing: Children's: *Boys*

[Dresses are not mentioned]
Boys' suits
Pants
Shoes
Mittens

Clothing: Children's: *Girls*

Skirts
Dresses
Stockings
Shoes
Mittens
[The store also did alterations.]

Yard Goods, Cloth, and Sewing Materials

Batting
'Beaver' [$4.25 a yard, so it is probably felted fur]
'Bosoms' [?]
Buckrum
Cambric
Canvass
'Crape'
Damask

Delanes
Diaper
'Dowskin' [possibly a shammie]
Flannels
Frocking
'Fry's Repellant' [Water Repellant Cloth, $1.40 a yard]
Fustian
Gingham
'Highland Plaid'
'Ladies Cloth'
Linens
Lining [for sleeves, etc.]
Muslin
'Net'
'Rush' [Ruche]
Sacking
Serges
'Shambre' [Chambray?]
Sheeting
Silk
Smocking
Ticking
'Tule' [Tuille]
Cottons [un-dyed and prints]
Velvets
Worsteds

Ruffles
Ribbons
Binder tape
'Rubber Tape' and elastic cloth bands of some sort
Twists, Braids, Cords, Trim
Wadding
Lace
Laces

Buttons : brass, cloth, glass
Rings and 'Stapels'
Hooks and Eyes

Yarns: woolen, cotton
Needles and pins by the 'paper' or individually

Knitting needles [but no crochet hooks]
Shuttles [probably for tatting]
Spools
Thread
Dyes [indigo, madder]

Housewares

Curtains
Wall paper
Rugs

Kitchens:

Dishes [sets, plates and bowls; platters and meat dishes, ashets, covered dishes and nappies; 'boats' and sauce dishes, tea sets, creamers; bowls, pitchers in several sizes, glass dishes [possibly for condiments and pickles], tumblers, glasses
Tin ware
Pie Plates
Knives (butcher knives, kitchen knives and others for table use)
Forks (for cooking and for table use)
Apple parers
Table sets of knives, forks and spoons
Jars and crocks
Oil cloth
'Washing Machines', ($5.50)

Dining Rooms

Carpets
Castor Bottles
Lamps and Chimneys

Napkins
Table covers

Living Rooms

'Pictured Box'
Mirrors
Clocks

Bedrooms:

Bedsteads
Blankets
Combs
Covers
Curtains, 'Mascate Curtains'
Hand Mirrors
Trunks

Hardware

Augers, bits and drills
Axes and ax handles
Brooms
Brushes
Castors
Files and tool handles
Pitch forks
Hammers
Handles [probably leather handles for bundles and cases]
Hoes
Hooks, 'Wardrobe hooks'
Lanterns and lamps
Locks: mortice, padlocks, hasps
Mauls
Mouse traps
'Curtain Paper' [?wallpaper or perhaps fancy window shades]
Rakes
Sandpapers
Screws
Screwdrivers
Scythes, snaths,
Shoe blacking and brushes for it
Shovels
Sprinklers [?watering cans]
'Steelyards' ($1.65) and 'scals'
Whetstones

Construction Items

'Blind Hangings'
Castors
Caulking
'Cupboard Catches'
Door bells; pulls, knobs in glass and brass
Door handles, knobs in porcelain, brass and glass; latches, latch plates
Nails from small to spikes
Lead [white lead to mix with oil for paint and for solder]
Linseed Oil by the gallon
Putty
Shingles
Sash fasteners
Tacks and brads – carpet, upholstery
Windows - cases, glass, locks, springs
'Zinc' [probably sheets for sink surrounds]

For the Sheds and Farms

Brooms and brushes
Cattle Cards
Curry Combs
Horse Blankets – 2 grades, $3.00 or $6.10 each

Stirrups
Whips ($1.65)

Sundries

Animal traps [for foxes not mice]
Bee's wax
'1 Bracelet & Ornaments $1.11'
Candles
'1 Casket $25.00'
Dusters
Envelopes
Kerosene
Ladies Pins
Matches by the bundles and boxes
Paper by the quire and smaller lots
Paper rolls [many were sold to the churches and used to cover tables at church suppers – as they continued to be into the 1940s.]
'Parasole' [1 sold at $2.50]
Piano cover ($12.00)
Rulers and perhaps a protractor
Slates [for children]
Soap, soft by the gallon
Starch
Tallow
Tobacco: cut plug, Navy, snuff, for smoking
Tobacco pipes
Twine
Wicks (by the ball or by length, for candles and lamps)

Unidentified items

Cloud
Redicate [? Reticule]

IV

What's in a Name?

One of the things which has fascinated me about New Englanders was their similarity to and differences with the people I had studied and about whom I had written articles and several books. Those deal with notable and enlightened Scots living between c. 1660 and c. 1840. Many of my pieces have been studies of groups of academics, scientists and medical men, and of others belonging to intellectual discussion clubs. I even have one paper on notable Scottish women. All together, my Scots number about 2,500 people. They were generally upper- and middle-class, ranging from rich noblemen to medical men, lawyers, and merchants down to a few fairly poor scribblers and teachers. They include both well-educated Highlanders and Lowlanders. So, I came to a consideration of Vermonters with well-known comparison groups, but ones unlike the people from the Northeast Kingdom. Some of the differences between the groups are due to the times in which each lived. My Scots generally lived earlier and in cities, had better educations, and were often professional men, or socially prominent aristocrats. Still, there are other things which bring out clear social differences in the worlds of Scots in the Old World and a more lower class lot of people in a corner of the New. One point of comparison centers on names and naming conventions and what we can make of them.

What follows is an impressionistic assessment. It is in no sense a meticulous statistical study of the occurrence of names or a careful inquiry into why they were chosen. My sources for the names are my 120 volumes of daily reminders, many letters, scrap books, and other materials which are rich in very unusual names. After working in, on, and from my Vermont manuscripts for about a year, I began to note down odd names as I came upon them. Those have been supplemented by names taken from my Barton store-keeper's Day Book and from the Census Records on line for 1850 and 1860 for both Glover and Albany. Some come from local histories. Many of the names are very odd.[77] Azuba, Lovisa or Zuar are not to be met with every day or among every people. Euphrada, today (2014), seems to be borne by only one American woman living in Detroit who is lucky enough to have her address listed on the net. I had no clear idea what I would do with the names when I began listing them, but, I was sure, some use for them could be found. What follows is the product of that search for a use.

Scotland in the eighteenth and nineteenth centuries was comprised of two quite distinct cultures. Highlanders, declining 40% to 30% of the population, occupied the larger portion of Scotland, a country about the size of Maine but climatically more varied and with more rugged terrain. Highlanders lived in a society which was poorer than that of the Lowlanders because Highland land was often useless for the growing of crops and not even good for grazing. Many Highlanders spoke only Gaelic, a language which few Lowlanders understood. Scots, generally, were among the most mobile people in Europe. Highlanders often went abroad as mercenary soldiers; Lowlanders went as soldiers but they also often went with skills given them by better educations obtained in a more commercial society. They sometimes went as merchants, medical men, teachers or as skilled artisans as well as mercenaries. Highlanders had low literacy rates while Lowland rates in the eighteenth and nineteenth centuries were among the highest in Europe – but not as high as in nineteenth-century Vermont.[78] Scots and Vermonters had distinctive naming conventions which reveal something about their cultures and societies.

In 1700, there were still Highland Scots who had, like some Icelanders today, no last names but used patronymics instead. 'Alastair mac Colla mhic Gilleasbaig' would translate literally to 'Alistair, son of Colla son of Gilleasbaig'. Some were born and grew up as, 'Rob, son of Alisdair the left-handed'; others with names like 'Íain Donaldson', were 'John, son of Donald'. Built into such naming is the assumption that the person and his father would be known to others in a localized and clannish culture. Some with surnames occasionally changed them if they took up land held from a man with a different name or surname or when they settled among clansmen having a different name. That signified a change in loyalty in a society in which, until 1747, those who held land might also owe military service to their lairds. Such name changes often boggle genealogists because MacArthurs could become Campbells, or Stuarts become Camerons. Scots often prized land above their blood relations, although this is not always recognized today. Sometimes men went by the name of the main clan in their area or by that of their own subgroup. The MacIver Campbells were known elsewhere as Mac a'Ghlasraich (their Gaelic name) but, sometimes, when living among MacDonalds in Lochaber, became 'MacDonalds'.[79] Highland surnames varied and often indicated loyalties or ties to land, not blood lines. Vermonters did not change names when they moved to new farms.

Highlanders of high status certainly had both given names, surnames and patronymics but some chiefs still commonly went by the clan name only. 'Clanranald', 'MacDonald of Sleat', or 'MacLeod' needed no other names because a clan could have only one Chief. Others were primarily known by the name of their principal estate such as 'Cameron of Lochiel', often merely 'Lochiel'. If you were a Fraser connected with Simon, Lord Lovat, the chances of you or your brother and your son and nephews being named Simon were very good. Simon, the 11th and 12th Barons Lovat, were trailed by many who bore their given names out of loyalty and respect for the Chief of the Clan Fraser. Because of this, it is often difficult to trace the ancestry of Simon Frasers or to follow the Army careers of men named Simon Fraser. On the other side of the Highlands, Archibalds, but not Simons, proliferated among Campbells who gave sons the name of the Marquis, 9th Earl, and 1st and 3rd Dukes of Argyll – all Archibald Campbells. Clan loyalties and the possession of land supported social hierarchies but did not promote Bible reading or shape Highland naming conventions. I have never come upon a Levi Campbell or Eliazer Fraser or a Zuar Cameron.[80] Naming was also affected by the fact that Highlanders used fewer names than did people in the Lowlands and elsewhere. Campbells used only about twenty – which accounts for some of their many Archibalds. Vermonters used many names but had no clans.

Among Lowlanders and the Ulster Scottish settlers of the seventeenth century (who tended to come from the Western Lowlands of Scotland), there was less addiction to naming sons for a chief, even if one existed and was recognized. Those people more often followed European conventions shared to a degree by all Scots. First sons tended to bear the given name of their paternal grandfather, second sons, that of their maternal grandfather; other younger sons were named for uncles and important relatives on both sides of the family. The philosopher David Hume,[81] a second son, was called David after his mother's father, Sir David Falconer. His older brother, John, was named for their other grandfather, John Home. John's eldest son was a Joseph named for his grandfather Home but John's third son was named for John's brother, David. The variance in Highland and Lowland naming conventions seem to have been shared further down the social ranks and points to the cultural diversity of the two regions in Scotland.

Scottish women's names seem to me to have followed fewer conventions. In both the Highlands and Lowlands, girls were commonly named after grandmothers, mothers and aunts but great ladies, such as Elizabeth, Duchess of Argyll and Countess of Dysart, seem not to have had many namesakes among many Campbell girls. The nieces of David Hume bore the names of their mother, grandmother, and another relative. The names of Lowland girls seem also more varied and sometimes a bit fanciful. There were Alisons, Nancys, Janes, and Janets, often related to forebears in no discernible order although many names must have been once borne by close living or dead relatives or family friends. There were Scottish Charlottes but no Lotties, certainly no Elzadas – to cite the names of two of my own great-aunts.

Aristocrats were more careful to follow customary naming procedures than the lower orders but neither Highlanders nor Lowlanders of any degree named many children with odd Old Testament names. In the Highlands, this undoubtedly reflected lower literacy rates and the fact that a full Scottish Gaelic Bible was not available until 1801; some Irish Gaelic Bibles were read before that date.[82] Still, Highlanders in the eighteenth century did not have a tradition of Bible reading, attended churches irregularly, and were probably more attuned to the names found in Gaelic poetry which shaped their literary but more oral culture.[83] In the Lowlands, there were more church-goers because there were more kirks in smaller parishes and many more ministers. There were more Bible-readers but their attention was, perhaps, more focused on the New than the Old Testament. Educated Lowland Scots, while religious, were not given to naming children after Hebrew heroes in Numbers or the Books of Chronicles. I suspect that religion in Lowland Scotland was more focused on the Gospels, Acts, and the Pauline epistles because Kirks kept attention focused on those books. That was likely to be true of all forms of Presbyterianism and particularly true in the Established Church of Scotland's 'Moderate' or modernizing wing. In the North of Britain, one seldom finds men named Hiram, Phineas or Peleg. I have never come upon a Josiah Campbell and it would be very odd to find one even in a clan which, unlike the sometimes Catholic Frasers, was usually associated with the Evangelical wing of the Kirk.

In Northeast Kingdom towns, like Albany, there was for most of our period no real Established Church to direct believers. Houses of worship existed there during the mid-nineteenth century for at least four sects – Congregationalists (1818, 1842-, in some form), Baptists (before 1842, 1857-1919), Wesleyan Methodists (c. 1830s-, in some form), and Roman Catholics (1840-1995).[84] In neighboring Craftsbury and in much of Caledonia County, Presbyterian churches also existed. Methodists [originally Anglicans with a difference][85] tended to support a more emotional form of piety which often focused on the 'blood of the Lamb' and strict adherence to what they took to be the saving and moral messages of Christ. Methodist hymns tended to give renditions of the Psalms and other verses which look forward to our redemption by Christ. They sing of His love and of His redemptive death for us. It did not find much place for the historical books of the Old Testament. Presbyterians in the Northeast Kingdom had the discipline of a Presbytery, better educated ministers, and their Kirks did not employ lay preachers as did both the Methodists and Baptists. The Kirks were, perhaps, less given to revivalism and included some 'Anti-Burghers' who wanted a sharp separation of religion from the state, something the Old Testament world did not know.[86] Presbyterians, like the Methodists, focused on the redemption of Christ and not on the Old Law and the religion of works. Baptists and Congregationalists, probably the largest of the Northeast Kingdom sects, were less-disciplined-bodies than the Presbyterians. They often had less well-educated clergymen and left more to individuals working out their own salvation. Doing that made the reading of the entire Word of God more central to religious life. Those sects had less fixed forms of worship and were perhaps closer to their seventeenth-century roots in a Puritanism probably more oriented to the Old Testament which described a gathered people living under God's rule. Catholics were also not much given to reading the Old Testament and were not encouraged to read books like Numbers since their rites made relatively few references to the historical books but many to the Psalms. Most church-goers probably had Bibles but the parts they read were not all the same.

Predictably, in a mostly literate, mostly Protestant society, the Bible was the most often read and pondered book, certainly one discussed every Sunday – if you went to church as most did with varying regularity. It should not surprise us that many children received Biblical names. What is surprising are the peculiar and striking Old Testament names chosen. The names suggest an intensive reading of what often seem the driest parts of the historical books of the Old Testament. Or, perhaps, naming was somewhat accidental or relied upon sortilege,[87] or upon the texts which had been preached upon in the churches the families attended about the time a child was born. There were certainly a lot of unusual Old Testament names but we cannot be sure that the many James, Johns, Matthews, Stephens, Pauls and Marys and Annas were not equally Biblical and picked from the New Testament and not just from lines of forebears and relatives. There were few from the Apocrypha but Phineas, the father of the Maccabees, some would have found in the Apocrypha. The apocryphal books were sometimes included in the King James Version of the Bible if it was printed in Britain. Susannah was there too. Other names were picked, not because they named relatives of the baby, or friends of the family, but because they, too, had religious significance. Names like Patrick, Christopher, Benedict or Wesley fall in that category. Catholics tended to eschew Old Testament names but not the names of saints like Francis, Thomas or Dominic. Of course, some of those names were passed down and became common in particular families – one thinks of the many Enoch Rowells who have lived in Albany, Vermont, since the early 1800s.

Many Northeast Kingdom Protestant men seem named for Old Testament heroes admired for being steadfast, faithful, or accomplished. New Testament names seem to come more often from the Pauline epistles than from other books. There were, however, fewer holdovers from a more puritanical time than one might expect. Male names such as Remember, Welcome, Luther or Calvin seem rare in nineteenth-century Vermont as were girls' names like Mercy, Prudence, and Silence.[88] There are fewer women than men named in the Old Testament and Vermont women's names drawn from the Old Testament seem less common – although many were quite exotic Old Testament names, such as Azuba, the wife of Caleb – one of the spies sent by the Israelites into the land of Canaan – or Tryphena [Tryphemia in one manuscript],'a woman who works hard in the Lord', as the King James Version puts it. There were certainly plenty of Sarahs, Miriams, Ruths, and Esthers from the Old Testament and Marys and Marthas from the New, and even Judiths from the Apocrypha and Genesis. Still, women's names seem on the whole more secular and chosen without an eye to the moral exemplars who first bore them. Perhaps girls were not seen as needing the reminders which boys needed to be heroic, virtuous, and steadfast. Daisy or Violet would not bring to mind what Deborah or Judith did – but, the latter names seem less common that the first. Names are an indicator of values prized so that is significant.

Nineteenth-century Vermont naming conventions point to people still clearly enthralled by the Bible. Its mythic account of the origins of things, its prophecies and its revelations of moral standards; the 'Good News' of salvation informed most things in the lives of those people. For perhaps a majority of readers, the Old Testament was as interesting reading as the New. For many, like Benjamin Emerson who possessed a big Bible (see p.44), the sacred texts came glossed and supplemented by commentaries on geography, weights and measures, histories of peoples mentioned in the Bible who had dealings with the Hebrews, as well as the sacred history of God's chosen people. For the Rogers, Tenney, Darling, and Emerson families mentioned in these essays, their Bibles high-lighted the names of heroes and priests, prophets and kings. Vermonters could find them easily if they had a concordance which came with some interpreters' Bibles. Those were often owned by Sunday School teachers.[89] Bible study was not restricted to the Hebrews but conveyed some knowledge of the Medes and the Persians, Assyrians and Egyptians, the Greeks and the Romans.

Other sources of names were not ignored. For both men and women, a surprising number of the names suggest the impact of Latin, Greek, and the classics in translation on the picking of names. That surely points to the Orleans and Caledonia County academies or equivalent schools operating through much of the time covered in the manuscripts I have used – in Craftsbury, Albany, Glover, Barton, Coventry, Brownington, Newport, Derby, and in Danville, Lyndonville, Peacham, and St Johnsbury. There was also available in the numerous district schools an education which included bits of classical material. If you had used the series of generally six books in Town's or McGuffey's graded readers, but did not go to grammar school, you might still would have known of Horatio, Brutus, Caesar, and others whose names surface as Horace or Horatia, Julia or Juline, Livia, Marcus, Antony, or something akin to their Latin or Greek sources. Indeed, a surprising number of names, like Ulysses, have Greek origins. One wonders if Delia was a shortened form of Cordelia, or if it had some relation to Delos and things Delian. Names derived from the classics tended not to run in families but then, people in the Northeast Kingdom showed less attention to the perpetuating of a set of family names even though there was a fairly high proportion of people of Scottish and Scots-Irish descent living in the Northeast Kingdom.[90]

The Vermont names do not seem to show a great acquaintance with English literature. A few women's names, like Rowena or Eulalei, suggest that the namers had read novels by Sir Walter Scott or the poetry of Edgar Allen Poe. Oscar might suggest some acquaintance with James Macpherson's Ossianic poems. Samantha had some currency before she appeared as a character in the novels of Maretti Holley written c. 1873-1910. There do not seem to be a lot of names from Shakespeare and other canonical English authors. Since women often named daughters, this probably tells us a bit about what some mothers had read. The diversity in the provenances of names male and female suggest that the women read more polite modern literature than did their men. That is also suggested by the manuscript sources which show men reading newspapers, agricultural magazines, and political pieces, but mentioning few novels and poems. Women often took ladies magazines which had not only fashion news but poetry and stories. There were few if any libraries in the Northeast Kingdom, but the books of one family were often borrowed by others.[91]

What is somewhat remarkable is that the names of American heroes, politicians and great men are not numerous. I have yet to come across a George Washington Something or Thomas Jefferson Whatever, of which there were many Virginian exemplars. My manuscripts do have several Harrisons and Tylers. In my own family, my Uncle Lee was named for General Robert E. Lee, but his brother Arthur, my father, seems not to have been named in memory of a President, although Chester A. Arthur was born a Vermonter – and was not a Democrat, which would have mattered in that family.

There seems little evidence of names reflecting an admixture of French and other stocks in what was still a fairly homogenous population. Most were of English, Scottish or Scots-Irish descent and the rest mostly Irish and French. There are a few Patricks, Paulines and Bridgets who came from Irish families named McGuire [or MaGuire], Mullaney, Gallagher and Sinon. French names in my manuscripts are often mis-spelt, which suggests that contacts did not go, in most cases, much beyond business dealings. In Barton, (twenty miles from the Canadian Border), French families named Nault and Frechette show up in the store account as 'Naud' and 'Frishit', or some other variant but seldom with accurate spellings. But in East Albany, some Irish and French families were accepted by their Protestant neighbors and joined in town affairs. Their children attended the district schools and the Academy in Craftsbury. That was true of other towns. There are also a few given names derived from place-names, like Archill, a town in Ireland. Women's names such as Daisy, Pansy and Violet, tend to be English in origin but some who bore them had Scottish surnames. French equivalents seem lacking and are outnumbered by the names of female saints.

Compared with Scots, most of the people of the Northeast Kingdom lived in an homogenous single culture, a society in which few spoke another language or lived very different lives. Their world did not know the social and economic inequalities so common in the Old World. In Vermont, naming practices do not seem class-based since there was hardly what could be called a class system. Some elder sons took father's and grand-father's names while younger sons took names which tended to run in families. In one line of my family, James, Jesse, and Robert are repeated in all the collateral lines to the confusion of those who would compile genealogies. But, this was not always the case. Many names fell outside the names traditional in a family and that is not just because of the numbers of children. Naming, thus, points to other features of the society such as its lack of deference, both to elders and social betters, or to preferences for accepted and common names. Indeed, locally, it would be hard to find many who were all that much better born or well off but not hard to find the bizarrely named. Their names surely reflect a lack of deference to tradition and a confidence often found in societies without great social inequalities.

How equal the Vermont world was can be seen when we consider its 'social pyramid', the term sometimes used to describe the structure a society has when social grades are considered. The Vermont pyramid was neither steep nor sharply rising. In both Scotland and Vermont, social grades were assigned primarily by ownership of land which in agricultural societies generally determines income, power, and the opportunities each affords. Scotland's land was held principally by about 600 important families and the social pyramid was shaped like a long stalagmite, very broad at the bottom but extending up, thinly, a very long way. On a map of Albany published in 1878, the names of twenty-two farmers appear in very bold type and twice as many in a smaller but still a larger than normal type face.[92] Those sixty named men owned much of the roughly thirty-six square miles covered by the township and paid different sums to have their prominence noticed. Their lands were not all equal in value but the discrepancies in value were likely not great and real wealth may not always be indicated by small case type.[93] The census information about property and wealth, taken in 1850 and 1860, shows a society of relative equals but one in which inequalities were growing (see below, n.69, p.357). Still, few were poor enough to be 'on the town'. Well off farmers by 1890 seemed to have made about $600.00 a year plus a good subsistence from their farms. Others might make do with a third of that. Working men might make only 70 cents to $1.00 a day with their board. That gives a ratio of about 3:1 or 2:1 in income when compared with the well off. It does not take account of wealth defined in terms of landed property or other capital items. In Scotland, by 1800, a peer [there were about 200 Scottish peers] was usually in receipt of more than $11,000 a year (in then current US dollars) but the daily wages of Scottish workmen were less than in Albany at the same time. Unlike Scotland, Vermont land was widely held and seldom entailed before 1843, after which entails were prohibited. Vermonters had much more access to small capitals available through mortgages, loans against property, or sums obtained from the full profits of farming. They might not name their farms but their plots were often as large and productive as those of the 'bonnet lairds' in Scotland. Rough equality meant independence which left them generally less deferential, even to fathers and other relatives whose names they often ignored when naming their children.[94] 'Bonnet lairds' and well-off farmers [renters of large amounts of land for long terms] in Scotland were seldom very independent of the dominant landowners in their locality. In Vermont, every adult male could vote; in nineteenth-century Scotland the number of voters rose roughly from one in eight males in 1833 to one in three by c. 1900. Women got the vote at about the same time in both places, in the USA, in 1920; in Scotland, in 1928.

Rough equality of status meant that the expectations of life for Vermonters were not all that different – something also promoted by the easy transition of farmers into merchants and merchants buying and running farms. There was, however, in both societies an incentive to leave the land. In Scotland, land usually went to the eldest child; younger children often left the farm, even the country. In Vermont the land was divided – and once divided and divided again, would not support all those who wanted it. Rough equality remained possible in Vermont only if many left. Vermont had few industries to absorb surplus people and those it had did not supply work to many. It is hardly surprising that large numbers of Vermonters left for 'the West' or went to work in the mills of southern New England. Towns like Albany produced many such young people; many of them did not return. Some probably shared the feelings expressed by one girl mentioned below (see pp. 195-196): she said she would not leave Brighton, Massachusetts, and the attractions of the Boston area to go back to Albany. Land in 'the West' – however one defined 'West' – cheaply satisfied the land-hunger of those who 'went West'. Many left the State as the frontier moved west and sheep-farming became less profitable after the Civil War.

Vermont children in the nineteenth century appear to have been named very freely and, perhaps, more imaginatively, than children elsewhere – as can be seen by a glance at the Census information available on-line for Albany. Some names simply seem made up since they cannot be traced on the web. Some were very rare in the period and had virtually disappeared by 1930. Many others are quite uncommon today. According to various indices on the web, the more exotic and strange names for both men and women went into a steep decline in use after c. 1880. A few revived for a short time but today few would name a baby Cornelia, Media or Ithiel. The decline in the use of many names is a sign of increasing secularism but also of changing interests and reading, and of TV and the movies. Less Bible reading, fewer students taking Latin and having exposure to classical culture bears upon naming practices. So too did the cessation of teaching German after World War I and the current popularity of Spanish, and African names among Blacks. Those changes correlate with the ending of the relative isolation of communities like Albany and with their members' greater integration into a wider American society which is anything but homogenous. In that process, economic changes, war, and the mobility given by automobiles all played parts. Names also tell us a bit about reading and the differences between what women and men read and were encouraged to be. But, considering names also allows us a glimpse into a non-deferential society of relative equals who had some engagement with ancient worlds full of mythic heroes. That world lasted until the 1940s but has largely gone. There is more to names than one first suspects.

Appendix to Chapter IV: Vermont Names[95]

Women's Names

Abba, Hebrew, Old Testament [OT]; stern.
Aboina, possibly a French or Indian name; no known meaning.
Ada, OT; 'adornment'; or from Germanic roots; meaning 'noble. This was a popular name c. 1880-1912 and, as a short version of Adelaide or Adeline, can come from a variety of sources; in the case of Vermonters, its source is likely the OT.
Adelia, Old German; noble, kind.
Addie, probably a nickname for the previous two.
Adusha, unknown but the names is East Indian.
Alfrata, unknown; possibly a place name.
Almira, Arabic; princess.
Alzada (Elzada, Zade), said to be English but having no known meaning; in the single Vermont case, it may be of French Canadian origin.
Amanda, Latin; worthy of love.
Amorette, French; little love.
Amorilla, unknown, possibly Spanish; a city in Texas; usually a male name.
Anabella, English; but probably from Latin 'amabilis'; common in Scotland since the 12th century.
Angelina, French; angel.
Antina, Hebrew; grace or favor.
Armelia, English variant of the German Amalia.
Armenia (Armina), unknown origin as a name; perhaps a whim based on geography.
Arthuza (Arethusa), probably Greek, the name of a wood nymph.
Asenith, Hebrew or Aramaic; she belongs to her father.
Augusta, Latin/English; sobriety, feminine form of Augustus.
Aurilla, Latin; golden.
Avaline, possibly French; a hazel nut tree.
Avilar, unknown.
Azuba, (Agubah, Ajubah) OT; the Wife of Caleb, one of the Spies sent into the land of Canaan by the Israelites.
Birdina, English; little bird.
Briget (Bridget), Celtic; pre-Christian goddess of fire and poetry or the Irish Saint, Bridget of Kildare.
Brilla, unknown.
Bula[h], perhaps meant to be Beullah, Hebrew; bride; metaphorically, Bride of Christ.
Capitiana, Spanish family name but otherwise unknown.
Celera, Latin; a word for swiftness.

Celeste, Latin; heavenly.
Chastina or Chastine, Latin; pure, chastity.
Chloe, Hebrew; green herb.
Clarisa, Latin; bright or famous; variant for Claire or Clarice.
Cleora, Greek; glory.
Cornelia, Latin; feminine form of Cornelius, from a family name.
Delia, Greek; pertaining to Delos: or, Welsh; mythic goddess of fire and poetry: or, a shortened form of other names such as Cordelia.
Delight, English.
Diana, Latin; goddess of the moon, forests, the hunt, and childbirth.
Diantha, Latin/English/Dutch; divine flower.
Dora, Greek; gift or gift of God: shortened form of Dorothy or Theodora.
Dorcus, Greek; woman of good deeds.
Doris, Greek; gift: or, pertaining to Delos.
Edna (Ednah), Hebrew; pleasure: or, Gaelic; kernel: or, English; friend.
Elvira, German; true: or a Spanish literary character.
Emiline, German/Latin; peaceful home.
Emena, unknown.
Endora, Hebrew; fountain.
Esta, OT; star or myrtle tree.
Ethel, Old English; shortened form of Ethelrade, noble.
Eulalie, Greek but forms are present in most European languages; to speak well; also the name of an 1845 poem by Edgar Allen Poe.
Euphrada, unknown; possibly Greek coming from a reference to Phrada, a place in present day Afghanistan where Alexander the Great made a speech – in which case, good Phrada.
Etta, Latin and English; little one: abbreviation for Henrietta.
Euphemia, Greek; well spoken. Effie is a shortened form.
Fanny, English; short for Frances.
Farilla, Italian or Spanish family name; its origin as a first name is unclear.
Filora, unknown, but Flora is a common Gaelic name.
Hannah, OT; God has favoured me.
Hannorah (Honor, Honour or Honora), probably English; honor.
Horatia, Latin; feminine of Horatio.
Hortensia, Latin; a family name but also referring to gardens.
Hulda, OT; mole or prophetess: or, Norse; a sorceress.
Ida, Greek; a nymph: or, German; hard working, prosperous.
Ila, Scottish; derived from the Island of Islay.
Ina, Nordic; an ending for diminutives used as a name.
Isabella, New Testament [NT], Hebrew; God's promise; the mother of John the Baptist.
Jensine, OT; a blessing of God.
Jersuha, OT; possessed by a husband; wife of Uzziah and daughter of Zadoc.
Julia, Latin; from a family name.
Julianna, Latin; Jove's child.

Juline, Latin; youthful or Jove's child.
Lala, Hawaiian; famous or cheerful.
Lauritta, Latin; bay or laurel plant.
Lettie, Latin; shortened form of Lettice or Letitia, joy.
Lilla, Hebrew; lily; in this case; or, perhaps a shortened form of Aurilla (Latin; golden).
Lillias, Scots; lily.
Lizzie, English; shortened form of Elizabeth.
Leona, Latin; lion-like.
Loise, Germanic; famous warrior; of, a variant of Lois.
Lona, ditto or unknown.
Lora, (used for Laura?), probably not from Spanish but from Latin; laurel.
Lorinda, Latin; laurel or bay plant.
Lorissa, Greek or Latin; cheerful.
Lotta, French or Old German; variant of Carol, Karlotta and Lottie; diminutive form of Charlotte, the feminine form of Charles, or a free man.
Lottie, English; also a shortened form of Charlotte.
Louella (Louilla), Old English; famous warrior.
Lovisa, Swedish and Old German; fighter.
Lucia, Latin; graceful light.
Luciann (Lucyann), unknown; (Lucy, Latin; light; Ann, Hebrew; prayer).
Lucina, Latin; light.
Lucinda, Latin; graceful light.
Mabel, Latin; lovable, dear.
Mahittable, OT; God rejoices.
Mamie, (in this list a nickname for Armenia or Armina), place-name used for a first name.
Manitte (variant of Manette), Latin; star of the sea.
Mariah (Maria, Moriah), Latin; star of the sea.
Mariett, perhaps a variant of a French or Spanish form of Marrietta.
Marville, unknown; probably a family name.
Matilda, Old German; mighty in battle.
Media (Medea?), probably in this case a made-up form honoring a relative named Medab. see same name in men, below.
Melvina, probably from Ossian and so from Gaelic; smooth browed, slender.
Mercy (Mercie), English or French.
Merinda, Australian aboriginal name meaning beautiful woman — but this is very unlikely.
Minnie, unknown (sometimes a diminutive for Wilhelmina).
Mona, probably from an 1884 novel but really unknown in this context.
Meeda, Gaelic or Irish; thirsty for the Lord; or a shortened form of Almeda.
Mondana, unknown.
Moranda, Italian family name; no meaning has been found.
Nabby, unknown.
Narcissa, Latin; narcissus or daffodil.

Nettie, English; diminutive for Henriette, Annette and so on.
Nora, Norah, English; from the names Honora and Eleanora, honor.
Odessa, Greek; wandering quest.
Oramel, unknown.
Orpha, unknown.
Orphenia, unknown.
Pamilia, Greek; honey.
Pansy (Pansie), English or French; a flower; or from the French 'penser', to think.
Parmelee, English; perhaps derived from a place name.
Patience, English.
Peace, English.
Permilia, Latin; sweetness.
Phileba, Greek, perhaps created by a Platonist who admired *The Philebus*, a dialogue on hedonism and knowledge.
Philena, Greek; lover of mankind.
Polly, English or Irish; a nickname for Mary.
Prudence, English.
Rhoda, Greek/Latin; rose.
Rosetta, Latin; rose.
Roselein (Roselin), Old German; gentle horse.
Rosinda, Old German; famous warrior.
Rowena, Celtic or Welsh or Anglo-Saxon or Old English; the name of a character in Sir Walter Scott's *Ivanhoe* (1819).
Sadie, Hebrew; princess: or, English; diminutive for Sarah.
Salina, Greek; moon goddess.
Sally, English; nickname for Sarah.
Samantha (Semantha), English; a name almost certainly taken from a series of 10 novels by Marietta Holley, 1873-1910.
Saphainie, unknown.
Sapone, unknown (or an Italian soap maker).
Sereno (Serena), Latin; clear tranquil, serene.
Silence, English.
Saloma, Hebrew; peace.
Sophia, Greek; wisdom.
Surippta, unknown.
Tabitha, Aramaic; a gazelle: or, Greek, NT; Acts (where she is raised from the dead).
Temperance, English.
Thema, unknown; name of an Egyptian Queen.
Theoda, unknown.
Thirza, Hebrew, OT; Numbers; one of the five daughters of Zelophehad); she is my delight. .
Tryphemia (Tryphena, Tryphine) Greek, NT; Romans, 'a woman who works hard in the Lord'.

Vilona, unknown.
Viola, Latin; violet.
Violet, English, flower name.
Waite (Waity), probably English and sometimes a boy's name.
Zilpah, Hebrew, OT; Genesis; Leah's maid, a droop or frail.

Men's Names

Aaron, OT; Exodus; mountain of strength.
Abel, Hebrew, OT; Genesis; the shepherd son Adam and the first to die.
Abijah, Hebrew, OT; Chronicles and many other books; worshipper of Jehovah, judge in Beersheba.
Abner, OT; 1 and 2 Samuel, 1 and 2 Kings, 1 Chronicles, *passim*; father of light, a commander.
Adam, Hebrew, OT; Genesis; the first man.
Adna, Hebrew, OT; Nehemiah; rest or pleasure.
Alaina, unknown; today sometimes given to girls.
Alden, Old English; old friend.
Alonso, Spanish/Italian; ready for battle.
Alphe, Hebrew, the first letter of many Semitic alphabets.
Alvah, Hebrew, OT; 1 Chronicles; his highness (in reference to the descendants of Esau).
Amasa, Hebrew, OT; 1 Chronicles and 1 Kings, Samuel; nephew of King David a captain of the Israelites, burden.
Anasa, probably a mistake for the foregoing.
Anson, English; no clear meaning other than son of Ann.
Aphram, unknown; see Ephram..
Antonie (Anthony), Latin.
Archil, probably a mistake for Achill, an island in Ireland.
Asa, Hebrew, OT; 1 and 2 Samuel, 1 and 2 Kings, 1 and 2 Chronicles, *passim*; a King of Judah.
Ashbel, Hebrew, OT; many OT references; second son of Benjamin; a fire.
Asil, Arabic; pure.
Augustine, Latin; great, magnificent, to increase.
Bartholusmus, unknown.
Byron, Biron, Old English; barn.
Calvin, French Reformer.
Cyrus, Hebrew, OT; Chronicles, Ezra, Daniel, Esdrus, Bel; Lord, a King of Persia; also Greek.
Darius, Persian/Greek; Ezra, Danile, Zechariah, Esdras, Macabbees; maintains possession.
Dian, possibly Latin; divine; now given to girls.
Duran, possibly Durand, and so French; if so, firm, enduring.
Eber, Hebrew, OT; Genesis; father of Peleg.
Ebert, variant of Eberhard, Old German; [here, more likely made up or taken from a relative].

What's in a Name?

Elias, variant of Elijah, Hebrew, OT/NT; (Hebrews, Ezra, Nehemiah, Chronicles, Esdras, Sirach, Maccabbees, Matthew, Mark, Luke, John, James, Romans); the Lord is my God.
Eliphalet, OT; God delivers.
Elisha, Hebrew, OT; (Genesis, Numbers, Samuel, Kings, Chronicles, Jeremiah, Ezekiel); God is my salvation.
Elzear, French from the Hebrew; probably Elzeard; God's help.
Enoch, OT/NT (Genesis, Ezra, Sirach, Hebrews); Hebrew; son of Cain, a builder; a prophet; Enoch was translated and did not see death: (Jude and Luke); a prophet of the Lord's coming.
Ephram (Ephraim), Hebrew, OT; Genesis, Numbers, Deuteronomy, Joshua, Judges, Samuel, Kings, Chronicles; fruitful.
Erasmus, Latin/Greek; to be loved.
Erastus, NT, Greek, Acts, Romans, Timothy; loving.
Ezra, Hebrew, OT; Kings, Chronicles, Ezra, Nemehiah; helper.
Fraid (Frait), unknown, perhaps a family name or made up: or, possibly Fred.
Galen, Greek; physician.
Ged (diminutive of Gerard or Gerald), Germanic/French; spear.
Harmon, (French, Harman), Old German; a soldier.
Heman (Hemand), Hebrew, OT; Psalm 88; faithful.
Hermand, Old German; soldier.
Herod, Hebrew, OT/NT; Matthew, Mark, Luke, Acts, Romans; a King of Judea.
Hilas (Hilos), unknown.
Hiram, Hebrew, OT; Samuel, 1 and 2 Kings, 1 Chronicles; builder of the temple and a hero of Freemasonry; King of Tyre.
Ichabod, Hebrew, OT; Samuel; 'The glory has departed' (refers to the capture of the Ark by the Philistines).
Ira, Hebrew, OT; 1 Chronicles; a captain of the Israelites.
Irville, unknown; possibly a family name or a variant of Orville.
Isa, Arabic for Jesus.
Ithiel, Hebrew, OT; (Nehemiah); God is with me.
Jabez, OT, 1 Chronicles; born in pain.
Jared, Hebrew, OT/NT; (Hebrews, Genesis, Chronicles, Luke); descending, an ancestor of Christ.
John Wesley, after one of the founders of Methodism.
Josiah, Aramaic and Hebrew, OT; Esdra, Sirrach, Baruch; the lord saves, a King of Judah.
Josius, form of James; see also Archbishop Josius of Tyre.
Laban, Luban, Hebrew, OT; Genesis; white or shining, name of Jacob's trickster father-in-law.
Levi, Hebrew, OT; Genesis; the third of Jacob's sons, joined; a priest.
Lizzen, unknown.
Loren, English, a form of Lorenzo.
Lot, Hebrew, OT; Genesis; a righteous man said to be an ancestor of Jesus.

Lucas, Greek; derived from Luke.

Luther (Luthur), Old German; soldier of the people; perhaps for Martin Luther.

Manasah, Hebrew, OT; Genesis, Chronicles; brother to Ephraim and son of Joseph of the coat of many colors; making forgetful.

Marcellus, Latin; derived from a family name.

Medab, unknown, possibly a form of Medan - a son of Abraham and Keturah in the Old Testament.

Media, OT; Esther, Isaiah, Daniel. see Media, above, in Girls; or from the Assyrian tribe of same name.

Merle, shortened form of Merrill: or perhaps from the French word for blackbird; merle.

Medow, unknown.

Milo, Greek/Latin/German, uncertain, soldier, perhaps peaceful.

Milotus, unknown, in this case possibly Zelotus; a classical Greek writer. In Acts, Paul visited Miletus.

Miron (Myron), Greek; fragrant oil or perfume.

Mortimer, Old French; dead sea or lake.

Nahum, OT; one of the 12 Minor Prophets, comforter.

Noah, Hebrew, OT/ NT/A; peaceful, long-lived, comforter.

Noel, French; Christmas.

Obediah (Obed), Hebrew and Aramaic, OT; Ezra, Esdras; servant of God.

Octave, French; born eighth.

Olin (? Olline), Old English; holly.

Orange, possibly a family name.

Oraston, unknown, possibly a family name.

Orel (Oarel), Latin; golden.

Oren, OT, 1 Chronicles 2: or Irish and Gaelic; pine tree; fair, pale.

Orlando, Spanish variant of Roland (Old German).

Orlin, French or Spanish; famous land.

Orville, Old French; character in a Fanny Burney novel.

Oscar, Gaelic; a dear friend, a character in Ossianic poems.

Osmond, Norse; God's protection.

Otis, Old English; wealthy.

Pardon, English.

Peleg, Hebrew, OT; Genesis; son of Eber, in whose days the earth was divided.

Philander, Greek; loving mankind.

Phineas, Hebrew and Aramaic, OT; Numbers, Maccabbees; grandson of Aaron the Priest.

Pliny, Latin; possibly in memory of Pliny the younger.

Reuben (Rheubin), Hebrew, OT/NT; Genesis, Numbers, Deuteronomy, Joshua, Judges, Kings, Chronicles, Ezekiel, Revelation; behold a son; the first of Jacob's sons.

Rolla, Germanic; a variant of Roland but possibly a nickname.

What's in a Name?

Romanus, Latin; Roman.
Roscoe, Norse; deer wood.
Royal, English; kingly.
Rufus, Latin; red haired.
Ruman, German; said to be a South German variant of Roman.
Salem, Hebrew, OT; name of Malchesidick's Kingdom and the name of a Massachusetts seaport.
Salmon, English; probably a family surname.
Seba, Hebrew, OT; Genesis, 1 Chronicles; a son of Cush.
Seth, Hebrew, OT; Genesis; the appointed one.
Shubain, Gaelic, from Suibhainn.
Silas, Greek, NT; Acts, *passim*; Paul's right-hand man.
Silsam, unknown.
Trestrum (Tristram), probably Celtic; a Knight of the Round Table; or, from Pictish and Old French; sad.
Tyler, English; a tiler; a Masonic office or perhaps for a President.
Uhla, unknown.
Vida, probably from Hebrew; beloved.
Zadok, Hebrew, OT; there are many OT references to this High Priest of the 1st Temple; righteous.
Zalora (possibly Zelosa), unknown; in the form Zelosa is today a girl's name.
Zapher (Saper), Arabic; victory; it was borne by a Vermont Lieutenant-Governor, Zapher Mansur.
Zebulon, Hebrew, OT; many OT references to the sixth son of Jacob and Leah; a gift or honor.
Zenus, Greek, NT; a lawyer named in Titus 3:13.
Zuar, Hebrew, OT, Numbers, *passim*; Bright or Shining; father of Nathaniel, Captain of the Tribe of Isschaar.

Family names used as male first names include: Alexander, Allen, Dana, Dewey, Emerson, Forest, Freeman, Gilman, Granville, Hanson, ?Lindol, Lyman, Marin, Mason, Merrill, Miles, Proctor, Ross, Rushford, Russell, Salmon, Sanford, Schuyler, Selden, Stillman, Taylor, Van Armbaugh, Van Doven, Walton, Warner, Wheaton, Willard, Wilson, and Woodman.

V

Jabez Page: 8 October 1793-25 November 1876

'And Jabez was more honourable than his brethren; and his mother called his name Jabez, saying, Because I bore him with sorrow. And Jabez called on the God of Israel, saying, Oh that thou wouldst bless me indeed, and enlarge my coast, and that thine hand might be with me and that thou wouldst keep me from evil, that it may not grieve me! And God granted him that which he requested.' *1 Chronicles* 4: 9-10.

1. A Business Career 1814-1876

Jabez Page was the grandfather of Mary Abby Tenney, the second wife of Cornelius Rogers.[96] That accounts for the possession of some of his papers by the Rogers family. When I first looked at the Page papers, the scraps seemed incomprehensible and too skimpy to be useful. Tempted to toss them out, I put them aside. When I looked at them again some years later, they turned out to be interesting. Most of the Page items are receipts and cancelled notes relating to Jabez Page's business activities. Other items concern land he bought or sold. A few are letters to him and his wife or to his daughter Lucyann. From those, supplemented by the Albany Town Records and other family papers, one can construct an account of a small businessman working in Vermont between c. 1814 and the 1860s. What follows is the account of Jabez's life reconstructed from the surviving records and fragments, mainly cancelled notes[97].

This note, probably issued by Jabez Page and his wife or business partner, was cancelled by destroying the signatures of the debtors.

Jabez Page; 8 October 1793 - 25 November 1876

Jabez Page's father, Ebenezer Page of Danville, and Ebenezer's brother Israel, were farmers who 'For Value Received' gave their note on 1 May 1809 to 'Robert Johnson or his Order' for two 'Likley New mikles Cowes With Calves By their sides the one eight years Old and the Other Four Years Old sai'd Cows to be Delivered in Four years From this Date'. That somewhat odd note was witnessed by William Knowlton and Theodore Willa, who made his mark – one of only two illiterates to appear in Jabez's records which must have the signatures of at least 200 fairly ordinary people. In October 1809, the men signed another note for $4.00 payable to Simeon Fairbush. In 1810, they gave Fairbush two more notes for 'value received'. On 6 May 1815, Ebenezer promised to pay Simeon Fairbush 'two middling likely cows' by 1 October of that year. And, he borrowed $16.00 from Fairbush. Both of his notes were witnessed by Salina Danice [?]. Even though the sample is not large, the notes show that the Pages were farmers with property and used to making deals. By 1816, Ebenezer lived in Walden (perhaps twelve miles north) where he paid 46 cents 'direct tax on property'. His brother, Israel Page, remained in Danville where, in 1817, he was farming but also seems to have had a business. He was either kept a store or inn or was a drunk because, in January that year, he drew on M. Casron [Carson?] to pay the bearer of his note for 'Sixteen Gallons of Whiskey' which was to be charged to his account. Those men were doing a variety of things and not wedded to one place. Jabez was not much different but more successful.

Who Jabez's mother is not known but she was a pious, Bible-reading woman who is likely to have had a difficult labor when he was born. His name seems to have meant, 'he causes pain', 'sorrow' or 'trouble'; it may well describe his mother's delivery of him. She may have hoped that all her travail and pain would be made up for in his life. He became a pious man and, as a Bible reader, would have been mindful of the meaning of his name, the obligation it entailed, and the hopes it implied. God answered Jabez's prayers; his requests were fulfilled and his 'coast enlarged'. The biblical passage from which his name derives also suggests that he was likely to have been a first-born son. They often got a better start in life and were, indeed, 'more honourable' than their brethren. His start certainly included enough education so that he could become an effective businessman working in a trade where some technical knowledge was required. Where he learned his skills as a dyer, fuller, and woolman is not known but there were few regular apprentices on the frontier in those days. He became literate and studious enough to function as a County Justice of the Peace when that office still conveyed the right to hold a court anywhere in the county. His children were more regularly schooled. One taught school, another thought about it, one son became a lawyer while another went to 'the West'.

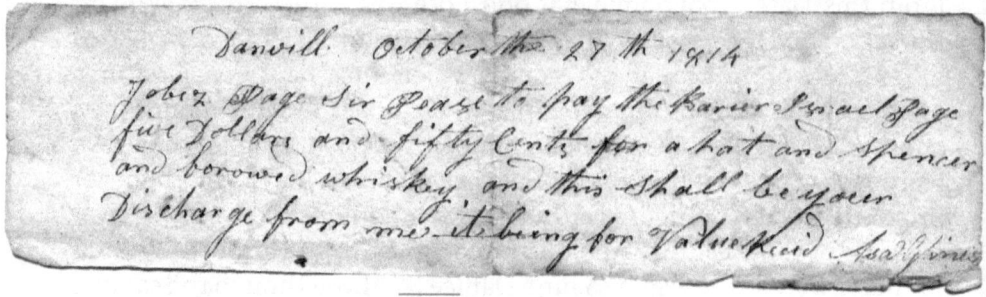

Bill drawn on Jabez Page for $5.50 which was owed by Asa Glines.

Jabez Page first appears in my records in 1814 when he paid his Uncle Israel $5.50 because of a bill drawn on him to pay for Asa Gline's 'hat and Spencer [a short jacket], and borowed whiskey'. On 6 May 1815, Jabez purchased from Joseph Pierce of Walden, where he was then living, most of 'Lot Number one in great Lot Number four' for 'one dollar'. Lots were often about 100 acres so this may have been a substantial purchase. The dollar recorded showed, as it would now, that it was bought for a price he did not want disclosed. It was a speculation. Jabez would farm but his principal interests were never those of a farmer. He was by then dealing in wood ashes[98] and was probably already something of a speculator in land. This first known land purchase was of a wood lot where he presumably cut the wood on the property, sold some as timber and burned the rest to make lye or to sell the ashes to others to make lye. In 1816, he agreed to buy 'good Clean green maple ashes', from Adam Amsden and others who were clearing their fields. That suggests Jabez had an ashery in which to process ashes to make lye. By the following year, if not before, he had gone into the wool business. In 1817, he gave a note for $12.00 to Mary Coburn of Cabot, Vermont. She was in the wool trade and sold out to him in 1821. Jabez still had enough cash to buy, on 17 March 1817, a piece of land in Walden, Vermont. For that he paid his father $200.00.[99] The $200.00 was then about a year's wages for a working man. At age twenty-four, he seems to have had quite a bit of ready cash or else a reputation for being a reliable businessman. A bit later, Jabez collected $20.00

from John and Luther Batton on what was obviously a running account since in the following year there are receipts from 'Boock Counts to this Day' and another for 'Dressing Cloth'. Those imply previous entries in now missing account books. He seems by then to have had a partner in the wool business since, in 1819, Jabez and Abrm Brown cleared their account with Mary Coburn in Cabot save for their 'notes of hand'.

The nature of Jabez's business is made clearer by a receipt from a Montpelier store, Hubbard & Spalding, where he 'bot of a bucket' [25 cents] 'a quarter cist' [chest] of Roman Vitriol and some 'Fustic'[a yellow dye made from a Mexican or Caribbean tree]. Later, he purchased more vitriol and something else illegible but costing a quarter. Those chemicals were used in preparing dyes or bleaches for either spun wool, woolens or linen cloth. More purchases in September 1820 confirm that. They included madder, redwood, indigo, fustic, and logwood. All were used as dyes – yielding crimson, red, purple, probably blue or green, yellow, and black. Oil of vitriol (sulphuric acid) in dilute forms could safely bleach linen. He would have used alum or stale urine as a mordant or color-fixing agent. All that points to the growing importance of Vermont sheep-farming and the growth of Vermont's cloth industry. In March 1821, Jabez paid Mary Coburn $240.00 'in full for the rent and use of my Cloathers Shop and tools and of all Book Accounts and other Demands up to this Date except Notes of hand'. His business was not confined to one town since he was already dealing with people in Montpelier, Cabot, and Albany, where he had purchased cloth to the value of $7.00 from Winslow Fay. Jabez seems to have been doing well and there are no further mentions of a partner. In 1820, he rented for $10.00, and repaired for $8.00, a house in Cabot – which may tell us where he was living or that his business needed a larger shop.

By the late 1810s, he was doing well enough to marry and found a wife in Lucy Perkins (c. 1796-1826), who is likely to have come from Danville since his children later called 'uncle' someone there named Perkins.[100] Jabez and Lucy probably had two or more children before Lucy died at about age thirty. The elder child was named Lucyann (c. 1818-May 1841). She became a mill-worker and died unmarried. The younger, Louisa (c. 1824-?), married Lyman P. Tenney whose daughter Mary Abby preserved the records and scraps.

By 1820, the Pages were settled in West Albany, a bustling little center where Page was not the only one dealing in wool. He and others there bought raw wool, had it carded, spun and woven, and then dyed bolts of cloth in their shops.¹⁰¹ He operated a kind of 'putting out' system since he was not doing the carding, spinning, and weaving on his own premisses but organizing this trade from the shearing to the sale of a finished product. That kind of business had not changed much since 1500 when English 'woolmen' worked in much the same fashion. He would have been at home in the Chiltons and other wool-producing areas of England anytime from c. 1450-1840.

One of Albany's attractions may have been the prospect of water power for his 'cloathery'. It seems likely that by this time he was expanding his operations beyond the dyeing of cloth. In 1821, he bought, for $100, some land from Norris Scott of Albany. That land was a sixty acre lot on the south side of Lot 76 near the sawmill, below which he was living.¹⁰² With the sale, he acquired the 'privilege of waters' so he could run 'a fulling mill and Carding Machine'. He also had the obligation to bear one third of the cost of all repairs to the dam, races, and pond. His fulling mill was built there. But, wool was not his only concern. He was also listed in the Albany town records as the owner of a 'cow 3 yrs old, 1 horse 3 years old, &' and of something illegible which may be a 'wool hall' worth $30.00. In 1822, he had five cows three years old and had bought from John Culver, for $400, land to keep them on. He was farming on a small scale which he continued to do all his life.

Page was now settled and a respected member of his new community. He was chosen as a 'petty juror' (1821, 1822) and was listed as a private in the militia company (1821-30). The town records for 1822 show that he was fully equipped with a gun, spare flints, and other accouterments; two years later he had none of those items. Later entries do not list his arms. He left the militia c. 1831. In 1824, he was elected to what seems to have been his only term as a Selectman.¹⁰³ By 1827, he had risen to be a collector of the road tax with the power to lock up in the Irasburg jail, delinquents who refused to pay.¹⁰⁴ He still held that post in 1829 when he paid a surveyor for laying out a short new road connecting two existing ones. His service to the town in other posts continued for many years: Petit Juror (1846), Grand Juror (1824, 1839, 1847, 1850), Surveyor of Lumber (1828), Lister (1843), Auditor (1844, 1845), Justice of the Peace (1851), and Town Representative in the State Legislature (1832).¹⁰⁵

As befitted a solid citizen and creditable businessman, Jabez Page went to church. He joined the Congregational Society around 1822 and paid pew rent and support for the minister totaling $16.00 in 1827. The

Jabez Page; 8 October 1793 - 25 November 1876

Coventry Falls and Troy Village (overleaf). *These villages are examples of two kinds of developments in the Northeast Kingdom. Where there was water power, tanneries, fulling and other mills followed stream courses. Villages about a common tended to be at the intersections of roads and their shops made things from wood, cloth, and leather which required skills but little power.*
Source: Walling, 1859.

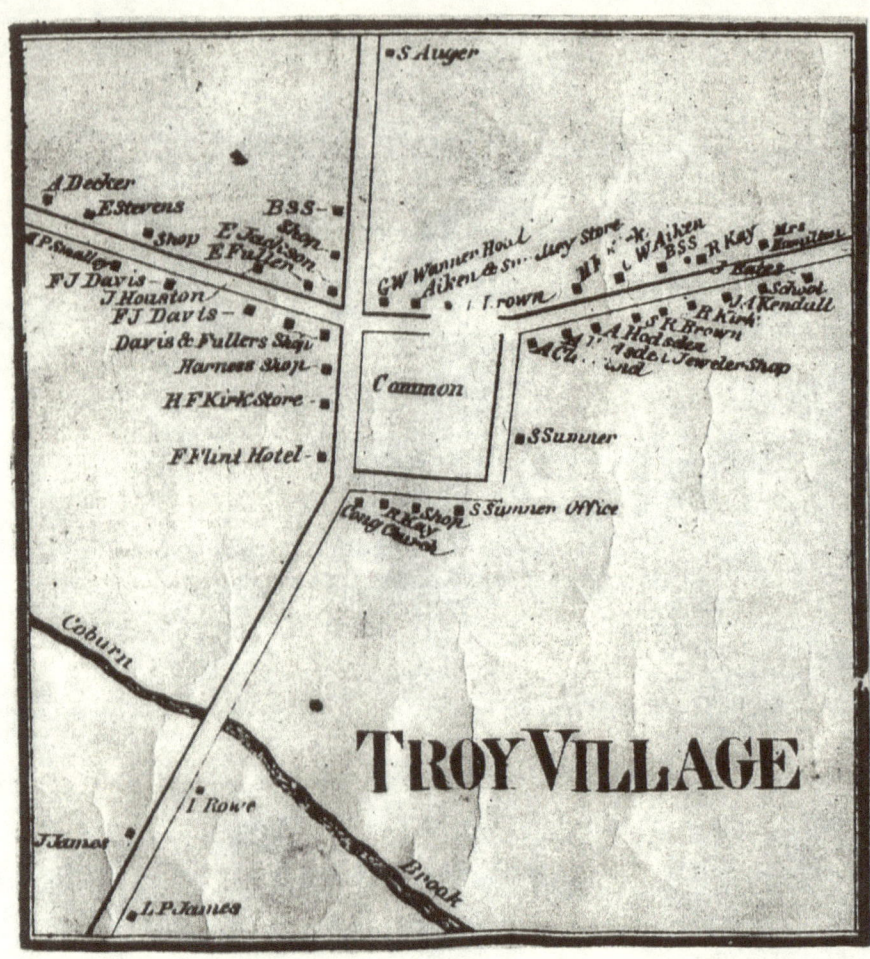

next year he paid a dollar less but again paid $16.00 in 1829. In 1830, he gave $20.00 to the 'first Cong Society of Albany'. Those sums, which probably included his pew rent, were often not fixed. He probably paid at the high end of the scale. There are no later recorded subscription payments to the church but in 1848 he paid a pew rent of $5.00 for a seat in the second row, not at the back.[106] In his final settlement in 1873, he left his pew to his son Chester. Over the years, he handled some Church business. In 1829, he was paid $5.00 by the Society for 'value received'. In 1836 and 1837, he was involved in real estate transactions on behalf of the Church or its minister, Elias Kellogg. The Rev. Mr. Kellogg remained his friend even after the minister left the town and, eventually, Vermont.

The grand list report of Jabez's taxable wealth was down in 1826 to $24.00 and was even smaller in 1829 but it increased over time. His property was not all of the kind that was taxed as 'wealth' or personal estate. His notes and bills show that he was involved with a variety of activities and that he was likely spending some of his money on an enhanced lifestyle. In June 1826, Jabez bought some silk thing for $3.00 [or it may also have been '1 Silv Barret a 18fr $3.00']. More interesting is an 1827 bill for 28½ yards of cotton cloth, ¾ yard of cambric, ¼ yard of buckram, a dozen silk buttons and 3 'Skains' of silk, a mourning shawl, 2 flags and half a pound of tea. Those were all bought at Paddock & Clark's store in Craftsbury, which then had better stores than did Albany. Some of those purchases may relate to the death of his first wife in 1827. Others likely pertain to his remarriage which must have occurred fairly soon thereafter. He had three children in school by 1831-32; one of whom seems to have been by his second wife. Some bills he paid in grain, presumably supplied by his farm or given to him in payments for dyeing. A Craftsbury storekeeper, Lyndon French, was promised at his store wheat worth $3.49 in 1827. In 1831, Jabez paid $14.00 to George Bosworth in 'merchantable grain'. Hard cash was in short supply and replaced by barter. Page also did errands for friends since he was more likely than they to be traveling. In 1826, he ordered from French, '105 lights of sash' and a bedstead to be delivered to William Hayden I. In 1827, Page was again dealing for, or with, William Hayden.

Page's business did well and it helped others too. In April 1826, he promised to pay James Rogers for wool, at his house in Albany, $4.77 in 'good merchantable wheat'. Rogers was a son of Jesse Rogers I (see above, p.6). Other receipts show that between 1825 and 1828 Page had been buying raw wool from others and paying 'Wells and Enos', an

Albany firm, to card it. In August 1834, he was billed $4.50 by Eliphalet Rowell for carding and dressing about fifty-three rolls of wool.[107] Like others in the wool business, he provided a market for those who raised madder. In 1827, Jabez, gave a note to Enoch Rowell of Albany for $5.00 worth of madder. Another was later given to the Rowells for $5.00 or the equivalent in wheat, but does not specify what he paid for – perhaps for more madder. The surviving records are but a fraction of the deals he must have been making.

Page's wool business seems to have expanded over the next few years. The first reference in his papers to fulling comes in December 1829. About that time, he registered eight land transactions. All concerned land and mill rights along the Black River. In January, he bought for $100.00 from John Catringer of Lower Canada [Quebec], a bit of land along the Black River. Several transactions took place on 11 May 1830 when Page bought another bit of land on the Black River from Samuel English, for which he paid $75.00. At the same time, he purchased from James Rogers '2 Acres 96 Rods be the same more or less'. That cost him $200.00 more, and is likely to have been either a grist mill which the Rogers family once owned on the river or land they had bought, logged, and were willing to sell. For $350.00 more, Jabez bought from Ezra Perkins contiguous land down to the bridge which adjoined pieces he already owned. By the end of the day, he had spent $625.00 plus his legal fees – recording fees were 24 cents a deed. He now had the water he needed to run his mill and land on which to build.

Despite its complexity, his business was not a large one. The evidence for that comes from a record of his operations running from 1825 to 1831. There is a reference to the fulling of cloth in December 1829 but it is about the only one in the day book in which he recorded his jobs. He may have fulled cloth as a matter of course but there are no surviving references to, or receipts for, fullers' earth or soaps, which fullers needed. As a dyer, he seems to have been dyeing about two or three pieces a day with the pieces varying in length from a yard or two to about twenty-five feet in length – perhaps eight yards plus a selvedge. His dyes ranged from black and greys, to browns, (including snuff colors), blues, greens, yellows, reds, and white. He dyed a lot of flannel – most of it red and perhaps used for underwear. Much of the cloth appears to have been locally woven and destined for local use, or, if not, then sold on by those who had made it for themselves and not by him. Much of the cloth was fairly heavy such as that used for greatcoats and surtouts. There are also a few references to blanket cloth.

Blankets for home used would have been fulled but were often left undyed. Some pieces were lighter, such as serges, used for 'men's wear', and shalloons used for other clothing. He probably also dyed yarn but there are no records of that.

Unfortunately, little about his marketing arrangements or the extent of the area over which he carried on his business is known but something of the scale of his business can be inferred from the surviving bills and notes. He used a printer from Danville and gave notes to people in Cabot, Walden, Irasburg, and Barton Landing [now Orleans]. In November 1834, he borrowed $100.00 at the Barton Landing Bank. He wanted news from a wider area. In 1831, Page had forwarded to himself newspapers sent first to Danville to his friend Ezra Perkins, whom his daughter later described as an 'uncle'. By the 1840s, Jabez was borrowing from local men and trading with merchants in Montpelier, Barton, and Craftsbury. He was known and working in four counties. Still, the small scale of his business in those years made it reasonable for him also to farm. Doing both, he got ahead.

Up to 1836, most of the land Jabez bought seems related to his wool business which peaked c. 1840. After 1836, he began to buy land which seems to have been his way of saving, securing his old age and the welfare of his children. From then until the end of his life in 1876, he purchased at least five properties, three of which seem to have been used to dower daughters. The remaining land and properties of all sorts went to his son Chester. Page bought forty-four acres in 1836, more in 1837, fourteen in 1841, half a lot in 1843, bits in 1846, and ninety acres in 1849. For the last, Jabez and a partner paid $475.00 for land owned by Norris and Mary Darling just north of West Albany village near where the Darling's sawmill was located. The decade of the 1840s ended as it began: he added another small piece of land to what he already owned. Some of this property was resold for a profit. Beside his farm and several retained purchases from the 1820s, he then owned in excess of 200 recently acquired acres, water and mill rights and buildings, such as his fulling-mill and dye-works which may have been separate from his shop. He had diversified his business activities in other ways.

By the 1840s, Jabez very likely had become a local money lender since there are several receipts for relatively large sums in which the interest to be paid is carefully stated. He was lending but he was also borrowing as he had done in the past. He bought his shop, tools and land in 1822 by giving a mortgage to Nathan Beede, a local cattle dealer. Later he took a mortgage from Walter Buck whose interest payments were to be made in 'good grey cloth'. Later still, he held at least four mortgages. One he seems to have assigned to the borrower's relative presumably for fair value. In 1853, he took an $800.00 mortgage on land a partner had bought. That does not seem to have been discharged in his lifetime. If it was not paid off, that too can probably be added to his land holdings or the interest to his income. Two years later, he sold, for a $275.00 increase on his purchase price, a bit of land he had bought in 1849.

After 1847, Jabez was buying items which may have been used to set up a child who was getting married or to make his family seem more genteel – a 'China Tea Sett' ($4.75), twelve plates and another set of nine, some sauce plates, a pitcher and a salt and pepper set and 'a sett of knives and forks', six tumblers and enough cloth to make small items and lots of thread and silk in skeins. That would have been used to make thread. All those things were bought in Albany from a Mr ?Hayden. The US Census for 1850 listed Jabez's worth as $1,000. Ten years later his personal worth was given as $400 but his property in Albany was listed at $1,800. Later censuses did not list property values but his surely increased even though he began to sell land in the 1860s.

Always in the background was an agricultural scene which is not much noticed because it was ubiquitous. Of the five chits from 1850, two concern his farm. Page got that year, from a man in Danville, a pair of steers, which 'we promise to keep well and break & work in a farmer like manner and return ... in three years from the first of last Oct^b'. He (really his hired man) was working his farm with borrowed oxen. The other is a bill from J. C. Dow who wanted settled an account for $4.13 before Dow began 'My drove'. Albany was a center for trade in cattle and Jabez owed money to a cattle dealer. Later, men like Cornelius Rogers and his relative, William Beede, sold cattle from Albany (c. 1880-1900) but that activity had already begun by 1850.

His domestic and civic life flourished. By 1831 he had three children in school for whom, in 1833, he paid $9 for three months tuition – about half of the school year. Two years later, he was paying for four children and continued to do so until 1837. By 1842, he had only two children enrolled. The last of his children seems to have left school in c. 1847. They were children of his second marriage to Orphenia Livingston (c. 1806-1860). While the children were in school, he was sometimes a school director. On 7 April 1830, he paid $6.50 to Sally Rogers for 'school wages' – probably the payment for the term running from the first of the year until mud-season – roughly from January to sugaring, some time in March. The rest of Sally's pay would have come from boarding round the district at the homes of her pupils. By 1854, the Pages lived in a fairly new farmhouse overlooking Page Pond. He had land worth several thousand dollars and his farming allowed him to sell grain. He had served in many local offices. He had long run a profitable business and was a member of the Congregational Church who paid for a good seat. He was a better man than most. All that was recognized in 1854 when Jabez Page was elected a Justice of the Peace by the Freemen of Orleans County. He was then authorized by Governor Stephen Royce 'to exercise the duties of the said office' in the whole of Orleans County. His election and commission entitled him to hold a Court and to function as a Magistrate throughout the County. It was the capstone to the career of the Honorable Jabez Page, J.P.

Jabez Page's 1854 Commission to be a County Justice of the Peace.

Jabez Page lived for twenty more years but of his later life little is recorded. He probably had more or less retired at about age sixty-five in 1858. His second wife died in 1860. The photographs of him and his wife were probably taken as a pair sometime before 1860. They show a couple well dressed but prematurely aged, prosperous but looking somewhat sadly at the world.[108] Their mouths are a bit sunken; like most old people in the nineteenth century, they had probably lost many teeth. He has the look of someone who may have been more honorable than his brethren but had not been given all he had requested. But then, that was (and is) the look of many old New Englanders. Needing a housekeeper and mate, he married for a third time not long after 1860.[109] He appears in no town records as an office holder after 1862. He bought no more land. As the Vermont woolen industry declined, to be replaced by dairying, he probably sold or closed his woolen business.[110] The last surviving receipt, from 1862, tells us that he was reading about the Civil War in *The Standard* [the ancestor of *The Newport Daily Express*]. A year's subscription cost $1.25.

Jabez Page (1793-1876).
Reproduced with the permission of the Albany Historical Society Museum.

Jabez Page; 8 October 1793 - 25 November 1876

Orphenia Page (1806-1860).
Reproduced with the permission of the Albany Historical Society Museum.

In 1864, Jabez and his third wife, Anne, made a settlement on his son Chester which looked to their ends. It was done in the form of a property transfer and is recorded in the Albany Town Records. There, Jabez and Anne Page, granted 'one Equal undivided half of all we now own of the said pieces of land above named together with one Equal undivided half of all the Stock, and farming tools on said premises' to Chester Page, if and only if, he fulfills the standard conditions set out in a bond 'for the support & Maintainance of the said Jabez & Anna D. Page during our natural lives'. When Chester confirmed the bond, he was to get 'the other half of all said real as well as personal property as we now own'. Presumably he did so but the confirmation was not recorded in the land records.

Jabez Page's business career paralleled that of his Vermont. Ashes and the making of lye were common concerns of pioneers who cleared the land. They, and probably he, were often speculators who sold plots when they had cleared land which could then be farmed or grazed. Through much of his life, his income came principally from a wool trade which boomed in the 1810s but died when sheep-farming became no longer profitable – as it was not for many by the 1840s. His dealings in ashes and wood, land, and money-lending supplemented his income as a wool man and farmer. He had insured a comfortable retirement.

He may have had other interests too since, in his time, Albany was a bustling place offering investment opportunities. Albany and towns like it were a bit more 'industrial' than we often think. At various times in Page's life, the town had one or more grist mills as well as saw and planing mills. It supported a cooperage and, later, a small tub factory and a creamery which made butter. It had a carriage maker, a harness maker, a millinery and shoe shop, a blacksmith or two, a tin smith and, for a while, even a still in which the Rowell's made 'potato liquor'.[111] Towns like Craftsbury, Irasburg, and Coventry were then able to support more stores than they do now. The small businesses, dealers in livestock, and general trade allowed more than one small hotel to operate in the town. Albany might bustle but the survival of promissory notes and promises to pay in wheat point to the shortage of cash and credit. Neither Albany nor Craftsbury had a bank but relied on men like Jabez or Isaac Sanders for needed loans.[112] Neither town was on a navigable river or connected by rail to other centers. Neither was able to sustain its growth. The young left for better opportunities – going West if they were farmers or wanted adventure, to southern New England for factory jobs, and elsewhere within the State as they married and found work. They could do so partly because they were fairly well educated. The town had plenty of district schools and for a time an Academy (1855 - c. 1880).

2. Other Dimensions to Jabez Page's Life

One would like to know more about Jabez Page's personal life, feelings, and beliefs but there are only a few scraps from which to construct an account of him. One is a verse preserved in his daybook in 1831 which suggests that he had been lucky in love and had a happy second marriage:

> Life is a shadow so they say
> Full of trouble every day

Only those who courting go
All the sweets of life do know.

He seems to have been an ambitious man but one who was also kindly and contented.

Other scraps and letters which point to the mobility of Vermonters[113] and concerns for absent family members. One such, from 16 April 1830, is a letter from a fairly young woman who lived in Springfield, Massachusetts, perhaps Jabez's second wife's niece. Larded with the sentimental pieties of the time, it bemoans the uncertainties of life and the sinfulness of the world. Its writer was sure that those relatives who have recently died have exchanged this 'World of Sin & sorrow and disappointment for a World of Happiness'. The writer thought that in towns such as Springfield, people have become 'grand' and 'real friendship' has vanished as it will not have done in Vermont, where her aunt lived among better people. She wondered how many cousins she had there and wished her mother might see her relatives again before they all leave this world. She was certain they would all meet again. Her idea of Heaven makes it seem like a happy and eternal family reunion. Family ties, even to people uncertain of how many cousins they had, were of importance in a world in which ties were becoming less oriented to relatives and more toward neighbors, work companions and class associates in industrial towns. The writer's own world seems bounded by Springfield, Pittsfield and Lennox, Massachusetts, but even more by the humdrum events of ordinary days, sicknesses, and her present duties. The Pages shared the piety of the writer but had fewer of her concerns for vanished friendships and the consolations of family life which they appear to have enjoyed.

Seven years later, Jabez and his wife, who had recently visited relatives in Danville, were expected to go to Pittsfield, Massachusetts, where their daughter Lucyann (c. 1818-1841) was working in a textile mill. Many Albany girls went to work in the mills in southern New England. Lucyann was one, and, like many, she moved around. In 1835, she was in Hookset, New Hampshire. Writing home in late January, during a thaw, she could see from her windows the Merrimack River from which the ice was out. The high water was nearly to the house and lapping at the windows of the mill. It was so high she thought they would not work on the morrow. She had not been well but had not been sick enough to lose time in the mill – except around Thanksgiving. She told her parents, sisters Louisa and Betsy, and an aunt, that she had left the spinning room for a job in the dressing room.[114] She thought she would like it better 'after I get learnt'. She made less money, $1.00 a week, but had the prospect of her wages rising to $2.00 as her skills improved. This new post was a more skilled job and a cleaner one. She thought it better than teaching school. Just as well – her penmanship was excellent but her grammar was shaky. She worried over her inability to go to church many Sundays since she lived so far from one. She wanted 'never to wound the Cause of Christ'. A bit later, still in the Hooksett mill, Lucyann, who again had been unwell, received advice from her step-mother. Orphenia thought she should come home immediately if she was not well and should not wait until she really got sick and could not travel. If she got sick in Hookset, she would have to live without an income. Her father could not go down then but might later. Being away from the supports of home was not easy for a single working girl – or her parents. She seems to have recovered and sometime around 1835/6, moved to a mill in Lowell, Massachusetts. There she lived with relatives named Perkins who also wrote to Albany. Lucyann was probably in Pittsfield, Massachusetts, by 1837; if so, she had moved again.

Jabez received a letter dated 30 July 1837, probably from his first wife's sister or sister-in-law, 'M. Perkins'. It is the sort of newsy letter one might expect from a religious woman eager to improve her family's prospects in this world and the next. Her health and that of her husband are noted – they were all well. Mr. Perkins was willing to go to the South or West if he had a chance. That seems to refer to work on the railroads; the 'West' meant the 'Old Northwest' – principally Michigan, Illinois, Wisconsin and Minnesota. Mrs. Perkins reflected that 'some wander in the world for the sake of earthly good which we shall soon leave   This anxious desire for riches is not justified   I hope we shall not indulge it att the loss of the true riches which cost no less than the life of the Son of God'. That led her to praise Sunday Schools and 'pious youth' who told children of their Savior. Her own son, aged twelve, asked her to tell his Vermont relatives that he had read the Bible through for the second time. The boy was working in a mill and had fifteen minutes each noon during which he could read a chapter.[115] His parents were also working there but Mr. Perkins felt 'more anxious than ever about giving [the children] an education'. She asked that some flannel be sent with Mr Hayden, who was to go there in September.[116] Homespun flannel went one way, thread went the other. Orphenia Page, in the letter mentioned above, asked her step-daughter to send her some 'yarn that will do for thread' so that she could make 'two or three quilts'. The local stores had none good enough for her. She also knew it would be cheaper in

Jabez Page; 8 October 1793 - 25 November 1876

Lowell. Railroads would allow stores, such as the Barton general store noticed above (pp.69-72, 90-94), to make those transactions easier. Religion and their work marked these lives.

There are also few vignettes of home life in Albany. A letter from late 1830s or early 1840s shows Lucyann's stay-at-home sister, Louisa (1824-18??), busy and moving about. She had been visiting in Danville and Peacham for three weeks. She was about to go off to help a new mother for a week or two and thought she would 'work out some' if '<u>Pa</u> and <u>Ma</u> does not go their journey this fall'. They appear to have intended to go to southern New England; they would have stopped to see friends along the way.[117] She seemed lonely since she was the only 'girl; there is in this neighbourhood'. Looking forward to the return of someone from Lowell and of her sister, she hoped Lucyann was enjoying health and would 'be prospered'. She could not leave Albany until she had done her wool. She had had 'thirty weight' to spin. Jabez business involved them all. Strawberries were ripe. She had a new dress but clearly felt somewhat harried. She had interrupted doing the washing to write and hurriedly finished her letter before the stage passed the house. In the end, she married a local man, Lyman Tenney.

Lyman P. Tenney, J. P., c. 1870s.

The next surviving letter in the collection of Page documents was written fifteen years later, on 4 August 1855, by the Reverend E[lias or Elice] W. Kellogg (1795-1861). Kellogg's family came from Craftsbury and he had been a schoolmaster in Albany and then the minister of the Albany Congregational Church from January 1827 until 1834.[118] During that time, he successfully carried on an evangelical awakening which expanded his Church's membership from about forty to over seventy. He and Jabez were like-minded men who kept in touch. Kellogg's form of address, 'Dear Br & Sis Page', referred to religious and social relationships which had survived his twenty-year absence from Albany, not blood ties. He and his wife went West from St. Albans, Vermont. He regretted that they had not seen Jabez's son, John, as he passed through St. Albans before they left. The Kelloggs were to settle and to acquire a farm in what must have seemed like paradise after the stony fields of New England. The minister, a man probably well into his fifties, was then in Lee Center, Lee County, Illinois, on his way to a new home somewhere in the West. They had made a good trip to Galena Junction, Illinois, thirty miles from Chicago. There, they stayed with the family of a niece of Mrs. Kellogg. Before that, they were '2 nights on the Lake & 2 nights put up at public houses at Detroit & Chicago'. They had seen something of those cities on their way out. For a month, they stayed with friends and then were united with their children who had been boarding in a town sixty miles from Lee Center. Mr. Kellogg had suffered a bilious attack which had prevented his working but he looked forward to settling soon, although perhaps a bit further west. If he was still preaching, he intended to farm on the side as he had done in New England. When the Kelloggs resumed writing this letter two days later, his plan was to go to Wisconsin but he would do just as Providence should direct: 'The trial of remaining so long homeless demands a good degree of patience & faith even tho we are with our children'.

Much of his letter dealt with the wonders of mid-western agriculture. Kellogg was struck by the yields of the corn fields – thirty to forty bushels an acre – and at the prices of grain. Wheat was bringing $1.65-$1.75 a bushel and even oats brought 40-50 cents.[119] Of that, he seemed to think twenty-five cents was profit. It was 'difficult for a Vermonter to conceive of the vast extent of grain now on the ground & just harvested, or of the amount that it must yield, should corn come in as well as it now promises'. It was an 'Egypt to all the States east of Indiana'. People were getting rich but also 'avaricious'. Like the girl in the Massachusetts factory town, he thought little of a society in which people had no concerns for others and were so focused on profits. One wonders what he might say today of the agri-businessmen or hedge-fund managers.

Kellogg noticed other changes which had transformed the region between his visit there in 1850 and 1855. In 1850, the area had lacked wood and water. Now forests were being planted and cisterns were conserving the supply of water. The railroads, which had attracted Vermont workers in the 1830s and 1840s, had remade the country. Timber and much else came by the lakes and rivers and then was taken by trains to all points. After thanking them for news and mourning the death of an in-law, he asked for the addresses of Vermonters already in the area in which he was going to settle. Like him, many of them would have gone with the capital necessary to start life over again in 'Egypt'. It would be good. Charlotte Kellogg, his daughter or wife, was teaching in an Academy. He had sent her piano from St Albans on 14 April; it had arrived without injury on 4 June at a cost of $14.90.

The Kelloggs did not go to Wisconsin but Providence moved them roughly 270 miles south-east – from the north-central to the south-central part of the Illinois. In March 1860, Mr. Kellogg wrote from Wayne Center, Dupage County, Illinois, to express sympathy with 'Dear Brother Page' whose wife, Orphenia, had died in February. Her death had been announced in the *Vermont Chronicle* to which the Kelloggs and other migrants subscribed. Mr. Kellogg wrote a letter full of religious consolation. Orphenia was surely in Heaven and bought with the blood of Christ. We may suffer but there is a cup of mercy and, in the end, Jabez would go up to his reward with her – and his first wife – 'who had enter[ed] upon the marriage supper of the Lamb'. 'The Lord's ways are all good & wise benevolent & just', and while we may not understand them, we can 'fondly expect to meet... in the upper sanctuary of our God'. Kellogg may still have made part of his living as a minister. He had the lingo and a fluent pen. Did he convince Jabez he had riches yet to reap? Maybe. From Kellogg's letters we can conclude that the Pages were more than ordinarily religious – but such evangelical piety was fairly conventional for the time and place and in their class. It also looks as if Jabez's son, John (1830-1857),[120] and perhaps another daughter had also gone to the West. The young were constantly leaving towns like Albany which affected the communities in which they had lived. Such towns were never wholly stable communities. Much of rural eastern America was like that, a place where folks bred new generations of internal migrants who, after they left, linked the stay-at-homes to a wider world.

***

Those vignettes of Vermont life and of the lives of ex-Vermonters do not add up to much that is novel. Their value lies in the reminders of an earlier age, in which now tiny towns had life and communities, which in the twentieth century would be weakened by lack of jobs, by migration, by television and the internet, and by the increasing demands for specialized work and educations, which small towns can no longer supply. For some like me, the stories they tell are interesting for personal reasons. I am descended of the Rogerses, Darlings and Bosworths mentioned in the Page records. I have William Hayden II's account book and pictures of many of those folks. Now in my eighties, I even sometimes use a Bosworth cane which belonged to my great-great-grandmother, Mary Lovisa Bosworth, George's older sister. But, I am not so old that I would not like to try the Rowell's potato liquor or perhaps its rival, Shortell and Timmins' Green Mountain Rye, which was drunk by some of those folks. I occasionally drink from my souvenir glass made for that company.

This thin mid-nineteenth century glass holds 3.5 ounces and advertises the company's rye whisky. Rye is again being made in Vermont.

VI

Leonard Watson (c. 1835-1912): Rail-hand, Farmer, and Jack-of-all-trades

1. A Varied Life to 1870.

Jabez Page of Albany was a successful small businessman, farmer, and local notable. He did not do one thing but many. His world included not only the towns of northern Vermont but also southern New England, which he visited and knew through correspondence with relatives, as he did the Old Northwest, and California. An almost equally pious and successful fellow, two generations younger, was Leonard Watson who worked in many places as a young man but lived most of his adult life in Sutton, Vermont. Then, he more or less retired to a small village farm a few miles away in West Burke. Jabez was not a record keeper; Leonard was. About 1970, I purchased a box of his daily reminder diaries. They run in an unbroken series from 1859 until 1911. There are seven others kept by one of his sons and his wife, and several others whose authors I do not know but can be sure that they were women because they contain recipes and discuss cooking. By 1911, Leonard was an old man struggling to do what he had always done. If he started a 1912 diary, it has not survived and would have had little in it because he died on 24 March 1912. Sophia, his wife, lived on in their Burke house. By the early 1920s, their son, Ebert, and his wife had joined her. I remember Ebert, in the early 1940s, as an old man with a cane shuffling along the street on which my great-aunt Elzada lived with her husband.[121]

Leonard Watson was born 6 March in 1835 or 1836.[122] His name suggests that his family was one of the many Scottish families which settled in Caledonia Country and then spilled over into nearby towns as far south as Newbury and north to Greensboro, Craftsbury, Albany, Irasburg, Barton, and Westmore. He grew up on a farm in Burke or West Burke where his education was mostly practical. He probably went to a district school for only a short time since his grammar and spelling show few signs of much education. Although he read local and Boston papers, and sometimes subscribed to magazines such as *The Boston Journal* and *The Farmers Magazine*, he was probably not much of a reader. He could cipher well enough to keep accounts although he remarked that his calculations of interest on money might not be correct.[123]

Leonard escaped military service in the Civil War. This was possibly because he had some form of recurring and acute 'rheumatism' which afflicted him early and lasted throughout his life. Some attacks kept him housebound for days. Those, even when he was young, could last two weeks but usually 'put him on the sick list' for only a few days. His diaries suggest that his rheumatism was brought on by long exposures to cold, rain, and the stress of heavy labor – that might have exempted him from military service.

From 1859 through the early 1860s, one can follow him somewhat uncertainly from the notes of expenses he kept in the first of his daily reminders. He made money as he could. At first, he seems to have been working for himself and others. He sold pelts in 1859, did farm labor for others and perhaps himself. Some of the expenses suggest he had set up a small-holding or was, perhaps, working on his father's farm. On 7 March 1860, he 'Commenced to work at the State House for Mr A Bemis'. Whatever he did in Montpelier did not last long. By late 1860 and in 1861, he was dealing in cattle or working as a laborer. By the end of 1861, he had been in Lowell and Boston, Massachusetts, doing something not described. Among his entries is one for fifteen cents for 'Drink' spent during a stay in Brattelboro. At this stage of his life, he was not teetotal. There are entries for odd items in 1863 and 1864 – a sewing machine belt, cloth, marbles, and traveling expenses; none of them allow for the construction of a coherent account of the life he was living or the circumstances in which he lived it.

In June 1864, 'I commenced work for Lorenzo Warren a starting to ?cast of [off?] Gunbarrels'. Ten days later he had 'Signed on Boston Comma....' [?] and went to the Boston area. He saw a bit of the city and its surrounds and on 4 July 'I selbated to day, all day and Evening'. The next day he decided to return to Vermont – perhaps repelled by urban life or drawn back by a girl. On 6 July, 'I came home'. He visited his father. His later wife is named in his book with repeated fancy writings of her future name, 'Sophia Watson'. He was already contemplating a union with Sophia Hunt (1842-1937), a Westmore girl. Still, he was at loose ends. On 24 August 1864, there are entries for the expenses of a trip to Canada, perhaps to buy sheep. This jaunt cost him over $13.00. By then, he seems to have had a small-holding, probably in West Burke. There, he also did carpentry and farm work for others and bought and sold animals. Also in 1864, he made an extended trip to Derby Center, Montpelier, Burlington and, in the end, to Boston. That trip may have involved the buying of cattle which were then shipped south and sold.

His account book – really jottings during the years 1859-1865 – shows him living a humdrum, hard scrabble-life which went on until he married. He was back home sugaring in the spring of 1865. During that year, he went to at least one dance with Sophia – 'Fi' of 'fi' as she usually appears in the diaries. They probably married in late 1865 or early 1866.

Leonard is not likely to have been a very romantic lover since some of the diary's early references to his new wife merely call her 'the woman.'[124] Perhaps there is a better reflection on their sex life in his later description of his rutting pigs as zestfully 'having a love Feast'. One suspects he and Fi had them too. They had a long and happy marriage. By 27 December 1866, they had a baby whom they named Bradbury (1866–1891).[125] Two more sons were born, Ebert, usually called Ebe or Eber (1868–1952), and Ira (c. 1876–1905).

In early May 1866, Leonard took a job as a section hand or as boss of a section gang on the Connecticut and Passumpsic Rivers Railroad. This line, in the end, ran north from Brattleboro, to Newport and Derby, Vermont. Through junctions at St Johnsbury, Wells River, and White River Junction, it connected to western Vermont and points to the southeast and 'the West'. At Newport, it connected with lines to Canada and Island Pond, and, from there, to eastern New England. The rail line did not come into the village of West Burke but there was a stop on the western edge of town to which he would have walked to go to work. Leonard and his crew generally labored five days a week. If snow, ice or washouts were problems, then they worked on the weekends too but took off other days. Not all of them worked every day. Indeed, they and the Railroad showed a casualness about regular labor which seems to have marked Vermont day-laborers in the nineteenth century. The Railroad may have employed no more than it needed each day and the men did not work when it suited them not to do so. Leonard's work as a railway man was arduous but it did not consume all of every day. There was time, on 7 June 1866, to spend the forenoon with others chasing a thief in a sort of informal posse. The stealer got away. When Leonard wanted to go to auctions, he went; on other days he went fishing. He took time off for funerals, to go to the 'circus' in Lyndon, and did some visiting which cut into work time. He liked to attend fairs and, through the years, often went to the ones held annually in St. Johnsbury, Lyndonville, and Barton. Sometimes he went to 'the horse trots.'[126] He still farmed on the side and some days that was his principal occupation although his main job was working for the Railroad.

Farming in 1866, Leonard did all that a farmer then did. He had a few cows – maybe three – and wished to buy a farm which suggests he was renting or looking after a property owned by his father. He worked in a wood lot, sugared somewhere (he made 948 pounds of sugar that year), raised potatoes, planted grain and gardened. Despite his wishes, in April and May, he and his wife moved to a new place in West Burke. Their place was likely to have been on the edge of the village nearer to the tracks. One of his first acts at the new house was to make soap. The house was probably dirty and had a pile of available ashes. He liked to make soap and his diaries record soap making every spring until the very end of his life. He, or he and Fi, bought the furnishings for their new house at local auctions. He put in a large garden and had a few sheep in a field. In 1868, he had some wool carded; his wife probably spun it and then worked it up into stockings or woven items. Leonard could do some of his farm work on weekends but would have milked one or more cows every day and cleaned the stalls and fed them. Presumably his wife fed the hens and perhaps his pig or pigs. He also bought and sold pigs, cows, and sheep with some frequency – then and later. The Railroad was steady pay but other things were more interesting.

By the end of 1867, he was hiring men and seemed to be organizing the work in his section, usually about a ten-mile piece of track. Sometimes, he and his wife boarded another worker for about 50 cents a day – about half what the man made each day.[127] The variable gang of four to six men was responsible for keeping the track in good order. They often cleared sections in the winter and shoveled snow at junctions and switches. Each spring, they cut weeds along the track (they might otherwise catch fire when dry), filled in washouts, and ditched the sides to insure good drainage. They replaced rails, ties and spikes, points, junctions, and switches. They laid lay-byes and shimmed plates which were too low. Their section of track probably ran from West Burke to South Barton, or, perhaps, up to the height of land which formed the St Lawrence Divide. Pumping the handcar – he called it a 'turtle car' – up that slope would have been hard work; the ride home was easier. Summer or winter, the work went on and sometimes was enough to bring on his rheumatism. It also had its dangers.

In 1867, a brake malfunctioned on the handcar and badly damaged it. There was a minor crash in March 1868, and, not long after, a hand car (not in his section) was destroyed when it was hit by a train. In the following year, the horse of someone he knew was killed by a train running into it. On 20 January 1870, a major derailment happened

Leonard Watson (c. 1835-1912): Rail-hand, Farmer, and Jack-of-all-trades

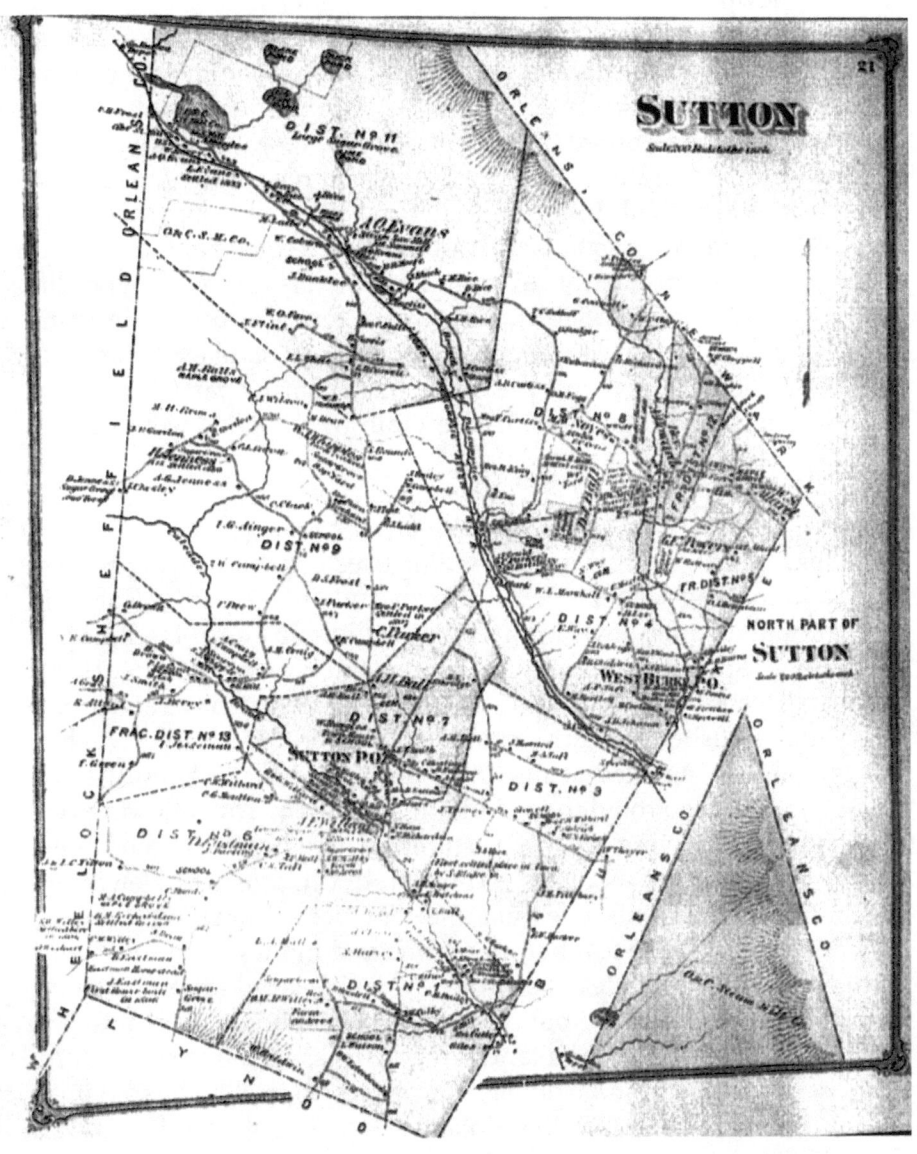

Sutton. Leonard Watson's house is shown between the two roads on the lower right. His uncle Henry Esterbrooks's house is the last on the road to Lyndonville.
Source: F. W. Beers, *Atlas of Caledonia County Vermont* (New York, 1875).
I thank the Bailey/Howe Library for this image.

north of Newport where an engine and its tender went off the tracks. Had it been in his section, his crew would have been setting the jacks to prize it back onto the rails and fixing them once it had moved beyond the accident site. That was dangerous work. About two weeks later, 1 February 1870, he recorded in his diary, 'I came very near being caught to day by an Extra train'. No one had informed him of the 'extra train'. The telegraph reached Barton in 1868 from the south but there was a gap north of that town so he could not have been told of a train coming south from Newport, as the 'extra train' probably did. He bought life insurance in February 1870, taking out a ten-year policy, insuring himself for $1,000. He also went to church more regularly after 1868, attending all day on 23 January 1870. He was ill during part of February. By the beginning of March, he had left railway work and went back to farming and fixing up his house.

2. Farming, 1871-1904

Leonard continued buying and selling livestock, butchering his own meat, and making soap. He could also do, and did, carpenter work – in fact he could do most anything at all. He could fix a pump-log if he had to,[128] shingle a house, or do simple masonry. But life was not all work. He and Fi still went to dances, two in the winter of 1869, to fairs and 'horse trots', and he fished when he could. There were no 'drunken fights', like the one he reported at his home on 18 August 1867, but he was social enough to go to Eden for Christmas in 1869. The following year they had Thanksgiving at Dr. Carpenter's where he 'had a good time'. Most years, until the 1880s, he did not note Christmas or New Year's celebrations. He and his wife went once or twice a year to Westmore to see her parents and to fish but more time and money went into fixing up his house with the idea of selling it. They replaced rotten masonry, repaired and painted, and put on many new clapboards and shingles. In November 1870, he even planted maple trees in the front yard. All this cost him about $250.00 dollars but was worth it when he sold up in March 1871 for 'Eleven hundred dollars – $150.00 down and a note for the rest'. The note was paid off annually over the next three years. He could now move out of West Burke to a real farm. He and Fi migrated to a farm in the southeast corner of Sutton (see previous page) about a quarter mile from a school house and on a road to Lyndonville. It was a good location. Their move was complete by 7 March 1871.[129] The next day Leonard went to sugaring.

They had not bought the place outright but worked it for his uncle, Henry Easterbrooks. The understanding seems to have been that they

Leonard Watson (c. 1835-1912): Rail-hand, Farmer, and Jack-of-all-trades

Sugaring. Sap was gathered from wooden buckets (above) and, later, from galvanized pails. It was taken in tubs (below) to the sugar house where it was concentrated by boiling.

The postcards are probably from a numbered series since the numbers shown are not dates.

Sugaring. Note the pile of firewood stacked by the sugar house (above). It usually takes about forty gallons of sap to make a gallon of syrup. Oxen had largely gone from Vermont farms by 1920.

would eventually come to own it but the sale was not completed until March 1873. Then, in an agreement like that of Jabez Page with his son Chester, Leonard agreed to give Uncle Henry '$210 a year his lifetime & Aunt Ab[by]'s'. When they died, the farm would be his. Henry and his wife were assured of retirement incomes; the Watsons got a farm.[130] In 1875, their agreement seems to have been turned into a formal mortgage but Henry retained some interest in the place until his death in 1888. In that year he received a final payment of $102.00. In the end, the farm had not come cheap but the cost of it was somewhat offset by the sale of Leonard's West Burke house.

By 1871, the rail-hand had matured into a solid citizen who owned a good watch and read the *Boston Tribune* or *Boston Journal*. He could afford to pay $1.00 a pound for tea and was going to School Board meetings, probably as a member.[131] He worked hard in their first spring. His rheumatism flared and he had to take on a hired man to help. But, he had arrived and settled into the annual work of a Vermont hill-farmer.

That was a routine which varied little from year to year until he left his farm in 1904. There were first of all the daily chores. Cows had to be milked to produce the butter checks. Their manure had to be mucked out. About once a week or so, he churned the cream he had separated from the skim-milk; that went to the pigs.[132] Sheep were 'greased' and 'snuffed' in the winter to leave tup marks and to prevent their infestation by mites and so on.[133] The pigs, which he needed for food and sale, had to be fed, kept clean and the boars castrated. Piglets, some of which were born in the winter, needed attention as did cows and mares at calving and foaling. That often happened in February or in the spring. The hens were fed and eggs gathered. Sometimes, there were also geese and turkeys to feed. Chores were a daily necessity and a drain on time for both him and Fi who would have looked after the poultry and maybe the pigs.

Once the chores had been done, January saw work in the woods. He chopped trees for wood which went to the wood piles in the house and sugar places.[134] Some trees were sold for lumber, some as pulp wood, and some cut for cord wood suitable for stoves in nearby towns. Some of that he split. Tending to the woodpiles was done not only in the winter but on days in the spring and summer when there was no other pressing business. The wood drawn to a mill and sold for timber had been stripped of bark, which was sold to tanners. Some of the milled wood he kept and used as lumber, some paid the mill owner for the cutting and planing. His swamp yielded cedar for fence posts and sometimes for shingles. In winter evenings, he picked over beans for home use or sale. Another winter task was rolling the snow on his sugar place and the town roads so they would be packed down for easy access in sugaring and for sleighs.[135]

Leonard on his own farm-roads used a small snow roller but on town roads larger rollers of the type shown were used to pack the snow for use by sleighs and pungs. It was cold and dangerous work, especially on hills and on icy terrain.
Courtesy of the University Press of New England and Allen F. Davis.

Leonard was usually sugaring by mid- or late-March. However, sugaring began in late winter with opening the roads, then washing the wooden buckets, and tapping the trees. That then involved pounding a nail into the tree from which to hang the wooden bucket and then boring a hole and driving in a spout to get the sap. There were two or three buckets to a tree. He seems to have tapped 500-600 trees. Then began the long process of gathering the sap, which went first into a tub on a sled and then into the evaporator pans to be boiled down so it could be made into hard sugar in 'the sugaring off'.[136] Occasionally, he boiled all night or went at it at 4:00 a.m. Syrup was not much made until c. 1900 because, when he began, there were no tin cans in which it could be easily stored.[137] Each year he made a few fancy sugar cakes using a caker or mould for the cakes. Some were then nicely wrapped and sold to stores and to discerning clients. All this went on from some time in February or March until as late as early May – usually for about five or six weeks. It ended with Leonard making soap, using the ashes from the evaporating pans and the fires in the house. To do that, he set up his 'leeches' and poured water through the ashes to leach out the lye. The fat for the soap came from the kitchen and the trying out of the fat from animals he killed for meat.

When sugaring was over, it was time to attend to the crops. Manure was spread as were phosphates and bone meal which he bought during the winter. Ashes from the house and sugar places were spread on the potato field and the patch in the garden. Then came plowing, seeding, and the harrowing in of some seeds. Normally, he planted (in this order) oats, wheat, potatoes,[138] barley, 'ingen [Indian] wheat' (buckwheat),' sugar wheat', corn, and sometimes late in his farming career, millet. Oats and some of the wheat and barley were for the stock. Some wheat was threshed and ground locally for the family which also bought flour at stores. 'Ingen wheat' and millet were cut and fed green to the cattle. Some of it was probably plowed under as fertilizer for a future crop. The field corn was chopped by hand and used as ensilage. Also in the fields were turnips, fed to the sheep, pumpkins, fed to pigs, and, late in his career as a farmer, squashes [probably Hubbard or winter squashes] marketed in Lyndonville.[139] Cabbages, carrots, and beets were grown in fields and sold locally or stored for the family's use in their root cellar. There was also a bean patch. He staggered the planting dates so not all the corn, potatoes or 'ingen wheat' ripened at the same time. Threshers for the oats, wheat, barley, 'ingen wheat', and beans came in the fall; few farmers had their own threshing machines. After everything was planted, there was cultivating to be done; the corn and potatoes had to be weeded and hoed.

In the family garden, they raised an increasing variety of vegetables. Lettuce, beets, peas, potatoes, sweet corn, turnips, parsnips, cabbage, string-beans, shell-beans and pea-beans, cucumbers, and tomatoes were all planted. One year they put in 'watermelons'. There were eventually strawberries and raspberries and in the orchard various apple trees and plumbs. He grafted many of his apple trees. In 1897, he set out some 'Cranberry bushes', high bush cranberries. The farm was self-sufficient in most of the foods the family ate. They sold some of their surplus and dried, smoked, pickled, preserved or canned the rest. Fi worked as hard as he did – and looked after the children as well.

Off and on in the spring, summer, and autumn, Leonard cut brush and sometimes blasted stumps or pulled them out to enlarge his fields or to make plowing easier. When he seemed to have little to do, particularly after plowing, he picked stone, improved a ditch or cut more brush. If he was a Selectman, as he was for many years, he would often do some work on the town's roads and bridges. He was good at this and trusted by his neighbors. And, there was for him an almost ceaseless quest for new animals and the disposal of dry cows, old sheep, piglets and shoats, colts, and other stock born on the farm.[140] He sometimes bought ten cows a year, a couple horses, sheep and rams, sows and hogs, and a pair of oxen.[141] This was a somewhat social activity which he enjoyed and often did well at. He would buy a cow for $25 and sell it quickly for $30 or keep it a while and then sell it on for a larger profit. Typical of his dealing was his buying a pair of oxen for $150.00 in 1872 and selling them a few months later for $190.00. He liked his animals but he was unsentimental about them, except, perhaps, for two horses, Charley and Snip. He kept them for years and found them good homes when they got old.[142]

When planting was done, it was soon time to begin haying. For some of his early years as a farmer, he lacked a mowing machine and did a lot of cutting by hand or hired a neighbor to come in and machine-mow his grass – sometimes sown grass.[143] Cutting with a scythe is very hard, blistering work. When he could afford them, he purchased a horse-drawn mower and rake. He had to harvest enough hay to feed, in the end, over twenty cows and enough oats and straw to provide bedding for a lot of animals. Haying was no sooner done than he began on his 'rowan' [rowing] – cutting a second crop of short hay after the first crop had been harvested. By sometime in September, that was all done and he could bring in his crops.

He picked apples in September and October. Many were peeled, cut up and dried but some were turned into cider – twenty gallons in 1871. It would have been difficult to drink that much before it fermented; some became 'hard cider'. There is no indication that he sold any. More apples went into apple-sauce. The peels would have been used to make jelly. Cabbages and the root crops were harvested in October and November. His wife seems to have picked the garden stuff and preserved, pickled, and canned a great deal. She began with cowslips and dandelions in the spring and ended with beets. Her subscription to *The Woman's Journal* would have been of use. There was a lot of corn to husk for corn meal or hulled corn which they sometimes made.[144] Then, it was time to bank the house with leaves and replenish the meat supply.

Pigs were often killed in November. He would butcher one day, hang the carcass, and salt the meat a day or so later. Beef creatures were butchered in late fall or in December, hung for a day or so, and then cut up. Some of the meat would be salted or corned. The family often seem to have eaten chicken on Thanksgiving day – a feast which did not figure much in his diary. Butchering was not just for the family but an occasion to make a bit of money by selling some meat to other folks or to stores in Burke, Lyndon or Lyndonville.

At the end of the year, one could clean out the hen house, fix up the sugar house,[145] build a bob sled, go back to the woods or cut ice, as he did after the first year or so of living on the farm. Ice kept his cream cool and unspoiled until it was churned – and then cooled the butter. Throughout the year, there were many such miscellaneous chores to be done. He was always busy.

By the spring of 1873, he had a farm with probably four cows and a calf, ten lambs, three horses and a pair of oxen. He sold several hundred pounds of sugar and kept all they could use. He had a small butter check and a bigger one for wood. He was improving his place with rapidity. In 1875 the farm had more cows, one ram, seventeen sheep and twenty-three lambs. Shearing that lot would have given him over $50.00. The sale of lambs brought about $75.00. The roughly 600 pounds of sugar he made realized $54.00. The sale of meat and lard,[146] and cord and pulp wood probably would have come to more than $100.00. All that would have paid the mortgage, his life insurance, and the fire insurance on the farm. In addition, there were the butter checks,[147] money from hides (about $10.00 in some years), the sales of produce, boarding a teacher, casual work for the town[148] and others, and the profits made on selling and trading animals (at least $40.00). By the 1880s, he had a bit of interest on money saved.

By the late 1870s, he had a house which had been refurbished with paint and new wall paper, a barn with a new add-on, a horse barn, a hen house, carriage house, two small sugar places, and a fair amount of stock. He had added several more dairy and beef cows, six or more pigs with their piglets, and had maybe fifty-five sheep, two oxen, three or four horses (Snip, Charley, Old Canada, and the Old Mare which had a colt every year), hens and geese. He never mentions a dog. While it is difficult to calculate his income, in the 1880s, it must have been in excess of $600.00 in cash, to which one should add the value of his consumables. After basic expenses of around $300.00 (mortgage, taxes, insurance), this family was more than solvent. He was, by then, a respected member of the community. After Uncle Henry died in 1888, he owned the farm free and clear. The following year he put up a new barn with a 'bridge' to drive hay into the structure above the main hay mow. The barn and the house had running water by 1889. He had given his father a note for $600.00 which he paid when an insurance policy came due. This was either his own term endowment policy or one on Uncle Henry's life. By then, he had also helped put in telephone wires in his district but it is not clear that his family had a phone.

Unpacked snow could be very deep and a problem to horses and people. This is scene is a barnyard with Cornelius Rogers driving his homemade sleigh in c. 1900.

By the 1880s, his equipment included a large sleigh, a buggy, one or two wagons, a stone boat and a sledge, a sap tub on skids, plows, harrows, a mowing machine,[149] rakes, and other gear used to skid logs and do other work. He had churns and separators but he bought a new (and fancy) separator in 1898 to replace his old one. His herd was then composed of thirteen or so milk cows, several beef creatures and cattle to trade. His flock of sheep numbered between fifty and sixty. He did not know it but his life had more or less peaked in 1890. He was about fifty-five.

When he sold the farm in 1905, it was a modern and prosperous concern. He sold it much as Uncle Henry had. He took a mortgage which gave him an annual income which he then supplemented from other sources. But, he was not done with farming. He purchased a new place in West Burke where, within a few years, he had refurbished the house, built a small barn and shed and added a hen house. There, he had a cow or two, pigs, and room for the animals he could not resist buying and selling. His small fields were enlarged and were still planted to potatoes, 'ingen wheat', cabbages, and other things. He again planted maple trees in his front yard although he no longer sugared. He continued to chop, draw, saw and split wood as he always had. He had a large garden and Sophia still preserved a lot of food. Their root cellar was full. He continued to make soap but increasingly his diary recorded entries like 'Sickness prevents me from worki[ng]', or, 'Stayed to home pretty much'. His farming days finally ended when he died not long after his last entries in 1911. There was more to his life than farming and to that we will now turn.

3. Other Things

Like so many members of rural communities in nineteenth-century Vermont, Leonard Watson was rooted in a social context defined first by family and neighbors. His extended family was large but somewhat difficult to define since some of the uncles and aunts seem to have been honorary and were probably not blood relatives. Still, his diaries mention at least seven real uncles living in the area. His wife's relatives added more. This meant that if he and Fi went to Newport, Barton, Westmore, Newark, Burke, Lyndon or Lyndonville, there were always people who would give them a meal or a bed. He and Fi reciprocated – more in their middle and later years than when they were starting out. Their Sutton farmhouse, like the Rogers household in Albany, tended to have visitors during the summer months. It was from his family circle that he sometimes borrowed things he needed and money before he had a connection with a bank – something which seems to have come only in the mid-1880s.[150] His Uncle Henry provided a farm; his father later provided the capital to build a barn. His wife's family had land on Willoughby Lake where his sons camped and where he and Sophia visited. Others borrowed or were loaned tools and money. It is difficult to tell quite how he felt about his relatives since the diary entries are so brief. He seems to have been a bit impatient with Uncle Henry but, with him and others, he was there for them in their old age and when they were dying. He 'sat up' with several as they neared their ends, including Uncle Henry, his own father, his son, Ira, and several neighbors. His kindness and sympathy is clear from the diaries.

It is also unclear just how he got on with members of his immediate family. His wife does not appear in his diaries very often but when she does, there are no signs of tensions in their relationships. Few of her domestic activities are noted but in many of those he helped. He pared apples to be dried and helped make mincemeat and sausage. Not all men would have done that. His wife had money to spend and seems to have been fairly independent – but, it was a long time before she appears in the diaries as driving alone to places. That may reflect their lack of a buggy before c. 1876 more than anything else. Later, she drove the team from Sutton to Lyndonville and Burke and took the 'cars' to Barton and St. Johnsbury where she occasionally went to visit or to shop. She wore fairly expensive shoes and, in middle age, had a fur coat. If she needed a hired girl, one was found. When she was ill or had teeth pulled, it was noted. She was active in the Ladies Aid at her church and he accompanied her to meetings. They seem to have pulled together and to have enjoyed the social activities they shared – dancing in their early years, going to 'socials' and suppers later. He attended church more often than she – presumably because she stayed home to mind the children and to cook the Sunday meal. She seems the one most interested in temperance meetings. Perhaps she had reasons to go.

His relations with his sons are a bit more uncertain. He noted their births but the diaries do not name them for some time. Still, Leonard liked to fish and took the boys fishing with him when they were quite young. They worked with him in the woods, boiled sap, worked on the farm and learned to be responsible early in life. Brad, when he was ten or eleven, was 'sent over to Burke to get some Gin and Alcohol' for his father who was feeling very rheumatic. It was not the boy's first time out alone with the wagon and probably not his first five- or six-mile trip one way. By then, he had cut grass in the fields and stoked the fires under the sugar house pans by himself. The boys were taken to fairs when Leonard went to see the stock, watch the horse races, shop, and enjoy the midway. And, they enjoyed celebrations on July 4th, Thanksgiving, or Christmas – if there were any as there often were

Leonard Watson (c. 1835-1912): Rail-hand, Farmer, and Jack-of-all-trades

'Camp Meeting' in Lyndonville.
Reproduced from Allen F. Davis's Postcards from Vermont *with the permission of the author and publisher, The University Press of New England.*

not.[151] Brad and Ira were sent to Lyndon Institute, the local high school, and probably graduated. Ebe did not go or go for long. Most years they all went to 'Campmeeting' (see previous page), the annual religious revival meeting held in Lyndonville in August. By 1886, Leonard seems to have established saving accounts for Ebe and Ira in the Lyndonville bank. Perhaps the best evidence of how he felt about his boys is to be found in his entries concerning the deaths of two of them.

On Monday, 9 February 1891, Leonard was working in the sugar place when a friend came to tell him that 'Brad was hurt he was killed instantly and was brought home in his Casket at half past ten P.M.'. The friend then went to tell Fi. It had been a stormy day and the young man, who worked for the Railroad, had been hit by a train along the tracks south of Lyndonville. When his parents went to the site several days later, they discovered that he had been hit, carried about 330 feet, and then thrown over two guard rails before coming to rest.

Brad's parents immediately bought a lot in the local cemetery. 'We had the funerall of our dear boy at One clock P.M.' and buried him there on Thursday, 12 February 1891. His father took what comfort he could in the fact that 'Their was a good many came and Elder Henderson preached   I paid him eight dollars' (see opposite) – about what he then gave to his Church over the course of a year. A day later, he noted with a grim sort of pleasure that Brad's girlfriend, Orpha Bedell, had sent them a very nice letter. He and Fi visited her family and they kept up with the girl until she died of TB a year or so later. After that, both sets of grieving parents kept in touch for many years.

Leonard settled Brad's affairs, collected his insurance, and then began to memorialize his son. Beginning in April, he fenced the graveyard, painted the fence and then laid out more lots in the cemetery. He moved his son to a better location in September and moved him again about a month later to a plot nearer the entrance where he had 'put in a foundation for a monument'. That was installed on 28 October and cost him $160.00 – half a farm laborer's cash income for a year. For many years thereafter, he planted flowers and bushes, manured them, and visited the grave on 17 August.[152] He also noted in his diary the name of a portrait studio in Boston where he may have had a photograph enlarged and colored as did others who wished to memorialize a loved one. When Leonard's father sickened and died in 1892, he cared for him but there was no expressions of grief such as the death of his promising oldest son had evoked. He looked after his father's grave for some years but gave it far less attention.

Leonard Watson (c. 1835-1912): Rail-hand, Farmer, and Jack-of-all-trades

Monday, Feb. 9, 1891

I was down to the Suggar place and J. W. Silsby called, and told me that Brad was hurt he was killed instantly and was brought home in this Casket at half past ten P.M. J. W. Silsby went up after Hi. It was a stormey and windy time sure

Tuesday 10

We are a makeing prepperations for the funerell to day. It has blowed and snowed hard to day

I have been up to the burying ground and selectted a lot

Wednesday 11

To day I have been down to the mills to get some things

Thursday, Feb. 12, 1891

We have had the funerell of our dear boy to day at One oclock P.M. Their was a good many came and Elder Henderson preached I paid him Eight dollars

Friday 13

To-day I went up to the Corner and got Orpha Bets Bedell letter and was glad to get it I can tell you sure

Saturday 14

Hi and I went down to Orcutt falls to see what we could hear about the accident from whear he struck the ground to whear he was picked up it was 20 rods and over thay guard rails. And then we came back and got went off to McIndoes, and went over to Mr Edward Bedells to see Orpha Their daughter. We came up on the Eight Oclock train

The diary pages which give the account of Bradbury Watson's death and funeral.

The Watson family monument in Sutton showing the face dedicated to Bradbury Watson.

The death of his youngest son, Ira, was a more protracted and difficult business. The boy seems to have graduated from Lyndon Institute in 1893 when he would have been about seventeen. What he did next is uncertain but he was not a rugged fellow or in robust health. In 1895, he took 'the Teachers examination' and probably taught in Lyndon or Lyndonville. He had a girlfriend there not long after, Miss Flora Campbell. In 1897, he was teaching in South Wheelock and still seeing Flora. Then, he went off to Buffalo State College – now the State University of New York, Buffalo – to take a course at its famous Normal School. He stayed for over a year of classes. In the autumn of 1899, he went to Southern Pines, North Carolina – probably to the Baptist College there. He probably planned to qualify as a minister. On 21 May 1901, Ira and Flora married and settled in Lyndonville but it is not clear what, if anything, he was doing. By the fall of 1904, Ira's health had deteriorated to the point that he and Flora gave up house-keeping. His father quit farming and took him back to Southern Pines where he bought a house. In January 1905, Ira weighed less than 100 pounds and had his lungs examined. He was on crutches by the end of February. The boy made it home, fished again in Willoughby Lake but died in August. By that time, his father had moved to West Burke. There was little on Ira's funeral noted in the diary but Leonard and Fi kept up with Flora even after she remarried. The Carolina property was rented but not sold until November 1911. It was as if his parents could not rid themselves of the place where they had tried to save their son's life.

Relations with Ebe were different. Eber, by c. 1900, was an odd-job-man often working for less than a dollar a day at a miscellany of things from carpentry to slaughterhouse work. His parents did not go to either of his weddings and never mentioned the name of his first wife – whom he may have divorced around 1910 when there is an enigmatic reference to 'a bill' which Ebe might get in court. What Ebe did not get was the family farm. But, he was given money more or less equivalent to what Leonard had spent on Ira's education – about $248.00. That was more than Ebe was likely to make in a year as a laborer earning 80 cents a day but with no regular job.

Other relatives counted for far less but friends were cherished by Leonard and his wife and shared many of their experiences. If they kept Thanksgiving or Christmas, it was with friends, only some of whom were relatives. Their friends by the 1880s were store-keepers, physicians, and mill owners. When they celebrated the 'Glorious Fourth', it was with the same people, most of whom also went to their or another Free Will Baptist Church in Sutton, Burke or Lyndonville. They met some of those people at privately organized 'sociables', and at Grange meetings.[153] Oyster suppers (maybe three or more a year, held by the Churches, the Grange and other groups) offered other places to socialize. So did auctions. Leonard went to several of those each year often buying nothing.[154] The family went to one or more fairs a year – at Lyndonville, St. Johnsbury,[155] and Barton – and sometimes to the circus at St. Johnsbury. They still attended 'horse trots' in Lyndonville and horse shows in Lyndonville and St. Johnsbury. The boys went to dances and 'masgarades' but their parents no longer did so. Most summers, Fi went off with friends, and sometimes with the young boys, to pick strawberries, raspberries and blueberries, and to picnic, in fields not close to their farm.

Leonard saw people at the Post Office at Sutton Corner, about four miles away, to which he went often more than once a week, and the various mills he dealt with to mill his lumber, grind his corn, or make cedar oil from cuttings from his swamp. He knew all the store-keepers in the area because he tried to sell them produce or bought things them.[156] Such contacts make it understandable that he should have made a successful washing machine salesman in 1891-92.[157]

Most years, he and Fi went to things that could be called cultural events. Sometimes they went to school exercises at the local district school which had been attended by their sons. There, poems would have been recited, songs sung, and papers read. They often went to the Graduation Exercises at Lyndon Institute which went on in the evenings for most of a week. They began with a sermon on the Sunday before graduation, after which came five or six days of 'exercises' at which there was music, the reading of poems, prize papers and the making of speeches. This all culminated with the graduation ceremony. They also went to readings, lectures, plays and 'conserts'.[158]

Leonard's socializing was not irrelevant to his civic involvements. He was probably elected a School Director in 1871 and remained one for many years. As such, he (and others) hired teachers, paid them, sometimes boarded the one at the school on the edge of his property, kept the school houses in repair and even sometimes painted them. He bought supplies for the schools and cut the grass around them. For a longer time, he was a Selectman involved with road work, the care of paupers, and much else.[159] Road work could be as simple as cutting brush for the town and looking after ditches and washouts. In the winter, it meant keeping the stretch of road past his farm open and getting others to plow in their areas as well. He aided the men who worked the snow rollers when those were introduced in the 1880s. On one occasion, he supervised and worked on the construction of a covered bridge.[160] He seems to have been a good carpenter and boss.

He always went to Town Meetings which were then usually held twice a year in Sutton, in March and September; other towns had different dates. In March 1886, he was chosen as the Town's Representative for the Legislature and went to Montpelier at the opening of the session in October. At first, he was clearly awed as he visited the State House and government buildings, heard speeches by the out-going and in-coming Governors and met other Representatives. He went to look at nearby Northfield, the site of Norwich University, got his committee assignment, and helped elect 'a Senator for Congress'.[161] He heard a lecture one evening and made a trip to Alburg to see 'the Iron Bridge'. His Committee was to report on it. After that, he visited nearby St. Albans and Swanton.[162] The session lasted a month. At its end, he was gratified to spend his last night in Montpelier with the Chairman of his Committee who evidently found him interesting. They dined and chatted late into the night. That was the highpoint of his civic engagements but it was not the last of them. He was several times picked as a juror in the County Court and served in 1901 as a Grand Juror. Named as a Commissioner, he valued several estates and was involved from time to time with the Caledonia County Probate Court in the settling of estates. When he moved to West Burke, he soon started going to meetings of its Improvement Society.

His Church provided his other principal social sphere. As a young man he seems to have had no particular confessional allegiance and does not seem to have attended any church regularly. After his marriage, he went to 'meeting' more often. By 1870, he had visited the Congregationalists in Westmore and probably the Methodists in Burke where Universalists, Methodists, Congregationalists, and Baptists shared a single meeting hall until 1871. In every year but two after 1872, he was present at the evangelical but non-sectarian 'Campmeeting' held in Lyndonville.

After moving to Sutton, he and Fi attended the Free Will Baptist meetings there. It was the only Church at 'the Corner', about four miles from where they lived.[163] By 1873, he was going to some Monthly and Quarterly Meetings and turned out in 1875 to hear 'the Gospel Preachers' – traveling evangelists who visited the parish. He noted in that and the following year that he had attended a baptismal service which seemed a novelty to him.[164] By the late 1870s, he was sometimes going to Sunday morning services, staying for Sunday School and going back in the evening for 'the Prair meeting'. Usually, he went only to the Sunday morning service conducted by an Elder, a layman acting as a minister.[165] Those men were sometimes local, sometimes preachers from outside hired for a term.

The big religious festival of Leonard's year was the summer 'Campmeeting' in Lyndonville (illustrated on page 151). That sometimes went on for two weeks. Leonard attended for as many as three days. This was sponsored by the Methodists and the Railroad. The Methodists ran a non-denominational show which imported a few notable minsters but also used talents from the local sects. The Railroad benefitted from the crowds whose members often came to Lyndonville by train. In some years, Leonard was involved with providing chairs, tables, and other amenities for the assembled crowds. At its fringes, the August 'Campmeeting' had a rowdy element and, as elsewhere, may have raised the rate of illegitimate births.

Some years 'Campmeeting' was preceded by a Temperance meeting to which he and Sophia went at least once. There were also local temperance groups which saw them now and again, as in 1877, 1886 and 1897. Such meetings probably did not end his cider-making.

Their parish constituted an active social scene for a largely homogenous population.[166] Monthly, Quarterly and Yearly Meetings were not only prayer sessions and places to discuss stoves and stable repairs but also featured dinners or suppers for those who attended. They were catered by people like the Watsons. The Ladies Aid Society met monthly and welcomed men. The Watson family was very much in evidence at other affairs during the year. Donation Suppers, often held in December or January, raised funds to support the Minister or Elder. Oyster Suppers, and Chicken-pie Dinners or Suppers came usually in the winter months. 'Sociables' tended to come after sugaring in the spring and in autumn after the harvest. The annual Church 'Picknick' was most often held in July or August after most of the haying had been done. Those occasions gave participants something to look forward to and to do on special days of the year. Beginning in 1879, their Church 'had a Christmas tree', which, by the 1890s, Leonard sometimes cut and set up.[167] The family strung popcorn the night before and then helped to decorate the tree on the following day. Going to the Church's evening 'tree' was sometimes the only observance of Christmas noted in the diaries. Christmas had not quite come to areas of Vermont settled by

Presbyterians. In other parts of the State it was kept with enthusiasm (see below, p. 189).

The Watsons were much involved in other parish activities and became more so after Leonard and Sophia were baptized on 6 July 1894. Others who probably entered a stream with them included three couples with whom they had long been friendly and the two children of one of the couples. After that, Leonard was more involved with parish activities such as finding ministers, raising the money to support them ('getting Minister Money'), and canvassing for money to keep up the church building. By the 1890s, he was giving at the donation dinners and putting $1.00 or $1.25 in the collection box once a month. That meant that he was giving the Church better than $15.00 a year. Judging by the 'Minister Money' he collected, he must have been one of the largest contributors to the parish funds.

Their usual religious activities did not exclude other religious experiences. In 1884, Leonard and Fi went to Burke 'to a Spiritual meeting and I got enough to last me a hundred years or more'. They were not recruited into the Spiritualist craze which swept over New England in the nineteenth century. In their old age (1909), they tried Christian Science but seem to have rejected that too, although the meeting was held in the home of one of the couples baptized with them. They may not have seen the Christian Scientists as a separate sect but as an additional set of religious instructions to heal those sick in body or mind – the view of it held by some of my Emerson relatives.

The Watson's world was one governed by the periodicities of the agricultural year, the round of Church functions, and the other events to which they went – Town Meetings, fairs, and graduation exercises. It was a stable predictable world in which good neighbourliness counted for much. When families were burned out or barns struck by lightning, Leonard was one of many who gave money to the victims. When there was a barn to be raised, everyone pitched in, as they did in his case. This was a society which did not have much in the way of formal support structures. The police power at the disposal of the State or local authorities was virtually nil. Very little crime and violence came to his attention. Over a period of more than forty years, he reported in his area four suicides and one murder (train accidents killed more), five or six thefts and frauds, and not much else. Religion, family and neighbourliness, the need to rely on others, and, perhaps, a satisfaction with life based on little knowledge of alternatives and perceptions of similarity in the social condition of one's neighbors made for social peace. One should not romanticize this time and place but nineteenth-century rural communities were not bad places in which to live. That may have been so partly because there was a realistic acceptance of limits and hardships. Death was more directly and more often experienced than is the case today. Few died with all their teeth or had escaped the illnesses which beset the Watsons and others from childhood to the grave – 'disetery', 'dipthera', fevers, measles, infections, boils, earaches, toothaches, eye infections, broken bones, serious cuts from axes and knives, rheumatism, tuberculosis and 'canser'. Leonard reported teeth pulled without anaesthetic, skin cancers cut out in a similar fashion, visits to physicians who could do little, and a lot of resort to patent medicines – which were probably, in many cases, as effective as the medicines made or prescribed by doctors. His was a world reliant on the 'placebo effect'. Life could be hard and it often ended early.

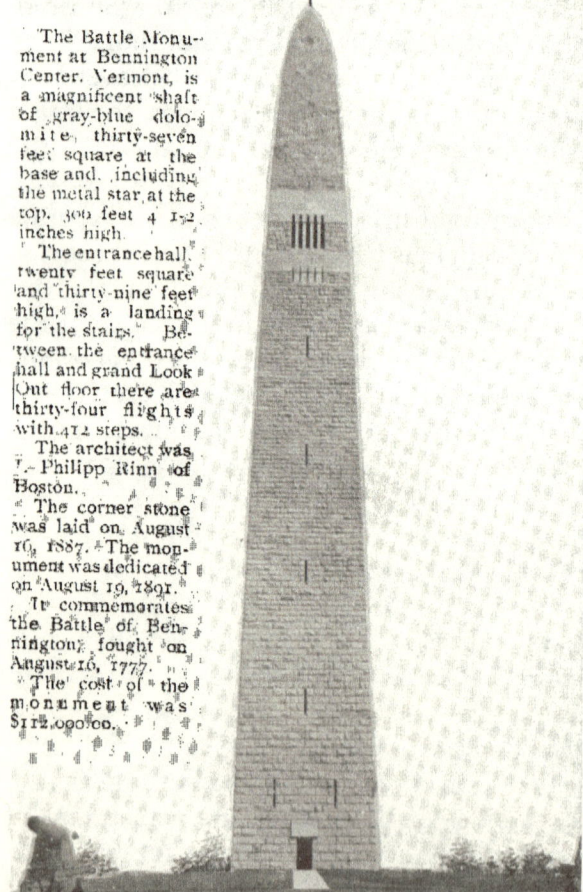

This image of the Bennington Monument is reproduced from a postcard sent in 1908.

Leonard Watson (c. 1835-1912): Rail-hand, Farmer, and Jack-of-all-trades

Leonard Watson's world was centered on local activities and people but he was not restricted in view to the twenty-mile radius of his usual shopping, business and other concerns. The Watsons were travelers as were many of their class in nineteenth-century Vermont. As noted above, he had traveled to Lowell and Boston as a young fellow, had seen much of Vermont, and had even been in the Eastern Townships of Quebec. He and Fi, in 1867, spent a week visiting relatives in towns in southern Vermont. But, they did not travel again until 1891, after he had been in the Legislature, built a new barn and seen two boys off their hands. Instead, they entertained others whom they might eventually visit. Their first occasion to do the latter was on a four-day August trip to southern Vermont and Bennington in 1891. There, they were present at the dedication of the Bennington Battlefield Monument (opposite) by President Harrison – after which they 'was out all night'. Two years later, they went north to Jay Peak, and then visited relatives in Brownington, the site of a once flourishing county grammar school housed in what is now the Old Stone House Museum.

This 1830s grammar school was falling into disrepair by the time Leonard and Sophia Watson visited it. It is now the heart of a flourishing county museum having several other buildings.

On 22 August 1894, they went to Old Orchard Beach, Maine, which they reached in nine hours by train from Lyndonville. They were there nine days, during which they saw notable beauty spots, such as Biddeford Pool, Ocean Park, and a house open to tourists which he called the Spring House and said was 'the nicest house that I ever saw'. In Old Orchard, they heard a political speech 'by a United States Senator' – actually the Speaker of the House of Representatives, Thomas 'Czar' Reed.[168] They went to Sacco, Maine, on the 'electric cars' on 29 August and returned to Vermont two days later.

One of the electric trains running along the Maine coast c. 1900.

In 1895, they made two trips. The first took them only to Hardwick to see relatives and the granite sheds and then to the quarries in nearby Woodbury which supplied the sheds. The second trip was to Bury and Compton, Quebec, in the Eastern Townships. They again made a stop in Brownington on the way home through Newport (opposite). They now spent some time each summer in Westmore with Fi's elderly parents and the fish in the lake. The boys camped there but whether they roughed it or had a cottage is not clear. The Watsons took a longer tour in 1897 visiting Manchester, N.H., Boston, and Pepperell, Massachusetts, Providence and Pawtucket, Rhode Island. They stopped in MacIndoes Falls to see the Bedells, the parents of Brad's girlfriend, Orpha. They were away two weeks and stayed with relatives, friends, and with some of Leonard's customers for butter and maple sugar – a nice testimonial of how he seemed to those who did business with him by mail. There were now more trips to Barton and Newport to see Fi's mother and other relatives but they did not make another long trip until they went to Southern Pines in 1904-05 and again in 1905-06. The costs of Ira's education may explain some of that. After their trips to North Carolina, there were no more long jaunts, but then, Leonard would have been seventy in 1905 and his wife was not much younger.

Newport had essentially two ports, one for light goods and tourists going to Canada, and another principally for its lumber trade. That was a mile or so away from this one.

4. Retirement – If You Can Call It That: 1904-1912

When Leonard and Fi left their farm in 1904, life changed in many ways but in others it remained much as it had been. In October of that year, they took Ira to Southern Pines where they bought a house and tried to cure their boy.[169] Leonard quickly found things to do. He bought and sawed his fire-wood, worked for the town's surveyor helping to lay out and install a new 'water Sistam'. He built a hen house, worked on someone's barn, and set out trees. They did a bit of local sight-seeing, going to the local spa, to Pine Bluffs, and to a winery where he bought two bottles for sixty cents. He saw a few baseball games – one 'a great game 13 Inins and a tie'. In early May 1905, they returned to Vermont and bought their new house in West Burke. Much of that month was consumed in moving. He moved out the house's previous owner, brought his and Fi's things from the farm in Sutton, and settled in. He drew manure onto his new fields, worked on his old farm, worried about Ira, labored on the new house and on constructing a hen house. Ira died early in September. After his funeral, they got ready to go South again and did so on 8 November 1905. In Southern Pines, he again worked for the town and improved his house by painting and putting in a sewer and more plumbing. He made a sidewalk and set out more trees and rose bushes. He and Fi did more sight-seeing and visited 'an Experimental farm'. On his birthday, they rented horses and took a trip to Aberdeen and, the next day, to a place called Lake View. They returned to Vermont the third week of April, stopping off in Washington for two days to see 'the Public Buildings and the Public Library',[170] and other places of interest. As after their first trip South, he spent time improving the place in West Burke: it got new carpets. Then he went to Willoughby Lake on an extended fishing trip which lasted almost two weeks – and then, he went back for a few more days. As he remarked one day in July, 'Fishing is the Business now days'.

But, what might be called his regular life resumed. He tended his garden, looked after his hens, his cow and several pigs and worked on a friend's barn for the better part of two weeks. He painted inside their house and planned more repairs. Auctions gave him another cow, wood to build with, and new furnishings. He had time to go to the school graduation exercises, Ladies Aid meetings, to Camp Meetings, to Barton Fair and the West Burke Improvement Society meetings. He returned fairly often to Sutton to attend his old Church, to get more things from the farm, and to see old friends at sociables. By April of 1907, he and Ebe were working on the new house and its barn, to which they added a shed. There was no let up in his drawing of wood and manure, his butchering, and general work. The next two years saw more of the same with perhaps a bit more 'lofing' and time off to read *The Farm Journal* to which he still subscribed – along with *The Caledonian Record* and the *Boston Journal*. Early in 1911, he decided to have a new barn built but he did little on this project other than cut wood for rafters and stringers and draw it to the site. Even that may have been too much for him since his entries more often contain lines like 'Cant do anything'. Still, he collected swill from local people to feed to his pigs, went to auctions, to the fairs and chicken pie suppers but he had noticeably slowed. Old friends were dying.

By 1911, he was setting things in order. He sold the house in Southern Pines at the end of that year. He had his Burke place in good order; Fi had new clothes. Ebe, now married again, was doing a bit better with a wife who had a name in the diaries and made chicken pie for her in-laws. As he paid Dr. Burke's bill of $10.00 in 1911, Leonard must have known his life was drawing to a close. One wonders what he made of the changes he had seen during his relatively long life. He was born before President Andrew Jackson died and when Abraham Lincoln was in his late twenties. When he died in 1912, William Howard Taft was getting ready to contest the office of President with Eugene Debs, of the Socialist Party, with Woodrow Wilson, the Democratic candidate, and the 'Bull Moose' Progressive, Theodore Roosevelt. The age of Jackson and the frontier had given way to an industrial society clamoring for legislation Jackson would barely have understood and would have opposed. Taft ran on a Republican platform supporting workman's compensation, anti-monopoly regulations, tougher regulations for interstate trade (enforced by a Federal Trade Commission), and bank regulation. He wanted such 'legislation as may be necessary more effectually to prohibit corporations from contributing funds, directly or indirectly, to campaigns for the nomination or election of the President, the Vice-President, Senators, and Representatives in Congress'. He advocated public works to reduce floods, improve arid lands and to promote trade. He was for an end to 'lynchings and other forms of lawlessness'. About the only reactionary note in his platform was advocacy of a law to curb 'undesirable immigration'.[171] All this was to make a better America and to insure its continued progress. His vision was largely shared by his opponents in the election. Taft, a conservative, hoped for a new world – one few Republicans want today. Leonard had lived through a lot of US history but what he made of it cannot be known. There is no known obituary and his Sutton gravestone testifies only to his affluence and the importance to him of his family.

VII

The Education of a Vermont girl: Mary Abby Tenney (1847-1914).[172]

As we have seen (p.xxi), one of Jabez Page's grand-daughters was Mary Abby Tenny, the daughter of Louisa Page Tenney and her husband, the Honorable Lyman Tenney, J. P. The Tenneys were a well-off family living on a good farm north of the present village of West Albany. Tenney held as many town offices as Jabez Page and acted as something of a lawyer for farmers needing wills, executors, witnesses, and legal advice.[173] Mary Abby and Julia, her slightly older only sister, had antecedents which were more than respectable. There was enough money in the family to insure that they got as good educations as were to be had for girls in north-central Vermont in the mid-nineteenth century. Julia went to Albany and Craftsbury Academies, taught for a while, studied for a term or so at the Normal School in Johnson, and then married and settled in the Eastern Townships of Quebec. About Mary Abby's education, more is known.

Nothing survives to show where the Tenney children went to primary school but it would have been in the one-room district school of District 7 situated virtually on the edge of their father's farm, perhaps 200-300 yards from the house.[174] The chances are that Mary Abby's education was in no way remarkable but that she attended more regularly than many because of the farm's proximity to the school building and the affluence of her parents. They did not need her help around the farm and house. Still, in 1862, she attended only two terms, missing the spring and fall sessions and was present only about half the time. She often stayed home when it was too cold and sometimes when her mother washed.

Most district schools were quite small – ten to twenty-five pupils distributed over what we might think of as grades one through eight. There seem to have been three or four terms of about ten to twelve weeks each year. Vacations came in the middle of winter, during sugaring and 'mud season', and around haying time. Schools did not keep on Fast Days, public holidays or when the weather was too harsh. Another feature which makes them different from most of today's schools is that students progressed at their own rate working as the teacher directed. A bright beginning-learner would soon be in working with second year students.

At school in the 1850s, Mary Abby would have been taught to read and write by a succession of young ladies who probably had attended Craftsbury or Brownington Academies, the nearest grammar schools. Most of them would not have taken much if any Latin and would have had little or no science and mathematics.[175] Often they taught only for a term or two and then married or moved on. Mary Abby would have learned to read from primers and readers which taught morality and religion as they instructed the child to read and write correct if rather high-flown English.[176] There would have been some elementary instruction in grammar and spelling. Spelling bees or spell-downs remained popular means of teaching well into the twentieth century. At home, the school readers would have been supplemented by little books given out by the churches and Sunday Schools. One from Mary Abby's family survives which was published in Boston the year before she was born – *Children's Offerings to Heathen Idols*. It deals with the need for missionary work and concludes (on page 24) with a poem ending,

Oh! Let us not at last be found
Heathens, though born on Christian Ground.[177]

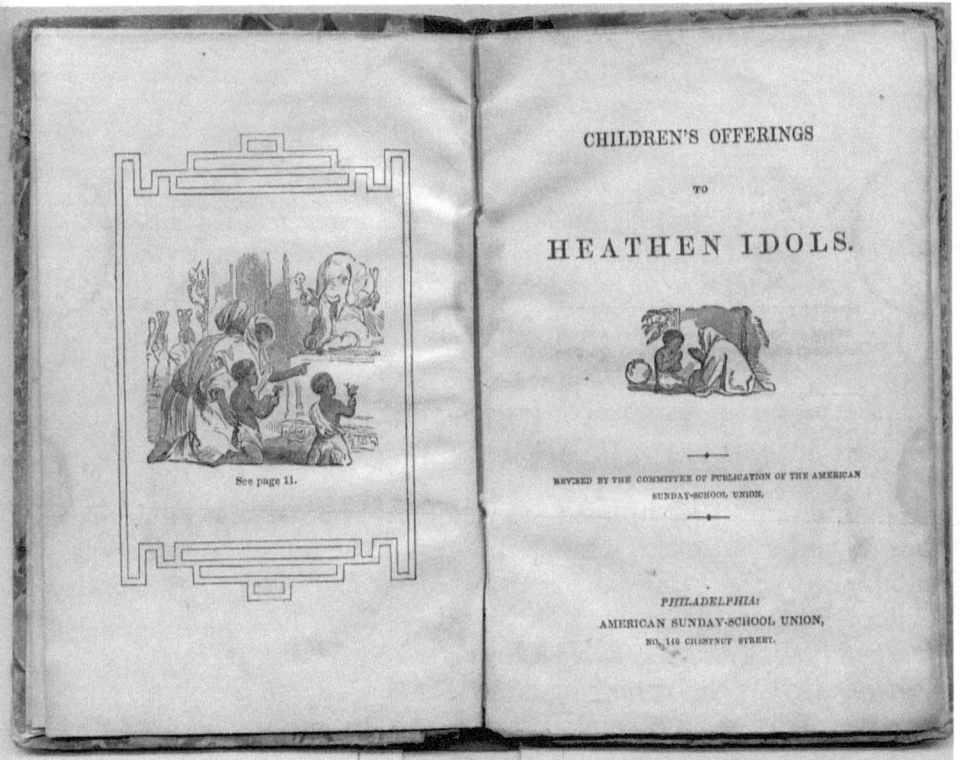

My Vermonters: The Northeast Kingdom 1800-1940

The American Sunday School Union was a non-sectarian Protestant society founded in 1817. As the American Missionary Fellowship, it lasted until 1960. It published books and periodicals for children and adults. Heathen Idols (1846, previous page) and Florence Kidder are uniformly bound and run respectively to 24 and 68 pages.
Florence Kidder (n.d.) belonged to Mary Abby Rogers's family. This may strike us as a morbid story but many of its readers would die as did Florence. Maybe it helped the young and their parents with its promises of a better life to come.

    By the time she had been in school a year or so, she would have been reading prose and memorizing verses. By then, she might have progressed to reading whatever booklets she received in Sunday School. Bible reading came a bit later. The other thing she would have learned how to do was simple arithmetic. She might, by the time she left the district school, have had fractions and worked simple exercises calculating areas and volumes, costs, and distances – perhaps even extracting square roots. It would not have been much but, for those who got no more, it would suffice for an uncomplicated life and gave a foundation upon which they could build. Mary Abby probably attended the district school until she was about twelve (1859/60) and then went to Albany Academy which had been opened in 1855 in what is now Albany Village. That was about a mile and a half from the Tenney farm – a not long walk except in cold or rainy weather.

INTERMEDIATE GRADE.

THE

INTERNATIONAL

QUESTION BOOK

AND

SCHOLARS' AID,

ON

THE UNIFORM SERIES OF THE SABBATH
SCHOOL LESSONS ADOPTED BY THE
INTERNATIONAL COMMITTEE

FOR

1882.

THE GOSPEL ACCORDING TO MARK.

BY

Rev. FRANCIS N. PELOUBET.

IN THREE PARTS.

I. SENIOR. II. INTERMEDIATE. III. PRIMARY.

PART II.

FOR YOUNGER SCHOLARS.

BOSTON:
PUBLISHED BY W. A. WILDE & CO.,
No. 25 BROMFIELD STREET.

The Question Book *was published by the Congregational Publishing Society of Boston. Other volumes in the series were for 'Older Scholars'. One owned by my great-aunt Alice Emerson (1859-1944) was entitled* A Hand-Book and on the International Lessons for 1882 with Questions. *Its 208 pages of small type were devoted to an exposition of the* Gospel of Mark *and came with a map of Palestine and a chronology.*

At Albany Academy, she would have studied a curriculum which prolonged, at a more advanced level, what she had been doing. There would have been more rhetoric and compositions, some of which she would have read at school exercises or elsewhere. There were mathematics drills and calculations but, for her, little or no algebra or geometry. The school also taught music and drawing but she seems not to have taken music lessons until 1864, some time after she had enrolled there.[178] She would have had some United States history and a smattering of English and European history. More poems would have been committed to memory and more things read at home. She would surely have read the Bible more intensively which would have given her a not yet archaic vocabulary of over 12,000 words and a sense of styles ranging over several genres.

There were other things she learned to do. Her diaries after 1861, when she was fourteen, contain many references to spinning wool and perhaps flax, some to weaving, many to sewing, making hats, doing fancy work (usually crocheting, embroidery, and tatting), and cooking. All that came – as it did to most girls – by watching, 'helping out', and being taught by her mother and other women in the family. She had her own flower garden in 1862 and worked on the farm picking hops with other girls. Hops were a cash crop for her family. She also looked after the chickens and hens whose eggs she sold. She drove the horse and carriage or the wagon on trips to Albany and Craftsbury (three or four miles). Occasionally, she rode side-saddle to visit neighbours. Longer trips she made in 1864 with her mother and father – to the railhead in Barton Landing (about 14 miles),[179] to Newport (23 miles), Montpelier (40 miles), St. Johnsbury (37 miles), White River Junction (102 miles),[180] Woodstock (95 miles), and Hinesburgh (about 66 miles). In those places there were sights to be seen, relatives to visit, and clothes to be bought. She visited several places each year as did many of her relatives. Their visiting ranged over several counties which points to their affluence and ability to take time off from work.

Besides home and school, there were two principal influences on her education – the churches and the community. Her Church taught her something about music and made her think about the contents of the Bible. The family were regular attenders of the Sunday services at the Congregational Church in Albany and, by her teenage years, she sometimes attended its mid-week prayer meeting. The Church provided entertainment with its weekly sermons and singing. It gave moral uplift and comfort during the crises which affected a population with fairly high death rates for all age groups.[181] At the end of 1862, there was a New Year's Eve 'watch service' in which the boys in the Army would have been prayed for. The several churches sponsored talks and were supporters of the Good Templars Lodge, a temperance society which she had joined by 1864. Her Church was almost co-extensive with her community. From her point of view, the few Catholics – French and Irish families mostly in East Albany – did not count for much.[182] But, there were no great divisions between her fellow Congregationalist and the Free Will Baptists who had a church on the Crick Road in East Albany. The Baptists, however, offered the spectacle of river baptisms which she sometimes watched. Baptists, Methodists and 'Congos' sometimes went to each other's 'donation suppers',[183] Sunday School picnics, and certainly shared an active and common social life. That may have included a common singing school to which she went on many Tuesday evenings. Mary Abby became a good musician and a thoughtful person good at many things.

There was also a secular community which kept her busy and taught her about life. Family affairs involved attention to a large range of relatives – in 1864 her family had twenty-six, mostly relatives, for Thanksgiving dinner on 4 December.[184] Her life took her into many homes to take tea, to dine, and visit, but also to tend the sick and 'watch' with the dying. She partied with girls her own age. They made and pulled molasses candy, talked to and about boys and young men, swapped photographs, looked at 'fashons' and, once in a while, thought about the Civil War and men who had gone to fight, including the father (illustrated overleaf) of her friend Mary Pine. In sugaring time, she went to sugar parties, in summer to barn-raisings and picnics, and all year round to 'sociables'. Letters from her girlfriends suggest they liked to be fashionable and were a sentimental lot who had crushes on each other as well as on boys. She was popular but also became a serious and reliable person.

Albany was also not without other sources of instruction. Her diary mentions attendance at a 'writing school', and at concerts, plays, and tableaux.[185] Lectures were sometimes given in the town. One, by a local teacher, was on 'Early Vermont Poets'– more numerous than one might imagine when so many wrote verses.[186] She mentioned a 'college meeting', meetings of soldiers, and once, a trip to nearby Craftsbury 'to a caravan'[187] where she had a 'good time'.

Mary Abby's diaries seem to have been given to her by her father and begin in 1862. He probably thought that keeping a diary would be educational and make her more methodical and responsible. If that was his intention, he succeeded. Year by year, she noted her activities and the letters she received. She also summarized her income and expenses for the year. In 1864, when she was seventeen, the diary shows her earning $37.00, including gifts of $3.00 from her father as 'spending money'. She had no allowance but she earned at a steady rate. Her earnings came from selling eggs, picking hops, and from either making or selling butter. Her major expense in 1864 – surely paid by her father -- was $50.00 for a musical instrument plus $2.00 more on rental fees and something else connected to her music. The next largest sources of expenditure were clothes and shoes (about $2.75 a pair). She received thirty-four letters for the year and probably sent about as many. Her diary for 1864, when compared with that two years earlier, shows she had become a conscientious diarist somewhat given to weather reports. She was methodical, serious, but able to enjoy herself. Letters from her friends show us a girl eager to look well-dressed and more capable than her mates. They looked up to her and sought her company. Her later diaries show more of the same.[188]

J. N. Pine, Mary Pine's father, survived the Civil War, in this photograph from c. 1870.

By 1864, music had become of increasing interest to her. She played the piano by 1862. Playing and attending singing school would have taught her to read music. Now, she wanted instruction in music so she could play another instrument. On 24 February 1864, she began to take music lessons from professional teachers. In the end, she played the piano, organ, a flute and a short-necked cello.[189] The instrument purchased in 1864 was almost certainly her cello. She took many lessons that year and by May she recorded board and tuition payments for music instruction in Coventry.[190] Sometime later she belonged to a local musical society likely to have included folks in Craftsbury, Albany and Irasburg.[191]

It is not known how long The Musical Association lasted but Mary Abby's ticket is from before 1875.

In 1865, aged eighteen, she returned to Albany Academy taking 'Arithmetic, Rhetoric Dramma & parsing' – for which she paid about $2.00 a term. She sang in a concert in Newport in March and attended the local 'funeral' for President Lincoln on 1 June; the preacher gave 'an excellent discourse'.[192] She continued with music lessons and singing school and had a part in a 'school exhibition' in November but by then she was no longer attending the Academy. From an educational point of view, perhaps the most interesting entry of the year came on 15 December: 'Went to Newport in a debate team to the teachers institute. Father carried up 7 or 8'. This was a girl who was learning to speak her mind and to argue. She did not record the outcome. That is the last recorded mention of an Albany Academy school function. For her, it was a sort of graduation exercise. Letters to her suggest that she may have learned to dance about this time but there is no record of her ever staying out all night dancing as did one of her friends.[193]

There were increasing numbers of boys mentioned in her diary as she aged but none seems to have been a 'beau' or fiancé. Couples appear more often in her entries but she generally had no partner. Of the thirty letters she received in 1866, she saved none from a man. An exception to her seemingly dateless life may be the visit to the 'Circus' in Irasburgh with 'T. J.', which was followed, in the evening, by a concert given by 'the Barker Family'. A short time later, she bought a corset, was photographed, and at the end of the year had a tooth pulled in one of the local general stores. Extractions cost a quarter, the corset was $1.75. She seemed a bit at loose ends. Visiting, music lessons, sewing on the new sewing machine, making rugs, and trimming her dresses took up her time while she recorded the marriages of others. In July, she drove to Newport to the 'horse trot' but went with a female friend as she often did. By then, she had probably begun to think about working in a cotton mill in Lowell, Massachusetts, but she was having eye trouble. Mill work, a friend told her, required good eyesight.

Nothing changed much in 1867. Julia interrupted her teaching to go to Johnson Normal School for a term; Mary Abby stayed home but visited her sister in May. She made a 'what not'[194] in the spring and, exercising a new skill, genteelly painted a sunset during the summer. She studied music and practised on her new organ, went to concerts, to Good Templars Lodge meetings, and to churches, and perhaps became a bit more religious. She attended Baptist meetings in June and the camp meeting in 'Leyndon'.[195] Indeed, she went with some frequency to the Free Will Baptist Church, on the Creek Road in East Albany, where she had first seen a baptism in 1864. The baptized were dunked in the Creek behind and down the hill from the church. Her family moved into a new house which she papered. Some unmarried men did show up and stayed the night with the family – 'wild' Wesley Paine, Isaac Chase, and a mysterious 'P. S.', with whom she went to a Christmas party. Her wardrobe grew and her picture album filled but she had no exciting prospects. What to do?

Living in Albany, but being twenty and unmarried, tended to mean more of the same. Ordinary excitement came in going to sociables, to musical events, to Lodge meetings, visiting others and being visited. Special excitement came with events like the dedication of the new Congregational Church and organizing its Sunday School, or going to Wesleyan Methodist 'love feasts'– or, perhaps, from the suicide of

'Uncle Silas Hovey', who hanged himself in July. Little novelties were found in surprise parties, making dried-flower or hair wreaths and having them framed,[196] berrying on unfamiliar hills, and singing in new venues. Her sister, who earlier had been engaged, had a new steady beau and seemed to live a better life. Both added to their wardrobes with Mary Abby buying a riding dress in September. Thanksgiving was celebrated at her grandfather's with thirty-five other people. Then, three days later, she decided to end her humdrum life by going to Lowell to work in a mill. This was a long-desired adventure which she had first spoken of in 1862 when one of her friends wrote to her about it. At that time, her father opposed the move.[197] She left Albany on Monday morning, 30 November 1868, at 5:00 a.m. and was in Lowell at 5:30 p.m. Public transportation was better then than it is now (2015) when the Northeast Kingdom has no trains or buses. She immediately found a boarding house and on the following day found employment at a Hamilton Corporation cotton mill. She went to work in its dressing room on Wednesday.

While Mary Abby's decision was likely rooted somewhat in the uneasiness of her situation, there were other things at play. She had had a persistent eye problem which may have made reading and sewing problematic. That now seemed better; working in a mill might not demand such close attention as did needlework done at home. She had recently been visited by an old friend and school mate from Lowell, Delia Darling (1847-1949). Delia ('Dill' to her friends, illustrated overleaf) had lived for about a year in Lowell, Massachusetts, where c. 1869 she married a retired American naval officer, Alden A. Honey (?-1881). Delia and Mary Abby both knew many other area girls who worked in southern New England mills. Mary Abby clearly intended to stay for some time in Lowell since her 'instruments' were sent down to her. Unlike most girls, she went, not to accumulate money for a trousseau, but for the experiences cities could provide. Her priorities at Lowell were seeing things, buying things, and enjoying herself at lectures, concerts and religious events.

Her job required her to be at work early so she quickly bought an alarm clock. She never noted when the work day began or ended but she was probably tired at the end of shifts since many diary entries note only, 'went to mill'. The mill worked a short day on Saturday. On her first Saturday, she walked over the town, bought a new skirt, and then went to a candy-pull at the home of an Albany girl. She found a church and prayer meeting for the following day. On Monday night, she and a friend went to the City Hall to hear a lecture by Mr Galiher on 'Ireland

Delia Darling Honey c. 1869. In this delicately coloured 7" by 5" oval picture, 'Dill' is probably wearing her wedding dress, gray silk trimmed with black. She lived to be 102, spanning the period from the Mexican War to the Truman Presidency.

and the Irish'. That cost her twenty cents. When General Grant visited the city, on 4 December, the mill workers were given time off to see him but they missed his 9:30 a.m. visit because they had not been released early enough. She seems to have done something special about once a week.[198] On 17 December, she began to go to concerts. Sometimes it was a lecture, once a festival in 'Dracot', or a 'watch meeting' (with a Joe Putnam), or a visit to the Lowell Library. A big outing came in mid-February when she and a friend went to Boston for several days. She was not the usual employee grinding on to save money. She did not always put in full days – but then she may have been doing skilled work not always needed – or, recurrent eye problems may have prevented her from working as hard as others.

She collected her wages on Wednesday, 10 February 1869– $30.00. Of this, $17.25 went on her board and room.[199] On Saturday, she and her friend, Carrie Nottage, bought tickets for Boston for the first of Mary Abby's many visits to the city – most of them occurring after her marriage. Following a Sabbath meeting and concert, the girls left Monday morning on a train which took them to East Boston where they met Delia Darling. Then followed a whirl-wind tour of the big city, the hurry and excitement of which is caught in her diary entries:

> Tuesday 16   Went to Boston City – Visited the State House, Library, Garden's – City Hall &c   Got back to E. Boston about 6 1/2, dinner .25 pictures .25 car fare .15
> Wednesday 17   Visited the Machine shops in forenoon, In afternoon went to the Natural History rooms,[200] bought rubbers .75   carfare .15   We arrived at E. Boston at 7. 00 o'clock,
> Thursday 18   Stormy, Came over to Tom Nottages this morning Bought candy paper .12   Carrie, Abbie and I stayed to Newall Nottage all night–
> Friday 19   Staid to Newell Nottage   In the eve we went to Morris Bros Minstrels got back about 11 o'clock[201]
> Saturday 20   Went to the Museum   Went into the play at two o'clock ticket .30   went through the Markets in the eve.
> Sunday 21   Stormy   In the eve we went to the Boston ?Metro house to church Rev Mr Algu's preached   car to & fery fare .10
> Monday 22   [rained, stayed at Notages and wrote letters] coffee .06
> Tuesday 23   Rain all day –we staid in Tom Nottages   Got cloth for ruffling   .14
> Wednesday 24   In the forenoon we visited the Navy yard [in Charlestown]   Went on board a Monitor & steamer &c[202] In the

> afternoon went to the City Fair .10   cloth for apron .50   Fans 1.50
> Thursday 25   At Newell Nottages to dinner.   Came back to Lowell on the five O'clock train. Very pleasant ride.

Then it was back to work – but no more regularly than usual.

Her time in Lowell was punctuated by frequent church-going, sometimes to hear notable preachers, and by attending two or three concerts and a lecture – 'Dr. O'lary's private lecture', which cost .25. On 17 March, she watched the Irish celebrate and on 25 March she took the afternoon off to attend a Methodist Conference. Three days later, she went to the ordination of five Methodist ministers. Two weeks later, she absented herself from work to observe a Fast Day. Since leaving Albany, she had attended services at Congregational, Methodist, Episcopal, and Adventist churches. Her curiosity was probably tinged with a bit of contempt for some of the things she saw.

Her diary entries stopped abruptly on 22 April 1869 and did not resume until 15 June by which time she had left Lowell and was back in Albany.[203] When and why she left is unclear but she was in Albany in time to celebrate her parents' silver-wedding anniversary on 17 June. They were given a surprise party attended by more than fifty people. The next day, Sunday, she was examined as to her fitness to join the Congregational Church in Albany. It accepted her and five others on 18 July when this diary ends. Her next diaries are lost, or resumed only in 1879.

At twenty-two, Mary Abby Tenney had seen a bit of Vermont and Massachusetts, had cultivated her musical and religious interests, and had developed a curiosity which led her to machine shops, museums and the Charleston (Boston) Navy Yard. She liked nice things and bought them but was also a worker able to do and make many things for herself. She could have earned her living as a seamstress, or, like her sister, as a teacher. Her education seemed over but it may not have been. What happened next in her life we do not know because there are no surviving diaries and few letters which are at all revealing.[204] The next surviving documents relating to her are letters from 1872. In the first, she was at home in January but by March her father addressed a letter to her at Seminary Hill, Montpelier, Vermont. A well-known Methodist academy, Montpelier Seminary, operated there, one which her son would later attend.[205] Was she in school taking teacher training, taking music lessons, or even giving them? And, who was the 'Geo.' whose name also appears in the salutation of one letter – a male George or her old girlfriend Georgia? Maybe the education of Mary Abby Tenney was not over but we can no longer follow her in her diaries or in the letters of her friends.

Three years later, in 1875, she became the second wife of Cornelius E. Rogers who earlier had married one of her close friends, Eliza (or Elizabeth) Darling. She had died of consumption in 1873. With marriage, Mary Abby became step-mother to a girl and a boy and later would have a son of her own, Andrew Tenney Rogers. At last, there was a man in her life but not quite the sort of man she may have dreamed of. Cornelius was not very religious, was not tea-total, and was a Democrat amongst Republicans. He did not sing, was not overly polite, and chewed tobacco. He was, however, clever, much better educated than she, and would be affluent and respected. He would do. He was a bit bossy but he would take her to machine shops and teacher training schools in New York City, to Boston shops and theatres, and, eventually, to Iowa, the West Coast, Arizona and Oklahoma. It may not have been an ideal marriage but it worked well enough for over forty years.

VIII

A Few of Mary Abby's friends: Teenage Life, 1862-1868

Much has been written on the educations of boys and girls in the nineteenth-century America but less about their social lives. What did Vermont teenagers do and how did they enjoy themselves? What did they expect from life in those years? Mary Abby's diaries and some of the letters which she received shed a bit of light on how girls her age and in her circle would have answered those questions. In considering them, it is important to remember that those girls were (with one exception) not poor, not badly educated, and were all fairly pious. They came from near the top of the rather flat social pyramid which characterized rural Vermont towns. It was also a pyramid in which a girl's expectations of life were qualified by the knowledge that life tended to be brief, that disasters could quickly ruin a family, and that there was a precariousness to existence which was not attributable only to the Civil War raging south of Vermont. Her friends, like Mary Abby, had 'watched' with the dying and had been to many funerals. Her friend, Mary Pine, buried her mother and a brother and worried a good deal about the health and safety of her soldier father. Another, Carrie Annis, was acutely conscious that her employment in the mills was dependent on her having good health and that the mills were not a healthy place in which to work. Their sense of the uncertainty of things is not so often shared by their descendants who are less often exposed to the dying of loved ones and the threat of incurable diseases early in life. In our world of social networks and public support systems not closely tied to families, there is less to fear and more to be careless about. We may live our lives less intensively than did they.

Mary Abby's life and the lives of her friends were characterized through the year by a round of activities shared with others. One aspect of that was constituted by life on the farm. Each day and week had its tasks. There was a usual washing day, a day for ironing, and another on which bread was made and cakes baked. Each activity had an accustomed time. The agricultural year also prescribed times for the taking care of newly butchered meat and the preservation of vegetables and fruits. Most young farm-girls, occasionally helped to get in hay when rain threatened. Mary Abby mentions picking over the family's wool but she would also have picked over beans, tended some animals, and done other tasks. Many of those things also provided some fun. Each summer she went berrying for raspberries with others. Sometimes they took a lunch and made a day of it. Hop-picking, which she did each fall for several years, put her in a gang of other girl-pickers numbering between four and ten and including Carrie Annis. Their work gave them about 50 cents a day but it was also a time of laughter. Summer or fall barn-raisings, to which they went, were accompanied by picnics and socials.

Mary Abby's family, like those of other well-off farmers, had visitors who came and stayed over throughout the year but were more underfoot for longer periods in the summer and autumn. She helped to entertain them and went with them as they visited others in the area. There were many weeks in 1864-1868 when she went somewhere for dinner, tea or supper,[206] or to stay overnight. Sometimes she went with her parents or sister; often she went alone riding her horse. All that was the usual round. To it should be added, in her case, piano and cello practice, singing, cards and other games, and reading, certainly of the Bible and devotional works but also magazines and papers. The lives of her friends were not very different.

The periodicity to their social calendars was not even much disrupted by the Civil War, which, surprisingly, figures very little in her diaries but was engaging many of her relatives. In 1864, Mary Abby's diary shows her going to church almost every week, attending singing school on Tuesday or Wednesday evenings, going to the monthly meetings of the Good Templars Lodge after she joined in March and, before that, to the temperance lectures which recruited for it. There were often winter get-togethers where girls or girls and boys pulled molasses candy,[207] sang songs, and had fun playing games. She made no mention of sugar parties but they would have been on most girls' dockets and may be concealed under some of the visits she made in March and April. She attended the Albany Academy graduation exercises for two or three days in May 1864 and went to an apparently public 'School Examination' in November. That she described as 'Very Good'. At the first, she read a composition. Others would have read papers or recited poems or sung. Thanksgiving was an annual festival but Christmas was not yet much celebrated in her youth. Hers was not a community much given to dancing but they did have winter parties and socials and picnics in the summer. Her Church offered some entertainment. In 1864, she went to at least three Sabbath School concerts at which she probably did not play because she had just started to take music lessons on her new 'instrument' – whatever it then was. There were also prayer meetings held in private homes which she attended.

Her social calendar was filled in with many other things. In March 1864, she was at the 'Sanitary Fare'[208] and appeared in a tableau with Mr. Henry W?. There, she also sang 'John Anderson my Jo', a song bound to appeal to folks who liked the Scottish songs which came to Vermont with Scots settlers. Boys 'called' on her too. Chester came twice, Wesley once but George, on 2 June, took her to Newport with another couple. That would have been for shopping and meant a meal out somewhere. They all had a 'tip top time'. Two weeks later, she went to a barn-raising. On 29 June, George drove her to Craftsbury where she had her picture taken; her sister Julia had had one taken in August. Mary Abby mentions going to two 'Soldiers Meetings' in Albany, probably meetings in aid of the Sanitary Commission. In September, she went to Craftsbury to 'a caravan' – probably a moveable sale out of wagons and tents. A bit later, she was taken up with getting new clothes to go to school in Coventry where she studied music during the fall and winter. She was home on 27 November for a Donation Supper in aid of a new school in the Crick District of Albany.

Eighteen sixty-five began with her making a winter trip to Waterbury and Stowe to visit relatives and to shop. On 11 April 1865, to the ringing of the local bells, she celebrated the end to the Civil War and 'the capture of Lee's Army'. There was a sugar party. The sweetness of victory did not last. On 14 April, the country mourned the President's death and observed a Fast Day followed by a local service for Lincoln noticed below (p. 367, n. 192).[209] On 16 April, 'she went up to the center to President Lincoln funeral surman   Mr Hadley preached an excellent discourse'. In the summer, she watched some Baptists get baptised in the 'Crick', for her as much a show as a rite. In September, she went to White River Junction to the State Fair and had another 'tip top time'. Eighteen sixty-eight added a dance at the Rowell's home, a circus in Irasburg, 'horse trots' in Newport, and, at the end of the year, a 'Christmas tree' at the Church on 25 December – the first one recorded in her books. In all three years, she rode to neighbours' homes on horse-back and at least once delighted in walking on the crust of the snow with friends.

None of this was at all unusual as can be seen in the letters to her from girlfriends. The earliest to survive was written by Mary Pine on 11 September 1862. She was then attending school in Williston, Vermont, but wrote from nearby Jericho during her September vacation. Her mother had died and she was away at school living with an indulgent uncle. Her language is of interest both for its odd turns of phrases and for showing the deficiencies of even a good education. She wrote:

> I am taking Music lessons of my cousin. I think I shall like it very much. But cannot tell as I have taken only two.[210] I have a very nice piano to practice on which cost $475 dolars. I suppose you can play very nicely. You spoke in one of your letters about my getting you a peace   I never have. for I had forgotten it until now. but if you would like me to get you one I will. Please say so when you write me again.
> I have not heard from Father for a long long time. I don't know as he intends to write any more but guess that I shall see one sailing along before long. I do so hope that he will come in Oct but am afraid he will not but when he does come I shall go to Albany, you bet. That is if he does   no doubt– but what he will.
> I had a good time yesterday. My Cousin & myself went to Williston to a Celebration. I wish you could have been there. There were three couple of us went off to ride after dinner   we run [raced] horses and one thing or other and at last came to the conclusion that we had a splended time. I expect that when I get up to Albany that I shall shock the good people I shall train[211] so hard. but how some ever I shall go it We will make the streets ring with our laughs. Do kens me both [212]....
> I have alway felt mad to think I could not [have] seen you when you were here last winter. but I almost I knew I should not before you came if you went to Uncle Nelsons first. If you should ever do that again   I should be [so] <u>mad</u> that I should not get over it so easy as I did this time – but I will hold on a little I shall get mad now. Yes! ....
> The last time I heard from you, before this time you talked of going to the factory. I hope you have given up the thought. I think you are very foolish to go. I would not go for any thing. I think your Father is wise not to let you go. ...
> Write soon
>   Love to all
>   Your trŭ & ct Mary Pine

Ten days later Mary Pine wrote again, saying she had suffered 'Hooping Cough' and still had heard no news of her father. She thought Mary Abby should visit her and George and Mondana Dike, a young married couple whom they both knew. She finished by including a caricature of 'my beau he is just a comeing a sparking ?' '[T]here is the dog going with him to keep him from all harm. I will make myself I am very handsome you see I have got my haris [hair] shingled'. Her letter (on following pages) included small sketches of the beau and his dog and a sketch of a girl with an upturned nose and a very full skirt. This girl wanted a boyfriend and to be in fashion. Before her next surviving letters from Williston (31 August and 8 September 1863), she had sent Mary Abby her picture, presumably a tintype for a now missing album. She also had been off visiting an uncle and other friends and was worried about a soldier brother who later died in the War. After speaking of her school, she went on:

> I have a very pretty room mate her name is Mary Warner from Milton. There are four Girls here besides myself, a jolley time. (Molley) Are you agoing to take Music this fall and are you a going to school? ... What are all the Girls all a doing up there this fall? Do they have dances[213] up there
> O!, Mary if you were but here to night. I am very lonely. I have got the (Blus) but I have to get over them I suppose. I shall have to close for it is most time for the male to go out.

By 7 March 1864, she had collected more photographs for her new second album and was enjoying music lessons and her room mates: 'there are three girls beside myself and we all room to gather and have a gay time all around'. As well as asking about Mary Abby's new cloths and her 'Beaw', and who was engaged or had been married, she recalled old times: 'How I wish I could step in that old school house once more. How we used to slide down the <u>hill</u> Do you remember?' But, the memories of sliding soon gave way to accounts of new dresses and a wonderful party:

> I have had my silk dress fixed up this winter I had it fluted with plain silk around the bottom of the skirt and the sleves as flowing and trimed with the same. The waist is cut with points and <u>Pastillions</u>.[214] I wore it for the first time to a party the last night of school last term. They danced. We only had a week and a half vacation. I went to a ball down to Hinesburg during vacation and danced until five o'clock in the morning. I had a splendid time I tell you. I think it is the best amusement I ever saw, I love to dance better than I love to eat and you know that is pretty

A Few of Mary Abby's friends: Teenage Life, 1862-1868

Mary Pine's 'beau' comes a courting with his dog.

... to Albany with him and see you went that be nice [Mary] if he will only come home I wont ask him to write I tell you if I should see him [peep] in the door I would jump 15 feet that is if I could I guess if you can read this writing you can French. I wish you would come down here this fall wont you I have been out to Mondana we had very good time now Mary dont you let any one see this if you do I will tend to yours case when I see you. have you had a letter from father lately. I wish you to tell Jennie McCoury I

think I wrote her last one I would like to have her answer it that is if she wants to how does your little brother get along and your big brother and Julie your father & mother and finely all of the folks at Albany give my love to all of them. Where is Lucy Jarustan and Laura Hovey and all of the girls I used to meet with tell me all about them and give my love to all of them and tell them I should like to hear from them. I will close for this time from a true friend Mary to a true friend Mary write as soon as you get this well. They have had two donations here this Winter. I attended both. One night I went, the first one they had, there were five couple of us about twelve o'clock started for home. We thought we would take a short ride, so we went three or four miles and the Gents went to a Hotel and ordered Oyster supper and we staidt and eat, and had a good time and then we went home, and when we arrived it was about half past three in the morning. We had a good time I tell you. Don't you tell any of the strict folks up there for they would think I was wild   But Mary you know better than that.

Those are the sorts of teenage nights not often imagined as occurring in Victorian Vermont. She was on the western side of the State where there had been more French and English settlers, not in the more dour and Calvinist Northeast Kingdom.

In September 1864, Mary Pine was back in Williston being looked after by her uncle but still worrying about her father. Her busy summer had included a trip to Burlington. There she had more photographs taken – 'a dozen of gems' – which she presumably exchanged for those of her friends. Her second album was filling up. She was hoping to go to Albany, where she expected 'gay times'. By 9 October 1864, Mary was sewing new clothes – '20 yards of cotton cloth to make up and one or two dresses and all of my clothes want fixing more or less'. The girls did a lot of dress-making and some fancy work. She was curious about Mary Abby's clothes for the fall and winter and about her boyfriends; she clearly missed her:

'How I wish you were here with me to day, we would 'raise cain', and talk over <u>good old times</u>. Do you remember that night we had a supprise party down to Uncle Dike's and do you remember our sitting in a carrier[215]   I have thought of that many times, How grand we thought sitting on Top was,   Didn't we have 'big' times about those days?   I am sorry that 'Wesley [Paine]' is getting wild. ___ I should think <u>you</u> could get him steady by talking to him in your low voice, I should think Mrs Paine would say, <u>Wesley Wesley</u>. I suppose you remember that I atand [attend?].

Then, her letter trailed off into her usual questions and topics stated in her own way:

Is Hellen marriade yet ? She has had rather serious trouble. Has she not? Mary will you ask your father if my father said anything about those things of late. I am very anxious about them. George and Mondana were out here a few weeks ago they were as full of fun as ever, Mondana is a trainer if there <u>ever</u> was one lived on this Earth, they started for Albany once this Summer and got as far as Stowe & then came back, I do not know why they did not go on. I am going to attend school this winter and Spring & than next summer I am going to try my distennty [destiny] in teaching. Oh! Mary please come down here & go to school this winter. It is called one of the best schools in Vt. Oh! You would learn so much. We would board to gather and have such a good time. You tell your father for me to <u>please</u> let you come there is a <u>splendid</u> Music teacher too & she is the handsomest lady in town & just as good as handsome. You would like her so much, & if you wanted to study French you could for they have a French teacher & a drawing teacher, I know you would like <u>ever</u> so much. Now <u>do do do</u> [one, two, and three lines under the do's] come. I will embrace you if you will, Our folks have come home from church, so I must close this long letter and get supper, I hope you will pattern this and write me a long letter. I remain as ever

            Your loving friend
              Mary

By 6 March 1865, she was thinking about teaching school but more immediately about the sugar season:

How I wish I could be up there this Spring in sugaring. I do not get much sugar down here. Do you remember the time we went way up to Billy Pope's to get sugar I shall never forget it in my life, and also another of our short walks up to the Center to Uncle nelson Dike's. How homesick we were and how we would go and how we did go if the snow was up to <u>our</u> necks. oh we had a good many good times and if you had come to Williston we would have had <u>another</u> I'll bet.

What seems to have been Mary Pine's next surviving letter was written from Jericho, 4 February 1866. She had been off on 'The 26 & 27 of last month' to a 'Chittenden County Teachers Association here at Jerico'. She had a good time seeing old friends. She was still partying:

I went to a dance two weeks ago last Friday. Had a splendid time. Danced until broad daylight. They are going to have another at Jonesville a week from next Wednesday. I presume I shall go but don't know. They always get up a dance the last night of school at Jo [Jonesville] so the school is out at that time. They don't think they have any time at all around here if they don't dance. I think you would like it well to dance. I do. ... I am going out to Huntington [Vermont] before long.

By her next letter, dated on Sunday, 22 July 1866, she had probably taught for a term or so and found a new teaching post but she was thinking about going to normal school or to a four year college. Her father 'has left it entirely to me about going to Col, he says I can go or take the money that it would take to go there and go to [normal] school. I don't know yet which I shall do,' She had had a dance date for the Fourth of July 'but the feller had a castrophe happen to him therefore Moll stayed at home. I was kinder sorry but did not care much .... I should liked to have spent the 'Fourth' with you ever so much, but could not'. She invited Mary Abby 'to come down in Sept and go to the Fair,[216] and by that time I shall be ready to go back with you [during the fall vacation]. We would have the grandest time imaginable.'

By the end of the year, she was 'attending school in this far off land' called Fairfax. She wrote on 26 December 1866:

How did you spend Christmas? Oh! I had grand times Christmas eve There was a tree at the church. The scholars all went Last evening there was a few couples permitted to go out for a surprise party. I was among the company. New Years the school are going to get up a grand affair. The ladies are going to have a tree and put presents on it for the gentlemen.[217] The 'junto' are going to get up an oyster supper. I am anticipating a fine time. I never had so good a time as I am having here.

By 17 March 1867, she was less ebullient and wrote, 'I would like to know who they were going to have you married to New Years? I think 'Thomas' must come oftener than he did when I was there last Fall. I hope I shall have an invite to the wedding if that is the case. For I partly claim Thomas myself as a brother'.[218] She was feeling a bit like an old maid. Two months later, on 17 May 1867, Mary Pine had graduated from the Fairfax Academy. As part of the festivities she 'had to read a composition, I was half frightened to death. We had excersises in the church and it was crowed, jamed full'. She immediately went to teaching in a district school in Williston. She had given up the idea of going on to college but 'I wish I might take a course but still I think it would seem a great while to think of studying four years'. Molly worried over some indiscretion in a letter she had sent to Wesley Paine but she was more taken up with the Good Templars Lodge she had joined.

> We have fited up a <u>very</u> large hall for the purpose and last Munday we had a public installation of Oficers   I am <u>inside guard</u>, so you can never get in without my seeing you. We have about 70 members in all and more are to join. There are more or less initiated every Munday night for that is the night we meet.

By October, her last letter is much about the time spent working, visiting the grave of her brother, and wishing she could do the same for her mother who was buried elsewhere. She still worried about her father who remained in the Army. The lively girl was being replaced by the more responsible young teacher. If she was Mary Abby's age, she was twenty and her youth was over – and with it her days of dancing much of the night since dancing all night was not for young teachers who wished to be employed.

What happened to Mary is not known but she and Mary Abby must have kept in touch. They met in San Francisco on 7 January 1906 and spent a happy evening together. Mary Abby noted in her diary, 'she has a fine home, – a pleasant husband'. One hopes she still danced and ate well.

Mary Abby had other correspondents who left some record of their studies, recreations and good times. One was Emma Webber who had been Mary Abby's fellow student in Coventry. Emma was not from Albany but perhaps also went to Coventry in 1863/4 because it was a local center of musical instruction. By 4 January 1864, she was at the Normal School in Johnson, Vermont, which she thought 'the best school I ever attended'. That summer, after teaching a short while in Barton Landing, Emma studied for a summer term in St. Johnsbury. Being peripatetic was normal for this group in which none seem to have pursued a regular course of study. Mary's sister, Julia, attended Albany and probably Craftsbury Academy, had a term in Johnson and also thought about going to a four year college. Mary Pine studied in Albany, Williston, and Fairfax. While in Johnson, Emma wrote a letter describing her life and courses:

Johnson Jan. 4 1864
Dear Friend
I did not think when your last kind letter came that I should neglect answering it for so long a time. But will promise better things for the future.
Perhaps you will wonder why I am at this place. Well be it known to you that I am attending school in this place: **having a nice time**. I like the school ever so much; think it the best school I ever attended. How are you spending your time this winter? At home or going to school. I hope to hear from you soon telling me all about yourself and your sister: she is teaching I suppose. I was much disipointed that I did not see you more while you were at Coventry; before I knew it you had gone home. I was very sorey that I did not see you more.
Our school closed nicely last fall at least most of the exercises.
We had just the nicest time last term. I think Coventry just one of the best of places. I like here very well, but not as well as C___ .
I am boarding in Mr. Robinsons brothers family, just one of the best of homes. I room with a daughter of theirs. We have nice times. I stoped at Mr. R___ when I came down; he brought me to this place. Their oldest little girl is a little beauty. Who do you suppose I saw last Sabbeth night at prayer meeting?
Mr Piersons and Sister (you can fancy I was supprised, and very glad too. The[y] were visiting their friends in the place. Monday evening I spent with them. It seemed like being at C___ again. I have not heard very much news from Coventry
Miss Daily and Mr Bean have visited for "better or worse". Hattie Wheelock is failing very fast. Charlie Cowles has been heard from. He is in N[orth] C[arolina], alive and well. I presume you have [heard] it ever so long ago.
I am studying Robinsons Algebra, Astronomy, Rhetoric and Parsing. There are 45 scholars; all of them are advanced. Mr Peal, our teacher, formarly taught in Craftsbury. He is very strict, but pleasant.
Are you going to attend school next spring? If so why not come to this place. You would like our teachers ever so much. Last week the scholars presented him with a silver cake basket. They were very much pleased.
Mary please write me very soon, will you not? telling me all about yourself and any news you may know from Coventry. Please

remember me kindly to your sister.
I shall look for a <u>letter soon.</u>
From your aff[ectionate] friend
    Emma A. Webber

    The books mentioned in Emma Webber's letter include two standard and recent texts by Horatio Nelson Robinson who, quite fittingly, had been an instructor at the U.S. Naval Academy in Annapolis. The first, was in a series of graded mathematics books which included arithmetic, geometry, trigonometry, and algebra for various grades, and finally calculus. Robinson's *New Elementary Algebra* (Ivison, Phinney & Co., NY, 1860; S. C. Griggs & Co, Chicago, 1860; 1st ed. 1854) also was published in an edition with a *Key* which gave answers to problems and further explanations of material in the text. The algebra book went through cube roots, binomials, and quadratic equations. Emma's astronomy text, *An Elementary Astronomy for Academies and Schools in which mathematical demonstrations are omitted* (same publishers, 1860), did presume some knowledge of spherical geometry, a bit of trigonometry and did give a few demonstrations. It was a text which would have given students a set of useful definitions ranging from simple things, like 'refraction' and the 'astronomical unit', to showing how the speed of light was determined. The students were taught something of the world system as it was then understood – it included planets now not recognized and lacked some we count. Diligent students would have been able to calculate local time, explain the seasons and the phases of the moon, predict, in general terms, future eclipses, and do navigational problems using the *Nautical Almanach*. The course would have made more sense and been more fun had it been accompanied with actual observations. Those might have been included since they were possible at Craftsbury Academy where Mr Peal had taught. Until the Academy burned in 1879, its scientific instrument collection included a telescope. Emma was almost certainly spending half or more of her time on mathematics and science – subjects which would not be needed in elementary teaching. Probably she aimed at teaching high school.

    Less clear is what Emma was reading in Rhetoric. The many rhetorics and grammars in use tended to fall into two groups. The first contained two sorts of materials – summaries of technical information structured within and by philosophic reflections. Commonly used versions of that sort were George Campbell's *The Philosophy of Rhetoric* (1776) and Hugh Blair's *Lectures on Rhetoric and Belles Lettres* (1783).

Both saw many editions and had imitators in nineteenth-century Great Britain and the United States. The other type of rhetoric books had less theory and were virtually anthologies of good prose to be imitated or emulated. That used at Albany Academy about this time was probably *The Progressive Speaker and Common School Reader ... by an eminent practical teacher* (Bazin & Ellsworth, Boston, 1858). It fell into the second group. However, its quotations and excerpts are interesting because the sources include not only standard English and American writers but also several Russian writers, such as Nicholas Karamzin, and, at least one Frenchman, Alphonse-Marie-Louis de Prat de Lamartine. Such books preached good religion, morals, patriotism, and the need for good style in both writing and speaking. Parsing would have been covered by any grammar. Then, perhaps showing the effects of her rhetorical education, Emma ended this letter with, 'Please throw the mantle of charity over this uninteresting Epistle as I have labored under many disadvantages'.

This frontispiece is a nice reminder that Greek antiquity vied with that of Romans and the Hebrews in academic settings.

By 18 June 1864, Emma was teaching in Coventry village's elementary school and was sententiously remembering 'the pleasant scenes of school-day life' and the times they had shared:

> Have you forgotten about "candy pulls" and Jimmie? I would like to see him. Poor Mr Taylor. I presume that he looks sad enough now the room is vaealed over Dea[con]. Cowls shop. He used to cast sly glanses that way did he not? ....' Mary please come down and see me this this summer I will promise you a ride on the hand car. Would not that be rich? Perhaps we could go down to Newport where friend Orcurtt lives. Is not that a temptation?

Perhaps of equal interest to Mary Abby was the news that Emma's

> Sister Eliza sailed for her distant home in California on the 13th of May. We have not heard from her since. We shall expect a letter ere long. It seems a long while to be in suspense.

When she wrote again, from Barton Landing on 1 August, Eliza had made it to San Francisco. The Confederate Navy had not been a problem but her worries were focused on the War.

> I have just been listening to a song sung by two of my little [school] girls "When this cruel war is over"[219]: When will this cruel war be over, that is now deluging our land in blood? Not untill the death song of slavery is echoed through our land & the clock of Destiny strikes the hour for freedom. Then may we hope to see the bright bow of promise illuminate the now darkened sky, and the clouds that have so long cast such deep gloom around us, threatening to deluge our land break away and morning succeed the dismal gloom of midnight.

Later she reported on boys they knew who had been captured by the Confederates. She then thanked Mary Abby for a photograph, 'the likeness of your "personal charms"'. Emma was an engaging girl who enjoyed parties, 'candy pulls', and good times. She was glad to have tintypes of her friends to fill her new album. Mary Abby's diaries show more letters received from this girl but none survive to tell us more about the things she enjoyed. Her letters suggest that reading rather baroque prose and romantic poetry must have been among them.

Another correspondent is more interesting because she was less well educated but was close enough to Mary Abby to be given a photograph and favored with letters of a personal sort. That was Carrie Annis. She had enjoyed hop picking with Mary Abby and other girls. By the Spring of 1864, Carrie was working in Lowell, Massachusetts, as a weaver at a Merrimack Corporation mill. In April, she fondly remembered Vermont sugar parties and hoped 'you will eat enough for me'. She told Mary Abby that she would come home for her wedding which seemed then in the offing but, as we have seen, did not occur.[220] Carrie's work left her little leisure, mostly Sundays, when she was often too tired even to go to church. One Sunday when she did go, it was to see some ladies baptized. She probably had gone to a Baptist Church which immersed them. In December, she pined for Albany parties and clearly had not had a happy Thanksgiving: 'I stayed in the house all day'. Most of her letters are really pleas for news and contain little about her own activities which seem centered on the mill and her boarding house. In January 1867, she looked forward to being again in Albany to pick hops 'as I did last fall.... if I am well and nothing hapens   I shall be at home most of the winter to hav som sleigh rides and to go to some of the Donations if I can get any one to go with me perhaps you will lend me Thomas once in a while if I cannot get any one else'. She wondered if Mary Abby had been to the 'the Center to the Donation   if so hue did you go with and what kind of a time did you hav   I would like to go to one and hav a good time but am doing very well whair I am'. But, 'I had rather be thair in the Winter'. By April, she was again writing, 'How I should like to be at home this Spring and hav some new Sugar face'. She would not be home until the mills stopped in July. Several of Carrie's letters mention her having company in the boarding house but she seemed to go nowhere and do little. Hers was the life of many working girls.

Mary Abby's only other known correspondence with girls her own age amounts to two letters, one from a cousin, Alice Cowdery, in St. Johnsbury, the other from another textile worker, Mary Brewer. Alice worked in her mother's dress and hat shop. On 15 May 1865, she wrote of going to 'levees', what was worn and by whom, and about who was married and engaged. Mary Brewer wrote from Brighton, Massachusetts, in 1868, in response to Mary Abby's enquiries about employment prospects. They were bleak. She went on,

I would not go back their [Albany, Vermont] for any thing   I

> have a great many friends at home that I want to see but more here   it is verry pleasant here in the summer   pretty warm ... but here it is so much better and in the winter it is splendid there is so much going on all of the time...

She was a convert to urban life and an enjoyer of its opportunities. She was probably doing some of the things which Mary Abby had done on her first trip to Boston.[221]

One could parallel that assortment of activities with what the boys were doing in the same years. If Leonard Watson and his sons were typical, they too were also going to dances, parties and candy pulls, going to more fairs, horse trots, horse shows and, later, to ball games, but also to church socials and picnics. As a young man, Leonard occasionally got drunk but diverted himself more often with hunting and fishing. Boys also found diversion at lectures and concerts. They too went to the 'Campmeeting', saw Baptists dunked, and did the other things which the girls did – indeed, they sometimes took them. They too came back late at night over dark roads. They were not all that much more adventurous but they may have been less interested in getting married. And, in those years always in the background was the reality of war. By 1863, they would have worried about being drafted.

Much of what they all did does not seem to us exceptional but one has to realize how new some of it was to youth in the Northeast Kingdom. These girls were better educated than their grandmothers but almost equally pious. They were probably more interested in fashions, danced more, and found diversions in temperance societies and school parties, musical events, and community activities such as fairs and the lectures of itinerant lecturers. Their mothers and grandmothers often had lacked such diversions. They all enjoyed sweets; food figures in many accounts of their parties and sociables. They led very social lives and were forever visiting others. They also had some spending money, not all of which seems to have been earned by them. They were eager consumers who used some of their cash to indulge interests in dresses and photographs. Youths of both sexes had a surprising amount of freedom and exercised it early. However, for this class, it seems not to have involved much sexual experimentation; that was replaced by early marriages. But, the girls' carefree times were short; adolescence could not be prolonged in a society in which all had to work when they could and when many married very early. Their youthful diversions seem very innocent and did not change greatly once they were out of school and married. Fun become less frequent but they still went to sociables and did what the seasons dictated – while they minded the babies and served food and drink to their men. In my family, Sunday afternoons candy pulls were still going on in the 1940s in a very different world.

IX

Robbie Rogers (1870-1896)

Among my family photographs is a wonderful photograph (opposite) of my grandmother and her brother Robbie taken c. 1872 when the children were respectively about four and two. The faces are clearly in focus but there is a soft blurring about the rest of the picture which is somewhat enhanced by the bluish watercolor wash which parts of it have been given. Both children are wearing white dresses and both have on little bar pins– gold, set with mother-of-pearl. Against the now somewhat dirty background, my grandmother's tresses are shown as brown as was her brother's shorter hair. Their eyes seem to be more or less hazel. Both children have the slightly uneasy, even apprehensive expressions which would be normal for any child held in place by a head restraint of some sort – as they almost certainly were. This picture, perhaps, formed one of a set of two or three pictures: the children and each or both of their parents. In its time, it was an expensive photograph, one which could be had by well-off farmers but not by more ordinary folks who were usually satisfied with small tintypes or with somewhat larger pictures taken on the occasion of marriages and important events. This picture was a sentimental indulgence by parents who loved their children and could afford a memento of the their innocence and sweetness, of the fragility and transience of childhood. It is touching but also revelatory of the time and of the outlook of such parents in the Vermont of the 1870s. It is so, partly, because we know a bit more about how they felt. That is revealed in a few letters of their mother which survive from about the time this picture was taken and from the diaries of their stepmother, Mary Abby Rogers.

The children's mother, Elizabeth Maria Darling Rogers, was the daughter of a prosperous saw-mill owner and farmer, Alden H. Darling. Lizzie, in 1867, married Cornelius Rogers, an enterprising cooper and wood worker, farmer, and cattle dealer. In a studio photograph, put into a locket frame meant to be worn or hung somewhere – probably a pre-wedding picture since Lizzie seems not to be wearing a wedding ring – she appears as a fashionably dressed, round-faced girl with dark hair and good looks who faced the world with an open and confident gaze (see page 64). Five years later, she was fatally ill with consumption

Robbie Rogers (1870-1896)

Robbie and Jennie Rogers (20" by 16"), c. 1872. This coloured photograph may have been made locally, or, a negative plate could have been sent to a Boston or New York studio for enlargement and colouring.

having endured several years of poor health. In the autumn of 1872, she and her husband traveled to New York City to consult doctors and to give her a change of scene and a rest. That, they hoped, would lead to her recovery. They arrived in early September and did not return to Albany until at least the end of October. Of the letters written by her, four were saved by Cornelius after Lizzie died in January of 1873. Both parents seem to have been sentimental people, if that is a term which can be applied to hard-headed farmers used to butchering animals and wives used to doing farm work of all sorts and to working harder than most of us would regard as reasonable.

The children were remembered in each of Lizzie's letters. One is even addressed to the 'Dear Ones at Home'. Lizzie missed them, sent them kisses, wished to see them, and hoped they asked for their parents. In one letter, she regretted she could send them nothing in an envelope, with the implication, that there would be presents aplenty when she and Cornelius returned. Another letter surmises that 'Little Robbie must be learning to talk very fast' and asked, 'has he out-grown that red dress trimmed with black'? And, 'what does he wear for shoes'? In her last letter, she wondered, 'Does Robbie wear his hat have you got his cape done?' This baby boy was as stylishly dressed on Sundays as his mother. When she wrote of the children she has seen in New York and New Jersey, they all seemed to be boys. Jennie, a bit older, was not so much on her mind although her mother would happily have seen the letters which her father-in-law told her precocious Jennie had written to her parents. Those children were cosseted and pampered but also expected to behave, to work hard, and to fear God.

After Lizzie's death, the children went to live with their Rogers grandparents who also had during that time their cousins, Lottie Rogers and her sister, Mary, whose mother had also died from tuberculosis. The elder Rogerses were pious, kindly, traveled (they had visited Philadelphia and New York) and as enterprising and capable as their two sons but they were less likely to have been as indulgent to the children. Jennie later remembered their piety, uprightness, and knowledge of the Bible. They taught her lasting lessons for she, too, remembered the Sabbath and always kept it holy.

In 1875, Cornelius remarried, wedding Lizzie's good friend, Mary Abby Tenney a woman of many talents, much style, and who possessed self-confidence and good sense. She had a reputation as a cook, seamstress, and musician. Twenty-eight in 1875, she was a bit long in the tooth. It is likely her marriage was initially one more of convenience than love. Love did come and was, for a time, passionate and intense; that one can infer from diary entries before and after her son's birth. Mary Abby made the two children of her friend her own and seems not to have put her own boy, Andrew (1881-1960), before them. Through her diaries, we can trace the short life of Robbie of whom she seemed especially fond.

There is little about his childhood in Mary Abby's diaries save for the usual entries about colds and other periods of sickness which seem neither unusual in frequency nor seriousness. He seems to have been a perfectly normal little boy who occasionally acted up or ate too many green apples. He had toys – blocks [cubes 2½ inches to a side] made by his father, perhaps a toy gun such as his father later made for Andrew, and an expensive little cast-iron cannon.[222] In 1882, his parents paid $6.00 for a bicycle for him.

The gun has a whittled stock with a fake patch-box. The barrel was a pasteboard tube, darkened and well varnished. The fixed trigger is guarded by a bit of bent iron. The sight was made using three pins.

His life, as one might expect, was structured by the farm year and the daily routines of the farm. He grew up helping with chores, working in the cooperage where, in winter, when he was not logging, Cornelius made buckets, butter tubs, churns, sap-vats, parts for wagons and sleighs, even furniture. Robbie might there have whittled out the yokes painted with red-lead paint which he and my grandmother used as children to carry pails of sap, milk and water. One of them still survives (below).[223] He would also have spent a lot of time with and around animals including the barn cats and the unmentioned cow dog which they probably had.

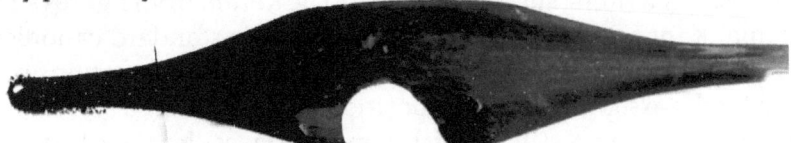

The three foot long yoke, painted with red lead paint, supported two pails, full of water, sap, milk or cream tied to it by ropes with fasteners. This yoke belonged to Jennie but Robbie Rogers had one too.

Robbie and his sister both attended the local district school in which children proceeded more or less at their own speed. There they would have used an elementary grammar and speller such as that which Jennie saved.[224] That was a rather nicely illustrated work which looked back to Noah Webster's interest in American English, its spellings and pronunciation, but also, explicitly, harked back to Demosthenes in its interests in oratory and action. Its last pages were filled with miscellaneous abbreviations and tables of weights and measures, the value of monies, and a multiplication table complete to 12 times 24. That they would have memorized.[225] This was a book designed to be used with a blackboard and slates.[226] It would have been supplemented by chap books read to the children and then read by them.[227]

Both children may have used a work by Frank B. Root called *Graded Lessons in English*; if not, then an equivalent. Their likely second grammar book was *Higher Lessons in English: A Work on English Grammar and Composition, in which the science of language is made tributary to the art of expression...* (New York, 1881, 1st edition 1877). It was by Alonzo Reed and Brainerd Kellogg of the Brooklyn Collegiate and Technical Institute, an institution their parents later visited on a trip to New York. It was part of a series in which the third volume was on rhetoric. The second book was dedicated to grammar and composition and designed to make it possible for children to express with clarity and feeling whatever they wanted to say. The authors did not see grammar as something to be learned by drill, or as a rote discipline to the mind, but as a set of skills leading to expression and the making of arguments both orally and on paper. The teaching of grammatical rules and prose structure was constantly related to expression and that to facial expressions and gestures. Grammar and rhetoric were one. The prose examples which the texts contain came from a surprising number of sources and were in their own ways both informative and interest-provoking. By lesson 80 (there were 145), students had been given sentences and short passages to analyze and parse. The sentences are pithy, sometimes proverbial, and their cited sources range from the ancient classical writers, such as Sallust, to *The Koran*, from figures such as Emanuel Kant and William E. Gladstone to the standard canonical writers of English prose and poetry. The lessons in expression were followed by the assignment of compositions to be written.

One of Jennie's, in a still childish hand, survives. It is marked, 'My first Essay' and dated, ever so faintly, 'Nov. 6 1880'. She was just twelve and had not yet learned to punctuate or to capitalize everything that needed capital letters.

Robbie Rogers (1870-1896)

My First Sea Voyage.
In describing to you My First Sea Voyage I will take you in your imagination to the Metropolis of the United States. Starting from Forty Second Street crossed Broad Way took the horse cars and rode down to the wharf, which was crowded with people and baggage. There were two boats lying at port the boston and the Lawrence   the Boston being so crowded I decided to take the Lawrence.   I went on board about four o'clock and she steamed out of port.   The first thing of importance I noticed was the Great Suspension Bridge which spans the East River [perhaps the unfinished Brooklyn Bridge, completed in 1883] The Abutments on either side towering two Hundred sixty feet [actually, 276.5 feet]   In going up the East River I saw several Sailing Vessels Steam Vessels   Ferry boats and Tug boats. Before passing out of sight   the streets of the city were lit up which was a Grand sight to behold   Soon a Light House came to view which shed its light over the waves.
It was now getting to be my bedtime   I went off deck to prepare for the slumber of the night
    I laid myself
    Upon a shelf
    And was soon rocked to sleep
    In the Cradle of the deep.
          Nicely

These 200 words probably did not reflect her own experiences but those of her parents or of visitors to the family.[228] The boats her parents took sailed from New York to New Haven, Connecticut. Robbie would have written such things but no composition of his survives.

The children also read through some set of graded readers such as Town's or those of McGuffey, which Jennie fondly remembered and re-read in her old age. They certainly read parts of Town's series since three volumes of their set still survive, including one from the second edition (Boston, 1858). That has inscribed on the flyleaf the name of their own mother who probably had used it when she was in school. The children were almost certainly given other books or booklets. Oliver Goldsmith's 'The Deserted Village' and 'The Traveler' still exist, signed by Jennie in an immature hand. They show evidence of having been used as texts. By the time the children left Craftsbury Academy, which they both attended, they had read a good many excerpts from great and not so great books and could write well enough to serve their needs. Jennie continued to read throughout her long life. She liked to read – newspapers, magazines, poetry, some novels and histories, and popular religious writings. Once in a while, she wrote a verse or two. She had been taught that it was genteel to do so.

Craftsbury Academy as it was rebuilt after the 1879 fire.

Among the other books which the children both studied in grammar school was the *Complete Arithmetic, Oral and Written* (New York and Chicago, 1880) by Daniel Fish (illustrated on the following pages), a book included in *Robinson's Shorter Series of Progressive Arithmetics*.[229] This has both the children's names in it and still contains one of Robbie's exercises.[230] Fish's work was a well-illustrated practical book with much of the text devoted to such things as measurements, the calculations of compound interest and even the returns on stocks and annuities. Robbie's surviving exercise contains his calculations of interest on loans running over several years. There is also stuck into the book a question from the next door neighbor, Henry Hayden: how much would be owing at maturity on a note of a given size and rate running from 1885 to 1888? Robbie got that to calculate.

NOTATION AND NUMERATION.

15. In representing numbers, objects are regarded as arranged in *groups* of *tens;* hence we have single things, or *units;* next, groups containing *ten* units, or *ten;* next, groups containing *ten* tens, or *one hundred*; and again, groups containing *ten* hundreds, or *one thousand,* etc.

16. This method of grouping is called the *Decimal System*, from the Latin word *decem,* which signifies *ten.*

17. *Notation* is a method of *writing*, or representing numbers by characters.

18. *Numeration* is a method of *reading* numbers represented by characters.

An illustration from Fish's Arithmetic explaining the decimal system.

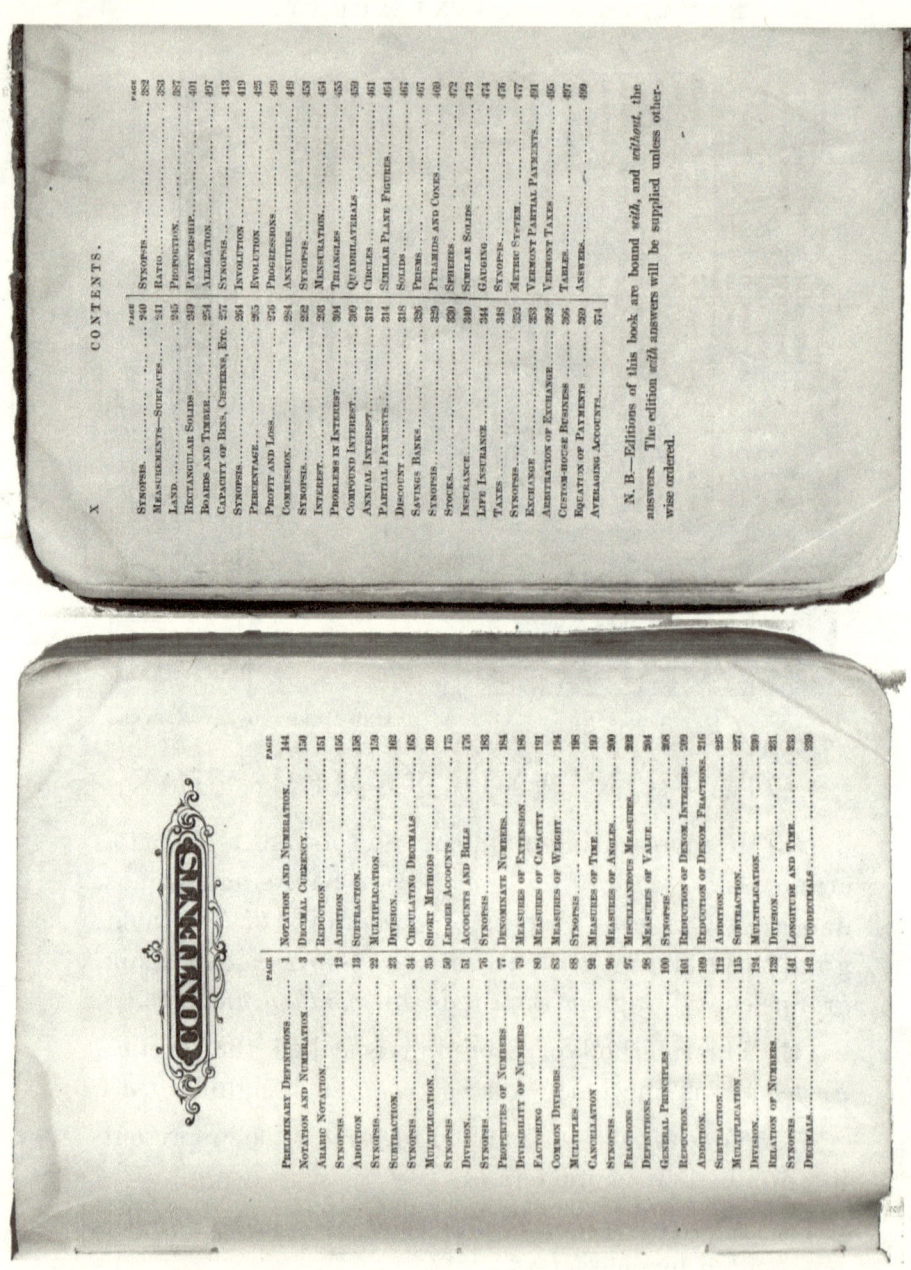

The contents pages of Fish's Arithmetic.

Both children are likely to have read Samuel Goodrich's *The American Child's Pictorial History of the United States* (Philadelphia, 1879) and to have used Charles A. Goodrich's *History of the United States for Schools* (Boston, 1854). The first book dealt briefly with the histories of the Greeks, of European countries, and the United States. The second was a book owned by Jennie. More restricted in subject matter, it came with colored maps and some illustrations. There were other things they almost certainly studied. One of them is geography. No geography textbook survives but there were bits of geographical knowledge in the other texts they used and they may well have studied the subject more formally since the family possessed Jedidiah Morse's *Geography Made Easy* (4th edition, Boston, 1794). That book had belonged to Jesse Rogers I, the first of the name to settle in Albany. Someone at the Academy may have taught them a bit of botany, as was being done c. 1910 when Jennie's daughter took such a course. Among Jennie's school papers, there is a foolscap sheet with plant and tree names prefixed or followed by numbers which may be page references to a botany book. Jennie, even in old age, had a surprisingly good knowledge of plants, particularly simples, and possessed a little book called *The Flower Vase containing The Language of Flowers and their Poetic Sentiments* by Miss S. G. Edgarton (Lowell, Boston, and New York, 1844). What else they might have gotten in the public schools is not so clear.

Instruction in the district schools and academies was supplemented by that of the Sunday Schools. There, the children would have received some instruction in reading the Bible and were been given cards with Bible verses or sentiments on them to memorize and to talk about on subsequent Sundays. As regular attenders, they would have gotten little books of piety which they no doubt read. They may even have had decks of quiz-cards such as Jennie later bought for her own children. Both children would have been encouraged to read their Bibles. Robbie at age nine was given a large-print Psalter by his grandmother which may have come with a bit of verse put in for him.[231] Most children of their class, by age twelve or fourteen, had read the Bible at least once if they were at all bright and had pious parents.

Following schooling of an elementary sort, both children proceeded to Craftsbury Academy where they got more of the same. Neither child went to school continuously nor completed a regular course of study. There is no evidence that either child studied Latin – Jennie certainly did not – or that they studied any other language but English or any science other than botany. They had little mathematics beyond arithmetic and, perhaps, some plane geometry. Still, they got a reasonable grounding in the basics of English literature, history, and geography. Their educations, while literary, had also been moral, polite in tone, patriotic, and religious and, given their circumstances, practical. Robbie seems to have liked school less but he attended the Academy until there was some upset; he was thrown out for not behaving and for lack of diligence. The following year, he went back but he never graduated. Jennie left the Academy to go to teaching when she was fifteen in 1883/4.[232] After teaching a term or so, she went back to school, attending an academy of some sort in Westfield, Massachusetts, where her father had contacts from his trade in cattle.

Their schooling would have been enriched, if that is the word, by what they might have found in the house to read. There were books but how many is unknown. We know roughly what families of this sort had on their shelves. Brought to Vermont by Jesse Rogers with his family were at least three books, two of which survive. They include William Scott's *A New Spelling, Pronouncing, and Explanatory Dictionary of the English Language...* (W. Creech and J. Robinson, Edinburgh and London, 1793). That contained a brief grammar, a short world chronology beginning with the creation (in 4004 B.C.) and a list of famous men, including many of the luminaries of the Scottish Enlightenment.[233] Other than Jedidiah Morse's *Geography Made Easy*, the third book was a work of natural history (perhaps by Oliver Goldsmith) which has been lost. The family also had a copy of Goldsmith's *An Abridgement of the History of England* (Thomas and E. T. Andrews, Boston, 1824) which had been bought second-hand at some time. From relatives, Robbie's family inherited a few history books, such as a *Life of George Washington for Children by E. Cecil* (Boston, 1859). Other presidential lives were to be found in a large tome by John C. Abbott and Russell H. Conwell, *Lives of the Presidents of the United States of America...* (Portland, Maine, revised edition, n.d.[1876 or after]).[234] The children's father had purchased another history by R. M. Devens called *Our First Century...*(Chicago and Springfield, Massachusetts, 1878). That ran to over 1,000 pages and had many illustrations. There were likely to have been more books of this sort which have not survived – big, expensive, well-illustrated, and sometimes purchased from itinerant booksellers. Those which have survived are well thumbed, some read to pieces.

There was more religious material. The family had a collection of Bibles and Robbie, like me, may have pored over the big illustrated Bible and Roswell D. Hitchcock's *New and Complete Analysis of the Holy Bible*. That included commentaries and histories and a revised version of Alexander Cruden's famous *Concordance*, first published in London in 1737 and not out of print since then. That could be supplemented by John Fleetwood's *The Life of Our Lord and Saviour Jesus Christ... together with the Lives.... of... Evangelists, Apostles and other Primitive Martyrs to which is added a History of the Jews* (Hartford, 1846; 1st edn, Glasgow, 1813). Fleetwood's popular work contained a good deal of theology. Among the lighter fare was John Bunyan's *Pilgrims Progress* (Indianapolis, 1859), which my grandmother could almost quote from memory, and many little books, mostly from their Sunday School or the Church – books published by religious organizations. Among those miniatures and chap-books were Jeremy Taylor's seventeenth-century the *Comforts of Piety ... carefully abridged* (Boston, 1831); *Arthur: A True History* (Philadelphia, 1838), 'By a Mother'. In that, industry, thrift and cleanliness triumph over their opposites. Another was the *Children's Offerings to Heathen Idols* (Philadelphia, 1846) noticed above (p. 167). Others included *Daily Food for Christians being a portion of scriptures for every day in the year* (Boston, n. d.); and *Good Daughters* (New York, 1861). These things must have made for long Sunday afternoons in the 1880s just as they tended to do in the 1940s when my grandmother thought I too should read them and not play outside on the Lord's Day. I preferred such things as *Inquire Within or Anything you want to know; or, over three thousand seven hundred facts* (New York, 1858). I suspect Robbie felt much the same.[235] There was, for days other than Sunday, a Hoyle's book of games which exists in tatters.

In Robbie's case, further education was provided by his father. Cornelius was not only a successful farmer but one with diverse interests and sources of income. Joining in his various activities constituted a very practical education for any boy who paid attention to his father's instructions and example. Their farm was principally a dairy farm selling butter to Nashua and Boston and sometimes to New York. It had a good milking herd of about sixteen cows. They churned their cream, fed the whey and skim milk to the pigs, and shipped the butter by rail from Barton Landing. Butter paid their basic bills. There were, of course, a few more cows freshening or drying off and there was at least one bull. The family also raised Devonshires, a breed of milk and beef cattle. A couple of beef creatures for their own use were slaughtered each year so they probably had at least one breeding pair.[236] They often had some steers or oxen.

In addition to butter, the farm produced between 600 and 1,500 pounds of maple sugar annually. That was worth, on average, about

$350.00 – more than the cost of the hired man for a year. Then, there were the profits from logging. Some of the wood was sold to local mills, some used in the constant building and repair work which seemed to go on continually on the Rogers farm. All the logs were stripped of bark which was sold to tanneries by the cord. More wood was cut for their own stoves and for the arch in the sugar place. Wood, in a good year, might realize as much as $400.00. Cornelius also scaled logs for others.[237] That activity in 1896 paid him $66.00. There were casual profits annually from the sale of a few geese, some pigs or a butchered beef creature, from eggs and wool from their sheep not needed for their own spinning. Pelts supplied by the animals they killed, which died, or which Cornelius trapped, were sold. Fox and other skins he took yearly gave him about $20.00 – the wages of an extra hired hand for twenty days during haying when an extra hand was needed. To that, Cornelius added the proceeds of his cooperage and wood-working shop. That was a diminishing enterprise but paid him something. Knowing about all that would have come to Robbie as a matter of course – as would the expectation of having an income like his father's when he was mature – more than $900.00 a year.[238]

And, there was cattle trading. For several years (1880s-1900) Cornelius, his younger brother Jesse (he also had a farm and later a store), Jack Beede (a cousin), and Robbie or a hired man dealt in cattle. Cornelius organized the trade and arranged the bank loan if one were needed. One year he borrowed $2,000.00 to finance his dealings. In late summer up to sometime in October, the men would buy in an area of about forty miles in radius. The size of the herd bought varied from about forty to over 300. Some of the cattle were put in lots near a railhead; others were driven to Albany and then to the railhead in Barton Landing. Cornelius purchased many of his cattle on credit, giving notes for them which he paid off once the animals had been sold. Once they had gathered enough stock, Cornelius, Jess, Jack, and Robbie or at least two of them would go south with the cows not sold locally. Among the places they sold the cattle were Concord and Nashua, New Hampshire, Springfield and Westfield, Massachusetts, and Brattleboro, Vermont. This trade must have been tiring but it was rewarding and came at a slack time of year. The year Cornelius borrowed $2,000, he cleared, after all expenses had been paid, just under $300.00, about 14% on the money borrowed and held for about three months.[239] For at least one year, when Cornelius seems not to have been involved, Jess, Jack and Robbie did the business themselves. Robbie learned to judge cattle, to deal in stock, and to bargain.

Robbie's further education included other lessons. His father and others had tried to bring a railroad through Albany in 1873 and were prepared to invest in that venture. Luckily, the towns of Albany and Craftsbury did not support him and his friends. That venture would have lost money since there was not enough to ship out and the local market for imported goods was too small. Cornelius was an investor in an Albany tub factory in the 1880s – in which he lost money as he also seems also to have done in an investment in a creamery in Craftsbury a bit later. He had stock in a Montpelier bank which paid dividends. Cornelius lent and borrowed money with some frequency and certainly, from time to time, handled funds belonging to the Church and Town. He bought land, which he then logged and sold or which he added to his farm. Robbie would have been aware of all that and, as he grew older, would have known a good deal about his father's business since even his sister as an old lady could supply details of those activities.

Ribbon worn by supporters of Benjamin Harrison who defeated the Democrat, Grover Cleveland, for the Presidency.

The other things which the boy would have picked up concerned the civic world in which he lived. His father was involved with his community in many ways. He served as a school director – which may be why his daughter could begin teaching at age fifteen. He helped to repair the local bridges and roads and was capable of doing simple surveying. He was for a few years in old age a Selectman trusted to help run the affairs of the town. He ran to be a Town Representative to the Legislature but his neighbors would not elect him. He was respected but once got only three votes for Town Representative – likely those of his father, his brother and his own. They were vocal Democrats in a Republican town.[240] Still, his neighbors were happy to have him do any number of other things requiring abilities to calculate and organize. Robbie appears in his step-mother's diary as involved in most of his father's activities; he would have learned how those things were done. By the time he was a man, he had done chores, sugared, logged, and driven the team to the mill or to the railhead with logs, butter, sugar or bark for the tanners. He had bargained for cattle and knew a good horse or cow from a poor one and he had some knowledge of business generally. The only place he does not appear is in the wood-working shop. He was not going to be a cooper like his father and grandfather.

Robbie's life was also involved with the usual events which diversified rural life in nineteenth century Vermont. His pious step-mother took him to Church with her – his father did not go often and attended fairly regularly only when the parish had a minister he liked and respected. Those ministers were the ones who had traveled and who gave talks on topics other than religion – such as accounts of visits to the Chicago Columbian Exposition. Like his sister, Robbie probably grew up to be a conventional Congregationalist who gave to missionary societies and despised Roman Catholics. The area's churches – both their own and the neighboring Methodist and Baptists – provided a good deal of their social life centered around Donation and Church Suppers, chicken-pie suppers, strawberry festivals, picnics, and similar occasions. Christmas was celebrated during Robbie's childhood at the Church with a tree and presents for the children. The family did not have a tree at home and Christmas itself was still a work day for his parents. Thanksgiving was the real family holiday. Then, they feasted on goose, turkey, and all the fixings with perhaps twenty or thirty of their relatives and friends.[241] At Easter, there were sometimes exercises in the district schools, to which they all went, and in June there was a Children's Day in Church on which children got to recite or do something.

The churches also sustained the singing school which trained people for the community's varied musical life.[242] Many local entertainments centered on music. They included concerts, given by a few traveling groups, and band concerts, and musical 'sociables'.[243] Those were held at the Albany Hotel ('the hall'), or in homes. There were also out of town singing 'conventions' to which Jennie went for years and which Robbie may have attended as part of an audience. Jennie was taught by her step-mother to play the piano and organ but Robbie seems to have been less musical. He is not known to have taken music lessons but in a family where most played something and sang, it would be unlikely that he was musically wholly illiterate.

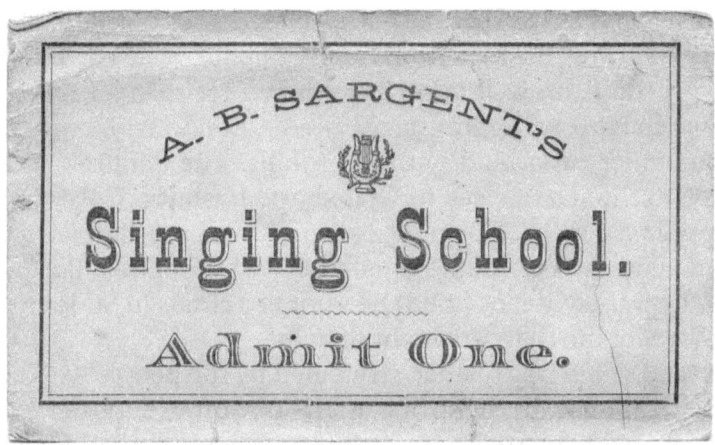

This ticket dates from c. 1890. A. B. Sargent was probably the father or brother of the noted Boston bandleader, symphony organizer, and composer William B. Sargent (1868-1957).

But, there was more than music. In February, the family, in some fashion, patriotically observed the birthdays of Washington and Lincoln. In late April, they celebrated Arbor Day by planting trees around the house.[244] They went to the local plays and 'Campfires', at which veterans of the Civil War told stories of their war and sang old army songs (see below, pp.250-53). Robbie very likely shared his sister's dislike of Southerners which was intense and rooted in those evenings. In May, Memorial Day involved 'exercises' organized by Civil War veterans. Then came the Fourth of July, a time when the children banged on pots and paraded through Albany village whooping it up.[245] Sometimes the day was an occasion for speeches, ball games, and fire works. In 1880, both Jennie and Robbie went to 'the Lyceum' but what and where that was is unclear. Probably it was a series of lectures on a variety of topics like the Chatauquas of a later date. There were also temperance lectures given by outsiders and attended by Mary Abby. She probably took Jennie to those and maybe Robbie. In 1881, when Robbie was eleven, both children 'went down to a Monkey show' in Albany village. Three years later, there was roller-skating in Albany. Jennie skated so Robbie is likely to have done so. There were picnics and promenades, and dances – 'kitchen junkets' – at their parents' house.[246] Other gatherings included one in 1884 at which the hired man broke his leg wrestling. Periodically, there were political rallies and speeches which Cornelius usually attended and to which Robbie went at least once. Before they were teenagers, the children could hitch up the horses and drive them. That extended their social sphere to include events some distance from home. Robbie, by then, was doing errands with the team well away from home. He seems first to have driven alone to Barton Landing at age twelve. Round trip, it was about twenty-four miles on a road with steep hills. The children drove to 'candy pulls', school exercises in Craftsbury, Irasburg, Coventry, and Barton Landing, to 'the Opera' at Newport, and the 'horse trots' in Barton and Lyndonville. Robbie usually went to the annual Barton Fair and, when he was eighteen, (1888) he went to a circus in St. Johnsbury. He lived a livelier life than we might imagine.

Their social scene was further diversified by the people who visited or stayed at the house. In the spring, there were often between five and a dozen loggers who for a day or more took meals and sometimes stayed over-night while they poked and peavied the logs in the Black River down to the mill in Irasburg. Some of those had been cut by Cornelius, others by loggers upstream or down. Later in the spring, there would be the crew which smoothed the road surfaces or men who showed up to repair a nearby bridge. The 'hulled corn man' came in the spring after sugaring as did peddlers of other kinds.[247] Annual calls were made by an 'old hatter', the 'sewing machine man' (he demonstrated his wares to local ladies at the Rogers house), a 'medicines peddler', a 'tin man' and a fellow who sold books from the back of his wagon. The 'old hatter' always stayed overnight paying his bill with goods. Most summers, this family entertained friends and relatives from Vermont towns but also from New Hampshire, Massachusetts, New York, Canada, and as far away as Iowa, and Nebraska. Almost every week, someone came to dinner (often unannounced) or the family visited elsewhere. For children whose parents had seen quite a lot of Concord, Nashua, and Manchester, New Hampshire; Lowell, Boston, and Springfield, Massachusetts; Albany, Buffalo, and New York City, and had gotten as far west as Iowa and Independence, Missouri, and north to Montreal, theirs was not a closed-in world bounded by horizons at the county lines. There were children in their village with such limited horizons but the Rogers children were not among them.

Using Mary Abby's diaries one can plot the family's normal range of travels. They routinely socialized within a radius of about ten miles. Their special shopping took them twenty to twenty-five miles to larger towns. Banking occasionally took them to Montpelier forty-four miles away. On that trip, they stayed overnight with relatives in the State Capital. Summer jaunts were about forty miles and usually involved staying overnight with friends or relatives. The children did not often go on those trips just as they did not go on the longer trips their parents took.

Until he was twenty-three in 1893, Robbie lived and worked on the farm but that and the family's social round was not his whole life. He now sometimes went to dances with a young man a bit older than himself who was something of 'a live wire'. This was Pat McGuire. Pat and his brother, Dennis, ran an Albany general store and brought the first telephone lines to Albany and the surrounding area (see n.75, p.357). Pat certainly did not belong to the Good Templars and was capable of raising hell. Both he and Robbie liked baseball and went to games. That Robbie went around with him suggests that he had found a sort of role model in this genial, somewhat older man. They went to the area's social events but not until 1893 did Robbie seem to have a steady girlfriend.

Albany, c. 1918. The view of the town had not much changed for many years.

After 1891, Robbie began to spend more time with his Uncle Jesse. He often worked on Jess's farm and went with him on the cattle buying trips. They got along. In the winter of 1893, they became partners when Jess bought one of the Albany stores (overleaf). In January, Robbie helped him to inventory the stock and to clean up the place. By 6 February 1893, uncle and nephew were in business together under the name 'J. B. and R. R. Rogers'. By 13 February, Robbie had left home to live with his uncle and his family in the village. About that time he started going to prayer meetings with a girl, Flora Gutherie – surely a sign of seriousness and a new found (or feigned) maturity. In either case, it showed an eagerness to please her. He was twenty-three and had found his niche in life.

The Rogers store c. 1900.

His new life also put him in competition with his brother-in-law, Ira Sanders, who also began as a store keeper in 1893, an occupation which he would leave after a short time. He found that he was not good at it, even though his father had kept store in Albany for many years. Both Robbie and Ira very likely got help in their ventures from Cornelius. The Rogers store was a general store like most of those established in small villages. Because Jesse Rogers eventually moved from Albany to keep what became, more or less, a men's clothing store in Barton Landing, it may already have had leanings in that direction. Whatever it sold, it was not the place where Cornelius bought hardware items, meat or flour but he ran an account there as he did with two other stores in the area. It seems to have done well enough but the family diaries contain little information about it.

After leaving home, Robbie shows up in the pages of the Mary Abby's diary when he helped with family matters, such as hiring a girl for his ailing grandmother or doing other similar things. He was less often around than was his sister and her family. They had a meal at the Rogers farm most every week. Robbie went more often to his grandparents and he continued to live with Jess and his family. While Flora Gutherie dropped from sight, he was clearly prospering. On 7 April 1896, he and his father went to Newport on business. His father attended to things at a mill and then gave his note for $160 on Robbie's behalf to a man from whom Robbie had purchased a wagon. Robbie then went off and bought a new suit of clothes. They both went back to Albany where Robbie had supper with his parents. That was probably Robbie's last happy day.

On the 9 April, Mary Abby's diary records that Robbie was 'taken very sick with pleurisy today at Jess's'. This seems to have been a sudden attack of some sort, possibly the sort of pneumonia which develops rapidly and to which the young often succumb. Given the medical parlance of the time, pleurisy would have meant pains in the chest, coughing, and a high fever. Whatever it was, he quickly became very ill. His sister, who lived in the village, was called to stay with him. In the evening, his father visited, as did Dr. Dillingham, who had seen him earlier in the day. He was later joined by Dr. Campbell, another Albany physician. His stepmother and Dr. Dillingham 'watched' with him all night. In the morning, Dr. Dillingham got Delia Darling Honey, now a widow and the local nurse, to 'care for Robbie'. Mrs. Honey had considerable experience as a nurse and mid-wife going back to the late 1860s.

By then, the physicians had decided that Robbie had pneumonia along with pleurisy. His mother described him that evening as 'very sick'. On the 11 April, Henry Darling, Delia's brother, came to care for him and stayed the night. The doctors looked in on him several times during the day and his parents went to him in the evening. They called on Dr. Dillingham themselves to check further on their son's condition. The following day, Mary Abby stayed with him and Delia came in the evening, having that Sunday morning been made a member of their church. On 13 April, the patient seemed a bit better but 'after we came away he had a terrible night– with pleurisy – Dr. Campbell with him all night'. In the morning his parents were told he was 'not as well'. They returned to sit with him all day and through the night. He was also attended by their friend, the Craftsbury physician, Dr. William Dustan [Dustin in her diaries]. He was their usual doctor and a frequent visitor at the Rogers home. 'We thought he could not live through the night' but he did and was 'comfortable' for part of the next day. His parents went home for a short time and then returned to be with him in the night, as did Dr. Dustan. Nothing helped.[248] 'Robbie tossed & rolled all night – no rest – and this morning [16 April] at half past seven he passed away. Oh! why could he not be spared?' From a pious woman who trusted in the goodness of God, that was a heart-wrenching cry. His sickness had lasted seven days.

Robbie was removed from his uncle's house and taken home to his parent's farm. His cousin, Henry Darling, came up to 'care for the body &c.'. Caring for his body meant packing it in ice because it was so warm. He was in a special coffin but it was closed and he was not on view, which bothered Mary Abby who wrote disconsolately, 'no one could see him'. Normally, the family would have purchased an ordinary casket at the Albany general store kept by Roscoe Cowles. He doubled as the town's undertaker. That would have been open so the body could be viewed. Robbie's uncle and aunt visited. His sister came up and two days later moved in with her family, staying until the 2 May. Her husband, Ira, did the chores for his father-in-law during that time. Other friends and relatives visited. On 18 April, there were more visitors and Henry Darling came to stay for a few days. Robbie's funeral was held that day at the house at 1:00 P.M.[249] The local minister preached on Job 37:21: 'And now men see not the bright light which is in the clouds: but the wind passeth and cleanseth them'. The text may have been less significant than the context which says that God's ways are unfathomable and 'he will not afflict'.

The body was then taken from the house to the cemetery over muddy roads, which were 'very bad going'. Robbie was interred in a muddy grave. The bearers included Pat McGuire and three other young men with whom Robbie had gone to ball games, races, dances and promenades, concerts and sociables. There were 'a good many' at the funeral and the procession from the house to the grave was larger than usual. Mary Abby's entry for the day ended: 'Beautiful flowers brought in'. They would have had to come from Newport or Barton Landing. The following day, his step-mother recorded, 'we have not much heart to work'. A few days later, the year-long process of settling Robbie's affairs began.

On 24 April, Cornelius and his wife went to Albany and brought home Robbie's effects and visited his grave. Three days later, his father and Jess went to the Probate Court in Newport which certified Cornelius as the administrator or executor of Robbie's estate. Robbie may have named his father as executor in a will or the Court may have chosen Cornelius as the 'next of kin'. Robbie probably had not died intestate because he had things to leave. The Court appointed two local men to appraise the value of the estate, principally his interest in the store. Jesse and Cornelius would not argue over that. While in Newport, Robbie's father bought for Henry Darling a ring for which he paid $5.00. For that one could get quite a nice bit of onyx set in a gold band – the equivalent of the old mourning rings. That same day, Dr. Dillingham was paid $15.00 for his attendance. No payments are recorded for Drs. Campbell or Dustan. The first may have been paid by Jess. Dr. Dustan probably gave his services to the family to which he was close. On 28 April, they began to inventory the goods in the store so that Robbie's share of the business could be ascertained. That took three days or parts thereof. Then things slowed – at least nothing is recorded in Mary Abby's diary until 20 May when they paid Robbie's subscription to the church– $1.50. Just before Memorial Day, his grave was tended so it would look well when Memorial Day visitors to the cemetery would see it. A little over a week later, Cornelius and his wife went to Newport where they ordered a stone for Robbie's grave and one for his mother, whose grave had remained with no marker since 1873. They sold Robbie's colt for $65. Like his forebears, he had a good horse. Toward the end of June, they gave Robbie's ring (probably a Masonic ring) to one of the pall bearers, John McLellan, who had been often at the house. By October, most of the business had been settled but not quite all of it. In December, they decided on inscriptions for the grave stones and bought Delia Honey some silver spoons for her 'kindness to Robbie'. These cost $4.75 and were likely to have been coin silver rather than plate.

By the end of the year, life at the Rogers farm had more or less returned to normal but Robbie's estate was still unsettled. Some bills were still to be collected or written off. Then, on 16 April, Jess and Cornelius 'settle[d] up business with Jess and Robbie – Robbie's part in all $1300 – all paid & debts'. It was a year to the day since he had died. A few days later, the estate cleared probate. There was, after all expenses had been paid, $236.45 left to Cornelius which he put in the savings bank at Newport. He had presumably paid himself back for what he had given to Robbie to establish himself in business. Later his daughter, Jennie, would be given a house worth a $1,000 which is perhaps what he had paid for Robbie's share of the store.

Robbie was long mourned. His sister kept two letters which seem to have meant much to her. One was from a friend in Andover, Massachusetts, and recommended that Jennie take her grief and burden to God who would help her bear it. The other, from a cousin, recalled Robbie and praised the man:

I always liked him so much, and he was so kind and helpful to us through Jacks sickness & death. How little we thought at that time he too, would be called away so soon by the same awful disease.... I shall write your folks & Uncle Jesse & Aunt Mary, how dear he was to them and your Grandpa and Grandma are so old & feeble to stand such a blow[250]... I will write you again when I am more calm myself.

His obituaries, clipped by his sister from the *Orleans County Monitor* and the *Newport Daily Express,* echoed those sentiments. They were probably written by a family member, perhaps by his cousin Delia Honey who often penned local obituaries:

His loss is deeply felt, not only by the afflicted family and relatives, but also by his many friends and associates. By his genial manner, his generous disposition and ready sympathy, he had endeared himself to a large circle of friends. By his business push and energy he was assuming a large place in the affairs of the community. His tact and energy must have won him large success. Though seemingly cut off in the very dawn of usefulness, he has possessed a large place in the memory and hearts of all who knew him. The funeral services were attended Sabbath afternoon, at the residence of his father, by a large concourse of deeply sympathetic friends and mourners.

For years, the family noted Robbie's passing. His grave was always decorated as long as Jennie could get there to do so. She never forgot his birthday. In 1898, Jennie named her last born son for her dead brother.

X

The Courtship of Jennie Rogers (1868-1963)

Robbie's sister, Jennie, appears often in Mary Abby's diaries where one can follow her courtship without much difficulty. The courting couple, Jennie Rogers and Ira Sanders, associated with others much like themselves – pious, interested in music, and eager to go to sociables, fairs, and races. But, when other young people are mentioned in the diaries, they usually came from families more similar to Jennie's and not his – but first, a bit more about Jennie.

Jennie Lena Rogers, was a cut above her future husband. Her father was better off, better educated and more accomplished than his future son-in-law or that fellow's store-keeper father, Isaac Levingston Sanders (1808-1890). Cornelius Rogers's income by 1883 was such that he and his wife could afford, and had already made, extended trips to New York City, Iowa, and Independence, Missouri.[251] For years, Cornelius was a town lister, a school director, and long an unsuccessful candidate for both Selectman and Town Representative to the Vermont Legislature. Cornelius was a sociable man who often went to church until about 1888, when he ceased to attend regularly save at Christmas. He read the thrice weekly *New York World*, kept bees and made metheglin, a spiced mead, from their honey. He and his wife entertained one or more people about every week and dined at the homes of others with some regularity. During the summer, their home was something of a hotel as they entertained relatives from the places they had visited or would visit. He bred good cows and drove a fine horse and almost certainly a hard bargain. The Sanders family lived a more frugal life, were less sophisticated, and played fewer roles in the town where Isaac had his store and lent money. There is no evidence that the Sanders family had many visitors or dined regularly with others.

Jennie's mother's family was rather like the Rogers family. Her mother, Eliza or Elizabeth Darling, was the daughter of Alden H. Darling, a farmer and saw-mill owner in Albany. His mill was on the road down from Lowell Mountain, whence came the wood he cut and the water which powered his saw. He was also a carpenter and maker of wooden objects during times when his mill could not run or business was slack. Bowls, choppers (using discarded hoe blades), and furniture, including bedsteads, and dollies' tea tables for his granddaughter, were among the things which he turned out. His wife was from a genteel southern New Hampshire family which kept up its ties with Vermont relatives through visits. Those were regularly returned.

As we have seen (p.166), Cornelius Rogers' second wife, Mary Abby Tenney, was the twenty-eight year old rather plain daughter of Lyman P. Tenney. They married on her birthday, 4 January 1875. Mr. Tenney, although not qualified as a lawyer, functioned as one, drawing up wills and other instruments for his neighbors and administering estates. He was the sort of man who was picked for Grand Jury duty and was said to be a 'side judge' in the County Court.[252] He was also a County Justice of the Peace. The Tenneys were a very musical family. One member is said to have played in a Philadelphia Symphony Orchestra; another, who lived in Hanover, N.H., made stringed instruments, one of which was probably the short-necked cello played by Mary Abby. The Tenneys had taken trips to Philadelphia, New York, and Boston. Mary Abby, Elizabeth Darling's classmate, became a formative influence on her step-daughter. Jennie's antecedents were, then, somewhat more cultured, refined, and up-to-date than those of her future husband, the son of a probable bigamist and a pious French girl (see above, p.31).

Ira D. Sanders was the son of Isaac Sanders who, as we have seen (pp.29, 31, 33), moved to northern Vermont in the 1850s. In 1856, he married Amanda (1835-1925), the daughter of John Sawyer and Mary Shortsleeves. Six children were born to them, three of whom died in infancy or early childhood. In 1863, the Sanders family moved to a farm located on the River Road between the villages of Albany and Irasburg. They stayed there only a short time before Isaac purchased one of the Albany village stores, that located opposite the present town hall, then the Congregational Church. He also purchased a home just to the south of the store. There, he and his wife lived. He 'kept store' from about 1865 until 3 March 1889. He also ran a haulage business from Albany to the railhead at Barton Landing.[253] Ira became an only surviving son and expected to inherit his father's store but the store burned, along with two adjoining properties, in 1889. After the store burned, the old man did not rebuild it and died in the following year. By that time, he had become successful as a local moneylender. He left enough money for his wife to live frugally but comfortably for thirty years after his death.

Ira, as a young man, tended store and drove the team to and from the railhead about twelve miles away. He carried butter tubs and other goods to the station and returned with the miscellaneous supplies needed for his father's store or by others. The store fire, coming a year

The Courtship of Jennie Rogers (1868-1963)

after he and Jennie had married, put him out of work, diminished his prospects, and reduced his expectations in life. He never regained the place he had expected to hold in the community.

Ira Sanders was a bit beneath my grandmother for other reasons. Isaac's second 'wife', Amanda, as we have seen (pp.29-30), was probably of French and Indian descent. She may have been raised a Catholic but she became a fervent Wesleyan Methodist and her family attended the Methodist Church in Albany – just slightly less respectable than the older Congregational Church. Being French, possibly part Indian, and possibly Catholic in the beginning, were not qualities which made one look good to people like the Rogers family. Amanda had little education, seems not to have been very musical, or much of a reader of anything but her Bible which she read daily. She dressed well but, in the privacy of her house, sometimes, smoked a pipe. The Sanders and Rogers households had little contact outside of trading at the Sanders store. That remained the case after the children married. Neither Isaac nor Amanda appear often in Mary Abby's diaries and then not as guests or friends.

Ira was a tall (5' 10"), clean-cut fellow who was strong and known as a hard worker. He had little formal schooling. Indeed, his wife claimed that he had not attended classes for more than three full years. He wrote with no facility and had a limited reading vocabulary. He was not overly polite but very direct, straightforward, and honest. A respectable and pious chap, he liked to sing and later on in life played horns (tenor and alto horns, trumpets, and the trombone) in the Albany Village Band. From the 1880s until the 1940s, he took part in musical entertainments – concerts, minstrel shows, musical evenings, and 'sociables'. Ira was serious in disposition, but, once in black-face, loved to clog and was sometimes Mr Bones or the End Man in minstrel shows. Otherwise, he never joked or showed much of a sense of humor or much imagination. He was reliable and clever in the management of equipment and animals – including grandsons. Like many of his breed, he was something of a-jack-of-all-trades able to cobble shoes, mend harnesses, do carpenter work and anything else required on a farm. When he bought a car, he tinkered with its mechanisms. He also had strong feelings which occasionally took a violent turn. He once had to be restrained when he wanted to horse-whip into marriage the man who had gotten one of his sisters pregnant. During a violent domestic dispute, he threatened to kill his wife, his children, and himself. He then left home for three days – the family never learned where he went. Tolerance was not one of his virtues. In the 1920s, he went to Ku Klux Klan meetings in Irasburg

My Vermonters: The Northeast Kingdom 1800-1940

Grand Benefit Concert

Newton's Opera House, Albany, Vt.

Friday Evening, December 18th, 1908.

PART FIRST

1	March. "Lead the Way"	Band
2	Character Sketch.	B. L. Shedd
3	Coon Song. "Susan Jane"	C. A. Sargent
4	Waltz Song. "The Ball Game"	Band and Chorus
5	Coon Song. "The Right Church but Wrong Pew"	A. M. Goddard
6	Baritone Solo. "Old Virginia"	Chas. Stewart
7	Coon Song. Selected	I. D. Sanders
8	Waltz Song. "When Dreams Come True"	L. Sanders
9	Overture. "The Village Bride"	Band

PART SECOND

1	Tenor Duett. "The Butterfly"	Sanders and Sanders
2	Song. "I'd Live or I would die for you"	Miss Lenore Sheehan
3	Cornet Solo. "O Promise Me"	A. N. Vance
4	Song. "When the Robins Sing again"	Miss June Annis
5	Tuba Solo. "Autumn Gold"	Hackett, Sargent, Band
6	Song. "All about You"	Miss Lenore Sheehan
7	Overture. "Golden Crescent"	Band
8	Song. "Love Me and the World is Mine"	C. A. Sargent
9	Finale. "Around the Circle"	Band

Social Dance After Concert.

Admission 15-25-35 cents.   Dance 50 cents per Couple.

Tickets on Sale at Cowles' Store, Dec. 14, 1908.
Committee: C. A. Sargent, A. M. Goddard, L. W. Sanders.

This programme is typical of the events at which Ira enjoyed appearing throughout his life. Others participating in the Concert include a telephone company foreman, the local MD, two teachers, the local band leader, and two farmers. The other Sanderses are Ira's wife and two sons.

and Barton – until he discovered the Klansmen were as interested in drink as they were anti-Catholic and anti-Semitic. He was against the use of alcohol and tobacco. As an attractive young fellow who sang well in singing school, one with prospects of running a store, he would have seemed to Jennie a good catch.

In 1884/85, the year the telephone lines were strung in Albany on poles sold to the McGuire brothers by Cornelius Rogers, Jennie Rogers, then sixteen, was teaching school. She had been given a place at an age when, as she often said later, some of her students were, 'bigger than I was'. During the part of the winter when 'school did not keep', she attended the Albany singing school where the teacher was A. B. Sargent, the father of the later well known Boston band leader, William A. Sargent, who is remembered for writing marches which are still played.[254] Singing school, church-going, and attending prayer and temperance meetings were all parts of Jennie's social life.[255] But there were other events where she met young men. On 20 January 1885, she and a boy named Waldo Lamphere went to the 'Soldiers' Camp Fire' at the village. My grandmother never forgot the stories about soldiers she heard at the Campfires. In Albany, some concerned prisoners were held at the Andersonville and the Richmond prisoner of war camps. Her 'date' seems to have been a 'one off' but, significantly, he was the son of one of the town's largest land owners. On 3 February, she went to Newport to the Singing Convention. To that she seems to have gone without a male escort and stayed over night. We can never be sure of such details since we cannot know how complete her stepmother's diary was. Going to Newport must have been something of an adventure for sixteen-year-old Jennie. She drove her horse first to Barton Landing, put it in a livery stable, and then 'took the cars' to Newport ten miles away. There were other such events that winter.

Jennie spent the spring teaching in the Davison District in Craftsbury and by May was driven back to school on at least one Sunday night by Ira Sanders. She would have known him for years as the fellow who worked in the store where the family shopped and who drove the wagon to Barton Landing with the tubs of butter which Cornelius Rogers sent to towns in New Hampshire and to Boston. This drive to Craftsbury must have seemed pleasant to both of them since, on the 4 July, 'Jennie went to 'Lydoville [Lyndonville] with Ira Sanders' – Mary Abby had trouble with the town's name and never spelled it correctly. Two weeks later, on 19 July, Ira drove her to school again. These drives were probably of about four miles which would have given them at least an hour by themselves and who knows how much time they lingered by the way.

They went to the Singing School Concert on 26 July but then there is nothing of interest about the pair in Mary Abby's diary until September. However, she did note numerous times when Jennie was in the village where she and Ira might have seen each other. Then, on 4 September, they had an interesting date. Jennie and Ira went to Newport to the 'opera' [we would call it a musical], a three-hour buggy drive each way. After that, there is nothing more until November. Ira does not show up in the diary as driving her to school, going to the Barton Fair, to 'horse trots', or doing other things which one might hope they did. Then, on 15 November, on a 'cold and stormy night,' he came to see Jennie. The following night, she went to an entertainment in Craftsbury. Ira is not mentioned and she may have been happy that the party she attended the night after that was with the 'Bowman boys'. By December 1885, she was being squired by Fred Robbins, who, took her to Irasburg on Christmas eve 'to the Christmas tree'. Over the next two years, he would periodically work for her father as a hired man, being paid about $18 a month and given board, a room, and his washing. She liked him. Members of his family owned several farms in Craftsbury and he would inherit one in a year or so but it was not large.

In January 1886, Ira was back to take her to a 'Musical Convention' in Barton where, perhaps, they both had a chance to sing – he was a tenor, she a soprano. That winter, she worked in Craftsbury at Doctor Dustan's for her board and room and took music lessons in the town. Ira was still around. By March, he was again driving her to and fro. On 3 April, he was 'up for sugar' and, three weeks later, he again brought her home and took her back to Craftsbury. Two other such drives are reported in June. Jennie came home to spend the Glorious Fourth (really the Third since the Fourth was a Sunday) with him. They spent it by going to 'Lyndolville to the horse trot' – a long drive each way. On the evening of the Fourth, he drove her back to Craftsbury.

Jennie's music lessons and period of domestic service were over in the third week of August 1886. On 24 August, she sang in 'the village concert'. Five days later, Ira came to see her at her house. She had decided to attend school again that year at Craftsbury Academy, but, after going back, she changed her mind on her birthday, 9 September. Ira may have been among the sixteen who came to her eighteenth birthday party or he may not have since that day 'she concluded to go to Westfield Mass.' There her father had contacts in his cattle-trade whom he and his wife had visited. By 24 September, she was in Massachusetts. There is no evidence that she regretted leaving Ira behind. Her stepmother's later reference to him as 'her old love' suggests that he had very much declined in her estimation.

This picture, taken in Westfield, and shows three Academy girls: Grace Gibbs, Jennie Rogers, and Clara Reed. All appear to be wearing the small bustles fashionable in the 1880s. Jennie wore a bustle until the 1920s.

Jennie attended a school in Westfield for which she paid tuition, board and room.[256] Her tuition covered lessons in music, drawing, and painting. It was a costly year, since, in addition to the unknown sum she took with her, her parents sent to her or had paid by May 1887, $138.87 – almost the same amount as her father paid the hired man for the eight months she was away. Mary Abby's diaries in the decade of the 1880s record only one other local person who went away to school or college.

When Jennie returned on 23 April 1887, she was given a small party to which, 'came 7 we sugared off'. She sat a teachers' examination on 30 April and by 16 May was again teaching school.[257] Fred Robbins was still working for her father and she was off with him on 13 May to visit friends, probably to a little party of some sort. On the 30 May, they went to a 'promenade'. There was little public dancing in the area where so many had religious scruples about dancing.[258] On 16 June, 'Jennie and Fred went to a Concert'. On 1 July they attended 'a Strawberry festival'. Ten days later, Fred took her to Irasburg with another couple. All this seems fairly intense. But, she also attended other social events in June and July to which she may have had another escort or none. None is mentioned for the East Albany Singing Convention, the Ice Cream Festival, held to raise money for the 'Congo church', or the meetings of The Good Templars after she had joined.

This photograph, taken by a guest in the 1890s, shows one of the rooms at the Darling Inn. The public rooms were equally homey with walls probably as cluttered.

The Courtship of Jennie Rogers (1868-1963)

During the August vacation, Jennie was visited by a friend from Westfield, Clara Reed, who came on 10 August and stayed for a little over a month. She would repeat such a visit at least twice more in later years. On 12 August, Fred took the girls to a promenade at the Darling Inn Hall in Albany.[259] Five days later, they went to one in Barton. On the 21 August, the girls went to an evening prayer meeting. Five days later, Fred took Clara, from whom he was now inseparable, to another promenade. Jennie's brother, Robbie (age seventeen), and his girlfriend tagged along. Jennie went with Ira Sanders. His courtship had resumed. Mary Abby recorded in her diary that Jennie had 'returned to her old love'. Thereafter, there was no looking back. It does not seem that Fred jilted her but his attentions were now on Clara and Clara's on him. He continued to be a member of the party on several occasions when the young people went to other things.

On 3 September, the Rogers family was visited by an engaged couple, Jennie's cousins, 'Mamie Rogers and her beau Will Farr'. Mary Abby recorded that the three couples, Fred and Clara, Ira and Jennie, Mamie and Will, 'set up tonight'. It seems to have been a usual thing before a wedding and is noticed at least one other time in the diary. Mamie and Will were married the next day. On 5 September, Jennie and Clara, planned a party which was held on the seventh: '15 in all   cake and coffee for refreshment   Ira did not go home untill about day light That Morn'. Jennie's parents seem not to have slept much either. The entry for the following day suggests that emotions had run high and had tired out the two girls: 'Jennie and Clara about sick a bed'. The following day was Jennie's birthday; she and Clara were taken to a promenade by Ira and Fred. On 10 September, they spent the day visiting but Ira brought the girls home. Fred took Clara to St. Johnsbury on 15 September where he probably put her on a train to go home to Massachusetts.

The next month was one of hurried clothes-making, both for Jennie and her step-mother. It was also one of social whirl. Ira took her to a promenade in Craftsbury on 16 September. On the 23rd, they went to a concert in Craftsbury. On the 28th, Jennie and her step-aunt, Julia and her husband, Solomon Corey, to the County Fair in Barton; Fred and Robbie tagged along. On the 30th, Ira took Jennie to a promenade in Irasburg and two weeks later they spent the day in Newport. That may have been the day they bought her wedding rings.

If she picked out her rings, she chose as an 'engagement ring' a rather flashy little reddish-gold ring set with two garnets and two opals. The four stones in a mount came high off the finger. It could not be worn while working or doing anything which required much use of one's hands (illustrated on page 87). My grandmother never called it an engagement ring but 'the ring Ira bought me before we were married'. The wedding band, if it was the one she had as an old woman, was a plain pink-gold ring with no inscription. That, too, she wore only on special occasions. Both rings were made larger for her in old age when she did wear them until the wedding band grew so thin that it cut her finger. Judging from the 1897 *Sears and Roebuck Catalog*, which shows similar items, the engagement-ring probably cost $3-5.00 and the other about one dollar. For Ira, the rings cost about a week's wages.

Amanda Sanders' wedding gift to her son and his wife was this quilt made in the 1880s. Aside from the centre squares, no piece is bigger than one by two and a half inches.

On 28th October, Jennie went to Irasburg where she probably had a music lesson, and then went to a Lodge meeting. After that, there was a promenade. On 10 November, she and Mary Abby went to Newport 'to traid'. The question had clearly been popped and she had said 'Yes!'. By the end of the ensuing week, Jennie had acquired three new dresses, one made of satin.[260] On the evening of 17 November, she and Ira sat in the Rogers living room sending out their wedding invitations. The following evening, they went to see the minister, almost certainly a Methodist and not Jennie's usual preacher, who was to marry them at the 'Congo Church'. Her step-mother began to clean the kitchen which she finished doing on the 21st. The day before, Jennie and Ira had 'stopped at Mr Sanders to tea', which meant they had eaten supper there.[261] There was no mention in the diary of either Mr. or Mrs. Sanders's involvement in the wedding preparations or at the wedding for that matter. Her gift to them was a wonderful log-cabin quilt, shown opposite.[262]

Mary Abby's entry for Thanksgiving Day, 24 November 1887 reads: 'Thanksgiving day – Jennie & Ira Sanders married by Rev. Mr. Collins A large company about 50 — after dinner they went to the Landing & took the cars for Newport: Went up to Julia's home – for a visit: They received a good many presents'. The courtship was over, the marriage begun. It was marked by wedding pictures.

The wedding photographs of Jennie and Ira Sanders. They were made in two sizes; these are from their small ones.

All this is interesting in a number of ways. Jennie Rogers was given a lot of freedom. She could leave school when she chose, go out with the boys she wanted to go with and even leave the community, with parental support, for the better part of an expensive year. There is no sign in the diary of her step-mother that her parents worried about her choices of boys or that they pressed her to marry or not to marry. They bought her roller skates, gave her parties, sent her off to Massachusetts for music and art lessons, paid for singing lessons and clearly wanted her to have good times which they willingly subsidized. They trusted her and she went her own way. They could pay her expenses and did not begrudge the money.

However, there is no sign that Jennie associated, except in large gatherings, with boys outside her class, if that is the right term to apply here. In Westfield, the story was likely to have been the same. Her friend there was, like herself, well able to afford a jaunt to Vermont and a special, perhaps even a fashionable school. Jennie did not seem to have many beaus although she was a good looking young woman and would have been attractive to men. Ira was not one of a large crowd. There is also a surprising amount of traveling going on in this set of young folks. By the time she married, Jennie had been to Buffalo or Albany, N.Y., to Massachusetts, to the Eastern Townships of Quebec and to Burlington, St. Albans, St. Johnsbury, and to many of the towns in the northern quarter of Vermont. Jennie had seen more of the world than many, certainly far more than her husband who never went to New York or Boston, and only, in old age, to Hartford, Connecticut, to see his sons.

The events to which she and Ira went while courting ranged within a radius of about twenty-five miles with most of the parties, socials and promenades held within twelve miles of the Rogers home. They and members of their set were clearly not afraid to drive at night or put off by cold or wet weather.

While she had known Ira for over two years, she had too little experience to judge what she wanted from life at age eighteen or nineteen. She and Ira had in common music, an interest in temperance and piety, but not much else. She was a bookish person whose reading throughout her life was rather like her step-mother's. Her husband read the local paper, farmers' magazines and joke books. She wrote the occasional verse and had once tried to paint, as genteel women did. For years, her living rooms had two still-lifes she had done while in Westfield – a vase full of roses and a bowl of fruit. His tastes were more earthy. She liked nice things but she would never have all that many until her four children could buy them for her. She would have happily emulated her step-mother as a hostess but there would never be the house or the money to support such a style of life. Her husband was neither so affluent, well read, nor as sociable as her father. Even though she must have spent considerable time alone with Ira, it is not at all clear there was much intimacy or deep understanding of each other. Her courtship may have been exciting and fun but it did not provide the insight into her mate and into life which she needed. She married a man who had many virtues but he would not do so well in life as had his father or hers.

The Sanders farmhouse c. 1910. On the first floor – kitchen, living room, parlour, bedroom; second floor– three bedrooms and storage.

The marriage started off well. The couple had a house in the village of West Albany. Jennie's parents provided a handsome trousseau and supplied her with furniture and continued their support in various ways for years to come. The house seems to have been well furnished with beds, tables, chairs, lamps, and other things. Some were moved from the Rogers farmhouse on 3 December and more came two days later when Jennie took her piano, but not her organ, which had been mentioned earlier in Mary Abby's diary. That was the first night in their new house, the beginning of what proved to be a long but not very happy married life. She may have thought to emulate her parents by marrying on a special day – in her case Thanksgiving – but in the end her marriage was not to be like theirs. The Sanders store burned. Ira tried to run the business from other premises but was not successful. He did not have much use for his stamp which read 'I. L. Sanders and Son'. Ira gave up his business to become a part-time barber and the pole-setter and linesman for the telephone company run by his cousins, the McGuire brothers. In 1900, he became a good, but unlucky, farmer on land on which his father-in-law held a lien. In 1906, his uninsured barn was struck by lightning and burned down, leaving him in a state of shock. Jennie had made what was in effect a poor choice, one made worse by fires.[263]

Ira Sanders' round barn finished in 1907. They were common in Quebec and northern Vermont.

The burned store, babies, and Ira's small income, abruptly changed Jennie's life by the time she was twenty-one. After she married, short trips continued for a while but the longer ones were virtually at an end. There were to be few trips[264] until she and Ira left the farm on which they lived for most of their married life between 1900 and 1921. There was too little to spend and Ira became hard to live with. All that was in the future in 1887.

The Courtship of Jennie Rogers (1868-1963)

Ira, too, may have felt let down. The fire which destroyed the Sanders store reduced his expectations in life. Not only had he failed to take over a business, he had become somewhat dependent on his father-in-law. In the end, he seems often to have resented his father-in law, a man lamed by an accident whom Ira derisively called 'Old Hippity-Hop'. Ira often found his wife an insufferable nag. His strong feelings sometimes took a violent turn. Two promising youths had made a mistake which led to years of domestic turmoil, short separations, and upsets among the children. Divorce was an unthinkable remedy to their problems – so they lived with them. Some of their disappointment and unhappiness seems reflected in this photograph of the family taken in their parlor in c. 1910.

This picture of the Sanders family, in their parlor, is from c. 1910. Back row: Elwood, Robert, Doris, and Leslie; front row: Ira and Jennie.

XI

Campfires and Other Matters: The Civil War and the Glover, Vermont, Grand Army of the Republic (GAR) Post No. 16, the Mason Post

In 1860, the United States Census showed a Vermont population of 315,098. Of those, about half were males (157,059), of whom perhaps 52,000-65,000 were men of fighting age. It is believed that 34,238 Vermont men served in the Union Forces in the Civil War with a few more fighting for the Confederacy – some say fifty.[265] Probably more than half of the Vermonters of an age eligible to fight actually served. Of those who served, 5,224 died in the War from diseases, wounds, and the deprivations suffered in Southern prisons. There were few families in the Northeast Kingdom which lacked someone in the services, mostly enlistees in the seventeen Vermont Infantry Regiments, several Cavalry units and three Batteries of Light Artillery. A few men served in the Navy or were attached to other units, such as the 19th Regiment of Coloured Troops which suffered great losses at the Battle of the Mine (or the Crater) during the Siege of Petersburg in the summer of 1864.[266] The War touched every community not only because of the volunteers but also because, when a State draft was instituted in 1862, and a Federal one a year later, the Selectmen of the towns were the ones authorized to pick draftees; community leaders decided who were to fill the quotas. The impact of the War on local communities can be gauged by the numbers of names on war memorials, such as that in Albany, or the numbers of serving men recorded in local histories.

The town of Glover in 1860 had a population of 1,250. If half were women (625) and, of the half which was male, about half that number were children and those too old to fight – that leaves 312 eligible to fight. Many of those were essential to the running of a farm or other concerns. Of those in that the eligible group, ninety-three (29%) actually served and at least twenty-two (24% of those serving) died in the war or shortly thereafter while still in military service.[267] Some spent time in Southern prisoner-of-war-camps. Glover's was a respectable but not extraordinary achievement.[268]

As in all wars, those who served did so for a variety of motives now hard to discern. Some thought, initially, it would be a lark; or, they joined because their friends were doing so. Others enlisted because they found it good to enlist in a moral crusade to end slavery and the political foolishness of Southerners – which has very slowly abated. Others saw it as their patriotic duty to save the country. Some were drafted. Of course, not all Vermonters were enthusiastic supporters of the Union. Cornelius Rogers and Chester Page, Jabez's son, hired substitutes to fight for them. Cornelius is said to have paid his a dollar a day. He and Page made more honest decisions than the well-heeled of today who let the poor fight at the expense of the nation, not themselves.[269] Some sat out the War in Canada. Others seem simply to have 'gone West'. As always, the War made some men richer. Others became poorer because of lost sons, their own wounds or because of lost productivity. Northeast Kingdom cattle-dealers and farmers experienced a surge in demand for food-stuffs and wool but that did not last for long after the War ended. Indeed, the 1870s saw a post-war depression worsened by the decline of Vermont's wool trade and by the financial panic of 1873 which created chaos in American markets and banking.

Initial reactions to the War differed but Vermont towns, after Fort Sumter was taken in April 1861, were soon abuzz with news, reports of battles, of the wounded, dead, and the captured. There was a surge of patriotism and a lot of scorn for the South which supported slavery and was willing to break the Union. The Vermont motto, 'Freedom and Unity' was seen as applying both to the State and to the United States of America.[270] American 'exceptionalism' of a Vermont variety was supported and articulated.

Girls like Mary Abby Tenney went to see boys enlist and leave to fight. She later attended Sanitary Fairs and other gatherings to support the fighting men.[271] Some of her friends, worried about fathers and cried over the graves of relatives (see above, pp. 184, 194). The Civil War deeply stirred emotions, produced rallies and aid meetings, and, even before the end of the War, occasioned meetings at which former soldiers gathered with their neighbours to tell them what their War had been like and what their Regiments had done. Such occasions, later on, were sponsored by local Posts of the Grand Army of the Republic and were known as 'Campfires'.

After the War, veterans had many other reasons to form groups to look after their interests concerning benefits, pensions, memorials, and the election of Republican Party candidates. The most successful of the veterans' groups was the Grand Army of the Republic. The GAR said it was founded to promote 'Fraternity, Charity, [and] Loyalty' amongst its members and in the larger public. This patriotic organization had a somewhat military structure. Its National Headquarters, initially in Detroit, Michigan, oversaw Departmental [State] offices, Districts, Divisions, and, at the lowest level, Posts. Inspectors went from higher divisions to localities; delegates from the lower levels were sent to those above. If Glover's Mason Post was typical, there were constant interactions among all levels. A military atmosphere was preserved by forms and rituals, by titles, and by the wearing of uniforms, caps, hats, medals and the badges worn by the members on official occasions, and by their trooping the colours on public occasions like Memorial Day.

Major Murray Clement, the Waltham, Massachusetts, husband of a Northeast Kingdom woman, is decked out in the uniform he would have worn at GAR ceremonies. The medals testify to his long service and show the campaigns or battles he survived.

Comrades at the Post level elected yearly a Commander, Senior Vice-Commander, Junior Vice-Commander, Adjutant, Quarter-Master, Surgeon, Officer of the Day, Sergeant-Major, Guard, Chaplin, Delegates and Alternates to go to Encampments and sometimes a Colour Bearer and Trustees. Other figures were chosen as they needed them. Among the latter were *ad hoc* committee members, auditors, and 'Patriotic Instructors'. In a small Post like Glover's, most members held an office every other year and then, as numbers dwindled, every year. Elected Committees dealt with the relief of members, entertainment, auditing accounts, visiting schools prior to Memorial Day, and other things as they arose.

The GAR held meetings and Encampments from 1866 until 1949, when its last National Encampment was held in Indianapolis. Fraternity at a national level was actively pursued through lobbying for veterans benefits – pensions, increases to them, hospitals and medical benefits, cemeteries, headstones and other memorials, and subsidies for Encampments and meetings to enable old soldiers to renew or sustain ties formed during the conflict. The GAR had and used its political muscle to get many of the things it wanted. Its enrollments and power peaked in the 1890s. By 1915, the old soldiers were rapidly dying off and the organization was in decline although it would not end until its last member died in 1956.

Many years ago I bought (for $1.00) a Minute Book kept at the Mason Post, No. 16 of the GAR, Glover, Vermont. The minutes (illustrated overleaf) run from 25 January 1894 to 14 October 1915]. The Glover Post, founded in 1866, was the sixteenth in the State and the third one in the Northeast Kingdom. It was named for a local hero, Captain Daniel Mason, who enlisted on 15 October 1861 and died in Texas of dysentery or some other illness on 20 November 1865 after the War was over.[272]

The Post usually met monthly on the 'Thursday of the Full moon' (GAR Minute Book, p. 57)[273] in the Union House, the Glover hotel (pp. 64, 105). Their 'hall' was the hotel's third floor ball room. Occasionally the Post met in a local school house (p. 40). Another hotel room was used for meetings by the Women's Relief Corps (1883-) which came into existence as an auxiliary body to 'aid and assist the Grand Army of the Republic and to perpetuate the memory of the heroic dead'. The WRC was, secondly, to assist the widows and children of veterans and 'To cherish and emulate the deeds of our Army Nurses, and of all loyal women who rendered loving service to our country in her hour of peril'.[274] Its members were wives and relatives of former members

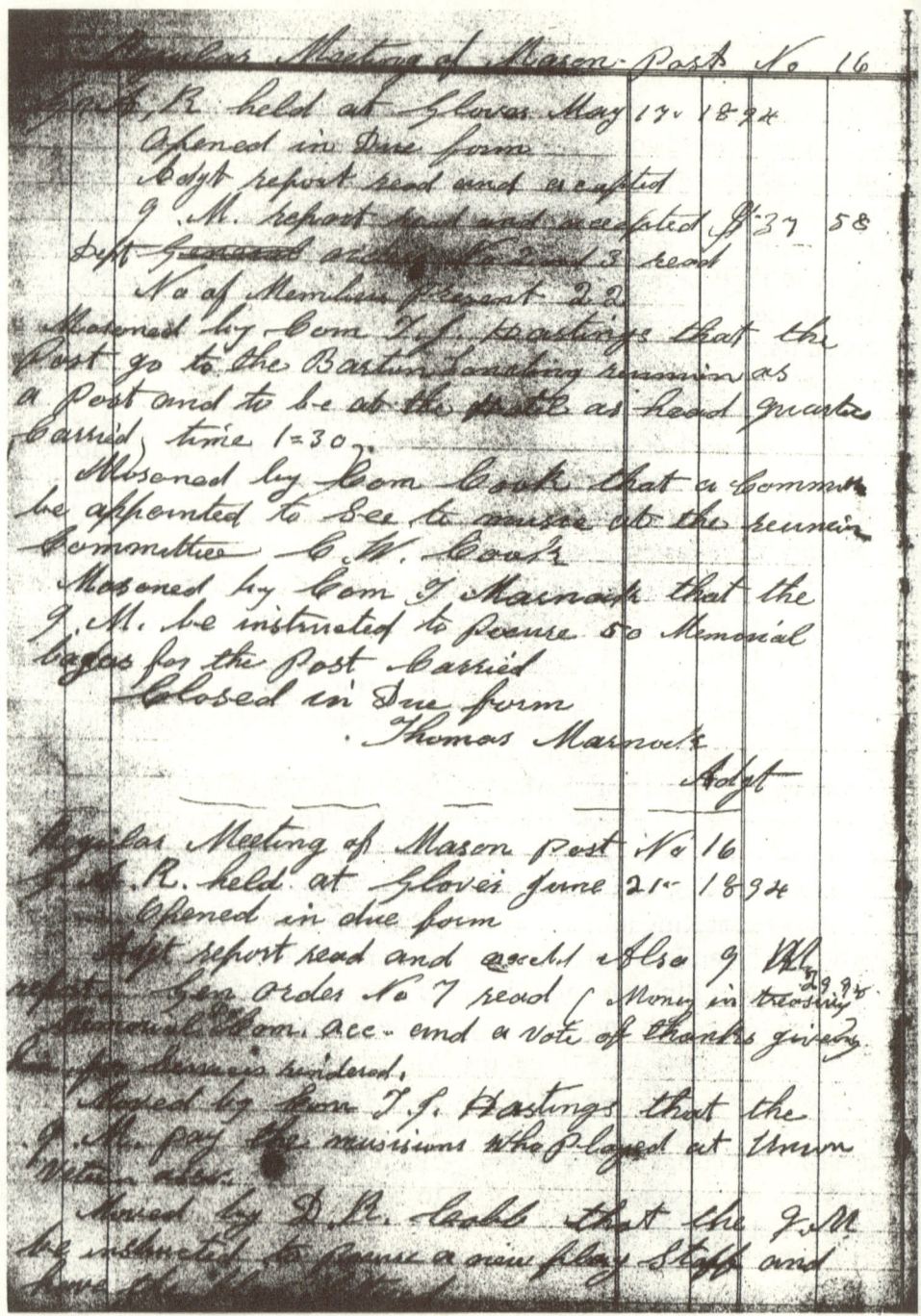

This minute, from 1894, details preparations for Memorial Day.

of the Union armed services (pp. 40-41).[275] When the GAR had a meal at the Union House, the ladies of the WRC took over the kitchen and served food in the hotel's dining room. That was large enough to accommodate members of both groups and seems to have held a large set of dishes used at the banquets put on by the WRC.

The Union House was an old posting hotel. It is shown as it was probably on Memorial Day, 1895. Most of the old soldiers wear a GAR badge or war medals. The building now survives as a nursing home.
The picture is reproduced with the permission of the Glover Historical Society.

From occasional notes, we can partially reconstruct the appearance of the GAR Hall. By 1899, when set up for meetings, the Union House dance hall sported a silk American flag and at least one other. The Post purchased a new flag in 1903 (for $3.00, p. 90), along with 'Woolen Buntin With painted Tale' (p. 89). In 1903, a fourth flag was given them by the WRC (p. 91).[276] There were some desks, chairs, lamps, and 'other furniture and fixtures', including an unknown number of 'spittoons'.[277] Their things were kept in side closets, as were minute and account books, a collection of maps (p. 47), and Rosters of members in the Vermont and National GAR Posts and other bodies. There was a Bible for the Chaplain's use and on which members swore oaths.[278] Also among the accoutrements of the officers, were belts, rank straps and ribbons, a quantity of bunting, and some 'Regimental buttons' (brasses which identified an infantry unit). The soldier's company number was often scratched on the reverse.[279] By 1912, a wad of Confederate bank notes had been given to them by Franklin McVey, President Taft's Secretary of the Treasury (p. 135). The Post had 'one of each denomination pasted onto a glass frame and hung in [the] Post room'. Also hanging on the walls were portraits of George Washington (given them by a member in 1894; p. 5), of General Ulysses S. Grant, and one of President Lincoln bought by them in 1910.[280] For the celebration of Memorial Day, there were '10 Memorial badges',[281] '10 Memorial flags', and as many as 150 flags with which to decorate graves. The members owned their own GAR caps or hats.

In 1894, the Post had twenty-five to thirty members of whom more than half annually held office or served on committees – about the same number came to regular meetings. By the end of the period covered by the minutes, membership was down to about twelve with thirty-five Associate Members, younger men who had been admitted to carry on the work of the organization. The admission of non-veterans was necessary since without them there would be no quorum and the Post could not officially function (pp. 42, 86). The wives of Associate members joined the WRC along with other younger women descended from veterans. By 1910, there were too few veterans to fill the offices.

The monthly meetings, presided over by the Post Commander or his Vice-Commanders, had opening and closing rituals since the minutes usually noted that they 'opened in form' and 'closed in form'. The opening was followed by the reading of the Adjutant's report and the report on news from the GAR's higher levels. Those were sometimes followed by reports from the Auditor or his committee, from the Quartermaster, and then by reports from other committees. New members were admitted, others transferred, suspended for non-payment of dues, pardoned for their inability to pay, or given a reduced rate. Other business was then considered. The business centred on the work of the committees which varied over time but included committees to audit the accounts, on memorials and funerals, the relief of the indigent, entertainment, on conferences and Encampments, visitations of schools, and on Memorial Day activities. The meetings varied but those were the usual concerns. Sometimes, the Post was visited by Inspectors or men from other Posts, and by those who gave talks – also given by local members and Inspectors.

At the end of every year, elections were held. They were often conducted in a somewhat informal way. After discussion, but apparently without formal nominations, there would be a motion 'that the Adjutant Cast one vote' for each of the officers whom he was to name. They would then be declared unanimously elected. It is not clear if this was to expedite matters or to determine the outcome without wrangling and to minimize hurt feelings (*e.g.*, p. 67). In 1907, a new officer was added, the 'Patriotic Instructor'. He was to visit schools before Memorial Day instilling patriotism in the young (pp. 110, 142).

If one looks at the recorded business, it is clear that routine matters took up much of the time but that other things mattered more. The sick were visited (pp. 14, 35, 87). Anniversaries in other Posts were noted and visitors sent to celebrate them (pp. 36, 37). Post members were named to go to Encampments and meetings. When they returned, they recounted what had happened at those events. Sometimes relief, in the form of a small sum, the remission of dues, or a loan, was granted to a member or his surviving family members who were having a hard time. Widows were sometimes given small sums (p. 61). Money was lent to members, either as a form of investment of the Post's funds or as charity.[282]

Every member's death was marked by a floral tribute (paid for out of the 'Flower Fund'). There was often a tribute to the deceased given at a meeting which was turned into a letter sent to his survivors and sometimes inscribed in the Minute Book. Typical of them was one from 1896 for Hiram Hunter:

> Whereas our Great Commander has seen fit in his Wisdom to detail from our Post Comrade Hiram Hunter   Therefore be it resolved that;
> We deeply deplore his loss as a member of the Post; Sympathize with the Widow and Children in this their Grate Affliction,
> Resolved That Comrade Hunter was a worthy Member of the Post, a worthy   Citizen of his Country and a truly worthy Soldier of the late rebellion   Resolved; that a copy of theses resolutions be spread upon the records of the Post, and a Copy of the same be sent to the Widow (p. 37).[283]

In some cases, concern with the dead meant buying a memorial marker to show his grave. They even searched for the burial places of long dead comrades whose graves they then marked or provided with a gravestone (pp. 13, 147). Akin to this were the Memorial Day ceremonies which the Post organized.

Memorial Day celebrations often began the Sunday before, in a church decorated for the occasion, and with a sermon directed to the veterans and their families (pp. 42, 62). Sometimes the chosen church was in West Glover. Vacant chairs were left among those occupied by the Post members to commemorate those who had died (p. 15). It is not stated, but it seems that only Protestant churches were picked for services– an indication of the social composition of the community in the 1860s if not in the 1900s. Memorial Day ceremonies were preceded by visits to local schools by members of the Post to keep fresh in young minds the memories of the War, the sacrifices it had entailed, and the need to defend the Union.[284]

On Memorial Day, the Post assembled and handed out flags to the children who would decorate graves by putting them in the holders marking the graves of old soldiers. Then, all marched a short distance to the nearest cemetery, preceded in some years by a band, for which they sometimes paid travel expenses and other costs. Glover lacked a band of its own. In 1910, those expenses came to $75.00 for the band; the speaker cost them $10.00; teams and bunting cost an additional $4.25 (p. 122). At the cemetery, there was a speech and prayers. No mention is made of firing a salute as is often done today. Then, all returned as they had come to have coffee at the Union House.[285] Over much of the Northeast Kingdom there were similar celebrations. Those of Albany c. 1900 were recalled by my mother in a short piece written as part of her autobiography (See Appendix I below, pp. 248-250).

The GAR's other principal out-reach activity was the presentation of Campfires (pp. 48, 55, 56), a responsibility of the Entertainment Committee. The Glover Campfires noticed in the minutes may not be distinguishable from Open Meetings where roughly the same things happened. Those often began as Post meetings opened to the WRC and then to the public (pp. 110, 114). At both gatherings, veterans told members of the general public about their wartime activities and sang songs dating from the War years. There might be stirring tales of heroism or heart-rending stories of deprivation in the prison camps of the Confederacy. My mother's family greatly disliked Southerners, whom they saw as cruel slave-owners, unreasonable and unpatriotic rebels, unfair fighters, and brutal prison-keepers. Those feelings were sustained by the tales told at Campfires.[286] Campfires in Albany went on into the twentieth century since my mother remembered going to them in Albany between 1900 and 1910.[287] In Glover, they seem to have stopped in 1899. The topics discussed in them and in the talks given in Post meetings allow us to glimpse how the Civil War was remembered. The known topics are listed in Appendix II below. Not surprisingly, the talks are very ordinary and do not to rise much above chatty reminiscences.

Charity and Loyalty to the USA need no comments but perhaps the GAR's third objective, Fraternity, does. At the Mason Post, that was locally long maintained by the monthly meetings and amounted to the promotion of good feeling among members. Sometimes the minutes noted that a meeting had ended in 'General conversation and a good time generally' (p. 51). Once, after a meeting held in the West Glover school house, 'all went down to Com[mander] James Abbotts and took dinner with the WRC and enjoyed a good social time When we repaired to the Store & smoked at Commander Williams expense' (p. 41). Fraternity derived from feasting, singing and story-telling, smoking, and, at one meeting in 1900, there was a novelty item: 'Post closed in form and repaired to the room of the WRC and were highly entertained by Mrs Clark a Member of the Quimby WRC with a talking and singing machine called the Gramophone' – perhaps the first heard in Glover.

Fraternity also meant visiting the sick and extending aid to those in need. In winter, it showed itself in socials and oyster suppers and, later in the year, in summer picnics (pp. 5, 17, 19, 36, 52, 71, 74) shared with the WRC (pp. 5, 19). The WRC room, adjacent to the Post Hall, was sometimes visited at the conclusion of monthly meetings for refreshments and occasionally 'entertainment' (pp. 22, 28). GAR members from as far away as Iowa and Michigan were welcomed at meetings and one man from Iowa was expeditiously admitted to the Glover Post (p. 130). Men from Glover could expect to be accepted in other Posts should they leave town.

Fraternity also meant sharing events with other Posts and visiting them. Over the years, visits were made to Posts in Albany, Barton, Barton Landing, Greensboro, Hardwick, Irasburg, Morrisville, Newport, St. Johnsbury, West Burke (pp. 19, 20, 93) and others not identified and possibly outside the State. Visitors to the Mason Post came from those places as well. Some were Inspectors or other officers of the GAR (p. 22). Many of the visitors gave talks or made 'remarks'. They were entertained and at least one dinner with the Department Commander ended with cigar smoking at the Hotel paid for by the Post (p.56). Fraternity was also shown by the sending of members to the annual Departmental Encampments with all or some of their expenses paid by the Post. Such delegates, when they returned, reported on what had been done (p. 2). One particularly expensive meeting would have been the Departmental Encampment in Montreal in 1899 (p. 64). Another involved defraying costs for some of those who attended the Gettysburg 50th Anniversary commemorations in 1913 (p. 134). Occasionally, delegates were sent to National meetings. Those generally dealt with the political activities of the GAR which the Glover Post certainly supported.

The GAR was a lobbying organization both nationally and at the local level. It pressed for adequate pensions and medical benefits and for honors and memorials for those who were deserving (p. 82). Indeed, on the first page of the Minute Book there was an order to pay for the printing of a 1893 resolution concerning pensions by the Sons of Veterans (p. 1). In 1904, the Post 'voted to except [accept] resolution of new pension bill' which was presumably sent on to someone. In 1911, the Mason Post instructed its Commander, E. H. Ney, 'to communicate with [the State's] Senators Dilingham and Page requesting them to use their influence in faver of ['the Salaway' or] Salarry Bill' then before Congress (p. 126). That was to provide more money and services for needy veterans and their widows. Nothing happened. A year later, the Post unanimously voted to write again 'to our Senators and Members of Congress'. This time, they wrote more stridently: 'For God's Sake use your influence to pass some bill for the relief of our poor and needy Soldiers and their widows' (p. 131). Such matters would have been taken to higher levels of the GAR by the Divisional and Departmental delegates. Fraternity very much involved looking after one's own. Its political functions as a lobbying group were largely successful and kept the Grand Old Party in power for years, particularly in single-party states like Vermont.

In 1894, attendance had often been in the twenties. By 1904, it was sometimes in the single digits and talks and Campfires had ceased. Meetings, as they appear in the minutes, now became routine affairs of listening to financial reports, noting the sick and dead, electing new officers, doling out charity, and reading Orders from the National Headquarters. The Post sent fewer visitors to schools, and social events seem less numerous. The WRC ladies were aging too. In 1910, the Post voted to remit dues for the year and ran down its savings account held at the Barton Saving Bank (p. 119).[288] Probably with that in mind, more was expended on the Memorial Day celebrations. On 11 August 1910, the Post voted to accept four Associate Members to fill up the ranks; this become more common, until, in 1915, there were over thirty of them. Finally, on 8 January 1914, the Post voted 'to draw out all of the relief fund and divide it equally among the old veterans' (p. 141). Meetings now often closed 'without form', probably because there were too few in attendance (*e.g.*, p. 129). Meetings of four or six veterans and four or five associates became common. The Glover Post of the GAR went on until c. 1933 when it disbanded. By then, there were few veterans left and the American Legion had pretty well taken over its functions.

The GAR also catered to a peculiarly American need to socialize in organizations. Posts such as the Glover Post had initially provided a place for men to share their experiences. Some of the stories and 'remarks' sound as if they had a somewhat therapeutic function. The meetings provided camaraderie and a place where one could hope to be better understood than among civilians who had not served and did not know the horrors of war or the misery of the camps. The GAR recognized services and honored those who had rendered them. And, it ensured that the honors continued. For those who saw the Civil War as a moral crusade to preserve the world's best country and the last best hope of mankind, it preached patriotism and an ideal of selfless service. The patriotic duty to serve, inculcated on the young, probably had some effects in 1917-1918, maybe even in 1941-1945. It also insured that Southern barbarism was not forgotten and not forgiven – but that did not much change the long held racist attitudes prevalent in the North as well as the South.

The generations of Vermonters before the Civil War, like those who fought in it, may have been more tolerant than those of my parents' generation. There was not enough local prejudice to prevent Black Alexander Twilight (1795-1857) from becoming Headmaster in the County Academy at Brownington in 1829. Albany families like the Haydens were fervent abolitionists (see pp. 25-26). George Washington Henderson (1850-1936), a former slave brought back to Vermont by a Civil War soldier, was educated in Vermont schools and graduated as the first African American Phi Beta Kappa from the University of Vermont. He married a girl from Belvedere. In 1879, he became the Headmaster at Craftsbury Academy. Eventually, he went on to Yale, was ordained, and had an academic career.[289] However, the GAR had no brief for equality and racial intolerance was growing.

Sixty years after the events which gave rise to it, many of the beliefs and feelings of those who supported and fought for the North in the Civil War had changed. The prevailing ideology of the University of Vermont, from which Henderson graduated in 1877, had become, by 1914, a Social Darwinist version of White Supremacy best exemplified by the successes of the Anglo-Saxon race. That was what my Uncle Karl (UVM, 1912-1916) was taught in history, literature, economics, and sociology courses. I have his lecture notes to prove it. Local politicians, including my father's youngest brother, upheld State Rights and found inspiration in the 1950s in the Senators and Governors of an unreconstructed South. The GAR had not changed any of that. Present day veterans' organizations do better because of legal changes and the integration of the present Armed Forces.

Appendices to Chapter XI

Appendix I: Memorial Day in Albany, Vermont (c. 1908) *by Doris Sanders Emerson (1894-1994).*

[This piece was written in the mid-1970s; her prose has not been changed.]

Synonymous with Decoration Day to me is the name of John Kelly who was a near neighbor to us in the village of Albany in the early 1900s. He was not a young man and I cannot remember of ever seeing him without a gray beard. Mr Kelly was a retired Civil War veteran.[290] At that time Albany could boast of quite a number of others who served in that war, namely Alonzo and Lew George, Mr Newton, Elijah Stone, Mr Sartwell, Nathan Shute, Herschel Markres, and Orange Whitcher. All returned unscratched by the ravages of that war with the exception of Mr. Newton, who returned blind, and Mr. Whitcher who had had a thumb shot off (He did it himself.).[291]

Mr Kelly stood out as the one man who wished to honor and to revere the memory of those left behind on the fields of battle such as Gettysburg, still known as the bloodiest battle of the Civil War),[292] or in the horrors of Andersonville prison.

Every Decoration Day, as it was then called, Mr Kelly would rally his cohorts and the town's people together to pay homage to those who served their country and never returned. And so it was on Decoration Day that Mr Kelly planned proper observance for them each year. He conducted a program in their memory for as many years as he was able to perform this patriotic duty and honor.

To start off the day, all those who wanted to march to the cemetery, gathered at the village schoolyard yard up from Pat McGuire's house. It is Decoration Day, and the old soldiers and school children make ready to march two by two to the cemetery. Each one carries a flag to put upon a veteran's grave. For us children, it was just a gala event, with the fanfare of the music and the excitement of the day and the people it brought together. The Albany Cornet Band, clad in their holiday attire, navy blue uniforms and caps with their highly polished instruments sparkling in the morning sun, led the parade. The band leader at this time was W. A. Sargent, until he left to go to Boston [or] another fine [musician] Bert Vance.

Following the band in the parade were the old soldiers, some with faltering step. Then came the older children down to the smallest who could make it alone to the cemetery walking two by two.

Mr Vance comes down with his baton and the band strikes up that beautiful march by Sousa 'The Stars and Stripes Forever'. As we march part of the distance, we will hear the dirge of the drums beating out their mournful tatoo. We know that is Jim Dow there with his big bass drum and his son Dwight with his snare drum putting in the beats for the measured tread with Reuben Miles playing the melody on his picolo. We arrive at the cemetery where the old soldiers break ranks and stand in lines for the school children to pass thru circling around, to get in place for the ceremony. Then Mr Kelly takes over as Adjutant [to the GAR Post in Albany] giving commands to his comrades which went something like:

'Attention Comrades!'
'Uncover!' Then all old soldiers removed their army caps.
'Salute the Dead!' All raised their cap over his left breast.
Now Mr Kelly reads from his [GAR] manual the meaning of the day. This over, he gives the command
'Cover!'

Each soldier replaces his cap on his head. Then the band plays a selection of martial music and they all disband to go thru the cemetery as they choose. Some visit graves; others will head back up street to the Methodist Church where there will be served a fine dinner which has been prepared by the Ladies of the Grand Army of the Republic [WRC] and the Methodist Church ladies. The menu will consist of home baked raised rolls, baked beans, brown bread, pickles, tea and coffee and assorted pies.

After the meal, the old soldiers will take time to rest and reminisce. Mr Kelly will go to his nearby home to rest and get fortified with a drink or two for the afternoon session held in the Congregational church and auditorium.

Soon the afternoon session will open with Mr Kelly using about the same procedure as used at the cemetery, and he will then proceed to read a ritual service. He will then go on with quite a long discourse of his own telling of their experiences and various battles of the Civil War in which they had so bravely fought.

Being quite young [she was 14 in 1908], and possibly not old enough to understand what he was talking about, I was not much interested in this part of the program. I preferred to go to the ball park to see the ball game and to be where the action was. However, after a repeat performance of this over several years, I now regret that I did not concern myself more with Mr. Kelly's discourse, as I now know what he said only as others have told me. The day's program brought to a close the Memorial Day activities in Albany Village. The Civil War Veterans have all passed on years ago, but each made his contribution to the cause of liberty, justice and union and so with Mr. Kelly, each year we honor their memory.

Since those days long ago, I have visited the Gettysburg battlefield, which gave a bit more meaning and interest to it all. As I rode over part of the battlefield which was studded with big boulders, I hoped that some of the Albany soldiers who fought in that battle were able to defend and protect themselves behind those boulders or crouch unseen in the bushes growing about the place. In more recent years, as the Civil War and Spanish War veterans have faded from the scene, the parade has added veterans from World Wars I and II and the Korean and Vietnam veterans and the Boy Scouts, the Legion and Axillaries and of course the children. Through my eyes, more vividly, I still see the parade as it was in my youth, a day to be remembered when the Albany Cornet Band clad in holiday attire led the way and of course Mr. Kelly added color and dignity to the day's activities.

Appendix II: The Talks Given in the Post and at Campfires 1894-1915.

1. 22 March 1894, E. H. Nye, 'account of how the Sixth Corps acted at the Battle of Winchester' (p. 2).
2. Memorial Day 1894, Address by the 'Departmental Commander Branch at the Church...Music and other exercises.' (p. 4).
3. 18 October, 1894, 'Short Storys for the good of the Order by several Comrades present' (p. 7).
4. 15 November 1894, The Inspector's 'pleasing remarks on the Nations Flagg' (p. 7).
5. Resolution to hold a Campfire at West Glover [there is no later record of this] (p. 7).
6. 13 December 1894, 'Visiting Comrade Ezra Clark made appropriate remarks' (p. 8).
7. 7 February 1895, Comrade Cook 'appointed to write a piece for the benefit of the Post' [about his service experiences] (p. 13).

8. 14 March 1895, Comrade Cheney 'requested to write and read a piece at our next meeting', given 6 June 1895; 'WRC present by request', (pp. 14, 17).
9. 4 July 1895 ? 'an informal talk of the war of about 40 minutes was heard' – they also had a picnic (p. 17).
10. 8 August 1895, E.H. Nye, 'history of the War at Battle of Fredericksburg in Virginia' (p. 19).
11. (Ditto), A. B. Smith of Rattery Post [West Burke], 'extended a invitation to comrade Smith to give us a history of his prison live (*sic.*) at our next meeting'; Although invited to speak, there is no record that he did but he was present on 5 September (p. 19).
12. 31 October 1895, Mr. A. Foss of Meade Post 99 [Barton Landing] 'favored us with a short address' [probably about his services] (p. 22).
13. 30 January 1896, 'the Entertainment Committee be instructed to put in a Campfire as soon as possibly convenient' (p. 28).
14. 19 November 1896, Oyster supper and Campfire planned for 20 November (p. 36) but there is no record of its being held.
15. 17 December 1896, T. J. Hastings, 'remarks on the character of [deceased] com[rade] [Hiram] Hunter' (p. 38).
16. 17 December 1896, visitors from George Meade Post, Barton Landing and Ellsworth Post, Hardwick; they made 'remarks' (p. 38).
17. 17 June 1897, 'Comrade Geo. Weeks from McLare 145 Missourea ... made some remarks';[this may refer to the Memorial Day oration of the previous month].
18. 9 December 1897, 'Recess for dinner after which the doors were thrown open and a Campfire was introduced. Several of the Comrades took Part among them was visiting comrade Agustus Larabee from Mich.' (p. 48).
19. 10 February 1898, Commander Williams, "Remarks ... right to the point on the pension question' (p. 50).
20. 10 March 1898, Comrade Marnock, 'Remarks', ' very interesting' (p. 51).
21. 5 May 1898, 'Remarks by Comrade Wm Williams on Our Navy' (p. 52).
22. 29 September 1898, Visited by Departmental Commander 12:00- 4:00 PM; 'recess for dinner   after dinner Post and Corps assembled in Post room for Campfire... After dinner exercises... 1st Speaker Wm Williams, Singing by Arthur Girls   Commander Harris next spoke   Mrs Gates next addressed us   C S Joslyn T Marnock and your Adjt spoke a few words' (p. 55).
23. 21 September 1899, Open meeting with WRC and the public invited. 'Comrade Chamberlain of Burnside Post [Greensboro] next addressed us   We next heard from Comrade Davidson of Burnside post   Comrade Williams came next who interested us for a few minutes   Comrade Marnock next spoke   The Adjt next had his words   Mrs Chamberlain WRC inspector was next called upon who next addressed us   Arthur WRC President next spoke   Commander called on Com Marnock to introduce Dept Com Buterfield which he done   Gen. Butterfield spoke to the satisfaction of all giving us a history of the encampment at Philadelphia'; the visitors were thanked and the

evening ended with 'some joking remarks' by Butterfield and the local speakers (p. 65).
24. 14 December 1899, Inspector Brunnen [Brunning] 'made a few remarks' (p. 67).
25. 20 September 1900, J. M. Currier, Senior Vice Commander of the Department, 'Gave the Comrades a Good Talk and some storys' (p. 75).
26. 11 October 1900, a visitor from New Hampshire 'Made some remarks' (p. 75).
27. 9 April 1904, Report by C. W. Cook 'on his visit to Washington and the Battle of Field of Gettysburg" (p. 89) [He had attended the June commemoration of the Battle fought in 1863].
28. 8 March 1906, 'enjoyed a Short literary Entertainment' in the WRC room after the Post 'closed in form' (p. 104).
29. 11 October 1906, 'Post took a recess Assembled in the M E Church and entertained the relatives of Capt. Dan Mason Welcom to the Guests by E H Nye response by Hon. Frank Clark Songs by Dr & Mrs Blake [of Barton][293] Capt Dan Masons Military record by Capt A W Davis read by the Adjt. Original Poem written and read by Rev A. B. Blake Prayer Rev. J M McDonald Mrs Borland presented the Post a Five Dollar Bill' (pp. 106-7).
30. 14 February 1907, 'Comrade Dwyer ...[gave] very good advice about attending meetings telling us how he enjoyed being among the comrades' (p. 111).
31. 14 October 1909, Comrade Sleeper from Newport 'made Some very appropriate remarks'(p. 119).
32. 10 November 1910, Comrade Nye made 'appropriate remarks' after his induction as Junior Vice Commander of the Department of Vermont GAR (p. 124).
33. 12 January 1911, remarks by A. P. Bean, Frank S. Philips, Harry Philips, by the Rev. M. H. Eddy and Commander Dwyer (Barton); William Williams (Glover) made remarks and gave 'advice', 'after which the Post Went to the WRlf Corps where installation of officers were concluded' (p. 125).
34. 9 October 1913, 'Commander Nye gave a very interesting talk in reference to his co[mpany's] annual gathering' (p. 199).
35. 8 October 1914, 'Comrade A. C. Sleeper of Newport gave a very interesting talk, Told of incident about the old soldier who came alone after all the rest dropped out and drunk a cold water toast to the departed. Comrade Bunning also favored us with some good remarks'. The Post then discussed the status in the post of the Associates. after which 'Commander Nye gave an interesting incident of Civil war days. Associate member Rev. G. W. Douglass gave a little talk full of interest, Had a very interesting meeting. Frank Phillips [a local poet] gave a nice selection' (p. 145).
36. 14 January 1915, 'Frank Phillips gave a recitation French Juniper –' (p. 147).
37. 11 February 1915, 'Rev. G. W. Douglass gave an interesting account of discussion in Grange meeting on which side will win in European

War'(p. 147).
38. 9 September 1915, 'Rev.   Jocelyn gave us a very interesting and inspiring talk.   Rev. W. E. Douglass also said a few words,   Commander Nye also favored us with a few well chose words.   Stories were told by different ones' (p. 152).
39. 14 October 1915, 'Com. E. H. Nye read a list of the No. of men in the different Vt Regiments & Batterys & the number of deaths & engagements of each. Quite a number of interesting stories of the Civil War were told by the old soldiers' (p. 153).

[End of the Minute Book]

XII

Another Farmer's Life: Arthur Frank Emerson (1896-1939)

1. The Education of Arthur Emerson

Arthur's sisters, who survived their brothers, were not ones for telling anything which was not flattering to their family. They said my father had been a very fine child, a good boy and became a man of whom the family was proud. They said he did well in the schools of Hardwick, Vermont, where he was born on 30 August 1896. There he was brought up and attended high school. His brother, Lee, said little about him although all that was all positive: Arthur was a good athlete, a progressive farmer, a 32nd degree Mason and a fine man. Lee never mentioned his brother's politics which may not have been something they shared. My mother had only good things to say about him and happily remembered being courted by a humorous fellow who was liked by everyone but who, in the end, put his family before her. Others echoed those praises and deplored his early death. The story does not begin or end there; I have tried to piece it out.

About my father's early years I know little. Next to nothing has come down to me about his childhood although I do have several of his early books and others owned by his siblings. One of his childhood books survives, possibly because it meant something to his mother and sisters. It is called *Happy Days of Childhood* – the title of a popular sentimental song from 1850. The book's stories, by several authors, are moralistic tales about homeless blind boys, who are made happy because of the care and concern of others, or stories about animals, such as the rats who laugh and sing, 'Long live the men who don't keep cats!' Some of it is written in baby-talk and more of it is meant to be an educational aid to reading, hence its division of words into syllables. It is reflective of the pollyannaish world in which the pious, the smug, and the philistine often lived when *Happy Days* was published in 1904. Its one story about Blacks does not give them high marks for intelligence. I doubt if an eight-year-old boy in Vermont would have found its pictures interesting or its poems diverting. One contrasts the boy fed cake with another:

> There was another boy
> Also his mother's joy
> And to him did she give all
> she could, could, could
> He only had dry bread
> Before he went to bed,
> But he smacked his lips, and
> called it good, good, good.

I wonder what my father made of it. I am sure he enjoyed more the falling-apart volume of Kipling, some of which he got by heart, or Longfellow's 'The Courtship of Miles Standish', which is also well thumbed. Those he would have read later. *Happy Days* looks unread.

It is very likely that he skated and played card games in the winter, rolled marbles in the spring and enjoyed a sort of baseball in the backyard during the summer as his younger brothers did.[294] Somewhere he learned to swim, perhaps at the Emerson farm in Barton which was close to Willoughby Lake. He seems to have been close to his uncle and aunt there who sent him an unsigned Christmas Postcard, (page 257), in 1906. Sent on December 24, his relatives expected it to arrive that day or the next. Posted early in the day, it would probably have been sent to St. Johnsbury, sorted on the train and made it to Hardwick in the afternoon or evening.

About my father's schooling I know more. For the year in which he is likely to have gotten *Happy Days* for Christmas, I have his third grade report card. His grades were As and Bs in almost equal numbers. He was poor in spelling (always) and, over time, erratic in deportment. He got one C in third grade, in drawing, and seems to have been best in reading and arithmetic. Later, his grades in mathematics and science courses would be good but not always high. As a young student, he attended faithfully. Graded school ended in the ninth grade with a graduation ceremony. Many of the children would leave school at that point.

He went on to Hardwick Academy, which, like most others in Vermont c. 1910, had classical and commercial streams and was not wholly public in its funding.[295] He took the 'Latin-Scientific Course' which required him to study four years of Latin and English and at least two years of French and German. Students like him also had three years of history (Ancient, English, and American) and four science courses (introductory general science; biology, zoology, and botany; physics, and chemistry). They included some time in the school's laboratory.

He had at least two years of algebra and geometry.[296] A good deal of writing was expected of the students by a faculty most of whom had university degrees.[297] Students were also expected to read six or eight books a year, half of which were not assigned in courses. The book lists, published in the annual booklet on the school, are varied and interesting. They included, over several years, such standards as *The Odyssey, Pilgrim's Progress, Robinson Crusoe, The Vicar of Wakefield*; and other novels, including *Ivanhoe, Rob Roy, Kenilworth, The Heart of Mid-Lothian, Guy Mannering, Quentin Durward*, and nineteenth century favorites like *Tom Brown's School Days, Jane Eyre, The Tale of Two Cities, Oliver Twist, Silas Marner, Treasure Island* and *Dr. Jekyl and Mr. Hyde, The Master of Ballantrae, The House of the Seven Gables, Uncle Tom's Cabin, Two Years Before the Mast, Quo Vadis* and *The Gentleman from Indiana*, and Ben Franklin's *Autobiography*. Homer, John Bunyan, Daniel Defoe, Oliver Goldsmith, Sir Walter Scott, Thomas Hughes, Charlotte Bronte, Charles Dickens, Robert Louis Stevenson, Benjamin Franklin, Harriet Beecher Stowe, Richard Henry Dana, Henryk Sienkiewicz, and Booth Tarkington are better writers than most eleventh graders read today. Poetry was not neglected but much of it was older. Thomas Blackmore, John Churchill, S. T. Coleridge, Sir Walter Scott, Alfred, Lord Tennyson, and John Ruskin figured on that list as did Rudyard Kipling. Among the plays were Shakespeare tragedies and Richard Brinsley Sheridan's comedies. The students staged a play or two a year. The regular work of the English and rhetoric classes was supplemented by courses in elocution. The school library encouraged more reading as did a rule requiring study after 7:30 p.m. Those with an average below 70, a 'D' average, failed.

Ordinary readings for his English classes were contained in four readers listed with thirty other texts to be mastered during the four years in which the students were expected to attend. My father would not have had any practical courses, such as shop or typing. He could do carpenter work and typed but those skills were not learned at Hardwick Academy but picked up from his father or came later. His demanding high school course was taken by about ten to twenty pupils each year from Hardwick and the surrounding area. He did well in high school and graduated from Hardwick Academy in 1914 before his family moved to Barton.

My father's high-school course was worth every penny of the roughly $10.00 it cost yearly – exclusive of athletic gear and the clothes he wore to entertainments, the annual balls, or in the plays in which

Another Farmer's Life: Arthur Frank Emerson (1896-1939)

What is most interesting about this Christmas card is that it was mailed by Arthur's Barton relatives in Barton on December 24 and received that day or the next.

My Vermonters: The Northeast Kingdom 1800-1940

Hardwick Academy and Graded School — REPORT CARD

Arthur J. Emerson — Ninth Grade
For Year Ending May 3, 1912

SUBJECTS	Fall Term 1st Half	Fall Term 2d Half	Winter Term 1st Half	Winter Term 2d Half	Spring Term 1st Half	Spring Term 2d Half	YEAR
Times Tardy	0	1	0	0	0	0	
Times Dismissed	0	0	1	0	0	0	
Days Absent	0	2	0	0	0	0	
Deportment	C	B	B	B	B	C	
Reading	85	87	90	92	90	85	
Spelling	65	76	83	71	80	82	
Writing	78	75	78	75	74	80	
Arithmetic	75	78	81	76	82	76	
Civics				63	80	89	
Geography							
History	86	86	82	79	78	80	
Language	68	79	73	82	80	67	
Physiology	72	78	87				
Drawing							
Music							

Anna M. Spaulding, TEACHER.

Hardwick Academy and Graded School — FORM 7

Arthur Emerson — 5 Grade
For Year Ending June 4, 1908

	Fall Term 1st Half	Fall Term 2d Half	Winter Term 1st Half	Winter Term 2d Half	Spring Term 1st Half	Spring Term 2d Half	YEAR
Times Tardy							
Times Dismissed							
Days Absent	0	6	0	0			
Deportment	0	0	6	0			
Reading	B	B	A	B	A		
Spelling	C	C	B	B	B		
Writing	A	B	C	C	C		
Arithmetic	C	B	B	A	C		
Geography	B	A	C	C	C		
Language	B	B	C	B	B		
History	C	B	C	B	B		
Music							
Drawing	C	C	C	C	B		
Physiology							

Edith Smith, Teacher

Hardwick Academy and Graded School

Arthur Emerson — Third Grade
For Year Ending ___

	FALL TERM 1st Half	FALL TERM 2d Half	AVER.	WINTER TERM 1st Half	WINTER TERM 2d Half	AVER.	SPRING TERM 1st Half	SPRING TERM 2d Half	AVER.	YEAR
Days Present										
Days Absent	0	0		0	0		1	0		
Times Tardy	0	0		0	0		0	0		
Deportment	B	B		B	B		A	A		
Reading	B	A		B	A		A	B		
Spelling	B	B		B	B		B	B		
Writing	B	B		B	B		B	B		
Arithmetic	A	A		A	A		A	A		
Language	B	B		B	B		B	B		
Geography										
Rhetoricals										
Drawing	C			B	B		B	B		
History										
Physiology										
AVERAGE										

Bertha Jennings, Teacher

Another Farmer's Life: Arthur Frank Emerson (1896-1939)

opposite: Arthur Emerson's report cards for the third, fifth, and ninth grades. Other years show the same courses being taken so these are indicative of the grade-school curriculum. Language here means English.

In the lower grades, there was a weekly attendance card; one of Arthur's is shown above.

The Ninth Grade Graduates at Hardwick Graded School in 1912. Arthur is in the next to the last row, two in from the right. He is holding his diploma which other boys have stuck in jacket pockets. That certificate is reproduced opposite. Many had no more schooling.

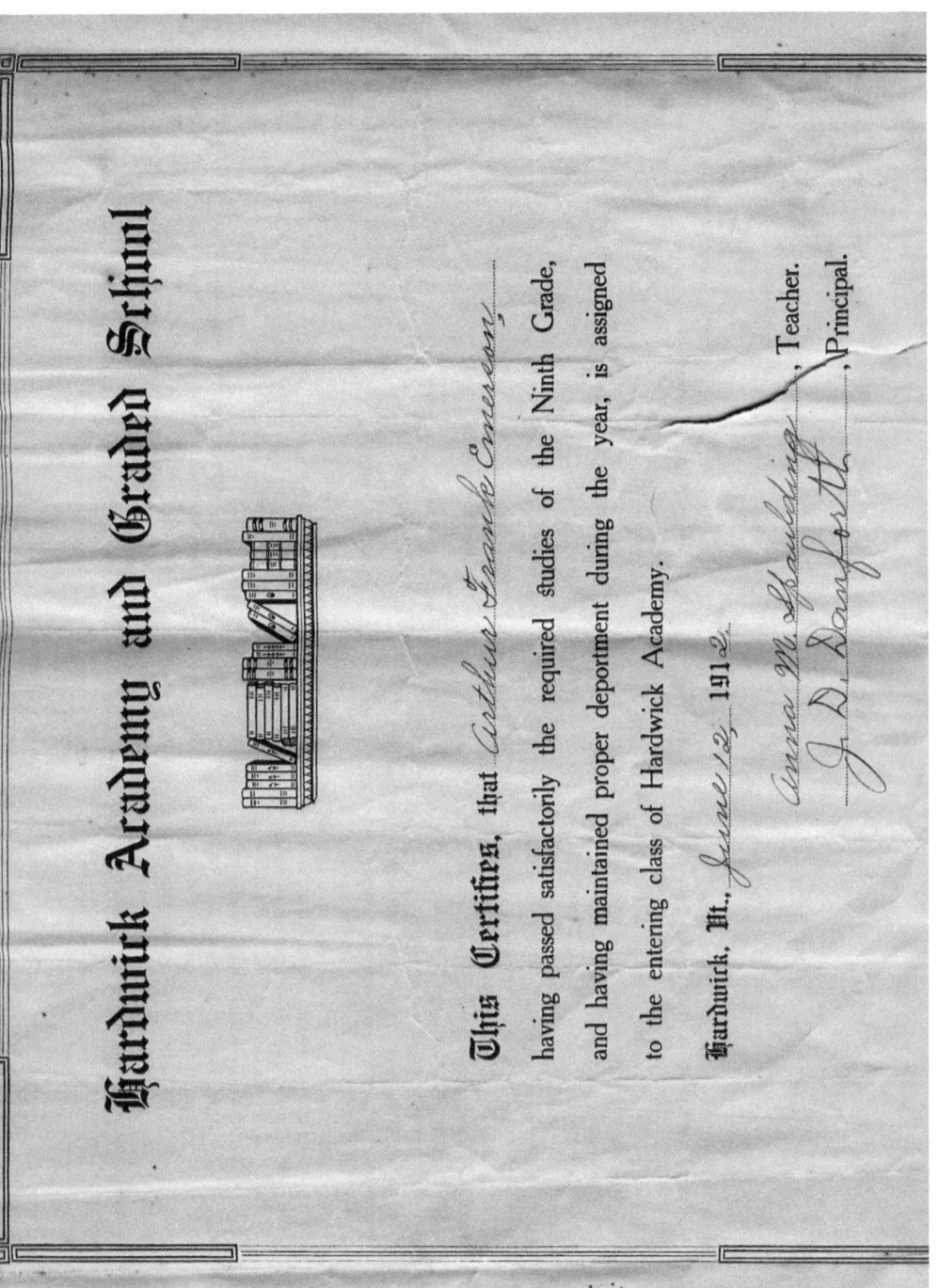

Expenses Per Term

Tuition, one-half due at the beginning, the balance due at the middle of each term, is as follows:

English (base)	$5.00
Languages, each	1.00
Physics	1.00
Chemistry	1.00
Elocution	.50
Extra Examinations	1.00
Typewriting	5.00
Grades 8 and 9	4.50
Grades 6 and 7	4.00
Grades 4 and 5	3.50
Grades 2 and 3	3.00
Grade 1	

The entrance of a pupil presumes a contract for a term, unless special arrangements are made. No discount will be allowed for absence for less than half a term. Pupils whose homes are in the Graded School District are charged only for languages, and in laboratory work, for actual breakage.

Rooms and board may be secured in private families on application to the Principal.

General Information

Each pupil in the grades, even if "promoted", will be considered on probation in the next grade above, for one term. If this probation period shows that the pupil can not do the work required, he will be assigned to the grade below.

Report cards showing the record of attendance, deportment, and scholarship of pupils, will be sent to parents and guardians from time to time.

A school library of over five hundred volumes suitable for individual reading for all but the lowest grades encourages the children to read for pleasure and profit.

All pupils who do not live with their parents or guardians are required to observe study-hours beginning at 7:30 P. M., and must hand in to the principal each week a house-report, signed by the lady of the house, showing how well this rule is observed. The following regulations apply to study hours:

I. Students are to be in their rooms at the beginning of study hours each evening, and are not to leave the house thereafter during the evening without an excuse from the principal.

II. Students are regularly excused from study hours to attend one evening prayer-meeting each week.

III. All students excused to attend entertainments must proceed directly to their rooms at the close of the entertainments.

IV. ALL excuses to attend entertainments or to be absent from the house during study hours, except as provided in Rule II and except school entertainments, must be granted by the Principal in writing and presented to the lady of the house before the student is excused.

Information concerning the school will be furnished by the Principal or Trustees.

Northeast Kingdom High Schools and Academies published annual guides to courses, costs, boarding charges, and so on. This is one from Hardwick Academy c. 1915.

he appeared. It gave him a good deal of knowledge on which he could build. After high school, he continued to read for his own amusement and seems to have preferred poetry to prose. Rhetoric, composition, and elocution classes made it easy for him to speak to large gatherings in which he seems to have been often witty and humorous. His voice, I was told, was low and resonant. He tended not to exhibit much emotion. A dead-pan delivery often made many of the things he said either sound impressive or, when he told jokes, funnier. At some point he won a silver medal in a Women's Christian Temperance Union speaking contest. Although he could talk well, he could not carry a tune but he liked to sing.

Arthur's Women's Christian Temperance Union medal for 'Declamation', c. 1914.

By the time he graduated, he would have been about full grown – 5' 7", slightly pudgy but muscular and broad shouldered with long arms. He had black hair and dark eyes which he described at different times as hazel or grey. Like his father and siblings, he was slow and deliberate in his speech and movements. At some point, while in school, he had rheumatic fever which left him with a damaged heart valve. Despite that, he played on the basketball and baseball teams. He learned to pitch well. No one noticed his heart condition, not even when he was called for a physical examination by the War Department in 1918. If he knew of it, he ignored it until he could no longer do so. In 1939, it killed him.

During those years, Arthur would have learned something about the qualities of stone and the ways of cutting it – the craft his father pursued, first for others and then as a stone-shed owner. Arthur would have gone to school with children who were Italian and Roman Catholic and may have learned the rough tolerance which playgrounds can encourage but sometimes do not. He undoubtedly went to Sunday School and read his Bible and other religious books along with the rest of his family. Indeed, in 1912, he signed a 'Forward Step' [298] card as 'Shorty Emerson....Christian Scientist', a choice he is unlikely to have stuck with but which long remained an option for his mother and sisters. By the time he graduated from Hardwick Academy in 1914, he would have considered going to university for four years as did his brother Karl. That option, he rejected. He liked the out of doors and probably saw his future in eventually having the Barton farm (opposite) his father partially inherited in 1914.[299]

That farm was bigger than most since its cow barn had stanchions for about twenty milking cows and spaces for half a dozen drying-off or freshening cows. Attached to the barn was the horse barn and beyond that the hired man's house and sheds. The house had been put together by Benjamin Emerson. To an existing small house, two others were rolled into place to form the middle section and a front part. The first was from across the road but the second was rolled about a third of a mile to rest on granite blocks and face the road. Many of the 600-700 un-surveyed acres were covered with trees, divided between the sugar place and forested land which was logged. Some was pasture land; not much was arable.

Arthur worked during the summer of 1914 on their newly inherited farm and then for two years (1914-1916) attended the Vail Agricultural School in Lyndon, Vermont. Its main town, Lyndonville (illustrated overleaf), was a railroad town with a lively commercial center and many amenities such as parks and some rather grand architect-designed houses. Arthur used its library and visited its power station. Located in Lyndon Center, Lyndon Institute was the local high school which also provided a year of additional study for those wishing to become teachers. The Vail School was located on the same campus but was a separate institution.

Theodore N. Vail (1845-1920), a public-spirited businessman who became the first President of the American Telephone and Telegraph Company, owned a 2-5,000 acre farm in Lyndon and established his school in 1910 as a joint venture with Lyndon Institute.[300] It was supervised by the University of Vermont and seems to have given college level courses in some subjects. It was the only institution of higher education in the Northeast Kingdom other than teacher training programs run by high schools. Arthur, unlike his farming forebears, would be a trained and scientific farmer – a new breed.[301]

Another Farmer's Life: Arthur Frank Emerson (1896-1939)

Frank Emerson's Granite Shed in 1909. The siding connected the business to the quarry in Woodbury several miles away.

Frank Emerson had his own business and, in 1910, a work crew of about ten to fourteen men.

Another Farmer's Life: Arthur Frank Emerson (1896-1939)

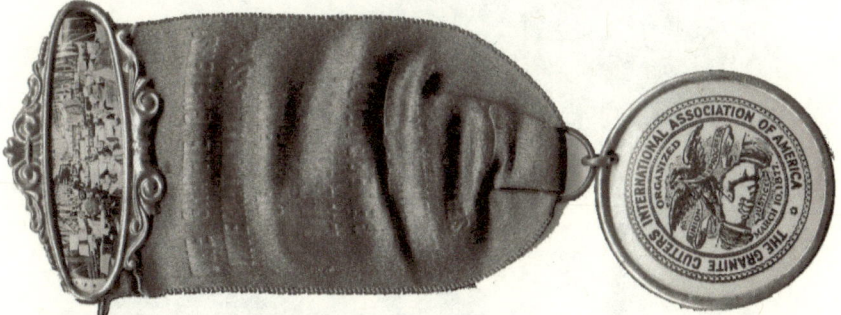

Frank Emerson is second from the left end in the first row. His workers were Scots, Welsh, and Italians – as Vermont stone-workers often were.

Frank Emerson's badge showing his membership in the Granite Cutters International Association of America. He wore it at a Hardwick Labor Day celebration in 1909. The union, founded in 1877, worked to improve wages, hours, and working conditions in dangerous shops.

The Emerson Farm c. 1915.

Another Farmer's Life: Arthur Frank Emerson (1896-1939)

For part of the time he was at Vail (he was eighteen when he enrolled), he kept diaries. They show a young man full of energy and curiosity who enjoyed life but did not always put his school work first. They also suggest he was trying to find himself. He thought about and visited sects and churches other than his own. He was not only 'Art' but 'Frankie'. He had an active social life but did not find a steady girl or wife. A leader among the school's athletes and on its school paper, he almost got thrown out for his pranks and acts of misconduct. Had he lived, he would have inherited and run a farm of over 600 acres. He was training for that role but there was more going on in his life.

It was not difficult to get into the Vail School. His diaries tell of others who applied and were accepted without much scrutiny. Probably he was too. It also does not seem to have cost much. There were no tuition fees for Vermont students[302] but he worked on the school's farm, waited on tables, and did other things which kept down costs. All his friends seem to have had such chores. In December 1915, he took a part-time job as a hired man so his boss could perform his jury duty. This was partly a favor to a friend but it also meant a bit of extra cash – and a few missed classes and meals. His noted expenses were mainly for clothes and for his social life. His parents seemed willing to pay generously for both. The cost of a new coat in his first year was $25.00 – about a month's cash wage for a hired man or a grade school teacher. In his second year, a suit, shirt, and belt, in which to graduate, cost him $25.00. Texts came to less than $10.00 a year. For the other books he bought, he gives no prices. It was possible to spend two years on the cheap at Vail and end up with an education worth having. What was that like?

In his first year, he took courses in chemistry [and received a grade of 92], soils [96], dairying [81], black-smithing [78], carpentry [82], fruit-growing [93], and was graded on his deportment [74]. In his second year, he took courses in bacteriology [82] and diseases [?], field crops [80], feeds [81], poultry [91], forestry [88] and practical courses in carpentry [90], black-smithing [78], farm mechanics [?],[303] farm drawing [90], and a laboratory course in vegetation [?]. The diaries have several references to the school's greenhouse in which he saw some exotics and a peach tree blossoming in March 1915. Visits there may have been part of the vegetation course. He once mentioned a civics course which may have been a part of each year's work although his mention relates to things done in the first year. There was also stock-judging from time to time. That was a practical part of the formal curriculum and was very

Four views of Lyndonville in 1912. Arthur borrowed books at the Library, visited the Power Station, and bought his cigars at a store on Main Street.

Another Farmer's Life: Arthur Frank Emerson (1896-1939)

The smaller park near Lyndonville railway station, and Depot Street.

Another Farmer's Life: Arthur Frank Emerson (1896-1939)

Lyndon Center was where the Vail Agricultural School was situated – just beyond the tree-line on the right. There are pictures of the schools facilities in Harriet Fletcher Lyndon Institute *(Images of America, Charleston, S.C., 2000)*.

The Vail Mansion was built almost haphazardly by continuous additions. It is now gone and has been replaced by buildings of Lyndon State College.

My Vermonters: The Northeast Kingdom 1800-1940

educational. He went eagerly to those events in both years. The boys learned to judge draft and other horses, sheep and pigs, and a variety of cattle. He mentions Dutch Belts, Herefords, Jerseys, and Ayrshires but there would have been Guernseys and Holsteins, perhaps others too. Some of those animals must have been brought in from Vail's estate, Speedwell Farms, of from other places such as Elmer Darling's Mountain View Farm in Burke. Darling was Vail's friend and another improving landlord. Some were breeds relatively new to Vermonters. In judging, his second year grade was only a 70. Another practical part of the course was being assigned work on the school's farm. He liked his duty in the milk room and creamery. There he indulged himself – by drinking cream, milk and butter milk, and in having butter fights with his friends. He also learned to make ice cream and sherbert. Mucking out the stables, and spreading manure or harvesting he liked less, but he did those chores too. He was learning much but not behaving well. His second year deportment grade sank to 59 – the lowest in the school. By 16 May 1916, he had accumulated 43 demerit points; the next worst student had 34. The class average was less than 20.[304] He was a 'cut up'.

Milk room friends. Arthur is on the right.

He tended to sleep when he was tired and work when he wanted to, so his schedule at the best of times was erratic. Sometimes, he was in bed by 8:00 p.m. and up at 3:30 a.m.; at other times, he went to bed late and tried to sleep-in. A 'normal night' was about 11:00 p.m. to 6:00 or 7:00 a. m. He either got up himself or was called by the 'waiters'. If he was working in the creamery, he did his chores before breakfast which seems to have been about 7:00 to 8:00 a.m. If he missed it, he did not mind much. He had made friends with 'cooke' who often gave him milk and doughnuts outside the scheduled breakfast times. He gave her maple syrup and sugar from his family's farm. If he was not working early, he had breakfast and then swept his room for inspection by one of the supervisors. Then came chapel, which he often skipped, then classes and labs. Dinner was at noon. Other work filled the afternoon. Black-smithing ran for three hours. Usually he was free by 3:30 or 4:00 p. m. That is when he took off for town, saw a girl, went to the movies, played ball or read. After supper at 5:30, there would be more chores if it was his turn. He does not seem to have been required to be in by a time certain each night – or he ignored it. There must have been a 'lights out' time because, in February 1916, he got permission to stay up late to study. That came after a night when he had read until 3:00 a.m.

Studies, the farm chores, the bit of time off in the afternoons was not all there was to life at the Aggie School. There was an active extra-curricular life in which he played his part. There was an Aggie Club to which he belonged. He was on the editorial board of *The Aggie* in both years he was there. It was the school's journal and independent of the Aggie Club. In his second year, he was Editor-in-Chief. He recorded visits to printers, to a State office about a 'cut' [an illustration], and sent admonitions to his associates to write their pieces and get them in on time. Working on this may have induced him to learn to type. He was elected Secretary of his class in both 1915 and 1916. He was on the committee to arrange graduation activities in 1916. 'Frankie' Emerson was involved in getting graduation pins made.

He belonged to the Athletic Club as would anyone who pitched, ran, pole vaulted (he pulled a tendon doing that in May 1916), played soccer and football and even tried to ski in February 2016. Most of those were not serious diversions but baseball was different. He pitched or played short stop. The end of his time at Lyndonville culminated in a series of games which took him to St. Johnsbury, Randolph, to other towns in between, and finally to Newport. The high points for him came in two games. On 29 April in the St. Johnsbury game, after the starting Aggie pitcher gave up eight runs in six inning, Arthur struck out seven in three and had scored against him no runs or hits. On 3 June, at Newport, he pitched thirteen innings and lost five to six. He noted only one football game in the diary. He 'played left end' in a pair of shoes he had tried to improve by nailing strips of leather across the bottoms. The team lost badly and got beaten up in the process. He 'broke a hunk out of a tooth'. Others were also hurt; one team-mate got a broken nose.

This is one of a set of fifteen or so pictures of the team taken in front of their dormitory in 1916.

The Lyndon Aggie *was the School's publication which Arthur edited. This cover shows the principal barn and cow shed, to which the creamery was connected.*

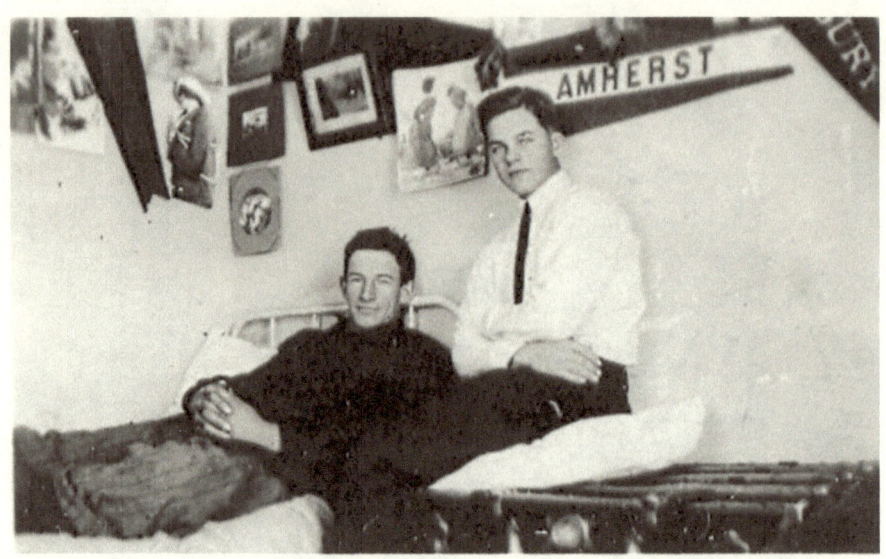

Arthur with his friend Lyman Morrill who was the Advertising Manager of The Aggie *in 1916. He became a Danville farmer and State Legislator.*

A sport which was even less organized was wrestling. This he seems to have done in his room.[305] There are several diary accounts of bouts. Of one, in April 1915, he wrote, 'had a wrestle up [in] Kirk's room, am getting slightly chewed up'. Nine months later, he recorded that he knocked out a friend who, on being thrown, hit his head on a table. There were other safer diversions. Going to church was among them.

His church going had social and intellectual dimensions as well as being a reflection of curiosity and a religious exercise. The social side can be seen in his attending the Baptist Church's candy pull (to which he went after he had visited the church), and in his presence at church suppers. Those may have been some of the 'Feeds' he recounts having had in Lyndonville village, a mile or so from his school. Lyndonville's churches also sponsored lectures. Seeing what was on offer and meeting new people was exciting to him and to those who sometimes went with him. But, there was religious curiosity as well. He wanted to know how others worshiped and what they believed.

He had been brought up a Congregationalist which in the Vermont of that day generally meant that Church congregations professed what their ministers believed.[306] That seldom meant reciting any creed or even conforming to a state-wide standard. In 1915, he visited the Lyndonville Congregationalists, Baptists, Christian Scientists, Roman Catholics (twice), and, in the next year, the Universalists. On the last occasion, he heard a sermon he liked – on love of your neighbor. At home, he went to the Congregational Church with his family but he was more skeptical than they. In early December 1915, he wrote:

> Went to church tonight, The preacher was a nutty old cuss   seemed like a dam street faker. Quite a few went up front in significance of their conversion. Carroll [their hired man] was one   the meeting   amused me immensely.

Two weeks later he wrote that he 'kidded hell out' of his more pious brother 'Karl, Aunt Alice etc, ... about the evanglist.' Sometimes Arthur also attended Sunday School if there was a young-people's class – or if he liked the teacher. In the end, my father seems to have preferred cool Pelagian moralism to the hot gospel of the Augustinians. Later in life, the deism and rituals of Freemasonry suited him well.

Arthur also went to town to mail letters, do errands, get sodas, have his hair cut, borrow books from the library, buy others, get a cigar or cigarettes, see athletic events and, in the winter, to watch the horses run races down the long straight main street into the town. Those races were famous and attracted horses from a large area. He was there in February 1916 to see Dr. Brown's horse break a record. About two weeks later, that horse was beaten, at a slower time, by a Newport nag. There was also skating in the town but, lacking skates, this was not for him. There were also lectures given in the town on topics like 'Hindus' and 'on [the] situation of Russian Peasant[s]', both of which he found 'very interesting'. Those were sponsored by the Women's Union Club, as was another he attended and judged 'not much good'. He did not even give its title. Most of all, he went to the movies. In 1915, there are at least three movies mentioned and nine in the partial diary for 1916. It is pleasant to note that, on 12 January 1916, he saw '"Birth of a nation" it was great. excellent music'. In his second year, he had a more or less steady girlfriend to take which may be why his movie attendance went up.

Lyndonville was a railroad town of perhaps 1,500, and had long had a theatrical and musical scene. In 1914-15, he saw at least five plays: 'Australian Merry makers', – after which 'Josh and I had a great time over the cigars and song'; 'David Garrett' was 'pretty good' in October. Two weeks later he saw 'her Second Husband'. In December, he went to 'the deep Purple' and in April 1915 to 'House of Lies'. All those were at the Music Hall or Opera House on Broad Street. At some point, he acted is a skit which survives only as a picture. His diary also mentions going to concerts, including one by the Tinkins Orchestra in October 1915. He even heard a bit of new music, jazz.

These dorm rooms resemble those at my college in the 1950s. They are replete with banners, pin-ups, pictures, and even a women's suffrage banner saying [in derision or approval?] 'We Want Our Rights'.

It looks as if Arthur was the 'M. C.' for this Phoney musical group.

Dances were also held at the Music Hall. He learned to dance, or dance better, in Lyndonville. In early 1915, he watched a dance at the Music Hall but by the end of February he had taken classes in the fox trot, the two step, and the waltz and, about a year later, went to dancing school in Barton with Ruby Wheeler, one of his girlfriends.

He spent some time reading. His taste ran to poetry, not novels, and to technical things, not light diversions. Among his poets were Alfred Noyes and Rudyard Kipling. He copied into his dairy part of Kipling's 'If you can keep your head...'; he was probably intending to memorize all or part of it as a party piece. In January 1915, he recited 'Gunga Dhin' at a social at Lyndon Institute where some of his girlfriends were enrolled in the teacher-training program. Later, he gave there renditions of 'A Stiff Drink' [unidentified] and Kipling's 'My Rival'. Other poems he probably intended to speak were variant lyrics to George M. Cohan's 1904 song, 'Life's a Funny Proposition After All'. That he copied into his diary at the end of June 1915. It is a humorous poem on women's changing fashions. Another beginning 'Farewell to the land....', is verse either by, or inspired by, Sir Walter Scott. One too long, and perhaps too dramatic, to give in such a reading was on Drake and the defeat of the Armada. He mentions reading De Quincy's 'Joan of Arc' and 'Ariel'. Other bits of verse also caught his eye and were copied.

Matheson Hall, the girls' dormitory at Lyndon Institute.

He read weekly papers such as the *Orleans County Monitor* and periodicals, such as the [*Farmers?*] *Gazette, Life,* and *Rural New Yorker*.[307] He bought a copy of the *Vermont Register*, an annual statistical collection. The only biography mentioned is a book on Lincoln which he read in the winter of 1915. Among his other reading were bulletins from US Department of Agriculture (which he sent for), and a book on butter-making, and unassigned texts on bovine tuberculosis, bacteria, and bulls. He bought three other unnamed texts for $3.50. He purchased a pamphlet on Herefords. From the Lyndonville Library, he borrowed 'Builders Three'. I have taught a good many boys his age but few of them had this sort of range.

He had a lot of friends at the school who joined him in many of his outings and activities. Like the girls, they appear as often under nicknames as their own – names like 'Doughnut', 'Egg'[Tas J. Egelston], 'Sherif', 'Uncle' or 'Uncas' [Lyman Morrill], 'Pig'[Art Reed], 'Gramp' and 'Wilts'. Others are last names only – Clark [Leslie Clark], Minnott, Hooker, King, Hatch– and closer friends such as Art [Reed], Tom [Walter M. Thomson], Mark [?], Kirk [Hugh Kirkland], and Harley [Leland]. At the end of the school year in 1915, 'quite a few went to the station' to see him off. It was a goodbye to someone whom they had enjoyed being with in classes, in the dorm, at dances (see p.285), picnics, ball games, movies, even at churches. Some had been involved in his free-spirited activities which had piled up demerit points and nearly gotten him expelled.

He minded breaking rules less than most of them. By the time he turned nineteen, Arthur had taken up smoking. He enjoyed cigars and smoked cigarettes and a pipe filled with aromatic Prince Albert tobacco. There was a rule that men could not smoke outside their rooms. He flouted it and noted in his diary that 'Karl told me Merrill [the Principal] sent a letter home saying If I was caught smoking outside room he would send me home for good'. He seems also to have been one of those who prompted the powers who were to draft a rule that no one could be seen in 'the front part of the house without a shirt or wearing a bathrobe'. Doing so brought five demerit points. He was scolded for other things. He played pranks in the dorm and may have lost a room-mate as a consequence. There were said to be no hard feelings but there were apologies. He was probably the one who tried to send to Coventry a first-year lad who had been assigned the room Arthur thought he was to occupy. The boy was anonymously warned to stay out of the Common Room. My father was also 'spoken to' on Leap Year Day 1916 for 'playing with [the] milk carrier'. He explained this: 'Nearly took a corner off a cow going around a curve'. He also liked a tipple. On 12 February 1916, after a good day, he 'Finished up my "Rye" tonight after which I turned in'. Since he did it in his room, that too might have cost him demerits had it been known. He cut classes to do things he wanted to do. Just after school resumed in 1915, he went to Hardwick where he and some friends 'had a little beer party, three of us slept in a bed Went to bed about 3'. He got up at 8:00 a.m. and returned to Lyndonville. Train service (over now torn up tracks) was then good in Vermont. He had missed a day. Still, the school's discipline seems not too rigid.

There were no onerous parietal rules which prevented him and others from visiting the girls' dorm at the Institute. Indeed, he saw quite a bit of the girls – to socialize, play cards, and have sing-songs. He recorded a dance at the dorm after a concert given by the boys. The dance had no accompanying music [10/2/15]. Sometimes those parties got a bit rowdy. A girl put dirt on his face and then, later, wrote a letter of apology which he thought funny. On another occasion, he seems to have force-fed cake to a girl – who got angry with him. His comment in his diary was: '[One should worry?]'. The closeness of the students may have caused worries to the administrators because there were two outbreaks of scarlet fever while he was there. Luckily, they came just before scheduled breaks so the year was not much disrupted. The students just went home a bit early. Another medical matter reported in the diary is funny given the experience of most of us. The aggie boys were lined up for tetanus injections on 6 May 1915. Those shots were new; few of the boys had ever had an injection before. Some fainted; others went white. Arthur was later grateful because, during the summer, he stuck himself with a pitch fork while haying.

Throughout the year and a half covered by his diaries he had three particular girlfriends – Ruby, Spikey, and Dimples. Ruby Wheeler was a high school girl from Westmore who lived not far from the Emerson farm. She was the youngest of the three and became a woman he tried to marry – but that was still in the future. She appears first in March 1915 when he took her for a drive and to a sugar party where they had sugar on snow and pickles.[308] He then went home and talked 'politics' until 2:15 a.m. There are casual references to her during the rest of the year including what is probably a special mention of her in connection with a 'social' at the Emerson Farm on 26 November 1915 when he was home for Thanksgiving. Chairs were brought in to accommodate guests at a costume party. He went dressed in 'a long tailed coat and glasses'. When it was over, he drove Ruby home and got back to the farm at 2:00 a.m. They had taken their time. He was up by 6:00 a.m. to do chores. She reappeared at Christmas. He and his brother, Lee, trimmed the Westmore Church and set up its Christmas tree on the 23rd. On the 24th, he 'called off presents' – Santa did not always do it yet – and was in two songs. He sang them in his 'long-tailed coat'. Ruby would have been there. The next day, the family had their own tree after dinner. He received 'slippers moccasins shirt etc'. His brothers Karl and Lee then went to the river and got some spruce gum but late in the afternoon, he went to the store and bought some 'P. A.' [Prince Albert pipe tobacco] and a pound and a quarter of chocolates. He then drove around to pick up Ruby. They went back to the Emerson farm and played games. Later, there was a lunch or supper after which he presumably took her home. Again, he got to bed at 2:00 a.m. but missed chores the next day and slept until noon. He saw Ruby several times in January. He took her to a play in Lyndonville called 'Stop Thief' on the 22nd. They also talked on the phone. On 7 February, he skipped school to attend a Barton Academy show in which his siblings, Lee, Flora, and Dorothy, and Ruby all had parts. Karl came from Burlington for the event but refused to visit classes at the school. Arthur went and had 'a fine time

Another Farmer's Life: Arthur Frank Emerson (1896-1939)

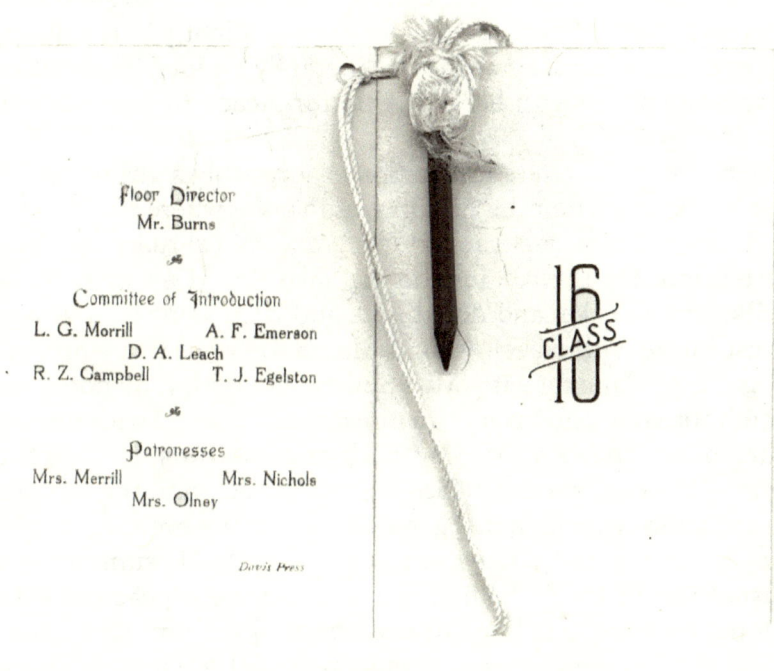

Floor Director
Mr. Burns

Committee of Introduction
L. G. Morrill   A. F. Emerson
D. A. Leach
R. Z. Campbell   T. J. Egelston

Patronesses
Mrs. Merrill   Mrs. Nichols
Mrs. Olney

Davis Press

SENIOR BALL
MUSIC HALL, LYNDONVILLE, VT.
FRIDAY EVENING, MAY 12

Dances
Grand March and Circle led by President
1. Waltz
2. Two Step — Florence Clements
3. Portland Fancy — X
4. One Step — Whitney
5. Waltz — Haughton
6. One Step — Giffin
7. Two Step — Little
8. Fox Troville — Peggy
9. One Step — Mrs. Olney
10. Schottische — X
    INTERMISSION
11. Waltz — X
12. Two Step — Peggy
13. One Step — Ayer
14. Fox Troville
15. One Step — Hunter
16. Waltz — X
17. Portland Fancy
18. Two Step — X
19. Waltz — Good Night — X

One of his surviving dance programs.

in French class and Latin'. He danced with Ruby at a Valentine's Day party on the 14th. After that Ruby figures but slightly in the diary. One guesses they had a tiff since they deliberately avoided one another. He did not even dance with her at the Barton Academy Junior Reception on 29 May 1916.

There are many references to Spikey, probably a girl named Hazel Gates [or Hoyt], whom he met in Lyndonville where she lived in the girls dorm and took the teachers' program. By February 1915, she had his attention. On the 13th, just before Valentines Day, he had a lunch of milk, cream, cake, and doughnuts and then went on a 'straw ride' to West Burke with Hazel. In mid-March, he went to a whist party, a play and then dancing with 'Miss Spikey'. On 6 May, he noted that he played horseshoes, and went to a musical and danced with her. He was in Barton for the Memorial Day celebrations of 1915. He watched the parade – 'Masons, band, boy Scouts, school, etc.' and then caught the train to Lyndonville for a ball game at 2:30. In the evening, he sat with Spikey whom he had walked to town and back. He summed it up in his usual way of saying he had had a good time – 'peach of a day'. In nid-June, they had a falling out and Hazel jilted him. He ignored her at a social to which she went with someone else. He peevishly wrote in his diary that he 'would not take such a dam kid as she is'. The next day he 'smoothed matters'; two days later they went to a dance but she could not dance because of a hurt foot. She must have limped through the Grand March but he danced with other girls. Later, 'she hated to see me say good by for it was our last night. Also other things which were rather personal' – so personal he did not enter them. Over the summer, she disappears but, by the autumn of 1915, he was going to card parties in the girls dorm where they played whist and 500. Spikey is probably the one who invited him to a candy pull at the girl's dorm on 4 December. After that she appears in the diary as the date of one of his friends.

His new girl was 'Dimples' whose real name may have been Peggie Smith but who, like Spikey, is also never given a full proper name so her identity is unclear. She comes into focus in January 1916 when he took her to see the 'Birth of a nation'. In early February, he would have taken her skating but had no skates; instead, they went sledding. By April, he was sending her new sugar-cakes made on the Emerson farm and began to spend more money on her. On Wednesday, 12 April, they probably skipped classes to go to a movie, then to a concert at the Opera House and on to Farrar's restaurant for a 'feed'. The next day he took her to hear someone play the piano, then for a walk, and to church. They saw each other at the Aggie School's sugar social on the 14th. By the 20th, she was miffed about something he said in *The Aggie* which had just appeared. He had to 'smooth things'– which he did. On the 21st they went into Lyndonville for ice cream. A week later, she was helping him get up his costume for a masquerade:

> I got cloths from Dimples for Masquerade this morn. Asked her for some corsetts she said didn't use them with middy blouses. I dressed like a girl   no one knew me   got a wig at 10¢ store and a sun bonnet. Had great time at dance. Came home before it was over.

On 12 May, he took Dimples to the Institute's Senior Ball and had a 'good time'. The next day they went to the movies and to dinner and the day after to church. On the 16th, they went again to the movies. Ten days later, when he had recovered from a sore foot, they heard the St. Johnsbury Glee Club and, the day following, attended a movie. All that looks like an account of a fellow in love with a girl who was more than interested. Perhaps she was but things may have been moving faster than Dimples wanted them to do. On 4 June, she told him she might not go to the graduation ball with him. 'There's a reason?', he asked; he recorded no answer. He only noted that he did not sleep well. He and Dimples walked out on the 5th – but with another couple. When they went fishing on the 7th, it was with another couple but they later went to a movie alone. There, his diary ended – presumably because of his disappointment in love. We get no diary account of the final events of the school year, of the Graduation Ball, of graduation, or anything else. Some of those activities can be filled in from other newspaper accounts and other sources.

Graduation festivities for the Vail School and Lyndon Institute began with sending out engraved or embossed invitations to its main events. On Wednesday, 14 June, the Graduation Ball was held at the Music Hall. The Hall was 'filled to its capacity'; more watched from the gallery. Arthur kept his programs from the graduation dances of 1915 but there is none from 1916. If he went with a girl, it cost him $1.00 but only $.75 if he went alone. On Thursday, the Alumni Banquet was held for the Institute; that of the Agricultural School came on the following day. Both had programs of toasts, speeches, music, recitations, even business reports. There were to have been two ball games but those were rained out. He was denied a last moment of athletic glory.

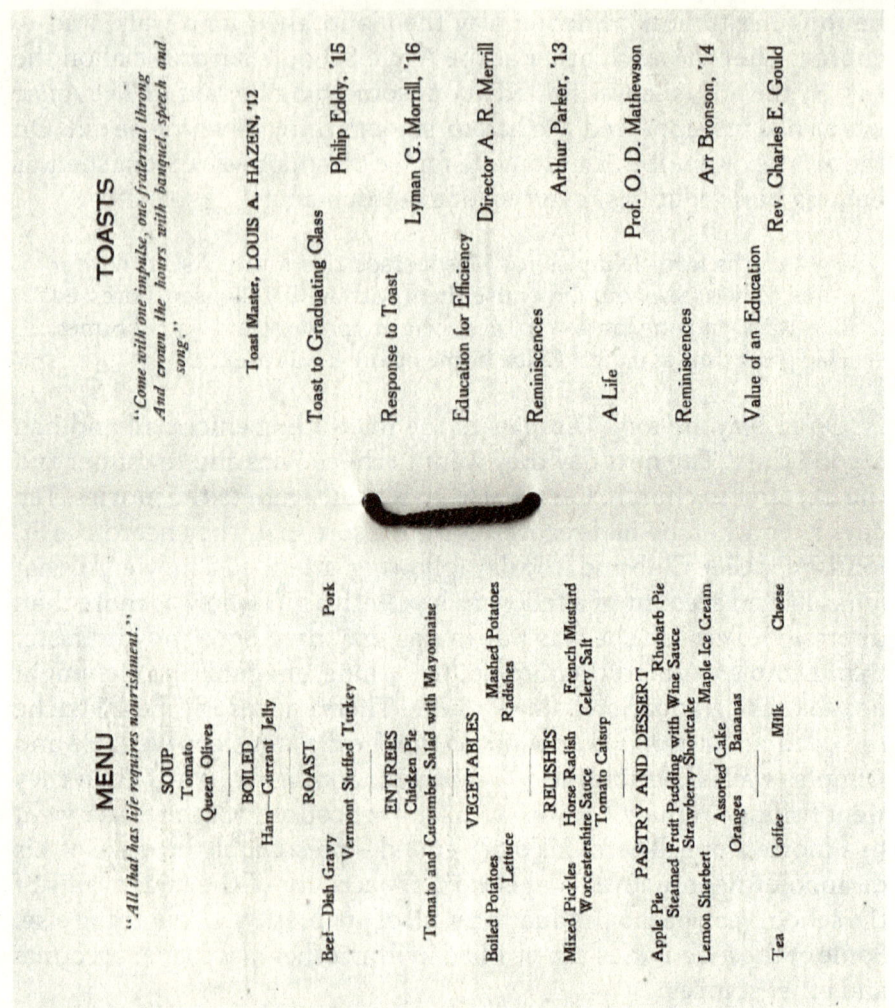

Menu and Toasts for the Alumni Banquet, Vail Agricultural School, 1916.

The Commencement Exercises were held in the evening of June 16 at the Music Hall. The very full program followed a pattern then common in Vermont high schools. There was an invocation, an address of welcome, and then, the reading of prize papers by the best students. In 1916 they heard about:

The Advantages of Rural Schools,
The Preparation of 'Bordeaux Mixture' [a fertilizer]
Vermont Names
The Treatment of Potatoes for Scab
Some Principles of Dress

and listened to the Girls Glee Club and two soloists. Three of Arthur's close friends spoke but not he. His contribution to the literary side of things had been Volume 5, No. 3 of *The Lyndon Aggie*, which had appeared under his editorship at the beginning of June and contained forty-seven advertisements in its twenty-five pages. Those had been secured from local and national companies located in Iowa, Massachusetts, New York, Ohio, and Vermont and from professional men. He and his friend, Lyman Morrill, had solicited most of those.

The address to the graduates, on 'Good Citizenship', was given by Loren P. Elliot. Then came two speeches not on the printed program.[309] Theodore N. Vail, the school's founder, introduced his friend, ex-President William Howard Taft, who talked about the need for education, the virtues of rural life, and liberty under law. While deploring lynchings, strikes, and socialism, he called for the equal application of the laws and their rigorous application to the 'trusts and the rich' – themes of his last Presidential campaign (see above p. 165) when he was defeated by Woodrow Wilson – really by Teddy Roosevelt who split the vote of the Republicans.

The *Vermont Union Journal*, which recounted all this on 21 June, also included his remark about 'the great necessity of women learning the science of good cookery'. The ex-President, said this was necessary to improve 'health standards'. It was also the remark of a man of such girth and weight that the Institute had had made a special chair for him to sit in. The paper went on, with a bit of a wink, 'Mr Taft closed his talk, which was that of a big man, who has come thru without the slightest trace of venom, the strenuous political life that as president of the United States and in the campaign of 1912 he must have lead, by urging all to go home and study our laws'. His friend Vail then praised the speech and introduced one more speaker, ex-Secretary of Agriculture, James Wilson. He spoke briefly – it was getting late – on Boys' and Girls' Clubs and the need to retain population in rural areas. Vail then gave another short speech to 'cheer you on your way, and try to say something you might carry away with you, something which might influence your future for the better, or aid you in your life work'. His message praised equality, said that possessions do not bring happiness, and that preparation for life's struggles and the pursuit of personal and larger goals requires knowledge and self control. Those bring happiness and 'rational contentment' to oneself and others.[310] The diplomas were then given out by the Principals of Lyndon Institute and the Vail Agricultural School. The evening closed with a benediction given by a local minister. This was a memorable time so it is sad that there are no diary entries for those days.

Arthur had from his years in Lyndonville an education as a modern farmer, good memories of a full life, and a copper watch fob which all the graduating boys seem to have bought.

Watch Fob purchased by men graduating in 1916 from The Vail Agricultural School.

2. Other Things in Arthur's Life

During his two years in Lyndonville, Arthur Emerson did much else which should be noticed because it helped to make him the man he became. Much of that relates to the farm and the community in which it was immersed and which, by the 1920s, he was helping to lead.

The Emerson farm in Barton was a fairly typical northern Vermont farm but it was larger than many. When it was properly surveyed in 1978, it turned out to be somewhat over 600 acres counting the section of scrub pasture land which had been given to the Town in 1952 as the Governor Lee E. Emerson Memorial Town Forest. The farm might have had seventy acres of arable land but most of it was pasture, sugar bush, and land which was logged or on which pulp wood was cut. Some of its acres were not good for much, but, taken as a whole, it yielded a good living to the family.

The farm house, as we have seen (see p.43), came in sections. Initially it had been only what Arthur knew as the kitchen, pantry, the back or summer kitchen, and a store room. Over all that, there was a bedroom and a loft which was never really finished off but in which one could sleep. To that, Arthur's Grandfather, Benjamin, had made additions. Beyond the ground floor kitchen were a living room, off which was a bedroom on the north side and a parlor in the front which faced east. Over those was a second story with three or four bedrooms connected to the loft. Later a large porch was added to the front. There was eventually a bathroom and flush toilet on the ground floor but that came later. From 1914 into the 1940s, there was a back-house reached by a corridor behind the sheds which would have been a cold walk on a winter night. There was no heat upstairs save for what went up through open registers. When Arthur came home late, he often just slept in front of the stove in the living room rather than in his icy loft bedroom.

Near the house were about twenty-five apple trees of various kinds – Transparents, Spies, and Macintoshes - which matured at different times. There were berry bushes with raspberries, gooseberries and currants. Blackberries or brambles the family picked in the fields and forest. There was also a large garden with all the usual things. They grew corn and potatoes in separate patches. In 1915, they were growing oats, corn, and hay in the fields. The last would have included some planted alfalfa and clover. There was also some millet that year but that was probably plowed under as a green fertilizer crop. In 1915, they raised about 400 bushels of oats. The oats were threshed by itinerant threshers as the other grains would also have been. Oats went mostly to the horses but some oats and other grains, and some dried shucked corn, were ground for the family at one of the two Barton grist mills. In the late 1930s, they had a patch of buckwheat; earlier the family had grown wheat for itself. They had all the usual farm machines which my father learned to maintain while he was at Lyndonville. Most of them were drawn by the horses in 1915, but, by 1939, the farm had a big truck, a pickup, and one tractor. In 1915, it had gas-run saw-rig; in 1938 or 1939, Arthur bought a small saw mill which he had not set up by the time he died. The Emersons usually had a hired man. He helped with everything but especially the milking.

This was a dairy farm which produced milk and cream. The Emersons milked by hand about twenty cows and had spaces in the barn to tie up more which were freshening, drying-off, or waiting to be slaughtered or sold. They also kept a bull.[311] Their milk went to a creamery in Barton which, by the 1920s, shipped whole milk south to the cities of southern New England. The family drank some milk and made its own butter. Like most farmers, they fed skim milk and butter milk to the calves and pigs, which also ate the family's garbage. In Barton, there was later a casein factory next to the creamery which turned some skim milk into a material used to make buttons but that may not have been there in 1915.

Dan and Daisy hitched to pull logs or draw a machine. Arthur seems to be standing on the whiffle-tree.

In 1915, the farm had three horses – Dan, Daisy, and Jenny. All the permanent animals had names including some favored cows. The horses were kept in a horse barn attached to the big barn. The other stock included some sheep, which were sheared in the summer by someone who came to do it. Some of those were eaten or sold as were the pigs. The last were sold or butchered in the fall and parts of them were smoked. Somewhere around the place, there was a smokehouse in which, very likely, the cobs of the shucked corn were burned for their smoke. Some cattle were sold as were the hides of any animals which died on the farm. A calf skin in 1915 was worth $1.25.

Sugaring came at the end of winter when mud clogged all the roads and things tended to be a bit slow. The schools, including the Vail Agricultural School, then shut down for about a month. Arthur did not miss sugaring in 1915 or 1916. The farm produced a lot of maple sugar and increasing amounts of syrup. Syrup could now be preserved in metal cans and shipped. Their poorest sugar was sold, even in the 1930s, to chewing tobacco companies as flavoring; the better sugar went to candy producers in St. Johnsbury. In 1915, the farm made about 600 pounds of sugar and an unspecified number of gallons of syrup. Nineteen fifteen was a good year; indeed, that year they ran out of cans. Like most farmers, the Emersons were more or less self-sufficient in sugar for ordinary uses including cooking. Sugaring was a lot of work but it came at an otherwise slack time and was enjoyed. In the end, there were sugaring-off parties and sugar socials where everyone ate all the could of sugar on snow, stirred sugar, sugar cakes, and the things which often went with those – potato salad, pickles, raised doughnuts, eggs boiled in the evaporating pan – all washed down with coffee. My father, like many others, drank sap and warm syrup. Sugar and syrup gave them much of their cash income. None of them became diabetics but their teeth were not good.

The sugar label used by Frank A. Emerson (c. 1922). The maple goods included syrup of various grades, sugar and sugar cakes. The advertisement is superimposed on the State's seal including its motto 'Freedom and Unity'.

My Vermonters: The Northeast Kingdom 1800-1940

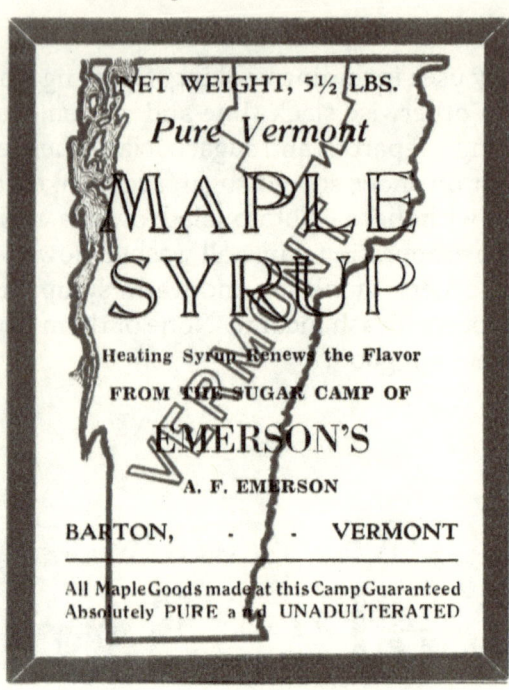

Arthur's sugar labels from 1938 and 1934. The later one advertises a half-gallon can and shows Orleans County; the older one refers to creamy sugar, which was not hard but soft.

Another source of cash was the wood which the farm produced. The logs were bought by mills in Barton and Orleans. Very good wood went to the veneer plant in Orleans. Bark, taken from cut trees, was sold to tanners. Some wood was kept or sold as firewood to others. Pulp wood was harvested but is not noticed in his diaries.

Later, vacationers at Willoughby Lake were be another source of money for my father. He sold them milk and cream, wood, and ice. The last was cut from the Lake and packed in sawdust until it was needed for cold cupboards and ice boxes. He understandably became a member of the Willoughby Lake Boosters which promoted tourism and vacations in the town.

Arthur Emerson worked at all that for years. He was up early to do 'chorse' – as he usually spelled it. He mucked out the stables, fed and watered the animals, milked usually four to eight cows – the hired man milked the rest – and did the same things all over again in the evening. He logged, skidded, and carted logs to Barton (usually five or six big ones at a time), and took loads of bark to the railway stations in Barton or Orleans. He sawed and split wood. He planted, cultivated, hayed, harvested, and looked after animals. He was the one who 'wormed the horse', doctored the colicky mare, assisted at the birth of a calf, helped the vet to 'alter' the male cattle and 'punched' (with his jack knife and later a proper cow punch) the cows who had bloat.[312] There was nothing done on the farm which he could not do and some things which only he could do. When they bought a Ford car in c. 1918, he was the one to repair the car's inner tubes, fix its ignition, and tinker with it when it did not run well. Being a farmer was being a jack of all trades and required some knowledge of increasingly complex mechanics – which he had acquired at the Vail School.

It was not all slog on the farm. He had a snowball fight with Karl on Christmas eve 1915 and broke a window in the kitchen door to the house. This seems not to have caused a ruckus. On 6 November 1915, he went hunting with a revolver but got nothing. Later, when he was home for Thanksgiving, he went hunting with friends and shot a doe on the backside of Mt. Hor, one of the hills flanking Willoughby Lake. It took the boys over two hours to haul it to a road but presumably it was worth it. Five days later, he went out again and shot a rabbit. He also took the muzzle loader which he tried to use. That suggests he had some experience with black powder and was foolish enough to take a chance with an old weapon. A month later, he killed a fox caught in someone's trap. The boys hung it on a tree for the trapper. He then did some target practice. He later bought a .32 caliber revolver either for himself to use or to raffle-off to raise money for his class. In the spring, he went gathering flowers in the woods for his Aunt Alice and, on a hot day in August, he went swimming in the Willoughby River with Karl. They then climbed Mt. Pisgah, the other high hill flanking Willoughby Lake. There was often time to fish but few catches are noted. He went to church and to more secular celebrations. When there was a sports day in Evansville, a village about five miles away: 'Lee and I win in most all sports'. Arthur and someone else won the three-legged race but no one could climb the greased pole. Not long after that, he went to a 'weding'. All this sound rather masculine but on 19 March 1916 he recorded that, while the family was at the Sunday church service, 'I got dinner'– which probably means he heated and then put out their usual baked beans and brown bread. His pious family did not yet cook on Sundays.

Top House. Mount Mouselauke is now known for its skiing but then it was for hikers and those who braved the rough road up in carriages to see the view.

Among the things one might not expect him to do is notice much in the natural world but he did. He liked moonlight and starry nights and more than once remarked there was 'a peach of a moon', or that it was 'A peach of a night'. For both 1915 and 1916, his diary notes hearing the first 'frogs sing'. He showed Dimples egg masses and hatching fish. In early May he found new-born muskrats and partridge nests and noticed the sand deposits high on hills around Westmore. He watched the northern lights in the summer of 1915 and saw an unexpected flight of wild ducks in January 1916. When he took a trip through central Vermont to Randolph, in May 1916, he was entranced by the beautiful scenery. On a spring trip to Newbury, to visit his brother Karl in 1915, he enjoyed fishing and climbing Mt. Moosilaukie, across the Connecticut River in New Hampshire. He took pictures of the mountain and streams on that trip with his new camera; so too did Karl. One of them bought a picture post card of the House at the top of the mountain, illustrated on the previous page. They also went to the Baccalaureate service in the school of which Karl was Principal. That was not the only trip he made to see his brother who seemed as eager to do those things as he.

At some point Arthur or his father acquired this Grange Badge which would have been worn at meeting outside Barton to identify his Grange.

By the time Arthur Emerson graduated at Lyndonville, he had done other things which were significant for his later life. He applied to join the Grange on 18 February 1916 and was initiated a month later. This was the formal beginning of an interest in, and public involvement with, farming matters which would culminate in the position with the Farm Relief and Rehabilitation Agency [FRRA] that he held at the time of his death. He would be a farmer but he would improve the lot of others and have some fun while he did so. Another was a trip to a church conference, the un-punctuated account of which has been transcribed here because it gives a fine glimpse of what interested a serious young farmer in 1916. It also contains his only reference to the War in Europe.

The Trip to the Convention [of young Congregationalists]

4:30 Jan. 13 Thur. 11 [a. m.]

3 classes this morning. Did chorse at Whipples [the man for whom he was then working]. He came last night didn't help. Cut dairying [class] got ready to leave for convention   Went down stayed with Karl over night. Surprised him as he didn't know I was coming. Mrs Irish got me supper. Nearly forgot my credential card had to run over to center and get it.

7. Jan. 14 Fri. 12.30

Breakfast met contractor who is putting in dam at Newbury he and his wife. Went to morning exercises at school saw Miss Hale. After exercises got my bag at the house went down to station. Karl came down to see Lee. All felows going to Conference were on train. Rawson Calkins, Wane French [Westmore neighbors], were on. On arriving at Bellows Falls we were given a warm drink at drug store and taken up to Vermont Farm Machine Works by Board of Trade. The shops were making munitions of war. There were 2 foreign inspectors there inspecting the goods. Saw Bob Thayer's brother there. Got into Rutland 5.30 that afternoon. We went to Congregational church registered, paid over 50¢ and got our assignments. I was going to room with Ned Carter. Lee exchanged cards with him and we roomed together. (Mrs. Wilkins 51 Kingsley Ave.) was a pretty good place. Evening went to Banquette, Shrine Theatre. All fellows from this way sat at same table. Yells and songs were given   ochrestra played. Ray Collins was toast Master, fairly good. Had lot of other interesting speakers, [Vermont] Gov. [Charles] Gates, [?] Benton etc.   Saw quite a few fellows from Hardwick.

7.30 Jan 15 Sat 12.

Meeting at church in morning   following men spoke: 'The Real object of scouting' - Franklin Mathews. 'Educating Farm Boys'- Jared Van Wagenen I considered this the best talk.[313] 'Physical Efficiency and Success in Life'- George Ja. Fisher M.D. After last talk we had conference picture taken, then went down to church. Afternoon had short service and the group conferences. At 3.30 the recreation went to House of Correction a very interesting place. The men were working marble. The building had cells, hospital, chapel, dining hall etc.   7.30 another meeting and a recital by Edward A. Mead. (The Passing of the Third Floor Back). Went down street after service.

9. Jan 16 Sun. 2.

Attended Congo church with Mr and Mrs Wilkins and children   Lee and I. Roberts gave the talk   was good. Didn't stay to Sunday school, took a stroll around city. 3 oclock another meeting. Mr. Wilkins went up with us. 'My Forward Step' I left mine.[314] Strolled a bit after this service didn't stay to the last meeting left on the 8 oclock. Rode up with Gus Bundies and a fellow from Newport. Had a feed in Bellows Falls. I stopped off at Hanover, [New Hampshire] stayed in [Lewiston] station [in Norwich, Vt.] all night. Lunch I had (clam chowder) made me sick.

5. Jan 17 Mon.

Started up hill to Hanover with a fellow in station 6.30. Looked the place [Dartmouth College] over a bit and hunted up Kirk's cousin. He took me all over works. Went to chapel with him. Went thro Gym (Largest in World), over to Skie jump and toboggan slide, and in quite a number of the buildings. Dinner at Common's hall. Saw Harley Lelands brother, had short talk with him. Left Hanover [Norwich] on 2 oclock all fellows were on[315]. But Lee and Rawson. Rawson missed train. Train was 45 mins late at Lyndonville. Conductor skipped me coming up. I bought Wanes purchase in Rutland. Went to Bed early didn't feel well. Kirk's cousin was a funny cuss more so than Kirk.

Jan 18 Tues.

3 classes, cut chapel and first class not feeling extra good today. Wrote a letter home, Ruby, and Mrs Wilkins went over to the Ville and mailed them.

The trip had probably not done his soul much good but he had seen interesting things and people.

By the summer of 1916 the education of Arthur Emerson was complete. He had learned a lot of practical things and some useful theories. He had something of a sentimental education and, in his own mind, may have failed the final in that course. He had heard some music, even a bit of jazz, and had been to many plays and films. He now knew something about sects other than his own. He had tested himself outside the very small world in which he had hitherto lived and had learned to make his values and priorities the ones which mattered, not those of others or the school's. He was more independent when he left the Aggie School than when he had entered. He had not become 'cultured' but he was better read and more accomplished than most boys his age. His athletic prowess had developed; he knew he could pitch thirteen innings of good ball.³¹⁶ He had shown a lot of curiosity but satisfying it came not so much in 'chimistry' but in doing what he could in a small town with more institutions than it now possesses. How intensely social his life had been! All that would continue as would his somewhat reckless expenditure of energy.

3. Being a Farmer, Being Useful

He resumed keeping a diary in 1918. He had no classes to go to but everything else was much the same. He went to a lecture and concert in Barton in January and to a band concert a month later – both at the Barton 'opera house'. Those may have been part of a series of events because just a month later he attended a 'patriotic meeting' at the same place. He 'took the Freeman's oath', a qualification for voting in Vermont. On 20 February, he went to Burlington to 'Kake Walk' at the University of Vermont where Karl had been enrolled. That was the University's annual winter festival built around a minstrel show. He took the train to Wells River and then crossed the State to Burlington. There he stayed at the Sigma Nu House, Karl's fraternity (and later Lee's at Syracuse). That evening, he went to Kake Walk which featured black-face acts and music. The next day he saw a movie, went to skate in the evening but found the rink closed because of a thaw and instead spent his time with Aunt Alice and his sister Flora, then a UVM student. He returned to Barton the next day the way he had come but had time enough between trains in Wells River to see another movie. In April, he went to Lyman Morrill's wedding in Danville and saw a number of his Lyndonville friends. With one of them, he talked all night. On 30 April, he went to a Red Cross Social at Westmore where he recited 'Gunga Din' – but, 'some of the old hens didn't seem to like it'. He went to Grange meetings and, although there are no notes of Masonic meetings, he was also going to them too. He went for his Army physical on 15 August and was given a classification of 1A and told to report for duty on 9 October 1918. There is no indication that he served. Responsibilities on the farm probably exempted him – and World War I ended in November.

Most of the 1918 diary, which he kept only half a year, is devoted to telling what he had done on the farm. Logging took up much of the winter and the care of the animals and 'chorse' were a daily necessity. All that continued for as long as he lived at the farm. He skidded logs, took them to the mills, trucked feed and shavings for bedding for the cows, and tapped 400 trees when sugaring came. His father tapped more. But it was not all work. Sometimes he drove to Barton, left his horse at the livery stable and took the train to basketball games in Newport and came back the same night, getting home very late. He went to Masonic meetings in Barton, played cards, and shot pool whenever he went to town and had the time. Ruby reappeared in his life. She seems to have been teaching somewhere in or around Newport from which she came home many weekends. He took her skating and saw her on most of the weekends she returned. They wrote or telephoned on the other weeks. Sometimes she also brought Dimples who seemed also to have been teaching in Newport. 'Rube' was now the one who interested him and to whom he wrote most of the weeks covered by the diary.

There were to be no more diaries and the rest of his young life can be filled in only by inferences from scattered documents and from the comments made by others. He fished, hunted ducks, snow-shoed on Willoughby Lake, attended Grange meetings, went to Church and, still, occasionally, to Sunday School. He went through the chairs at his Masonic Lodge, the Orleans Lodge in Barton, and was made Master in 1924. At some time, he had joined the Scottish Rite Masons [probably in St. Johnsbury] and was doing the same thing in their Lodge. By 1922, he was a 'Royal Prince of the Secret 32' [degree] in that Order. He was a member of the Keystone Chapter of the Royal Arch Masons in Barton, where, in 1926, he was Scribe. Eventually, he became its Master. He invested a lot of time is his Masonic activities and became a member of the Grand Lodge of Vermont.

His Masonic Penny inscribed on one side with his Mason's Mark and the other with a motto from the coin from which it was made.

He did other things which were more unusual. By 1930, Westmore had a fairly large summer population comprised of people whose incomes, despite the Depression, allowed them to maintain or rent summer homes on Willoughby Lake. My father supplied many of them with milk, ice, and fire wood. Among them was the artist, Paul Sample. The Samples were his customers for wood, milk, sugar and syrup. My father posed for Sample as did some of the other local people. Arthur

Order of Induction into Military Service of the United States.

THE PRESIDENT OF THE UNITED STATES,

To __Arthur Frank__ __Emerson__
      (Christian name.)   (Surname.)

Order Number __151__   Serial Number __20__

Greeting: *Having submitted yourself to a local board composed of your neighbors for the purpose of determining the place and time in which you can best serve the United States in the present emergency, you are hereby notified that you have now been selected for immediate military service.*

You will, therefore, report to the local board named below at __The Court House, Newport, Vermont__, at __2 P. M.__,
      (Place of reporting.)   (Hour of reporting.)
on the __9th__ *day of* __October__, 19__18__, *for military duty.*

From and after the day and hour just named you will be a soldier in the military service of the United States.

H B Cushman

Member of Local Board for __Orleans County, Vermont__

Report to Local Board for __ORLEANS COUNTY__

__Newport, Vermont__

Date __Sept 24, 1918__

FORM 1028. P.M.G.O. (See Sec. 157, S. S. R.)   3—5115

Induction Notice. There is nothing to show that this was appealed but he never served.

was almost certainly the model for the first man on the left in Sample's Thomas Hart Benton-like painting, 'Church Supper' (1933).[317] His sister Flora and his mother seem to be shaking hands, in the middle distance, on the left side of the picture.

In February 1923, his father died and his mother became the principal owner of the Emerson Farm in which his Aunt Alice still had a share. In any case, it was his in all but name. At some point, his mother deeded to him all or most of her share. Other obligations accumulated throughout the 1920s and early 1930s. He became a Selectman, a School and Village Trustee, Road Commissioner and the man who looked after the purity of the Barton Village water. He was involved with the care of the town's poor and was known as a progressive farmer. That reputation came partly through work in the Grange but also in the more politically radical Farm Bureau. He was one of the area farmers who established in Barton, in the mid-1930s, the New England Dairies Milk Cooperative [later the United Farmers Milk Cooperative]. By then, he had also taken up golf and belonged to the Barton Country Club and to the town's Improvement Club. He was probably Barton's most eligible bachelor. But, Ruby had gotten sick of waiting; she married someone else. My mother said his mother did not approve of her and had spoiled that match as she did others. After Ruby's marriage, he deeded the farm back to his mother and told her he would marry whom he pleased.

4. Courting and Being Married (1931-1939)

My parents must have courted for a bit more than a year beginning in late 1930 or early 1931. They danced, went fishing (my mother never liked to fish), took rides, went to the movies and to other entertainments in the area. She once told me that they had nice moon-lit rides along Willoughby Lake which was more of an adventure then because the road between the rock-face and the Lake was narrow and falling rocks more common then than now. They had what my father would have called 'feeds' at places like Shonyos in Lyndonville to which I remember once being taken. This was a restaurant run by a French family related to my great-grandmother Sanders. They probably did other things but my mother was reticent about talking of their courting days because they brought back memories with which she had a hard time dealing.

My parents married on 8 November 1932 but had no Church wedding. They drove 'down the line', to Newbury, where they were married by a minister whom they both liked and respected. Arthur probably met him when his brother Karl worked in Newbury. He had preached at a service before my father's graduation from Agricultural School and was known as a good speaker – always a recommendation to Arthur. Less than seven years later he would participate in my father's funeral. I think the witnesses were people whom the minister found. I do not know where they went for their very short honeymoon. When they returned, their marriage was announced by Mom's parents on a nicely engraved card and in a note sent to the local papers. There was a reception held by Lee's wife, Dorcus, to which many came bearing gifts. Somewhere among my mother's effects is a stack of cards, neatly tied with a green ribbon, which came on the presents which included pitchers, an 'hilarity set' (a glass pitcher and party glasses), a waffle iron, a cheese sandwich toaster, glasses, ashtrays, knicknacks, table cloths, and much more. Jane Willis, the wife of a local car dealer and a local 'character', wrote a humourous skit which was performed. My mother moved to the farm and life began over again.

To minimize the strains, my father had refurbished the hired man's house and added a porch to it but not enough insulation. His mother and his brother Russell were to live there. The place was big enough for them but too close to the main house for any of them to be really comfortable with the arrangements. My grandmother Emerson did not like to see changes made to *her* house; my mother did not want an interfering mother-in-law. The arrangement did not work and that quickly became apparent. Mrs. Emerson criticized and carped; my mother occasionally snapped back. Things were tense. Mom also missed having an income of her own. My father would buy her anything she wanted but he did not put her on an allowance or willingly hand over money on a regular basis. One reason for that was that she has some money which had come from the life insurance of her first husband who had died in 1926. Arthur thought she could spend some of that. His own cash was going into the improvement of the farm. At some point, they had a major row over whether or not my mother would invest in the farm. My father wanted to build them a new house. Mom was willing to have him do that but she would help fund it only if she had joint ownership. That, he, or his family, were not prepared to give her. It may have been legally difficult for him to do that because of the way in which the property was held – now by his Aunt Alice, his mother, him, and his three siblings. It was a sore point for as long as he lived. Still, things did not go too badly for a year or so. About a year after her marriage, my mother was pregnant; that helped smooth things over.

Another Farmer's Life: Arthur Frank Emerson (1896-1939)

Courting Couple, c. 1931.

Anxious new father, 1934.

I was born on Monday 26 March 1934 in the Cottage Hospital in Barton – more cottage than hospital. It probably had five or six rooms for patients who were mostly women having babies. I weighed in at seven and a half pounds, was 21 inches long, and, of course, was a welcome and beautiful baby – and probably the first Emerson not born in a family home. There had been the usual shower; more presents came after I arrived, including a dollar from Aunt Zade to start my bank account. I was later told that the year after I was born was a very good year in their marriage. It did not last.

By 1936, my mother had taken enough of her mother-in-law and wanted out. Caught in the middle, my father agreed to a new arrangement. She used her own money to buy a small house in the village in which she could again do hair-dressing as she had done before they married. He would spend some of his time there (he had a room), and he would permanently move to the town when his mother died. The plan was for them to buy a house on the edge of town which they both liked. It was owned by an old lady, who, like his mother, they believed, would not last long. My mother bought her temporary house and began setting hair in it. The move must have been hard on both of them.

What made this arrangement feasible at all was the fact that by 1936 my father had begun to work for the Farm Relief and Rehabilitation Agency which had an office in Barton. This New Deal agency loaned money to failing farmers to get them back on their feet and to minimize the dislocations in rural areas which the Great Depression had brought. He ran the local office and from it covered a large part of the northeastern part of the State.[318] In some ways, he was a natural for the job because of his popularity, education, and active involvement in farm organizations in the town and state-wide.

Sometime in 1937 or 1938, he became the State's Chief Debt Adjustor, in effect, the agency's principal loan officer for Vermont and a figure in the New England area. He made trips to Boston, Springfield, and New York City, more frequent ones to Montpelier, Burlington, Rutland, Bellows Falls, and Brattleboro. Dealing with poor farmers entailed a lot of driving and long hours on back roads. In his Barton office, he had a secretary, Mary Crowley, who looked after things but much of his work was done out of town. It may have been during this time that he became a Notary Public. I have no idea what he was paid for his work but it was likely to have been a good salary. He continued to look after the Emerson farm which was in the day to day care of his hired man and his mother, again the legal owner of most of it.

My parent's separation would have been hard for my father but the toll it took on my mother was not only emotional. While her schedule was of her own making and she worked at home, which kept her independent, she now had to look after a baby and a house, and do her hair-dressing as well. Among the other things she did was to make all my clothes on a sewing machine my father bought for her in 1937. Until I was about eight, I had few store-bought items save for shoes and things which others gave me.

Portrait photograph by Max Derrick, 1937/38. This was probably done when my father was promoted from a District to a State position in the Federal Relief and Rehabilitation Agency.

Another Farmer's Life: Arthur Frank Emerson (1896-1939)

I have many memories of my father and perhaps held onto them because he was no longer there after 1939. My mother and I often went with him on his business trips around the county and sometimes further away. Sometimes, I went alone with him. I was a very small boy when he took me into a field where men were haying. He picked up from the ground a tiny new-born mouse. Still blind and very pink, it did not even look like a mouse. He told me what it was and that it would not live since its mother had very likely been killed by the mowing machine, and, in any case, its nest was gone. He then tossed it back on the ground. It may have been that day that we peed in a stable gutter and, looking over at him I was astonished at the size of his penis – so unlike my own little 'whach-ya-call-it'. Another Emerson farm memory was seeing sheep being sheared and their fleece later being taken into the cellar of the farm's little house where bags of fleece were dripping lanolin into pans. He told me it was good for hands and to smell it. I rubbed some on and had a whiff. Those memories come from 1937 or 1938.

When we all went on outings, my mother would generally pack a lunch or take something to eat. I have a distinct memory of being taken off on a cold day in the winter of 1938 to visit some poor family. My mother had put a bag of cookies in the car. My father's visit turned out to be a bit longer than anticipated so she and I went into the house and sat in the kitchen to get warm. It smelled of poverty – too many snotty-nosed kids, wet wash hanging behind the stove to dry, and the smell of cooped-up people. It was a smell I would encounter later when I played with my friend 'Mutt' Gleason and peddled papers in Barton. Those farm kids needed my cookies and I was forced to share them, even to offer them. In the summer, we had picnic lunches by the roadside or at nice spots which my father had found. We ate sandwiches, a hard-boiled egg, and something sweet – cake or a piece of pie – and drank thermos-coffee which had evaporated milk in it. I liked those times and, after he died, noted many places where we had picnicked – at some we probably had. On longer trips, we went to restaurants. One trip was memorable because it included my first movie. We had gone to Barre or Montpelier, in 1938, and stopped in one or the other place to see a double bill, 'The Cowboy and the Lady' and a Charlie McCarthy film. I thought both were just great. I tried to do a Mortimer Snerd accent for days afterwards. Years later, I watched the 'Cowboy and the Lady' and wondered why it had ever been made. When I went for trips with my parents, we sometimes stayed overnight. I saw my first swimming pool in Rutland next to some cabins where we stayed. The lifeguard had white stuff on his nose – probably zinc oxide then used as sun-screen. Another 1938 trip was to Burlington. I remember visiting Aunt Alice whom we found sitting by a lamp reading a book. She gave me cookies and milk. I was taken to see the Ethan Allen Tower in Burlington and to Fort Ethan Allen, the Army Base. I saw my first airplane there. Sometimes my parents did not need a trip to prompt them to eat out. When that happened, we generally went to Mrs. Sawyer's in Barton who would cook a meal if given warning. Her food was good; later she sold baked beans, brown and white bread, cakes and cookies and would cook things to order. Mom often ordered things from her.

Another memory which was also probably from 1938 is of my parents hugging in the living room as my father was about to leave on a trip. I was beside myself with rage and tried to part them. My Mom was mine as I tried to make clear. It amused them. Usually when he went away, he would say with great seriousness as he stood in the door. 'Now Roger, I am going away so you have to be the man of the house while I am gone. You look after things and take good care of your mother'. I took all that very seriously.

Christmas, too, produced memories. In 1937, I got a tricycle. My trike was down cellar by the chimney clean-out which the jolly fat man was said to have come out of. I couldn't figure out how that was possible – Santa seemed to be the size of Mike Hanson, a very fat cattle dealer in the village who played Santa at children's parties. In 1938, I got a nice sled – a Fleetwood Flexible Flyer – which could take two people. My father rode on it at least once with me and then drew me up the hill afterwards. That summer, he gave me a 'station wagon', a cart with a handle. It was a sturdy steel thing painted brown with cream trim and called a 'Skyway'. Despite hard usage, it lasted most of my childhood .

It was probably in the summer of 1938 that I had two experiences with my father which were not so nice. One occurred in the summer after men had been cutting brush behind the school gym which stood next to my mother's house. They had left their cuttings which looked to me as if they would make good whips. I got a couple of those and, with one in each hand, I went across the street to the school playground and whipped all the children there. My father saw this and walked with his usual deliberation up the hill and took them and whipped me home. He kept saying 'How does it feel. You will not do this again'. I was hit hard enough to raise welts on my legs. My mother was very upset at my beating but my father, unrepentant, thought it was a lesson I needed.

The other experience was going swimming with him and being thrown in the water and told to swim. I got water up my nose and would not go near any lake for a couple of years.

My father took me to the Orleans County Fair in 1938. A friend and business associate, Lou Tilton, was in town and they decided to take the afternoon off and go to the Barton Fair. We parked in the infield and walked up to the Midway past the gypsies trading horses and cars. I am sure I got to ride on the merry-go-round but I have no memory of that. I do remember Floral Hall and the Midway. They were filled with booths exhibiting and selling one thing or another or offering games to be played for prizes. One on the Midway featured a Black man in a baseball mask: 'Hit the Nigger and get a cigar; hit him twice and pick your own prize!' It was a catchy pitch which stuck with me. Lou thought my father should have a go at this since he was a pitcher with good command of the ball. He refused but went on to a booth where he could throw at bottle-like things on a stand. He came home that day with two blankets, a tray, a braided leather whip, candy and some little things for me which did not last long and a small black pipe which did. The other Black at the Fair in those days was the woman standing at the entrance to the women's toilet handing out toilet paper to those going in. Around her neck was a sign which said 'Tips are my Pay'. I have no recollection of seeing her in 1938, but, when my mother took me to the fair in a year or so, there she was.

Another of my father's friends, a Mr. Marvin, invited us to spend some time with him and his family at their cottage on Caspian Lake in 1938. My mother bought herself a swim suit and slacks and we all went off. It did not work out too well. After a couple days, my mother decided she had stayed long enough and drove home with me. My father stayed a day or so more to fish and swim. I think Mom did not like the other women, did not like camping, and did not like the bugs.

Sometimes, after supper, when my father was in Barton, he would take me to Glover (three miles away) to see the animals in a small zoo there. It was maintained by the man who sold gas. Resident was a chained bear in a cage, to which one could gently toss a bottle of pop, but small boys should not try to touch the bear. We gave it pop. Behind that cage was a rank of cages on two tiers with raccoons, foxes, mink, bob cats, some birds, and I don't know what else. I liked to go there and did not see it as the cruel captivity it was because the animals were kept in quite small cages.

My father was a fisherman who fished the local lakes and often took out to them people who could not otherwise have gotten there. One such person was Mike Reynolds, the town 'morphadite'. Mike was a person of uncertain age and sex who lived somehow without really keeping a steady job. He would work the Fair as what today would be called 'a security guard'. And, he was always on hand to help out where there was free food to eat or casual labor to be done. Later, he lived rent free in the Barton Chamber of Commerce building in exchange for taking care of it. He was something of a character but probably not overly bright since, about 1941, he once tried to pick me up by my ears. My mother lost no time in twisting one of his and putting a flea in it. My father would drive Mike and me and out to places like the 'Old Auger Hole' where they fished. Sometimes, he took 'Old George Humphrey', a one-time farmer and partial cripple who served as the town's Constable. When I misbehaved, my dad would look serious and threaten to send me to 'Old George Humphrey who knows how to deal with bad actors'. I was scared of Mr. Humphrey. My father and he would stand there with their poles in the water while I ran around on the bank. They never seemed to catch much and mostly just talked about things in which I had no interest.

There was always a fishing rod in my father's car. He would drive along and decide to take little break by a stream which looked inviting. I remember once when he, my mother, and I were out and he felt the urge to fish. I was delighted to go down to the stream with him. We crossed a hot dry field of uncut hay which was going or had gone to seed. I excitedly ran through it to the brook. He fished for a while, caught a trout and told me to take back to my mother in the car. It was the last thing in the world I wanted to do. He told me I must or he 'would tend to me later'. I ran back crying with the smelly thing struggling in my hand. I never wanted to fish again and seldom have. Still, I am sure he was trying to be a good Dad.

With a farm to run and a government job to do, he still found time for other things. He went to Masonic meetings, was still a School Trustee or Select Man responsible for the Barton Purification and Filtration Plant and had time, in 1934 and 1937, to help plan and run the Barton Farmers' Day.[319] His touch in 1934 is not obvious but in 1937 it may have been starting the event off with a Western movie with plenty of gun-play. *Arizona Mahoney* (1936), starred Joe Cook and Robert Cumming. The bad guys, rustlers and stage robbers, were chased from Phoenix to Tucson. That was followed by serious talk and a good meal cooked by women instead of the local antique dealer, Earl Davis. The entertainment may seem corny in both years but the statements about farming were up-to-date and came from local innovators, like the man who built the potato barn in Greensboro.

Early in 1939, Arthur purchased a new car from the Ford dealer in Barton. I remember going there and smelling the smell of new cars for the first time. I met Melvin Willis, who was part-owner of the place and its salesman. He and my father had long been friends and were on a first name basis. My dad thought it funny to have me call his friends by their first names so I too became on a first name basis with Melvin – and Max Barrows, the School Superintendent, Lou Tilton, a functionary in the FRRA, Marion Redfield, the Barton Town Clerk, and others. My mother, mortified by this, had to break this habit after he died. He was amused by and had encouraged it.

There are lots of other things I remember from those years, such as going out with my father on Halloween with my jack-o-lantern to scare old Mr. Mossman and his unwed partner, Eva Baxter.[320] I have memories of wading in the water at the lakes, or of seeing honking geese flying over. There is only one other set which is important to relate. Those deal with my father's death in 1939 when I was just over five.

5. Arthur's Death and Funeral, 11- 14 June 1939

While my parents had not lived together for some time, they were not estranged in fundamental ways – or so my mother always insisted. His mother remained the principal but not their only problem. My parents' plan to reunite came to nothing because my father died before the two old ladies on whose deaths their plans depended.

On the day my father died, 11 June 1939, Mom had spent some of the day at his family's farm. Looking back on it, she may have hastened his death since she could not have been calm or left him to rest in peace, which is what he seems most to have needed. Not that he was one to rest. I had been taken up to see him a few days before and found that he was in bed but that he had walked to the toilet that morning although he had been told not to do so. He refused to be still. Having a cough and the need to spit, he spit bloody sputum into the pan of ashes under his bed. It must also have been hard for one who did not want to admit he was really very ill. His teen-age rheumatic fever had left him with a 'weak heart'. He had worked very hard that winter and the strain of running a farm and an office had done him in.

The 1938 autumn hurricane devastated his sugar bush. All that winter he had tried to get out as much wood as could be salvaged. He did not cut much or any of it himself but had a gang working through the week getting out timber and cutting pulp wood while he did his job for the FRRA. On the weekends and on a few other days, he skidded

SIXTH ANNUAL

Barton Farmers' Day

Thursday, January 25, 1934

MENU PROGRAM

COMMITTEE IN CHARGE

Wallace H. Gilpin	P. C. Brown
R. P. Webster	F. S. Whitcher
W. E. Hanson	P. D. Pierce
A. L. Loukes	C. S. Webster
Frank Sinon	Arthur Emerson
J. L. MacDermid	Fr. E. Marion
C. A. Nute	M. E. Willis

AFTERNOON PROGRAM

MEMORIAL AUDITORIUM

Orchestra Number.
Ballet Dancing and Comedy Skit.
Four-Minute Talks by:
    J. L. MacDermid, Orleans County Farm Bureau Agent.
    Fred C. Kinsey, President Orleans County Farm Bureau.
    R. A. Dutton, Irasburg, "The Farmer and the Legislature."
Dancing Tots; Impersonation Skit; Ballet Dancing
Barton-Orleans High School Agricultural students in original stunts.
Saxophone Solo, Miss Doris Webster.
Address, "The Future of Eastern Agriculture,"
                W. Arthur Simpson
Wheeler Boys in Novelty Stunts.
Stories by L. M. Kinsley.
P. R. Miller, "A 1934 Soils and Crops Program for Orleans County."
Vocal Solo, Wm. McLaughlin.
J. Joseph Fowler in Fifteen Minutes of Fun.
R. D. Aplin, Boston, Assistant Director of New England Milk Shed.
"Batiste," in costume and dialect readings.

Acknowledging Contributions for the Tables:

Potatoes	W. C. Leonard, Hawkins Bros., Labounty Bros.
Milk, Cream and Ice Cream	H. P. Hood and Sons
Rolls	C. H. & G. H. Cross Co., St. Johnsbury
Doughnuts	Ralph F. Hamblett, Newport
Cranberries	A. & P. Company
Butter	Swift & Co., through Comstocks
Coffee	At wholesale through C. A. Nute
Pickles	Through Mass's I. G. A. Store
Squash	Elliott Brothers
Cheese	Lyndonville Creamery Association
Pies	Barton Women

MENU

ROAST BEEF	BROWN GRAVY	CRANBERRIES
BAKED POTATOES		
SQUASH	PICKLES	ROLLS
	PIES	DOUGHNUTS
ICE CREAM	CHEESE	COFFEE

The Committee hereby acknowledges great assistance from E. W. Davis in preparing the dinner, N. R. Underwood in taking charge of the dining room, F. R. Adams in soliciting pies, and to a score of others not on the committee whose efforts make this dinner possible.

THROUGH N. E. UNDERWOOD:

State Mutual Fire Insurance Company, Rutland, Vt.
Merchants Mutual Casualty Co., Buffalo, N. Y.
American Fidelity Co., Montpelier, Vt.

THROUGH F. C. BROWN:

American Agricultural Chemical Co.
   Fertilizer, A. A. Quality
Dominion Lime Co., Ground Limestone
St. Albans Grain Co., Wirthmore Poultry and Dairy Feeds
Craver-Dickinson Seed Co., Timothy, Clover and all kinds of Field Seeds, Pop Corn—Poultry Feeds
Graylawn Farms, Inc.
Louse-Chase, Fly Killer and Kleen-i-cide
David Stott Flour Mills, Inc.
Columbus and Blue Ribbon Flour, are always satisfactory
Elmore Milling Co., Elmore Feeds, Millers and Distributors and Manufacturers of all good feeds
Sherwin Williams Paint Co.
   Paints, Varnishes and Lacquers
Bird & Sons, Inc.
   Bird's Roofs—the crowning glory of the home
Corn Products Sales Co.
Buffalo Corn Gluten Feed & Diamond Corn Gluten Feed
Ashcraft-Wilkinson Co., Helmet Brand Cottonseed Meal

MISCELLANEOUS:

International Salt Co.
   World's largest Salt producers, International Salt
H. P. Hood & Sons
George H. Soule Co., Maple Sugar Making Equipment
E. B. Dickenson, Representative, Newport, Vt.
First National Stores, Groceries
The Great Atlantic & Pacific Tea Co.

ACKNOWLEDGMENT

This day's activities and this program have been made possible through the co-operation and generosity of the following individuals and concerns outside Barton. The committee hereby gratefully acknowledges their help:

THROUGH R. P. WEBSTER:

Arthur R. Cone, Buffalo, N. Y., Field Seeds
Federal Mills, Inc., Lockport, N. Y.
   Flour and Table Cereals
Glenn Miles, Albany, Vt.
   Burgomaster Beer and Soft Drinks
E. W. Bailey & Co., Montpelier, Vt.
   Occident Flour and Pennant Feeds
Tidewater Oil Co., Tydol Gas—Veedol Motor Oil

THROUGH WEBSTER MOTORS:

Goodrich Tire & Rubber Co.
Goodrich Silvertown Tires & Tubes

THROUGH BARTON MOTOR CO.:

Firestone Tire & Rubber Co.
   Tires, Tubes, Batteries and Spark Plugs
Ford Motor Co., Fords
Goldberg's Auto Service
   Automotive Products, new and used parts
Standard Oil Co., Socony Products

THROUGH F. S. WHITCHER:

Joseph Breck & Sons Corp., Seeds and Hardware
Ralston Purina Co., Feed and Grain
Colonial Paint Co., Paints and Varnishes
Sargent, Osgood & Roundy, Farm Machinery
Dairy Association, Inc., Veterinary Remedies
Hunt, Helm and Ferris, Star Barn Equipment
Strong Hardware Co., Hardware of all kinds
Hagar Hardware Co., Hardware of all kinds

Barton Farmers' Day
Yearly the Last Thursday In January   1937
COMMITTEE

WALLACE H. GILPIN, Publisher	ARTHUR F. EMERSON, Farmer	GEO. E. MORSE, Milk Station Mgr.
FRED D. PIERCE, Druggist	C. A. NUTE, Merchant	W. E. HANSON, Cattle Dealer
C. S. WEBSTER, Banker	E. W. DAVIS, Furniture Dealer	L. P. COMSTOCK, Market
REV. E. MARION, Priest	R. P. WEBSTER, Feed, Chevrolets	ERNEST BLAIR, Milk Station Mgr.
J. L. MACDERMID, County Agent	F. S. WHITCHER, Farm Implements	H. M. SMITH, President Men's Club
FRED C. BROWN, Feed Dealer		

DEAR FARMER:

Plans are perfected for Barton's Annual Farmers' Day on Thursday, January 28, and this is your invitation, BUT we must have your registration card returned on or before Monday, the 25th. This must be done for two reasons. FIRST, no one will be admitted to the activities of the day without a badge and a badge is issued ONLY after registration is made. SECOND, we must know how many to prepare for. Our facilities are taxed to the utmost. In fact, the picture theatre will not hold as many as we invite and dinner facilities cannot be stretched beyond registration limits. Plans for dinner must be made on Monday night.

PLEASE CO-OPERATE.

The program will open at 10 o'clock with a Western feature movie entitled "Arizona Mahoney," and short comedies. Dinner will follow the movies and following dinner will come a fine program of instruction and entertainment. Dr. C. F. Dalton, executive head of the Vermont Department of Public Health, will be the chief speaker of the day and his topic will be "Farm and Public Health Problems." There will be other speakers including John Nicol-Mark, a humorist-entertainer from Boston, music, and other entertainment numbers.

Don't fail to register by Monday. Remember, no one will be admitted to the various activities of the day without a badge. You get a badge only after you register. And none will be issued after Monday.

The day is sponsored by the committee named on this letter head, and this invitation is extended for the committee by

> R. P. Webster, Invitation Chairman
> F. C. Brown, Secretary-Treasurer
> Wallace H. Gilpin, General Chairman
> Fred D. Pierce, Registration Chairman.

P. S.—If you want automobile storage apply to Webster Motors on arrival, if team accommodations, apply to F. S. Whitcher.

Barton Farmers' Day

Thursday, January 28, 1937

WHO'S WHO

MEMBERS OF GENERAL COMMITTEE
Sponsored by Barton Improvement Club
Dr. H. Monford Smith, President
Wallace H. Gilpin C. S. Webster Fred D. Pierce
Rev. E. Marion Fred C. Brown J. L. MacDermid
Ernest Blair C. A. Nute Arthur F. Emerson
E. W Davis F. S. Whitcher R. P. Webster
Geo. E. Morse L. P. Comstock W. E. Hanson

MEMBERS OF ORCHESTRA

L. C. Batchelder .... Flute
Philip Moulton .... Violin
Harold Domina .... Cornet
Mrs. Harold Domina .... Piano

MENU

ROAST BEEF
Donated through W. E. Hanson by Shonyo Bros., Lyndonville

POTATOES
Partial donation through W. E. Hanson by Lisle Bean, Glover

ROLLS
Donated by C. H. & Geo. H. Cross Co., St. Johnsbury

CHEESE
Donated by Lyndonville Creamery Association and New England Dairies

KRISPY CRACKERS
Donated through Comstock's Market by Loose-Wiles Biscuit Co.

BEETS
Partial donation by A. R. Wakeman, Barton

ICE CREAM
Donated by H. P. Hood and Sons

PIES
Donated through Woman's Alliance by Barton Women

COFFEE
Donated through Comstock's Market by French and Bean Co, St. Johnsbury

BUTTER
Donated by John P. Squire & Co., Boston

MILK, CREAM AND BUTTER
Donated by United Farmers' Co-operative Creamery

APPLES
Donated by C. A. Nute

DOUGHNUTS

PICKLES

DINNER COMMITTEE

Of Woman's Alliance of Barton M. E. Church

Mrs. Alice Rowen Mrs. Belle Urie
Mrs. Jayne Willis Mrs. Leah Rollins
Mrs. Mabelle Blake Mrs. Cora Jenness
Mrs. Angie Annis Mrs. Ruth Martin
Mrs. Carrie Scott Mrs Lettie Natole

Barton Farmers' Day 1934 (on previous pages) and 1937 (opposite, above and overleaf). The unsophisticated entertainment in 1934 and the film in 1937 may have been part of Arthur's contribution but this was a community effort involving local women, school girls (one of whom, Dorothy Reed, was a contortionist), the school superintendant, insurance men, and the local antique dealer.

PROGRAM

FORENOON

10 o'clock at Memorial Theatre, "Arizona Mahoney," and short subjects.

12 o'clock, Dinner in Memorial Building dining room.

AFTERNOON—1 o'clock. Memorial Auditorium

Introductions, announcements and acknowledgments.

FOUR-MINUTE MESSAGES BY:

J. L. MacDermid, Orleans County Farm Bureau Agent.
A. M. Hoyt, Manager Greensboro Bend Potato Warehouse.
W. A. Bailey, President of Orleans County Farm Bureau.
Enos Freehart, "Making Butter for the Local Market."
P. Don Clark, "A Farmer Looks at the 1937 Conservation Program."

Scotch Songs by Jock Chalmers of Essex Junction.

Goofus Dance in Spanish costume by Six Barton Girls and a Barton Young Man.

Dr. C. F. Dalton of Burlington, Executive Secretary of the Vermont State Board of Health, on "Farm and Public Health Problems."

Acrobatic Feats and Dance, Miss Dorothy Reed, Newport
John Nicol Mark of Boston, "Laugh and Forget the Milk Crisis."

The Barton Farmers' Day Committee hereby acknowledge assistance from the following to make this day's activities and program possible. To our guests we ask consideration for the products and services rendered by them.

THROUGH BARTON MOTOR CO.

Socony-Vacuum Oil Co. Mobiloil Gasoline and Oil.
Universal Credit Company, Automobile Financing.
Firestone Tire & Rubber Co., Albany, N. Y., Firestone Tires, Batteries and Accessories.
Ford Motor Co., Green Island Branch, Troy, N. Y., Ford V-8, Cars and Trucks.

THROUGH F. C. BROWN

American Agricultural Chemical Co., North Weymouth, Mass., Agrico and A. A. C. Fertilizer.
Hagar Hardware Company, Burlington, Vt., Wholesale Hardware and Paint. Bird's Roofs and Wallboards.
Sherwin Williams Company, Boston, Mass., S. W. P. Paints, Varnishes and Brushes.
St. Albans Grain Company, St. Albans, Vt., Wirthmore Poultry and Dairy Feeds.
Robert S. Wallace, Boston, Mass. Staley's Gluten.
Upson Company, Lockport, N. Y., Upson Board.
Graylawn Farms, Inc., Orleans, Vt., Insecticides.

THROUGH F. S. WHITCHER

The Star Line, Albany, N. Y., Barn Equipment.
International Harvester Co., Albany, N. Y., Farm Machinery.
Sargent, Osgood & Roundy, Randolph, Vt., Manufacturers of Farm Machinery and Milk Coolers.
Joseph Breck & Sons, Boston, Mass., Wholesale Seeds and Hardware.
Jackson Fence Co., Jackson, Mich., Fencing and Steel Goods.
Checkerboard Grain Co., Barton and Orleans, Dairy Feed Stores.
Mechling Brothers' Chemical Co., Camden, N. J., Spray Materials and Insecticides.
Colonial Paint Co., Brooklyn, N. Y., Colonial Paint.
Strong Hardware Co., Burlington, Vt., Wholesale Hardware and Louden Barn Equipment.
DeLaval Separator Co., New York City, Separators and Milkers.
John Deere Plow Co., Syracuse, N. Y., Farm Machinery of all kinds.
First National Stores, Grocers.
Dairy Association Co., Lyndonville, Vt., Kow Kare, Bag Balm, Grange Remedy.
S. D. Woodruff & Sons, Orange, Conn., Garden Seeds.

THROUGH R. P. WEBSTER

Arthur R. Cone, Buffalo, N. Y., Field Seeds (Arco brand).
E. W. Bailey & Co., Montpelier, Vt., Pennant Feeds and Occident Flour.
Tide Water Oil Co., U. S. A., Tydol Gas, Veedol and Tydol Oils.
Plastergon Wall Board Co., Buffalo, N. Y., Evenaire Insulating Board.
Flintkote Company, U. S. A., Roofing and Roofing Accessories.
The Great Atlantic & Pacific Tea Co., Groceries and Meats.
Old Deerfield Fertilizer Co., Mixed Fertilizer and Chemicals.
National Oil Products Co., U. S. A. Nopco XX Cod Liver Oil.
International Salt Co., Scranton, Pa., Salt that is Salt.
Ashcraft Wilkinson Co., Atlanta, Ga., Cow-Eta brand Cottonseed Meal.
Dominion Lime Co., Lime Ridge, Que., Agricultural Lime.
Webster Motors, Barton, Vt., Chevrolet Cars and Trucks.

MISCELLANEOUS

George H. Soule Co., St. Albans, Vt., Maple Sugar Making Equipment. E. B. Dickinson, Rep. Newport, Vt.
H. B. Cutler, Barton, Vt.

Another Farmer's Life: Arthur Frank Emerson (1896-1939)

One of the organizers, Mr Nute, had a store next to the creamery. It was popular with farmers who shopped there after delivering their milk. Mr. Nute is the man on the right end. I used to be allowed a macaroon from one of the bins on the left. Others held dried beans, peas and dried fruits.

logs and scaled them to estimate the number of board feet they would yield at the saw mill. He put in long Saturdays to insure that the mill would not cheat him on the prices it paid for his logs. His appointment book has a jotting suggesting that he was paid in excess of $890.24 for his wood with more than half of that (27,094 board feet) coming from the U.S. Bobbin Co. at South Barton which bought his rock maple. The rest – 17,663 board feet of mostly birch, bass and maple – went to mills in Barton.

His office job was also demanding. In the five months he worked in 1939, his appointment book, in which he recorded his mileage, shows that he had clocked 8,108 miles, roughly divided between trips to the larger Vermont towns – Burlington, Rutland, Brattleboro, Montpelier – and a lot of little towns in between. When he noted his hours of work, they tended to run to about eleven each day. Sometimes he worked all day in his office and then left Barton in the evening to drive eighty miles to Burlington for morning meetings. Usually, he left early in the morning to meet with farmers, bank officials, lawyers, or others in his Agency. Often he stayed away over night and came back by a different route, seeing people as he went. He needed the new Ford sedan he had bought in February. Busy as he was, he still found time to attend Farm Bureau meetings and probably some Masonic meetings too. All that work brought on his heart attacks.

He had been given warnings that he was not well and had taken a bit of time off during the winter and spring. In January, he recorded some 'sick days' and each month thereafter there were 'annual leave days', often taken after very busy times. Around 1 May, he had a 'bad spell' and did not work for a week. That was followed by another week of part-time work and then no work from 29 May until he died on 11 June. He died at the Emerson farm in the little room off the living-room. That meant my mother had to visit him in an unfriendly place which could not have helped either of them. His mother prayed a lot but did not encourage doctor's visits.

The eleventh of June must have been a tense day for my mother and her parents although I remember nothing about it until evening. Mom had his car and had driven up to the farm and stayed part of the day; she probably returned to the farm after supper. I was with my grandparents. In the early evening, as the radio news was finishing and I was about to go to bed, a neighbor came in with a message from the doctor. Art was worse and they should go up to the farm at once. Since there was no one to stay with me, I too was taken along.

Another Farmer's Life: Arthur Frank Emerson (1896-1939)

Gramp had a Model A Ford which I remember for its smell. It was always well-polished and smelled of simonize, but that over-lay a permanent aroma composed of the smell of gas, damp upholstery, and something more which I just thought all old Fords had. He got it out of the barn and parked it in the driveway while my grandmother dressed and bundled me against the rain and wind. It was not a nice night and my raincoat was at my home not theirs. My grandfather never drove at night and never drove very fast – indeed, he once told my mother never to exceed thirty miles an hour, a speed which he believed was unsafe. We putted along over the unpaved road for what seemed like a very long time – a time during which I was admonished to be quiet and good when we got there.

We drove into the yard, got out and went in. We were met in the kitchen by my grandmother Emerson and/or one of my aunts, I have forgotten which. She or they told us my father was very ill and that my mother and the doctor were with him. They probably told my grandparents that he was thought to be dying but I do not remember that. I sat with my Gramma Sanders by the kitchen door holding onto and being restrained and stroked by her. Gramp was by the stove, at the end of the kitchen table. The door into the living room was shut but I recall hearing people moving there. My father had been put in the small room off the living room so he would not have to negotiate the stairs. I do not know how long we waited but I remember it as being quite a while. I think I remember anxiously, asking questions about what was going on and not really getting much in the way of answers.

Eventually, there was a muffled sob and my mother burst into the kitchen crying and saying, 'Art's dead, Art's dead! What will we do? What will we do?' She clutched me and, sobbing, held me very tight, saying repeatedly 'Your Daddy's dead, Art's dead. What will we do?' I squirmed as I always did when held too tightly. I did not know what to make of all this and probably cried too, without really knowing why. The doctor came out and spoke to my grandparents. After a time, we all went away back down the hills to Barton. I think my mother came with us and that we stayed that night at my Grandparents' house but I am not sure.

The next day, arrangements for his burial began to be made. My mother was upset because her mother-in-law would not allow the undertaker to remove the body so that it could be properly embalmed. It lay in his death-room covered by a black tarpaulin. I was taken in to see him that day or the next and told by my mother to kiss him, indeed, more or less forced to do so. I did and learned that dead men are cold and clammy to the touch. I was repelled and somewhat nonplussed by the thought that he would never speak to me again. At the same time, he seemed so quiet and still, so there. That contrasted with the house which had begun to be busy with people bringing in food, flowers, and condolences. My mother had to share her grief with those whom she disliked. That put an edge on things which even little boys might sense though not comprehend.

Sometime between then and the funeral, Mr Hartwell, the Barton undertaker, managed to dress my father in a suit and lay him out in a coffin which opened to full length. I think there was a drape over his lower legs but his Masonic apron was fully visible. People who saw him in the church said he looked good.

The weather cleared and the funeral day, probably 14 June,[321] was bright and warm. The service was in Barton at the Congregational Church which was the one my mother attended when she went. The Emersons had associations with it too but it was picked because it was known that there would be many people coming to pay their last respects. There were. People came from all over the State. Business associates, like Lou Tilton and Mr. Marvin came from southern New Hampshire and Burlington; others drove up from Montpelier and elsewhere. Men came from the Grand Lodge of Vermont; other Masons came from what seemed like far away. Old school friends came from Hardwick, and more who had been with in the Agricultural School in Lyndonville. 'Uncas' (Lyman Morrill), showed up from Danville, where the Emersons had settled by the 1830s. All the people who mattered in the county and town were there as were most of those with whom he had played baseball. He had been a popular and a useful man. For about fifteen years he had been elected to all the town offices which required someone who was clever, trustworthy and could get along with people and get them to work in harmony. He had been active in most of the local organizations. The turnout for his funeral more than filled the church, then larger than it now is – perhaps 300 came. Later, many of those people sought out my mother to tell her how sorry they were that Art had died. Others spoke only to his mother – as my widowed mother noted.

My mother and her brothers and his family were marshaled in the downstairs vestry and came up to sit in the front rows. I was not with them but with my Sanders grandparents. I think that, like others, we walked up, stood silent by the coffin, looked at him and then made our way about a third of the way back in the church to their pew, number 62. That was a better vantage point for the spectacle which followed. Slowly the large building filled as the organ played somber music. Then, the swinging doors at the rear were opened so that those who filled the vestibule and straggled onto the outside steps could see or at least hear. The Minister, Mr. Vincent, began the service undoubtedly intoning, 'I am the resurrection and the life and he that believeth in me ...'. I remember little about all that but I was fascinated by the procession of Freemasons – maybe forty or fifty of them. They processed in wearing their regalia. All wore aprons but of many different types – white, blue, fringed, or ornamented. Others had chains about their necks from which hung squares, compasses, and other 'jewels'; those who I now imagine were tylers carried silver trowels. They marched up the north aisle of the church and each laid a sprig of evergreen on my father's aproned-body. After doing that, they filled the front of the church and conducted a short ceremony. Then, they processed up the center aisle and left the body of the church, eventually returning to the rooms of Arthur's local Lodges about a block away. The service ended and the family, including me, went one more time to view the body and then left for the cemetery. In the interval, the undertaker took off my father's apron and gave it to my mother. We got into the cars provided and went to Westmore where my father was interred in his family's lot overlooking Willoughby Lake. There was no place there for my mother to be buried.

The grave-side ceremony was short and conducted, I believe, by Mr Hutchinson, the minister who had married my parents less than seven years earlier. After that, those who attended were invited to the Emerson farm for 'refreshments'. That meant an assortment of pies, cakes, and cookies, coffee and tea. I remember sitting in a window chair by the roll-top desk in the living room where I had been told to stay out of the way. I looked longingly at a piece of lemon-meringue pie which had beads of caramelized sugar and egg-white hanging from the drooping peaks of its meringue. They gleamed amber in the light. I kept hoping no one would eat it, that it would be left for me. In the end, I got it. I was more concerned with that than with talking to the folks who noticed me.

6. Settling Up

The aftermath of my father's death went on and on. One dimension of it was legal. He died intestate. Probating the estate meant that an administrator had to be found and appointed by the Probate Court. His lawyer brother found one, Will Hanson, a local cattle dealer, whom Mom did not think was wholly honest although she was probably wrong. He did, however, take his fee. My father had settled estates without doing so. The Judge of the Probate Court forced Mom to ask for custody of me. Each year, until I was a teenager, she and I made an annual trip to the Judge's office to show her that I was being adequately looked after. Mom found that humiliating and deeply resented it. I learned early always to have a will and to keep it up to date.

Predictably, given the dispositions of the parties, there was an immediate fight about the division of Arthur's property. The farm, a property jointly held by all of his family members save his brother Russell, had been once mostly in his name but had been deeded back to his mother when she tried too hard to run his life. That meant that the only part he owned at the time of his death was a small wood-lot on which pulp-wood had been cut during the winter. He did not own the timber he had gotten out of the main wood-lot and sugar place – which had cost him his life. His family offered my mother her choice – his pulp and wood lot or the value of the wood he had cut elsewhere but not both. The value of either was about $1,000. She took the wood lot for which the family immediately gave her the money but kept the lot. His insurance came to about as much more. It was not much on which to raise and educate a boy. She was angered by this and enraged by their refusal to give her his personal effects – his razor, golf clubs, wallet, and so forth.[322] Her response was to attach and sell everything on the farm held in his name. That meant the farm was stripped of its two trucks, his dismantled saw mill, some wool, and various other things, including a few animals. She sold the three riding horses he had bought for us to ride – two too big and spirited, the other a pony. That angered his family who were now forced to replace expensive equipment. A few years later, when she discovered that he had held a bit of stock in a milk co-op, she forced the family to surrender that too since it was in his name. It was worth all of $40.00.

The toll my father's death took on my mother was great. She was a high-strung woman not always in secure control of her temper and emotions. She sometimes acknowledged that. She spent much of her life from 1939 - c. 1966 being depressed.

***

Another Farmer's Life: Arthur Frank Emerson (1896-1939)

This is to Certify that Companion *Arthur F. Emerson* IS A MEMBER OF

Keystone Chapter, No. 16, R. A. M.

Barton, Vermont

Dues paid to May first, 192*5*. $2.00

Barton, Vt., *June 23* 19*24*

Orleans Lodge, No. 55, F. & A. M.

Barton, Vt., *June 22* 19*34* $9.40

This is to Certify that Brother *Arthur F. Emerson* is a member in good standing of this Lodge, and that his dues are paid to May 1st, Nineteen hundred *thirty five*

Nº 821

THIS CERTIFIES THAT *Arthur Emerson* IS A MEMBER OF

Barton Improvement Club

OF BARTON, VERMONT

AND IS ENTITLED TO ALL CLUB PRIVILEGES

FROM *April 1* 193*8*, TO *April 1* 193*9*.

My Vermonters: The Northeast Kingdom 1800-1940

. Some of the items in Arthur's billfold when he died.

Another Farmer's Life: Arthur Frank Emerson (1896-1939)

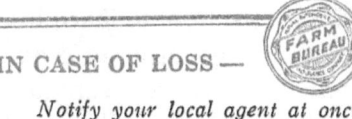

IN CASE OF LOSS —   F-27-453A
                                                POLICY NUMBER

Notify your local agent at once or phone the office of
Farm Bureau Mutual Automobile Insurance Co.
Located at...... BURLINGTON, VERMONT
Issued to..... ARTHUR F. EMERSON
Address...... BARTON, VERMONT

Ford	Coach	18-4330969
MAKE OF CAR	STYLE	MOTOR NUMBER

FIRE ☐   THEFT ☐   COLLISION ☐   LIABILITY ☒   PROP. DMG. ☒
Fire Coverage Carried in Farm Bureau Mutual Fire Insurance Co.

(Over)

BARTON COUNTRY CLUB
MEMBERSHIP CARD

This certifies that **A. F. Emerson & Family.**
Having paid the dues, is a member of Barton Country Club, and entitled to all its privileges until April 1st, 193 9.

H. R. Conner
Secretary-Treasurer

Amount Paid $ 10.

I am a member of the Willoughby Lake Boosters
This card Gives *Mrs. Arthur Emerson*
a special license to rave about
WILLOUGHBY LAKE, NATURES MASTERPIECE
My Membership Fee of fifty cents for
the year ending June 1st, 193......
has been paid to
P. W. Daniels, Sec.

Arthur Emerson was an interesting fellow but he was also a new sort of farmer. Like many his age, he went to school to learn his trade and he knew more about the world than did his father or men of his age. His farming was more scientific than theirs, more mechanized and less dependent on horses and manpower. While he still made his money from sugar, wood, cattle, and milk, he marketed his milk though a local creamery owned and operated by H. P. Hood & Sons, a Boston company – or, through a cooperative which was not town-based but operated beyond his town and probably had an interest in a Troy, Vermont, cheese-factory. He lived to see a lot of State and Federal government regulations and interference in agriculture and in other spheres of life. He must have approved of some or all of that since he was a willing and hard-working Federal employee. He was probably more tolerant than his family had been, making no distinctions in his treatment of Roman Catholics and others who went not to his Church – as attendance at his funeral and the sympathy cards sent to my mother showed. The Barton Priest, Father Marion, sent a very nice card to my mother. His death was a loss to the community which he had long served and perhaps to the State since he, like his brother, Lee, would have aspired to higher offices. He was popular and humourous enough to have attained them and used them to make Vermont more as Governor and later Senator George Aikin, a near age-mate, would have liked it. His politics seem not very ideological but addressed problems as they came and tried to find common-sense solutions to them in the interest all – not in the interest of power companies, banks, the railroads, and big business generally. He had a wider frame of reference than earlier Northeast Kingdom farmers had had. I have often wondered what I would have made of him had he lived – and what I might have become.

Epilogue

In the Preface I said this was a set of personal essays looking at a world now gone and past recovery. Barton, the town where I grew up in the 1930s and 1940s, had fifty or more working farms. I am told there are now about six or eight and one or two small holdings whose owners work at other jobs while doing some farming.[323] The small houses of the homesteads are still often used as homes but much of the land is no longer farmed by those who own the houses; it is uneconomic to do that. Much of it no even longer goes with the houses. Some land belongs to farmers who do not live near-by and is used for hay and grain crops to supply large dairying operations milking 200 or more cows – not the mere ten or so cows which could be accommodated on the eighteen-acre vacation-place I owned for a while in the 1960s and which was a subsistence Farm until 1966. Other places belong to those who bought them, as I bought mine, to vacation on. The Emerson farm has been broken up into at least three units and nearby neighbors are not mainly farmers but are 'summer people' or work in nearby towns. Vermont has more forest land now than it has ever had. Wildlife has returned but the animals offer little to those who live with them year-round. Employment for Barton village residents is often to be had only at a distance, or in local factories which resist unionization and keep wages low. Few of the larger businesses are locally owned. Even the Bank in Orleans is now owned by The Toronto Dominion Bank. The world of relative equals described in these essays has given way to a world of greater inequalities and a far steeper social pyramid. The Albany of William Hayden II had one rich man, sixty or so well off families about equal in their wealth, many others with perhaps half their capital, and a few with less. The really destitute were accommodated on one 'Poor Farm'. Today, while the poverty line has risen, such small communities have many very poor people assisted by various kinds of welfare. Not all that many are well off, and, depending on the season, there are varying numbers of wealthy people. The social pyramid plotted by incomes varies seasonally but its peak has risen and the pyramid changed shape.

The multifarious independence of the early period is gone as well. No one can be self-sufficient in food, construction materials, fuel, means of transport and much else, including clothing. How many girls now even sew and are willing to do so? We live, must live, in a world tied together by commerce which cannot be merely local in its capitalization, ownership, and payment of returns. Local self-sufficiency cannot give us the things we all desire and need, or the things on our lists of apps, most of which are not locally made. It has happened, and, barring man-made catastrophes, there is no going back. We should admire the independence and enterprise of our forebears but we must make our lives in a world unlike theirs. We can and should be proud of their virtues but we should also remember that their society was founded on the taking of land from indigenous peoples and exploiting them as Americans went West. Vermonters had a good record on slavery but were willing to settle on Indian land. My grandfather Sanders (d. 1945), who remembered the last of the Indian Wars, but forgot his mother's heritage, was given to muttering that 'the only good Indians are dead ones'.

The rather unsophisticated world described in this book cannot to be revived. Scattered communities which try to revive the past usually find they are unable to make it work even if they are permitted to do so. Usually, they are not. Living in older ways violates too many rules. After all, the nineteenth century had no septic systems and recklessly polluted the world – although not on the same scale or in the ways we do. Regulations protect us and were enacted to remedy clear ills and deficiencies. Welfare may be demeaning for some but it is needed in a world in which charity and family-ties no longer operate as they once did – and never so well as many believe. Federal and State welfare schemes also lessened the importance of fraternal organizations which carried out some welfare functions. As government programs grew, fraternal orders, like the Odd Fellows or the Modern Woodmen of America, declined.

The communities described above were rooted in the similarity of circumstances of those who formed them, mostly small farmers. Their people were independent and self-reliant but the first settlers in the Northeast Kingdom helped build each-others' houses and raised each-others' barns. They agitated collectively for charters for their towns. Those gave them a corporate existence and the legal rights to run their own affairs, to tax and spend for the common good, to create school districts, to be represented in State government, and to do whatever else was, in their minds, necessary, right and good. Some of that, formed 'the more perfect union' and belonged to the Federal authorities in Washington. On most of those things, they could agree. They were even, to some degree, responsible for the militia which was to protect them, some of whose officers they also chose. A militia, but not a well-regulated one, is now the aim of right-wing conservatives whose delusions include a notions of defending communities with hand guns and rifles in an age of drones. In the nineteenth century, a rough equality of wealth, status, education and power precluded much that happened elsewhere. There, the powerful could force their wills on dependants. In Vermont, a person who tried to rule would be voted our or down. Even clever and wealthy Miss Jean Simpson of Craftsbury could not sit only two or three terms in the Vermont Legislature.

Despite rivalries, dislikes and grievances, most of these honest and uncynical people got along well enough and had little difficulty working, playing, and worshiping together. They were constantly busied with social interactions of one sort or another. Few of those were violent although the Northeast Kingdom was not without crimes, including murders. But, the policing, so much with us now, was lacking because it was costly and seldom seemed needed. Those tight-knit communities resembled extended families. Informal and internalized controls worked among people who were often relatives. That is no longer the case in our more changeable world.

Such communities engendered loyalty and a sense of place for those who stayed. Those who left often maintained ties which brought them back for vacations and visits. But, community loyalty and spirit was constantly eroded by the emigration of many who went to cities in search of work, to the West for cheap land and better lives, or to places where they might pursue a chosen profession – or just to enjoy the advantages and anonymity of a large city. Emigration and the increased mobility of people generally weakened communities by removing many of the brightest and the best who did not find opportunities in Northern Vermont. In my parents' generation, seven of ten children left for opportunities they could not find in Vermont. Only five lived most of their lives in Vermont. Of their ten children, only two made a permanent home in Vermont.

For good or ill, the religious nature of the towns also altered. Within a few years of the first settlers, itinerant Protestant preachers appeared; churches followed soon after. The first were sects with a Calvinist background followed by the Methodists. Later, there were Universalists and by 1900 even a few Christian Scientists. Those sects catered to felt needs and differing beliefs but they all reflected the conviction that this world is not the end all and be all of our existence. The mystery of our destinies, the solace for our failures, was not to be had in this world, dispensed by psychologists and grief-counsellors, but required other sorts of people and a supernatural dimension to our lives. The religion of most of the early settlers was softened and eroded in various ways. Hell-fires were banked and the churches, like the secular world around them, became more interested in material progress, in comforting words, and actions dependent not on God's will but our own. Our wills and actions, not God's grace, loomed larger in sects like the Universalists or Unitarians and then among Congregationalists, Methodism, and even among Baptists. This has ended in the feel-good Christianity affecting even the older Calvinist sects. Today, only the charismatic sectaries of the region have the enthusiasm which often characterized the sometimes scandalous Camp Meetings of the nineteenth century. What was common among the best educated and the leading class of the early period is now marginal and odd and informed by literalism and an unsophisticated theology.

The early Congregationalists and Presbyterians ordained preachers only after fairly rigorous training but that standard broke down where the need for a minister was great but the stipend was low. The older sects – Presbyterians and Congregationalists – often had educated men leading them but the economics of religious life determined that many preachers would become essentially laymen – farmers not very different from their parishioners, who could afford none better. Those with theological training tended not to stay long but moved to better paying churches in larger towns or into teaching. Some who stayed preached enthusiastically; others touted doctrines of good works or differing sorts of heresies but hardly the orthodoxy of old-line Calvinists. The Rev. Mr. Elias Kellogg had little training, preached well, and farmed. The level of training of Baptist ministers and elders in Sutton was lower and other ministers gradually sank in learning but not necessarily in their knowledge of the Bible read literally. Most churches seem to have hired men like Kellogg – ministers with little training other than the earnest reading of their Bibles and a few other books. The piety of some early settlers, which rested on knowledge of the Bible and some theology, is seldom seen today. Even in the Kirks, maintained here and there in the region, the rigor of Scottish dissenters – the heirs of the Associate Presbytery and its splinters, the Burgers and the Anti-Burghers – weakened and in the end disappeared. In a democratic world, all desires and needs tend to be seen as equally meaningful and valid. Sects catering to those wishing for religious experiences not much grounded in theology serve those who want more, more regular, or more exciting ministrations.

There were few Roman Catholics in the beginning but many now.

Despite well-educated priests and a different ecclesiastical structure, they too have found life hard as costs increased. Their convent schools have closed as have most Catholic high schools. Attendance at churches has declined. There is a shortage of priests and vocations have fallen in the teaching orders of nuns. Their churches, too, have sometimes been forced to close.

Worse yet, if one is a believer, the nice white churches with tapering spires, once the hearts of towns, are now often quite empty and are finding it hard to survive. In Albany, the Free Will Baptist Church is a storehouse for wood; the Catholic Church is closed but used on special occasions; it may soon be sold. The Church in Albany village is a union of Methodists and Congregationalists. For some people, the convenience of televised services keeps them at home. For others, it is simple disbelief engendered, sometimes, by thought but at least as often by an unthinking acceptance of secularized values and a present-mindedness incompatible with a message about a Savior and the Heaven in which He supposedly sits at the right hand of God and rules, 'world without end'. Simple hedonism accounts for more unbelievers and is not countered by peer-pressures to attend and worship with a community of the like-minded, who in an age of greater mobility may no longer be relatives. Those who would like to return to a more godly world have to contend with doctrines of rights, and notions of equality and 'political correctness' which were not there in the nineteenth or earlier centuries but which increasingly challenge religious people on issues of historical truth, authority, race, and gender. With the decline of religious authority, the region has lost the cheap police exercised by its old churches. Weekly sermons deploring sin and sinners – which must have frightened some– no longer awe the area's present house-breakers, violent drug dealers, and petty criminals.

The people in the Northeast Kingdom a hundred or more years ago tolerated differences in their communities – but those were not great. Until very recently, their's was a 99% White world of farmers and small businessmen. The few Jews who appeared were given a guarded welcome but seem to have been accepted if not particularly well regarded or treated. Most of them were peddlers and, later, small merchants selling dry goods and shoes, or, in my youth, running junk-yards. The first sizable and different group was the Roman Catholics. Initially they were Irish, with the Italians and French coming later. It is interesting that in Albany, most of the Catholics originally settled in one section of the town. Catholics seem not to have been much harassed although their religious beliefs, like their priests, were sometimes despised. It was easier to laugh at them than to persecute them. By the end of the nineteenth century, some of the Irish and French played on the ball teams; attended the academies and even dated Protestant girls like my mother. Integration has come but it took a long time.

Sometimes it seems as if sports are the chief reason American schools exist. That has never been true in Vermont but the schools have changed – but not enough. In the nineteenth-century towns of northern Vermont, only low levels of skills and knowledge were required to run things – even to produce acceptable verses. Grade school educations, better then than now in teaching elementary reading and mathematics skills, were adequate to the demands made even on those who had authority. The local banks and corporations were not tied to large conglomerates and international companies as they often are now. Now, with each higher level of complexity, more knowledge is needed to run the system – and the banks are not the only examples which might be given. Road Commissioners, like Leonard Watson or my father, did not need to know much about State and local laws, about gradients and the runoff of agricultural wastes. They operated fairly simple and not very expensive equipment much of which could be locally made and maintained. Increased demands for safety, health regulations, competence in handling machinery, and much more have raised the educational requirements for running small towns beyond their ability to train and fund many of their managers or even the ventures they undertake. A Town Trustee or Selectman can no longer manage a water purification and filtration plant without special training as my father did. With all that has come, inevitably, interference by outsiders – Counties, States, the Federal Government, and their agencies, such as Conservation Districts, State and Federal Forests, Wildlife Sanctuaries, and so on. Town meetings no longer do all the business of their communities and cannot do so if health, security, and better amenities are prized. Those can be had only with some outside assistance – which brings the control of distant Federal government agencies, the State, and various national and State police forces. The politics which now matters is not only local but pursued at the State, Federal, and even at international levels.

As the integration of the towns into wider networks of producers serving larger markets increases, so does level of required knowledge and the locals' dependence on outsiders. My father, in the 1930s, made a living selling wood to local mills and to the people who burned it for fuel, bark to distant tanneries, sugar to St. Johnsbury firms and a few summer folks, and milk to a local creamery run by a Boston firm or to a local co-operative. Both shipped milk to more distant markets. The markets he served generally covered small areas and were nearly if not quite unregulated. Today, drinkable milk has to be pasturized and to understand its pricing, one has to think not only about its butter fat and protein content but about national agricultural policies (and politics) and about a host of rules imposed by various levels of government. The price of New England milk is affected by international agreements set by lobbyists to protect big American farmers and hurt consumers and by the European Union's protection of French and other dairy farmers. Milk prices are set for Vermont farmers who have, essentially, no voice in their determination. Roads, improved communications, agribusinesses, and banking operations of a new sort have transformed the world my father knew and worked in. He was a well-educated farmer but belonged more to Kipling's world than to the age of computers.

For others, outside ties came through visions of progress related to new inventions, new processes, better crops and seeds, and much else which built confidence in the nineteenth century. Their visions and their hopes were often realized out of the State. There, they often came with more regimented work forces, less control over one's working life and a constriction of one's interests. Leonard Watson might work at a large number of things but many workers, several generations later, tend to do one thing day after day, year in, year out. There was no 'idiocy of rural life' as Karl Marx imagined, but 'the idiocy of industrial life' today is, at best, compensated for by union-negotiated high wages and less work at repetitive tasks, or at worst, by being replaced by a robot. Many workers become redundant or have to be re-trained as processes, needs, and machines rapidly change. Most of Vermont's regional high schools no longer offer vocational training adequate to secure good jobs. That has become the function, not of 'shop courses', but of trade schools which are not located in most communities. Schooling is not poor in Vermont but it takes longer, is relatively more expensive than it used to be, is often not local, and demands more of students who want to do well in life.

As the cure of souls has changed, so too has the care of bodies. Most nineteenth-century illnesses found their best treatments in placebos which did no harm but allowed nature to work its own cure – if it could. A local 'doctor', like Albany's Dyer Bill (1792-1876), usually had no medical degree and seldom had a first rate medical education even for the times.

Such men set up practices without much concern shown by regulating authorities even where they existed. Doctors, too, were part-time farmers or shop-keepers. That sort of practitioner had become outmoded by c. 1890 and illegal not much later.[324] Today, anyone really sick in the Northeast Kingdom is likely to be treated by specialized doctors and surgeons in or from Hanover, New Hampshire, or from Burlington. He or she will almost certainly not die at home and will not be put in the ground without checks to see that the body is 'properly' disposed of by undertakers who have a monopoly on cremations and burials. There are no more private grave yards beside houses in the country.

Once, uniformity in socio-economic status, similarity of condition and education, like close family ties, and the small size of groups, made it easy to organize for collective action while the lack of alternatives made it necessary. By the mid-nineteenth century, many associations and clubs were beginnings. They boomed after the Civil War. Some of those were political and supported parties. Others supported singing schools, musical groups and bands, temperance organizations, Masonic Lodges and other fraternal groups, ball teams, and a host of other activities. Many had charitable or welfare dimensions. After the Civil War, GAR Posts and the WRC were added to this list, to be joined after 1919 by the American Legion. Many of those groups put on musicals, concerts, sponsored socials, lectures, minstrel shows and more. The small inns, hotels and taverns, which gave them places to sing or whatever, gave further life to the villages as did traveling merchants and traders. The hotels have been largely displaced by the more anti-social motels and the merchants are often now working for chain stores – or worse yet – Walmart, which has beaten down attempts to keep it out of the State and so, at a cost, to preserve small businesses. The peak for local associations came perhaps in the 1920s but it did not survive the arrival of television and mobility in and to wider markets.

In the 1940s, my mother and her friends were regularly going to meetings of the Grange, the Barton Literary Club, the Home Demonstration Club, to a Christmas Club, and church groups. She went less often to meetings of the American Legion Auxiliary, the Barton Improvement Society, and the Eastern Star. By 1960, Mom went regularly only to the 'Lit Club', 'Home Dem'; and to a Church group. Never much of a church-goer, for years my mother each Sunday morning watched the Rev. Mr. Robert Schuler and enjoyed the music from the Crystal Cathedral.[325] 'Televangelism' has to some extent replaced the lackluster performances of the local ministers. And, just as religiously, each Sunday evening my mother tuned into the Ed Sullivan Show and other variety and music shows. Where she had once performed in one way or another, she was now mostly a spectator. Old organizations withered and died. Barton by the 1970s had no town band, no ball teams, and no Golf Club. It now counts among the missing the WCTU, the Odd Fellows and Rebekahs, the Modern Woodmen of America, the Eastern Star, and probably other groups about which I have forgotten, and, it again lacks a bowling alley. Those who had amused themselves by going to community events before 1950, now stay home to watch shows which provide them better, and better presented, entertainments, or offer viewers up to-the-minute-news, major league ball games, and other diversions in which their participation is often turning on a television set or a computer of some sort. The screams of the eagle on Memorial Day or the Fourth of July are now more often heard on devices than at a local cemetery or park and soon TV will be replaced by mobile devices as it has been for many of the young.

The life lived by those I have described was also challenged by better roads and cars and by wars which made it possible to go outside the villages for entertainment, employment, and other services. Vermonters had been leaving the State for years but World War II caused an exodus. Many from the Northeast Kingdom went south to work in the shipyards of Bath, Maine, or Boston, the arms factories of Hartford, Connecticut, and Springfield, Massachusetts, or at the machine-tool companies in Windsor and southern New England cities. French-speaking boys were drafted, learned better English, and did not return. They could find jobs elsewhere and there were not farms or other jobs for all of them. The weakening of bonds to an old way of life can also be seen in things like the lapsing of Old Home Day Celebrations which had begun by 1901 and went on somewhat irregularly until the 1920s with few after 1937. Albany celebrated its centennial in 1906. That and Old Home Days drew many former residents back to the town. They came again for the bicentennials of Kingdom towns which produced a flurry of festive occasions and a lot of local histories. But, the Vermont, described nostalgically in the publications commemorating those is largely gone.

My Vermonters in Orleans and Caledonia Counties may not be wholly typical of small-towns in Northern New England but they come close. I think the lives described above show patterns found not only in the Northeast Kingdom but in of much of rural New England and America. The top echelons of that society were better educated, better off than many, but, still, not much out of the ordinary. They mostly went to Protestant churches, worked hard, were engaged in their communities and with their often large families. They knew a bit of the world and read more than their Bibles and a weekly paper. Uncynical, earnest and patriotic, they wanted their politics to be moral. They rallied round the flag when their conceptions of what was right were violated by foreigners or by secessionist slave-holders. They owned many things testifying to their patriotic belief that the United States of America was an exceptional place. Indeed, it was. Unlike Europeans, Americans had no powerful continental enemies to challenge or restrict their growing power, no rivals requiring high taxes expended on large armies and navies or the regulation of subject civilians. The United States had an expanding resource base, a well-educated population, and outside the South, a fairly well-functioning and integrated society less fraught with class or religious conflicts than many European states. While we may admire or be amused by the McGuffey Readers and the pieties and patriotism they inculcated, our task is not to return to those times but to rework and adapt their values and institutions so that we may cope with a vastly different world. We should try to keep from failing disastrously by wasting our resources, destroying our environment, destructively intervening in the lives of others and fighting one another. Will we make it? I do not know. I would not bet much on the future – but then I will not be around either to pay or to collect.

Epilogue

All the collections of papers I have used show a sentimental patriotism which seems often lacking today. The Emerson and Rogers families purchased mementoes which celebrated liberty, independence, and other values which they admired. Some are kitschy and mass produced but were eagerly bought as souvenirs not only of an occasion but of something more enduring.

These centennial moulded-glass goblets were bought by some Emerson in 1876. The fronts have a Liberty Bell flanked with the dates 1776 and 1876. A ribbon above the bell reads, 'Declaration of Independence'. The reverse reads, '100 Years Ago'. They belong with flags, medals, July Fourth celebrations, patriotic books and songs, and more – all of which the Northeast Kingdom people had in abundance.

Select Bibliography

Manuscripts
See Preface
[Albany] Records of Albany, Vermont [kept in the office of the Town Clerk].
[Barton] Various Minutes of the Orleans Lodge [once owned by Charles Barrows but now at the Lodge].
[Craftsbury] Town Records [kept in the office of the Town Clerk].
Craftsbury Academy, School Records, 1890-1917 [Held at the Adademy].
[Glover] Minute Book of the Mason Post, No.16, Grand Army of the Republic, 1894-1915 [now in the Glover Historical Society Museum].
[Sutton] Sutton Land Records, Vols. I-V [kept in the office of the Town Clerk].
[West Burke] Records of Births and Deaths [kept in the office of the Town Clerk].

Newspapers, Periodicals etc. (various issues)
Green Mountain Whittlins, (Vermont Folklore Society, 1948-).
Hazen Road Dispatch (Greensboro Historical Society, 1975-).
Forty Years of the Hazen Road Dispatch 1975-2015, (an anthology of its articles), edited by Gail A. Sangree (Greensboro, 2015).
Old Stone House Museum Bulletin.
The Orleans County Monitor (Barton, Vt.) [This is digitized for the years 1872 to 1922 and will soon be completely done.]
The Independent Standard [published first in Irasburg (1856-1866) and later Barton (1866-?) and then in Newport, Vt. It was the forerunner of *The Newport Daily Express*].
The Thrice Weekly World [later *The New York World*].
Vermont Union Journal.
Vermont Life.

Web-sites
BlackPast.org, 'Henderson, George Washington (c. 1850-1936)'.
P. G. Kearney, hhtp://wprokasy.myweb.uga.edu.Emerson2.htm [This is an MA thesis on the Emerson sisters, Hannah and Elizabeth.].
The Peacham Library Web-site.
Republican Party Platforms: 'Republican Party Platform of 1912,' June 18, 1912 [online in Gerhard Peters and John T. Woolley, *The American Presidency Project.* http://www.presidency.ucsb.edu/ws/?pid 29633.
The Vermont Historical Society web-site has online a number of letters of Captain Daniel Mason (?-1865).

Reference works

Dictionary of First Names, edited by Patrick Hanks, Kate Hardcastle, and Flavia Hodges (Oxford University Press, Oxford, 2006).

Dictionary of Scottish Church History and Theology, edited by Nigle M. deS. Cameron (InterVarsity Press, Downers Grove, Ill., 1993).

Vermont: A Bibliography of Its History [Vol. 4 of *Bibliographies of New England History*], edited by T. D. Seymour Bassett (G. K. Hall & Co., Boston, 1981).

Vermont Year Book [formerly Walton's Register and other titles] (various issues).

Books and articles

[Albany] *History of Albany Vermont*, edited by Virginia Wharton (n.p., n.d. [1991])

[Albany, St John's Church], Daniels, Paul Patrick, *The Bell Tolls No More to Call the Faithful from Their Chore* (n.p., n.d.).

Alexander, Joan, 'Glovers Civil War Places', *Glover History*, (Winter, 2007).

'Articles of Faith and the Covenant adopted by The Danville [Vermont] Baptist Association', (Danville, 1823).

[Barton], *A History of Barton, Vermont*, compiled and edited by Darlene Young (Crystal Lake Falls Historical Association, Barton, 1998).

[Barton Landing], Hoyt, Darrell, *Sketches of Orleans, Vermont* (Orleans County Historical Society, Newport, 1985).

[Barton], Hunt, Wally, *Wally Hunt's Vermont* (Orleans County Historical Society, Barton, 1983).

Beers, F. W., *Atlas of Caledonia County Vermont* (F. W. Beers & Co., New York, 1875);

___, *Atlas of Lamoile and Orleans Counties Vt.*, (F. W. Beers & Co., New York, 1878).

Bonfield, Lynn and Mary Morrison, *Roxana's Children: The Biography of a Nineteenth-Century Vermont Family* (1995).

Burklyn, (n.p., n.p., 1963).

[Cabot], *Cabot, Vermont: A Collection of Memories from the Century Past*, edited by Caleb Pitkin (Cabot Oral History Committee, Barre, Vt., 1999).

Cady, Daniel L., *Rhymes of Vermont Rural Life* (The Tuttle Co., Rutland, 3rd edn., 1921; 1st edn., 1920).

Clifford, Deborah, *More than Petticoats: Remarkable Vermont Women* (n.p., 2009).

[Coventry], *Bits and Pieces of Coventry's History*, 1977 (L. Brown & Sons, Barre, n.d. [1977].

[Craftsbury] *A Craftsbury Album*, edited by David B. Linck (Craftsbury Historical Society, n.p., 1989).

[Craftsbury], *Pageant of Craftsbury: Craftsbury Academy 1829-1929* (Cowles Press, St. Johnsbury, 1929).

[Craftsbury], *Souvenir Booklet of Craftsbury Academy* (Craftsbury, 1960-1961).

[Civil War], *A War of the People: Vermont Civil War Letters*, edited by Jeffrey D. Marshall (University Press of New England, Hanover, N.H. and London, 1999).
[Civil War], Coffin, Howard *Full Duty: Vermonters in the Civil War* (Woodstock, Vt., 1993).
[Civil War], see Harris.
Congregational Publishing Society of Boston for 1882 with Questions (Boston, 1882).
Daniels, See Albany.
Davidson, J. Brownlee, *Agricultural Engineering: A Textbook for Students of Secondry Schools of Agriculture Colleges Offering a General Course in the Subject and the General Reader* (Webb Publishing Co, St. Paul, Minn., 2nd edn., 1913).
Davis, Allen F., *Postcards from Vermont: A Social History, 1905-1945* (University Press of New England, Hanover, N.H. and London, 2002).
Dopp, Daisy, *Daisy Dopp's Vermont* (The Chronicle Office, Barton, 1983).
Emerson, Ralph Stanton, *English Roots of the Haverhill and Ipswich Emerson* (Gateway Press, Baltimore, 1985).
Emerson, Roger L., 'Hume and the Bellman, Zerobabel MacGilchrist', *Hume Studies* 23 (1997), pp. 9-23;
___, *An Enlightened Duke: Archibald Campbell, Earl of Ilay, 3rd Duke of Argyll, 1682-1762* (Humming Earth Press, Glasgow, 2013).
Fisher, Dorothy Canfield, *Vermont Tradition: The Biography of an Outlook on Life* (Little, Brown & Co., Boston,1953).
Fisher, Harriet Fletcher, *Willoughby Lake: Legends and Legacies* (Orleans County. Historical. Society, Brownington, 1988);
___, *Lyndon Institute* (Images of America, Charleston, S.C. , 2000);
___, *Lyndon* (Images of America, Charleston, S.C. , 2004);
___, *Hometown Album* (Lyndon Historical Society, Rutland, 2007);
___, *Remembering Lyndon: A Glance Back in Time* (The History Press, Charleston, S.C. , 2009).
[Glover] *History of the Town of Glover, Vermont*, (Glover Bicentennial Committee, 1983, 3rd printing 1993, Burlington, Vt.).
[Glover], See Alexander and Dopp.
[Glover] *History of the Town of Glover and Runaway Pond* [in verse], Harry A. Phillips (Northeast Vermont Development Association, Glover, n.d., [1930s ?].
Graff, Nancy Price, editor, *Celebrating Vermont: Myths and Realities*, an exhibition at the Christian A. Johnson Memorial Gallery, Middlebury College, with essays by Graff, W.N. Hosley, J.K. Graffagnino and W.C. Lipke (Middlebury College & University Press of New England, Hanover, N.H., 1991).
Graffagnino, J. Kevin, *Vermont in the Victorian Age: Continuity and Change in the Green Mountain State, 1850-1900* (Vermont Heritage Press and the Shelburne Museum, Bennington and Shelburne, Vt., 1985).

Graffagnino, J. Kevin, *et al.* editors, *The Vermont Difference* (Woodstock Foundation and the Vermont Historical Society, n.p., 2014).

[Greensboro], *The History of Greensboro: The First Two Hundred Years*, edited by Susan Bartlett Weber (Greensboro Historical Society, Greensboro, 1990).

Hardwick Academy and Graded School, (Hardwick, Vt., pamphlets for 1910 and for 1914).

Harris, Luther B., *A Prison Story: A Vermont Soldier's Memoir of Andersonville and other Rebel Camps*, edited by Denise Brown and Virginia Downs (Vermont Civil War Enterprises and Lyndon Historical Society, 2006).

Hazen Road Dispatch, see Periodicals, above.

Hemenway, Abby Maria, *Poets and Poetry of Vermont*, edited by Abby Maria Hemenway, George A. Tuttle& Co., Rutland, 1858);

___, *Vermont Historical Gazetteer*, 6 vols. (various places and publishers, 1861-1891).

Hill, Richard H., *North Williston: Down Depot Hill* (The History Press, Charleston, S.C., 2011).

Honey, Delia Darling, *The Honey-Comb: Poems by Delia Darling Honey* (William Bullock, Newport, Vt, 1936).

Hoyt, Darrell, [See Barton Landing].

Jaffe, Daniel, *A Nation of Goods: The Material Culture of Early America* [mostly mid-eighteenth century to c. 1920] (Philadelphia, 2010).

Lamoureux, Louis, 'Fall of the House of Hayden: The Dale Curse', *Vermont Life*, XVII (1963), pp.50-54. This was later reprinted with additions in *Mischief in the Mountains*, edited by Walter R. Hard and Janet Green [and nicely illustrated by Jane Clark Brown] (*Vermont Life*, Montpelier, Vt., 1970), pp.33-52.

Leyburn, James G., *The Scotch Irish: A Social History* (University of North Carolina Press, Chapel Hill,1962).

Lowell; The Mill City, Publications Committee of the Lowell Historical Society (Arcadia Publishing Co., Charleston, S.C., 2005).

[Lyndon, Lyndonville], see *Burklyn*, Fisher and Swainbank.

McCarthy, Molly, *The Accidental Diarist: A History of the Daily Planner in America* (University of Chicago Press, Chicago, 2013).

McIntyre, Kenneth E., 'Tales of an East Hardwick Boyhood', *The Hazen Road Dispatch 1975-2015*, pp. 87-89.

Malloy, Barbara Kaiser, *Newport and the Northeast Kingdom* (Images of America; Arcadia Publishing Co., Charleston, S.C. , 1999).

Meeks, Harold A. *Vermont's Land and Resources* (The New England Press, Shelburne, Vt., 1986);

___, *Time and Change in Vermont: A Human Geography* (The Globe Pequot Press, Chester, Conn., 1986).

[Morgan] *Lake Seymour: Illustrated and Historicized* (*The Historian: The Orleans County Magazine*, n.p., n.d., [after 1925]).

Muller, Margaret Hazen, "The Strange Tale of George Washington Henderson,'77," *The University of Vermont Alumni Magazine* (April ,1968), pp. 3-7. [a revised version appears in the *Hazen Road Dispatch*, 2015 in Newspapers above].
[Newport], see Mallory.
[North Williston], see Hill.
Orleans County, compiled by Sarah A. Dumas and the Old Stone House Museum (Images of America; Arcadia Publishing, Charleston , S.C. , 2011).
Phillips, Harry A., *History of Glover, Vermont and Runaway Pond* (Northeastern Development Association, St. Johnsbury, n. d. [c. 1940]). [in verse]
Polhemus, Richard V. and John F., *Stark: The Life and Wars of John Stark, French and Indian War Ranger, Revolutionary War General* (Black Dome Press, Delmar, NY, 2014).
Pope, Charles Henry, *The Haverhill Emersons* (Murray and Emery Co., Cambridge, Mass; Part I, 1913; Part II, 1916).
Rogers, Maj. Robert, *A Concise Account of North America*, (John Millan, London, 1765);
___, *The Diary of the Siege of Detroit in the War with Pontiac*...[1763/64], edited by F. B. Hough (J. Munsell, Albany, NY, 1860);
___, *The Journals of Robert Rogers,* (1st edn, J. Millan, London, 1765; edited by H. H. Peckham, Corinth Books, NY, 1961);
___, *Ponteach, or the Savages of America : A Tragedy*, edited by Tiffany Potter (University of Toronto Press, Toronto, 2010; 1ST edn, 1766).
Sherman, Michael, Gene Sessions and P. Jeffery Potash, *Freedom and Unity: A History of Vermont* (Vermont Historical Society, Barre, Vt., 2004).
Sherman, Michael and Jennie Versteeg, *We Vermonters: Perspectives on the Past* (Vermont Historical Society, n.p.,1992).
Swainbank, Dan, *Mr Vail is in Town: Theodore N. Vail, AT&T, and His Lyndon Legacy* (Lyndon Historical Society, Lyndon, 2011).
[Vermont], *Vermont Statutes, 1894*, Commissioners to edit the Vermont Statutes (Tuttle Co., Rutland,1895);
[Vermont], *Records of the Council of Censors of the State of Vermont*, edited by Paul S. Gillies and Gregory Sanford (Secretary of State's Office, Montpelier, 1991).
Walling, H. E., [Atlas of] *Orleans, Lamoile and Essex Vermont* (Loommis and Way, New York, 1859).
Wilkinson, Catherine Perry, ' A brief History of Medicine in the Greensboro Area' , *The Hazen Road Dispatch* (Greensboro, 2015), pp. 44-46.
[Woman's Relief Corps], *National Roster of the Woman's Relief Corps...1901*, (Bradford, Vt.).
Young, Darlene, see Barton.

Rogers Family Books

1. Texts, Chap-books[*] and Children's Books Owned by the Rogers Family to c. 1910

Anonymous, 'By a Lady of Cincinatti', *The Child's Bible with Plates* (J. Q. Preble, New York, 1834). [this volume is 2" by 1 1/2"]*

Anonymous ['By a Mother'], *Arthur: A True History* (Philadelphia, 1838)*.

Anonymous, *Children's Offerings to Heathen Idols* (Philadelphia, 1846)*.

Anonymous ['by an eminent practical teacher'], *The Progressive Speaker and Common School Reader ...* (Bazin & Ellsworth, Boston, 1858).

Anonymous, *Good Daughters* (New York, 1861)*.

Anonymous, *Daily Food for Christians being a portion of scriptures for every day in the year* (Boston, n.d.).

Anonymous, *The New American Pronouncing Speller* (J. H. Butler & Co., Philadelphia, 1872).

Anonymous, *A Brief History of the United States,* [part of A. S. Barnes and Co's. *One-Term History Series* (New York, Chicago and New Orleans, 1880).

___, ['By a Teacher'], *A Brief History of the United States* (A. S. Barnes & Co., New York, Chicago & New Orleans, 1890).

Cecil, E., *Life of George Washington for Children* (Boston, 1859).

Fish, Daniel, *Complete Arithmetic. Oral and Written* (New York and Chicago, 1880) included in *Robinson's Shorter Series of Progressive Arithmetics.*

Goldsmith, Oliver, 'The Deserted Village' and 'The Traveler' (? Dublin, 1777).

___, *An Abridgement of the History of England* (Boston, 1824).

Goodrich, Samuel, *The American Child's Pictorial History of the United States* (J.H. Baxter & Co., Philadelphia, 1879).

Greenleaf, Benjamin, *A Mental Arithmetic... for Common Schools and Academies* (Robert S. Davis, Boston, 1870).

Hall, S. R., *Outlines of Geography, Natural and Civil History and Constitution of Vermont also the Constitution of the United States...and the Declaration of Independence* (C. W. Willard, Montpelier, 1864) [the revisions of a similar book from 1827].

Robinson, Horatio Nelson, *New Elementary Algebra* (Ivison, Phinney & Co., NY, 1860; S. C. Griggs & Co, Chicago, 1860; 1st ed. 1854).

___, *An Elementary Astronomy for Academies and Schools in which mathematical demonstrations are omitted* (Ivison, Phinney & Co., NY, 1860; S. C. Griggs & Co, Chicago, 1860).

Reed, Alonzo and Brainerd Kellogg, *Higher Lessons in English: A Work on English grammar and Composition, in which the science of language is made tributary to the art of expression....* (Clark & Maynard, New York, 1881, 1st edition 1877).

Root, Frank B., *Graded Lessons in English.*

Scott, William, *A New Spelling, Pronouncing, and Explanatory Dictionary of the English Language....*(William Creech, Edinburgh, 1793).

Town, Salem, *Town's Graded Readers*, 6 vols (1837 ff; three volumes of the Rogers children's set still survive, including one from the second edition (Sanborn and Canton, Boston, 1858).
[Three lost chap-books: Humpty-Dumpty, Robin Hood, and Tom Thumb]

2. Other Books Owned by the Rogers Family up to 1920 and Still Surviving

Abbot, John C. Abbott and Russell H. Conwell, *Lives of the Presidents of the United States of America*...(Portland, Maine, revised, n.d. [?1876]).

Anonymous, *Inquire Within or Anything you want to know; or, over three thousand seven hundred facts* (New York, 1858).

___, *Picturesque Cuba, Porto Rico, Hawaii and the Philippines: A Photographic Panorama of Our New Possessions, Over three hundred Illustrations* (Mast, Crowell & Kirkpatrick, Springfield, Ohio, 1898).

'Barnes' One Term History Series', *A Brief History of the United States* (A. S. Barnes & Co., New York, Chicago & New Orleans, 1885).

Bibles [one for every member of the family and several more. None appear to have been King James Versions after 1848. Instead, they were revisions of the KJV published by the American Bible Society and others from 1858 into the 1880s. Those, in 1900, became the *American Standard Version of the Bible*.]

Bunyan, John, *Pilgrims Progress* (Indianapolis, 1859).

The Century Book of Facts...., compiled and edited by Henry W. Ruoff (King-Richardson Co., Springfield , Mass, 1908).

Devens, R. M., *Our First Century*... (Chicago and Springfield, Massachusetts, 1878).

Edgarton, Miss S. G., *The Flower Vase containing The Language of Flowers and their Poetic Sentiments* (Lowell, Boston and New York, 1844).

Fleetwood, John, *The Life of Our Lord and Saviour Jesus Christ...together with the Lives.... of... Evangelists, Apostles and other Primitive Martyrs to which is added a History of the Jews* (Hartford, 1846).

Foster, Charles, *The Story of the Bible from Genesis to Revelation told in simple language ...adapted To The Young* (Charles Foster, Philadelphia, 1883 [1st edn, 1873; by 1883 154,000 copies had been printed].

Goodrich, Charles, *A History of the United States of America... to which are added the Constitution of the United States and the Declaration of Independence* (Boston, 1854).

Hitchcock, Roswell D., *New and Complete Analysis of the Holy Bible* [including a version of Alexander Cruden's famous *Concordance* (first published in London in 1737 and not out of print since then); Hitchcock, too, is still in print].

Hoyle's Book of Games [the page listing its publisher, place and date is missing].

Morse, Jedidiah, *Geography Made Easy* (4th edition, Boston, 1794).

Select Bibliography

Talmage, Rev. Dewitt, D. D., *From Manger to Throne embracing A New Life of Jesus the Christ and A History of Palestine and its People* (Historical Publishing Co. And D. Appleton & Co, Philadelphia, 1890).
Ward, Mary O. and Augustus F. Kinnersley, *Songs for the Little Ones at Home* (American Tract Society, New York, 1852).
Wyss, Johann David, *Swiss Family Robinson* (Porter and Coates, 9th edition, Philadelphia, 1884).
Young, M., *New Guide to Horse Owners: A Complete Horse Doctor*...(New York, 1880)

Notes

1 Unless otherwise noted when first used, all place names refer to Vermont.
2 The best short account of Robert Rogers is that by Colonel C. P. Stacey, *Dictionary of Canadian Biography*, IV (University of Toronto, Toronto, 1979). The frontier world, in which he and other Scots-Irish migrants lived has been nicely described by Richard V. and John F. Polhemus, in *Stark: The Life and Wars of John Stark, French and Indian War Ranger, Revolutionary War General* (Black Dome Press, Delmar, NY, 2014). Rogers's play, *Ponteach*, has recently been republished with pictures of the Major and more of Indians with whom he dealt but not those who burned down his family home in 1748.
3 The original painting was by George Henry Broughton (1867). Our teacher (sacked for having an affair with the school janitor), read us part of Longfellow's poem about Standish's courtship. Next to it on the wall was a large print of a Winslow Homer painting, 'Fog Warning' (1885). It shows a man in a boat soon to be caught in a squall as his ship moves away into fog – or so we were told. The third picture in the room, was Guido Reni's 'Apollo and Aurora' (1614). Apollo is chasing away darkness and bringing light to the world. All three were in sepia tones.
4 *See* Polhemus and Polhemus, *Stark*, pp.2-4.
5 The Duke in question would have been Francis Scott, 2nd Duke of Buccleuch of the second creation, so the Bosworth line had no royal blood. The Dukes of Argyll had a pedigree back to Adam. It also included King Arthur, Old King Cole, Joseph of Arithmathea, some Trojans and their forebear, Japheth, the son of Adam and Eve. *See* Roger L. Emerson, *An Enlightened Duke: Archibald Campbell, Earl of Ilay, 3rd Duke of Argyll, 1682-1762* (Humming Earth Press, Glasgow, 2013), p.15.
6 I have left the phrasing largely untouched but I have expanded Lottie's abbreviations, added punctuation, and re-paragraphed the stories. She tended to make each sentence a paragraph. A few sentences have been rearranged in the interests of order and repetitions have been removed. Run-on sentences have been separated. I have made some small additions and explanations which are bracketed thus [...]. Dates and minor details have been corrected [*e. g.*, 1864 has become 1764]. Texts not in brackets are her own words; the quote marks are also hers. Other punctuation has been left as she had it.
7 My grandmother thought he had one contract 'out West', in Michigan, part of the Old Northwest. In an article about the Haydens and their house, Louis A Lamoureux sketched his career in New Hampshire, Michigan, and Canada. He built, in all, 586 miles of railway line and

made money doing so: Lamoureux, 'Fall of the House of Hayden: The Dale Curse', *Vermont Life* [hereafter *VL*], XVII (1963), pp.50-54. This was later reprinted with additions in a *Vermont Life* book, *Mischief in the Mountains*, edited by Walter R. Hard and Janet Green [and nicely illustrated by Jane Clark Brown] (*Vermont Life*, Montpelier, Vt., 1970), pp.33-52. Many dates have been taken from these sources.

8   This story differs significantly from the genealogical account compiled by Eldon Sanders, who, like me, was a grandson of Jennie Rogers Sanders. My cousin's account has the Rogers family deriving from Northern Ireland and coming to America prior to 1729 [?1720] when a Robert Rogers (c. 1729-1808) was born to Hugh Rogers (?-?) and his wife in Greenfield, New Hampshire. That Robert Rogers continued to live in Greenfield where he died. Jesse Rogers I (1769-1838), who settled in Vermont, was his eldest son and the only one of nine children who seems to have gone far from the Greenfield area. Aunt Lottie was not as likely to be correct as my cousin. Most of her stories derived from a grandfather born in 1806; but, he (or she) may not have remembered all the details. Jesse I and his son were friendly with the Haydens but a Welsh origin makes no sense of the Irish connections which she claims for the Rogers family. Irish origins fit the claim that they were relatives of Major Robert Rogers, who came from Northern Irish stock. The Major's family settled near Londonderry, south of present day Manchester, N.H., but the Major was born in Massachusetts. By 1738, his family was settled at 'Mountaloma', a few miles northwest of the Amoskeag Falls, near present-day Manchester. Naming an estate was a very British thing to do. This one was burned by Indians in 1748.

9   Eldon Sanders records six sons, all of whom lived to marry producing a plethora of Roberts, James, and Jesses who cannot now be linked with certainty which is why my precise connections to Major Robert Rogers are uncertain.

10 Eldon Sanders's genealogical records and Lamoureux, *VL* (1963), p.52. Lottie's account of the Wylies is of some interest: "The parents of Sally Wylie Rogers (James Wylie and Catherine or Catarina Carroll) came from Antrim, Derry County, Ireland. They were descendants of people who emigrated from Scotland in the 16th century and settled in the vicinity of Londonderry, Ireland. In 1718 a colony of the descendants of these people, a party of 120 families, with their religious Instructor, came to New England. They applied to the Government of Massachusetts for the grant of land for a township. After some time in viewing the country, they selected the tract afterwards comprising the town of Londonderry, first known as Nutfield [New Hampshire] . In 1719 a delegation of these people took possession of this land and the name was changed to Londonderry. They introduced the culture of the potato, until then unknown in New England. Also the manufacture of linen cloth, for many years the source of early prosperity. It was to this

community that James Wylie and his family came in 1770 and remained in the vicinity until the year 1800 when they came to Craftsbury, Vermont, to make their home. Their daughter, afterwards the wife of Jesse Rogers, one of the pioneers of Lutterloh, was born on the ocean July 22, 1770. One record says 'on ship board in Boston Harbor.' James Wylie died the day he was 100 years old, February 22, 1820. This I looked up in the town clerk's office as the exact date seemed uncertain. In some old letters loaned me to read, the date of death was given as April – 1820. So I looked it up to be sure. My great grandmother Sally Wylie Rogers was one of the original members of the Covenanter Church in East Craftsbury, which was organized in September 1816. Her mother, Mrs James Wylie, was another of the original members. She was 94 years old at the time. Sally Wylie Rogers used to come on horseback from her home in Albany to Craftsbury to church, a matter of perhaps 5 miles, following the [Bayley-]Hazen [Military] Road. She would come Saturday afternoon by sundown, stay over night at the home of one of the elders, attend an all day meeting, two sessions, and go home after sundown Sunday." This woman's sister, Molly, "opened a school just on the edge of Craftsbury and families 4-5 miles away sent their children to this school. This must have been about 1812-14. So Molly Wylie seems to be the Pioneer in School History in Lutterloh." Aunt Lottie thought this school must have been supported by the town but it was, perhaps, a venture school. The Covenanter Church seems also to have had members who were what Scots would have called 'Anti-burghers', believers who would not swear civil oaths. There were still some in Craftsbury in the 1940s during my childhood. They never voted because they scrupled to take the Freeman's Oath which qualified one to vote in Vermont.

11 A printed obituary for Jesse II clipped from an unidentified paper says that his father came to Vermont in 1806, 'to a clearing started the year before by his brother-in -law'. This story was repeated by the Newport *Standard*, another paper carrying his obituary. It may well have confused the date of arrival with his and others' petition for a charter for the Town in 1806.

12 Here Aunt Lottie was following Abby Maria Hemenway's *The Vermont Historical Gazeteer: A Magazine*, Vol. III, (Claremont Manufacturing Co., N.H., 1877), pp.55-57. The Haydens were described on pp.59-60. Other early settlers figure in Hemenway's account.

13 Greensboro was the town next to Craftsbury, where Lottie lived most of her life. In the early nineteenth century, Greensboro was a shire or half-shire town.

14 *See* the obituary for Jesse Rogers II cited in n.11.

15 These children are accounted for in Aunt Lottie's manuscripts. Their careers, locations, and progeny allowed for the extensive travels of her grandfather, her father and her uncle Cornelius: 'Robert, the eldest son

of Jesse and Sally Rogers, went to New York where he made a fortune and returned to Burlington [Vermont] to live. James had a family of 15 children and went to Iowa in a prairie schooner where he remained for the rest of his life. Mary married Nathan Beede and lived in Albany. Sally never married and died at her brother's home in Burlington. Jesse II remained on the farm to care for his parents and the farm was deeded to him in 1838. He married Mary Bosworth of Berlin, Vermont, May 1st 1840 and two sons were born to them, Cornelius E. and Jesse B.' [Until the early 1900s, the family maintained contacts with distant relatives in Hancock, Greenfield, and Nashua, New Hampshire and with others in the Boston area. New York visits were made to relatives in Brooklyn, in towns north of the city, and to other Rogerses in New Jersey. When my great-grandparents, Cornelius and Mary Abby Rogers went to California in 1905-06, they stayed with relatives during much of this six-month trip – notably in Iowa, Oregon, California, Flagstaff, in the Arizona Territory, in Tulsa and Enid, in the Oklahoma Territory, and in St. Louis. In two places they stopped at hotels owned by former residents of Albany.

16   Aunt Lottie is here following her *Gazeteer*.
17   A few receipts exist among the Rogers papers from the 1820s and 1830s for the sale of land, the carding of wool, and the sale of wheat to Jabez Page (see above, p.122). At least one other receipt concerns the similar activities of William Hayden II.
18   *History of Albany Vermont*, edited by Virginia Wharton (n.p., n,d. [1991]), pp.13-14, has a different story in which the discovery of the smugglers was made by Sally's son, Robert.
19   Aunt Lottie had some odd things to say about William Hayden II: 'I have been told that William II could neither read nor write. I would not know about that but think it might be so as no money was voted for schools in Lutterloh until 1814, then only 1 cent on a dollar. In those days, 1814, boys 14 years-old were doing a man's work and William was about that age when his father deserted the family. From then on he was the man of the family.' This seems incompatible with Hayden's success as a contractor and businessman.
20   Both men were coopers working in what must have been a small market.
21   His obituaries wrongly describe him as having been happily married for '57 years' [it was really for 43 years] and possessed of 'one of the best farms in the Black River valley.' [He had about 300 acres and wood lots elsewhere. His Hayden neighbors had about 450 acres.]
22   Like Jabez Page a few years later, Hayden was running a 'putting out system' in which he bought wool, gave it to others to card and spin, and somewhere had the cloth fulled and finished.
23   After legal changes in 1843, such entails were prohibited in Vermont.
24   Later in the manuscript the name is spelled 'Agubah'; 'Azubah' is correct. In eighteenth-century Scottish orthography, there is little

distinction between g, z, j, and y. In this very Scottish region, that orthography may have persisted.

25 According to *The History of Albany*, p.17. William Hayden I started a cloth business in Albany which employed several spinners and weavers. *The History* says he left Albany in 1830 having lost money because he had stood surety for someone. My grandmother's story was that the Rogers family lent William II money to go to Quebec where he became involved in the 1837 Rebellion. Gramma was sure he went to New Hampshire and then to Michigan or Wisconsin to work as a contractor on railroads. Lamoureux in *VL* confirms most of that in a different order and gives dates.

26 This two and a half story Greek Revival house, five bays wide and four deep, is now on the list of National Historic Sites. It was constructed in the 1850s and incorporated the newest of hot air furnaces and many elaborate and luxurious fittings. It is described in some detail in *History of Albany*, pp.167-171. The US Census for 1860 lists the Hayden property as worth $50,000, which would include the property, house, and furnishings – roughly the value of the estate left by William II, if a bad debt for $40,000 is excluded; *VL*, pp.52-53.

27 For Aunt Lottie and my grandmother, 'the West' was usually the Old Northwest running out to the prairies, not the land beyond the Rockies.

28 This account may not be accurate. See Lamoureux, *Mischief in the Mountains*, pp.48-51, 168.

29 My mother, Doris Sanders Emerson, remembered William Henry as an unsuccessful businessman ' "who kept and trained blooded horses".... William Henry left his family, when he died in 1910, heavily in debt. The property was sold but after paying the debts there was only a small amount for Armenia and Carrie. After seeing her sister Carrie through the terrible illness of TB, there was not much left for Mamie to live on. By now she too was in poor health. After selling the farm she spent a summer with us in my old home [in Albany].'

30 Jennie Rogers took a temperance oath at about age seventeen when she joined the Independent Order of Good Templars. She wanted me to take one when I was nine. What she and her brother made of their father's drinking metheglin and hard-cider we can only guess. Robbie, as an adult, was probably more like his father.

31 This fits with the family's abolitionist leanings and with its independence of local churches.

32 In the 1960s, I asked the owner of the house, the Rev. Mr. William Chadwick, about a tunnel but he had found no evidence of one in the extensive renovations he had undertaken. Lamoureux thought there were tunnels which might have been used for smuggling Chinese workers into the country before they could legally enter. Chinese laborers worked on railways but the story does not seem plausible to me. See *VL*, p.54.

33 Sprung floors have supports, which are not directly tied to the ceiling timbers of the room below. They have a bit of give and a softer feel when danced on.
34 'Miss Jean' was a remarkable lady from an extraordinary and arty family which until 1914 was *au courant* with the art communities of Paris and New York; *See* Sally Fisher, ' "All the World's a Stage": Miss Jean Simpson, 1897-1980', [1982], *Forty Years of the Hazen Road Dispatch, 1975-2015*, edited by Gail Sangree (Greensboro Historical Society and the Greensboro Association, Greensboro, Vt., 2015), pp.158–159; Allen F. Davis, 'The Simpson-Rodin Connection', *The Hazen Road Dispatch*, 30 (2013), pp.15-18.
35 My mother was sure the Sawyer name had been anglicized from Shonyo, presumably a name deriving from something French or Indian. Amanda died in Lowell where other Shonyos lived. 'Courtemanche' is a name common in Quebec.
36 This incidental information about the family comes from my family papers and from the autobiography started, but not finished, by my mother. Other dated references and quotations are taken from the diaries of Mary Abby Tenney Rogers.
37 Barton Landing grew up around the point at which the Barton River became navigable for boats plying Lake Memphremagog. The railroad reached Barton Village in 1857 and Barton Landing a year or so later.
38 His sons claimed never to have heard him swear other than to say, 'By turd'.
39 I remember this picture from my childhood – an old lady lying peacefully on a plump pillow wearing on her head a bonnet trimmed with lace.
40 *See* Ralph Stanton Emerson, *English Roots of the Haverhill and Ipswich Emersons* (Gateway Press, Baltimore, 1985). The early history of the Haverhill Emersons given there rests on too many suppositions to seem reliable.
41 My Aunt Flora thought we were all descended from some Lincolnshire knight, whose coat of arms she had someone copy for her. It seems to me a bit of pure fantasy and wishful thinking. If one is going to find an aristocratic ancestor, better a Scottish Duke.
42 Among the family papers is a printed 1825 'Articles of Faith and Covenant adopted by The Danville [Vermont] Baptist Association'. Some of the family went to a Baptist church until about 1914.
43 Other accounts say the reward was set at £50.
44 Penacook, N.H., was the site of her killing of the Indians; Haverhill was her home. Both statues had been defaced by vandals and in 2009 needed repairs. There are numerous web-sites containing material about her.

45 Job, 36:14. See P. G. Kearney, hhttp://wprokasy.myweb.uga.edu. Emerson2.htm. Mather's *Magnalia* went through several editions and is again in print.

46 'I am a miserable sinner, and I have justly provok'd the holy God to leave me unto that folly of my own heart, for which I am now condemmed to die. I cannot but see much of the anger of God against me, in the circumstances of my woful death. He hath fulfilled upon me that word of his, "Evil pursueth sinners!" I therefore desire humbly to confess my many sins before God and the world; but most particularly my blood guiltiness. Before the birth of my twin-infants, I too much parlied with the temptation of the devil to smother my wickedness by muthering of them. At length, when they were born, I was not insensible that at least one of them was alive; but such a wretch was I, as to use a murderous carriage towards them, in the place where I lay, on purpose to dispatch them out of the world. I acknowledge that I have been more hard hearted than the sea-monsters; and yet for the pardon of these my sins, I would fly to the blood of the Lord Jesus Christ, which is the only "fountain set open for sin and uncleanness." I know not how better to glorifie God, for giving me such an opportunity as I have had to make sure of his mercy, than by advertising and entreating the rising generation here to take warning by my example, and I will therefore tell the sins that have brought me to my shameful end. I do warn all people and expecially young people, against the sin of uncleanness in particular. 'Tis that sin that hath been my ruine. Well had it been for me, if I had answered all temptations to that sin as Joseph did, "How shall I do this wickedness, and sin against God?" But, I see bad company is that which leads to that and other sins; And I therefore beg all that love their souls to be familiar with none but such as fear God. I believe the chief thing that hath brought me into my present condition, is my disobedience to my parents. I dispised all their godly counsel and reproofs; and I was always of a haughty, stubborn spirit. So that now I am become a dreadful instance of the curse of God belonging to disobedient children. I must bewail this also, and although I was baptized, yet when I grew up, I forgot the bonds that were laid upon me to be the Lord's. Had I given my self to God, as soon as I was capable to consider that I had been in baptism set apart for him, How happy had I been! It was my delay to repent of my former sins, that provoked God to leave me unto the crimes for which I am now to die. Had I seriously repented of my uncleanness the first time I fell into it, I do suppose I had not been left unto what followed. Let all take it from me: They little think what they do when they put off turning from sin to God, and resist the strivings of the Holy Spirit. I fear 'tis for this that I have been given up to such "hardness of heart", not only since my long imprisonment but also since my just condemnation. I now know not what will become of my distressed,

perishing soul. But I would humbly commit it unto the mercy of God in Jesus Christ. Amen.'

47 My grandmother Emerson's paternal line went back to a Bradbury Carr who the Emersons thought came to New Hampshire in 1719 from Londonderry, Ireland, with the congregation of a minister named 'McGregory'. This sounds very much like the Rogers family story. Similarities continued. My Aunt Flora had found somewhere the story that Bradbury Carr was the first to grow potatoes in America. *See* Richard V. and John F. Polhemus, *Stark: The Life and Wars of John Stark*, pp.2-3. Some of the Carrs migrated to Cabot and Woodbury, Vermont, in the 1780s and 1790s, and married equally adventurous people named Lawson, Wells, and Nelson. All seem to have been farmers and stone cutters. From the Carr line of my family, I inherited a pewter charger once belonging to Mary Chase Morse (1726-?), the great-grand mother of Jonathan Emerson.

48 This group purchased about that time a six-volume set of David Hume's *History of England* (Boston, Little, Brown and Co., 1863) once in my library. Fairs and agricultural improvement groups go back to the 1720s in Scotland and lending-libraries were common there by the 1780s.

49 Transcription of a manuscript I own.

50 He was following this trade in Barton c. 1857.

51 It is not shown on the 1859 map of Barton but was close to Willoughby Lake.

52 *A War of the People: Vermont Civil War Letters*, edited by Jeffrey D. Marshall (Hanover, N.H. and London, 1999), pp.110, 161.

53 His two surviving letters from June and July 1863 describe interminable marches, in the rain, through Maryland, Northern Virginia and near the Pennsylvania border – on the way to Gettysburg. Sleeping on an Army-issued rubber blanket kept the men off the mud but they slept wet and in discomfort.

54 The gun was a .22 used by my aunt Dorothy to shoot woodchucks and porcupines from her bedroom window. The bayonet was real but may not have been used in the 1860s.

55 He appears in Abby Hemenway's list of such men given in *The Vermont Historical Gazeteer*, III, p.34.

56 The location of his granite-shed is shown on the bird's eye view of Hardwick published in 1892 by George E. Norris of Brockton, Mass. This is reproduced in J, Kevin Graffagnino, *Vermont in the Victorian Age* (1985), Plate xxxi.

57 The inventory is held at the Town Clerk's Office in Albany Vermont and is dated 24 December 1838. It was prepared by Dyer Bill, a popular physician, and Hiram Merrill, a local farmer. It cost $2.00 but it is unclear if this went to the appraisers or into the Town's general revenues. A quick way to value those goods is to think of $2-4.00 as being then a workingman's weekly wage. Particulars of the wealth of

the family come mainly from the *Books of Records of Albany Vermont* kept in the office of the Town Clerk of Albany.

58 In 1821, the house and 220 acres seem to have been valued at $400 but Jesse also owned another lot, and had 3 horses, 2 oxen, and 6 cows. His son, Robert, owned a watch by then; so, his father may be presumed to have had one too. The house built by Jesse's son, Jesse II, and his cooperage is shown on the F. W. Beers' map of the town in 1878 – at the bottom lower left.

59 This may be a listing only of what went on the ropes of the bed frames or bedsteads.

60 Spaces were often used as punctuation.

61 This was probably cooking gear such as bread tins and pans. There would have been wooden basins in which to mix dough and so forth. Those may have been deemed to belong to Mrs. Rogers.

62 These were probably used to pickle the pork and beef and then to store some that was salted but not, or not yet, smoked.

63 The house had eighteen-inch think walls and required a lot of bricks for a house forty- by thirty-five feet with an attached annex holding the kitchen and other rooms.

64 See Daniel Jaffe, *A New Nation of Goods: The Material Culture of Early America* [mostly mid-18th century to c. 1920] (University of Pennsylvania Press, Philadelphia, 2010).

65 Ten or so years later, Barton had far outstripped Albany. In 1859, it had seven mills or shops on Mill Hill. Twenty years later, the number given by Abby Hemenway is eight. Many were now larger and with new names and owners: *The Vermont Historical Gazetteer*, III, p.80. Eight is the number shown on the Beers map of the town 1878 [Map 9]. Mill Hill allowed the stream flowing out of Crystal Lake to power Barton's shops until a town owned power-plant brought electricity to the village in 1895. Those businesses are described in Darlene Young, *A History of Barton, Vermont* (Crystal Lake Falls Historical Association, Barton, 1998), *passim*. Barton, like Irasburg, Albany and Craftsbury owed its industry to water power. Lyndonville built an electric plant early, in 1890, partly because the rail-town's industry was not located near its falls.

66 He would have had less money had two ventures he sponsored come to fruition. In 1873 he was among those who promoted a rail-connection to Montpelier running down the valley of the Black River to Barton Landing. The railroad would have carried butter, logs, cattle, and sugar to more distant markets. About two thirds of the Albany voters in 1873 supported the railroad but there was not enough support to build it. In 1888, Cornelius joined others in an scheme to build an Albany tub factory. Their support of the tub factory came just as tin cans and pails were appearing. He seems also to have invested in the Hardwick Bank and, like many with spare cash, loaned money to neighbors. He seems

not to have taken mortgages on those loans; Isaac Sanders did and foreclosed on some.
67 Many of those things were inherited by my grandmother Sanders.
68 The original of this is held at the Scottish National Gallery in Edinburgh, Scotland.
69 The US census returns for 1850 suggest that Jesse Rogers was one of 71 men from 200 family census entries who had over $1,000 in property; he ranked eighth in the list of the wealthy. In 1860 there were 161 families worth $1,000 or more out of the 230 family census entries but the Rogers family had slipped in the rankings to about eighteenth. Consumption was fueled by the growth of wealth in a prosperous Vermont which would become less affluent after 1870 because of the decline of the wool trade. Listing wealth stopped after 1860.
70 The Sears and Roebuck Company issued catalogues by 1893 and, like other merchandisers, experienced greater sales after the institution of Rural Free Delivery in 1896.
71 It was said to have been brought back from the South by a Rogers relative who had spent the war there. My uncles claimed they fired it in the 1890s using match-heads for powder and priming.
72 The Arm & Hammer Baking Soda Co. offered decks of bird and animal cards – and advertised using racist cartoons. They went down well in a town where Minstrel Shows were regularly staged.
73 The first US postcard dates from 1861 but they became popular as collectors items in the 1890s. Allen F. Davis, *Postcards from Vermont: A Social History, 1905-1945* (University Press of New England, Hanover, N.H. and London, 2002), pp.1-2.
74 By 1840, there were drummers and fifers for the militia company in Albany; by the Civil War there seems to have been a band of some sort. There was certainly one by the 1880s which lasted until c. 1950. Bands gave weekend concerts, played at ball games, and on holidays like Memorial Day or the Fourth of July. Band members usually supplied the music for minstrel shows and other town entertainments.
75 Phone companies came to Vermont in the 1880s and 1890s. In Albany, a company was started by Dennis and Patrick McGuire c. 1888 to serve Irasburg, Albany, and Craftsbury, with eventual ties to companies in Hardwick and Barton and through them to a wider grid. Dennis ran the business side; Pat took care of other operations. In c. 1900, the McGuire brothers charged a dollar a month for service. Pat and my grandmother lived for a time in the same nursing home in Barton so I got to know Pat in his old age. He was a cousin and one-time employer of my grandfather Sanders. Pat had been a lively young fellow. In the mid-1880s, when he was in twenties, he worked his way out to California. He told me he had ridden on the tops of stage coaches when a fellow with a gun sat next to the driver. California disappointed him, so, he returned to farm in Vermont and to string phone lines. He was the last

man in Albany to wear a swallow-tailed coat to Church (c. 1915) – and to local dances. Both brothers eventually became bank directors – Den in Hardwick, Pat at the Barton Savings Bank and Trust Company.

76   The movies were shown by a visiting missionary trying to raise money for his African mission.

77   My list is attached at the end of this essay.

78   I have been unable to find figures for Vermont in those years but travelers agreed that Vermonters were highly literate. Among the many early cancelled bills and receipts held by Jabez Page, only two are signed with witnessed marks.

79   In this paragraph and in others below I am grateful for the advice of my friend, Dr. Ronald Black.

80   In a broadside mocking the righteous, David Hume created a character named 'Zerobable MacGilchrist' whom he wanted recognized as a throwback to seventeenth-century Scottish Puritanism. That, he believed, was still cherished by uneducated, lower-class Presbyterians. The name 'Zerobable' was a deliberate corruption of Zerubbabel, an Old Testament King and a reputed, but problematic, ancestor of Christ. Gilchrist signifies 'Christ's gilly' or servant. For an account of Hume's pamphlet and of the games he was playing, see Roger L. Emerson, 'Hume and the Bellman, Zerobabel MacGilchrist', *Hume Studies*, 23 (1997), pp.9-28.

81   David changed the spelling of his name when he left home to make the spelling correspond to the sound of his surname. He was actually a third son but the second surviving.

82   'Bible (Version, Gaelic)', *Dictionary of Scottish Church History and Theology*, edited by Nigle M deS. Cameron (InterVarsity Press, Downers Grove, Ill., 1993), pp.75-76.

83   The poems by many Gaelic poets included brave and bloody heroes, but also girls like 'Ishbel of the golden hair' and young men like Colin of Glenure, to cite only two attractive figures from the poems of Duncan Ban Macintyre (1724-1812). This folk poetry was not full of biblical names and figures.

84   This information comes from *History of Albany*, pp.257-59.

85   The Albany Methodists were Wesleyan Methodists who had adopted that name to distinguish themselves from George Whitefield's Calvinist Methodists. The Wesleyans were abolitionists while Southern Methodists supported slavery.

86   They came from a Scottish secession Kirk in which believers refused to allow any state authority over the Kirk such as that establishing it and limiting its powers. Christ the King was the Head of the Church and not to be limited by men. They took no civic oaths and in Vermont could not vote because they refused to swear the Freeman's Oath.

87   Sortilege involved being guided by opening the Bible at random and pointing, without reading, to a passage and then interpreting and

acting on what one found – or rather, what God had guided one to discover.

88 My reading has turned up no Remembers or Calvins and only two Luthers. I know of one Welcome, the man who gave his name to the Welcome O. Brown Cemetery in Barton.

89 Most concordances were still versions of that produced by Alexander Cruden between 1737 and 1769. Sunday Schools in this period enrolled many adults as well as school children. Indeed, my father attended off and on until he was about twenty (1916).

90 They did, however, sometimes give boys first names which were surnames and presumably taken from branches of the family. Among my ancestors were Russells; I had an uncle Russell.

91 Peacham was an early exception and shows its Scottish roots: 'The library in Peacham was founded on August 9, 1810 by a group of students of the Caledonia County Grammar School (Peacham Academy) as a resource for their debating society. They named their library "The Peacham Juvenile Library Society." For an original fee of $2.00, an individual could become a proprietor. For forty-five years, the Peacham Juvenile Library Society continued as it had begun, serving its member proprietors. There was no actual building for the library throughout its first one hundred years. The book collection moved from store to store in the village of Peacham Corner.' The Library Web-site. Scottish societies established many libraries and were often connected to academies or collegiate groups. The name of the Peacham group may point to an adult library as well.

92 More appear in those type faces in the detailed map of the village of West Albany and in the hamlets of Albany Center and South Albany.

93 My well off great-great grandfather appears in the smallest of the three type faces and may have paid nothing. That probably reflects stinginess and semi-retirement from farming and his work as a cooper.

94 In the 1860 Census, the family of William Hayden is listed as having landed property of over $50,000 in value and other assets worth $6,500. By 1912, the property had been sold and the heirs were nearly indigent. Rags to riches, riches to rags was more likely in Vermont than in Old World societies which knew entail. That and other restrictions on property might preserve an estate, even though it was debt ridden.

95 The sources and meanings have been taken from many sources on the web. They can be checked against those given in *Dictionary of First Names*, edited by Patrick Hanks, Kate Hardcastle, and Flavia Hodges (Oxford University Press, Oxford, 2006), a more authoritative source than those I used but one I found only when my list was done.

96 Mary Abby was the daughter of Jabez's daughter, Louisa, and Lyman P. Tenney, J.P., an affluent and respected farmer in Albany.

97 The notes were cancelled by the tearing out of the debtor or debtors's signatures.

98   Lye was an alkaline ingredient of soap, glass, and other manufactured items. An important part of the soap market was the cloth industry
99   Ebenezer gave him a quit-claim deed witnessed by Ashbel Hale and Patience Hale. The deed is dated from Greensboro, then a shire town, where it was said to be entered in Book 3 p. 111 of the land records. Those records later burned in 1831.
100 Another account says he married a Lucy Hitchcock on 2 November 1817. For that information, I thank Lynn Bonfield whose source is Jennie Chamberlain Watts and Elsie A. Choate, People of Peacham (Vermont Historical Society, Peacham, Vt., 1965).
101 See n. 17.
102 The shop was there but the first mention of his house in the land records comes in 1830.
103 *History of Albany, Vermont 1806-1991*, edited by Virginia Wharton (n.p., n.d., [1991]), p.22. His colleague in that office was Daniel Rowell, a member of the family from whom he later bought madder. He may have been elected again in 1848 and 1849 which is suggested by the records for that year which, however, do not explicitly show him to have been elected.
104 Irasburg was a shire town from 1812-1884. Courts sat there and some records were kept in the Court House to which the jail was annexed. After 1884, the honor of being the shire town passed to Newport.
105 Jabez Page was never re-elected but in various ways he served his town for over twenty years.
106 By then, the Church may have funded its activities mainly through 'donation suppers' and gifts and not from subscription fees which included pew rent.
107 These seem to be the fleeces from shorn sheep which were rolled up.
108 The photographs appear with the permission of the Albany Town Museum.
109 Her first name was Anne but her surname and her dates have not been found.
110 No 'clothery' or fulling mill in Albany is mentioned by Norris M. Darling in the *Vermont Historical Gazetteer*, edited by Abby Maria Hemenway, III, pp.47-54.
111 *The History of Albany*, pp.10-12.
112 For some time after 1830, the only bank in the County was in Irasburg, see Hemenway, *Gazetteer*, III, p.253.
113 This was not only within the State and the United States, but, for a few, overseas. In the volumes of Vermont poems mentioned below (notes 186, 270) there are poets who visited Europe, Britain, China and the Far East. They were tourists, teachers, lawyers, doctors, and missionaries. What is perhaps surprising is their interest in writing about the French Revolution, Napoleon, and the Greek War for Independence. Some Vermonters were well-informed about distant countries and even had

read Mme. de Stahl's *Corrine ou Italie* (1807) and other out-of-the-way books.

114 The dressing room was where the fibers were dressed for weaving by giving them some starch and a final twist. It was probably cleaner and less dangerous than the weaving halls.

115 That would have given him a large vocabulary – the King James Bible contains 12,143 different words – and would have taught him something about style and good writing.

116 This letter probably refers to William Hayden II who may still have been running the cloth business begun by his father (see above, p.18).

117 Like many later well-off Vermont farmers, Jabez may have taken vacations in the autumn after the crops were in and before the snow came It was a slow time of year for farmers.

118 Kellogg had been on the Town's School Committee in 1830 and served as Town Clerk from 1825 through 1832; *History of Albany*, pp.14, 22, 257.

119 .The record U.S. average corn yield was 164.7 bushels per acre in 2009. The price per bushel was $3.34.

120 During the Civil War, Chester Page in Albany paid $300 for a substitute so he did not have to serve in the army; *The History of Albany*, p.27.

121 The following material has been drawn mainly from his daily reminder diaries fleshed out with bits from the records of the Town of Burke, local histories and sources on the internet. His diary entries are all short and laconic. They often appear somewhat random. He did not always enter expenses and money received, or note all his transactions at the ends of the diaries, where there is a space to do so and where many costs and receipts were routinely entered. He did not identify people mentioned in his entries but most of them were neighbors or belonged to his or his wife's extended families.

122 His diaries twice mention his birthday but not the year of his birth. The first date comes from his tombstone and conflicts with the date recorded at the Burke Town Clerk's Office. That has him dying at age 76 – which would make him born in 1836.

123 Most of his daily reminders had charts which calculated interest for him. The diaries included more as time went on. Such sources are discussed by Molly McCarthy, in *The Accidental Diarist: A History of the Daily Planner in America* (University of Chicago Press, Chicago, 2013).

124 A somewhat similar treatment was meted out to his sons as babies. Bradbury Watson is not named in the diary for almost two years but appears only as 'baby' and only then when he was a new-born or was sick. The same was true of the Ebe (whose full name his father never gave) but this was less the case with Ira, his youngest and most promising son. He also had the shortest name.

125 There were many men named Bradbury living in the area – a tribute to a Baptist elder or minister, Bradbury M. Richardson, who had lived and preached in Sutton for many years.

126 Lyndonville had a main street used for horse-racing both summer and winter until the 1940s.
127 Board in nineteenth century Vermont usually included a room, food, and washing.
128 Pump-logs were tree trunks or large limbs bored with long augers so they could convey water. The ends were shaped to fit into the logs to which they were connected. Fitting the joins was precise work if water was not to be wasted.
129 The farm was on the present day Pudding Hill Road leading to Lyndonville and about four miles from Sutton Corner where the Free Will Baptist Church he attended was located. It is not clear from the deeds how much land the farm originally covered but it was over 122 acres – probably about 200. According to the deed of 20 March 1873, it cost the Watsons $2,500. Another piece of 'three hundred fifty five square rods' [about 2.1 acres] was added in 1882. A well, owned by a Harlaw Easterbrooks, was bought in 1890. The whole was sold in 1905 by Leonard and Sophia Watson for $3,500 to Gilbert Jesseman. Fi had been made a co-owner at some point. Sutton Land Records I:273; II:(1882); V:80.
130 It included, by c. 1878, two sugar bushes, wood lots, arable fields, and pasture land for about twenty cows. It had a small orchard and a large garden.
131 His early presence at meetings may have owed something to the fact that a district school bordered his property. He long served as its caretaker.
132 At this point in his life, the separator was likely to have been a can with a tap at the bottom to allow the milk without fat to drain away. Later, he had one which had a hand crank and worked by centrifugal force.
133 When he turned them out in the spring, he 'dipped them' in 'Alum water'.
134 That suggests Leonard had initially bought only part of his uncle's farm which is said still to be held by him on the Beers map of 1875.
135 He always hired an extra man for sugaring but Leonard did most of the boiling himself – he would not burn the syrup. It looks as if they boiled in alternate shacks in turn and that the sap was not always boiled soon after it was collected.
136 He also made some maple honey, or sugar with a stirred-honey consistency. Some of that was sent to customers as far away as California after he had become an established sugar maker.
137 He seems to have bought his first tin cans in 1901.
138 He planted Early Rose potatoes, introduced in the 1860s and popular not only for their color (pink) but because they matured in seventy-five to one hundred thirty days and were hardy.
139 Pumpkins, as a fodder crop, were introduced to American farmers in the 1880s. Leonard grew them for some years.

140 He recorded when his cows were 'served' and offered the services of his bulls and rams to others who paid him stud fees – as he paid to others from time to time. He tended to breed his own cattle to the best bulls in the area which he often did not own. In the end, he had a herd of Jerseys for milk and Devonshires for beef. That was more or less the mix on the Hayden and Rogers farms in Albany.

141 For years, he used oxen for heavy farm work but kept horses to go to town and take logs to mills. Each had its role.

142 Snip was 'traded off' to a good owner in 1899 and Charley in 1903. Leonard had had the latter thirty years or so.

143 He sowed clover as well and put grass seed in with his 'ingen wheat'. His land was well-fertilized.

144 Hulled corn was made by taking off the hulls or outer covering with lye, washing the corn, and then eating it cooked. It was peddled in Vermont in the spring by men diving carts full of the stuff.

145 He replaced his pans, arches, roofs, and much else during the time he farmed in Sutton.

146 In 1880 he got $9.24 for a hind quarter of beef.

147 In 1882, they came to $272.49 for better than half a ton of butter, sold principally in Springfield, and Boston, Massachusetts, and locally in Lyndonville.

148 In 1881 this came to $19.50.

149 He bought a new one in 1890 for $35.00.

150 He had a saving account by 1885 but perhaps not before.

151 On suspects that there was a lingering Presbyterian dourness hanging over the Baptist Watsons and people like them. That kept them working most holidays and minimized their celebrations until Leonard was past sixty. It would not have been so different in Barton where the stores were open on Christmas Day – or in Edinburgh, where in the early nineteenth century, courts still sat on 25 December.

152 The significance of this day is not known. Entries in the diary (*e.g.*, 1898) show that he was a cemetery trustee in the 1890s and may have been so for a much longer time.

153 He and Fi attended Grange meetings from January 1873 and were regulars for many years. His last recorded Grange meeting was in 1901 but he noted going to 'Farmer Meetings' after that which may have been the same. Leonard probably attended State Grange conventions in the 1880s. The local Grange met at their farm on more than one occasion as did the Ladies Aid Society.

154 When he bought, it was often equipment, animals, lumber and shingles.

155 On 15 September 1910, he recorded that he 'Saw the Aire Ship got up twice It was a success'. This was perhaps the first flight in Vermont of an airplane which is said to have happened on 24 September 1910 at the Caledonia County Fair. *See* Allen F. Davis, *Postcards from Vermont*,

p.287. Balloons were often seen at fairs, but there was no uncertainty about their ascension. In my youth (early 1940s), the balloons at Barton Fair had men jumping with multi-colored parachutes from the attached basket. I watched them from an attic window of my grandparent's house.

156 Throughout his life on the Sutton farm, some of his trading was bartering items for which there seemed to be no fixed price.

157 He 'took the agency for to sell the Washing machine' on 10 August 1891. Two machines were put in a friend's store. By the end of the month, he had sold twenty-seven washers. He peddled more in November and December, and was still selling them in the spring by which time he may have exhausted the local market. The profits probably were spent on the monument erected for his son and the family (p 154).

158 He recorded the following in his diaries:
- 14/2/79   'went up to the Lyceum', [in Lyndonville].
- 14/2 81   'up to the Corner in the evening to a lecture', [Sutton Corner].
- 15/1 84   'up to the Corner.. a Publick reading   Very good so they say'.
- 22/11/87   'Reading at the Corner by Miss Dunkley'.
- 5/10 /94   'entertainment' at the Corner.
- 21/1/95   'a Dramatic play', at West Burke.
- 21/2/96   'up to the Corner to a play'.
- 28/2/96   'up to the Corner to the know (?) Lecture'.
- 2/2/97   'down to the Ville tonight to hear the milk maids'.
- 13/12/00   'to the Ville in the evening to the lecture   a whack at the Universe'
- 2/2/01   evening lecture in Lyndonville.
- 16/2/01   'to the Ville to a slight of hand performance'.
- 14/2/02   'we tended the Lecture of Gearhart   Lectured [sic] from Buffalo'. [This was G. A. Gearhart, a Methodist and Chatauqua circuit lecturer whose topics in this year were 'Dangers that Threaten our Civilization', 'The Coming Man', and 'Footprints of the Centuries.' He was managed by the Mutual Lyceum Bureau and lectured widely for many years.]
- 12/1/03   'went to the lecture' in Lyndonville.
- 25/4/03   'the old Homested plade'. [in St Johnsbury; This was a popular play by Denman Thompson first produced in Boston in 1886.]
- 30/5/03   'heard McCall speak', [a Memorial Day celebration; McCall may have been a Massachusetts Congressman, Samuel McCall].
- 2/1/05,   'We went to a Negro school Exhibition in the Opera House' [in Southern Pines].
- 31/1/07,   'went to the lecture coarse' in West Burke.
- 20/6/08,   'School exersises...in the Evening to the Consert'.

159 He served as Selectman in 1891, 1892, 1894, 1896, 1898 and in most of those years gave in the report of the Surveyors of the Highways. *Sutton Town Records*.
160 The bridge had been washed away. He salvaged some of the old bridge, cut stringers and rafters on his farm for the new one, drew them down to the site and got the bridge up in about a week. He had it shingled a few days later.
161 The election of Senators was still indirect and was not done by ordinary voters until after the 17th Amendment was ratified in May 1913.
162 His committee was an important one and not one of those to which those thought incompetent were usually assigned into the mid-twentieth century.
163 That was a basically Calvinist Church which did not believe in predestination but in the need for adult individuals to freely and deliberately choose Christ and the salvation He offered. That they forfeited if they accepted Christ's offer but did not thereafter lead a godly life. It tended to be an austere Church, which may account in part for his not keeping Christmas until fairly late in life. In most years, Christmas was a work day like any other; Easter is almost never mentioned in his books. His religion was focused on beliefs in salvation through faith and moral living, not on ceremonies and theology.
164 This would have involved total immersion and may have been performed at a river bank as it was in Albany, Vermont, at about the same time.
165 Few of those men would have had much theological training but they would have known their Bible well. The Free Will Baptists made little distinction between Ministers and Elders and, in time, Leonard used the terms interchangeably.
166 His diaries have few mentions of Roman Catholics, the Irish, Italians, and increasing numbers of the French, all of whom were coming into the region in the late nineteenth century as farmers, stone workers, and general laborers.
167 It was about that time that the family went shopping for presents just before Christmas. Before c. 1890, that activity seems not to have been noted and there were no extra expenses entered in his records of money spent.
168 Leonard's error in identifying this man shows how little he followed national politics or knew its principal players.
169 A surprising number of Vermonters visited them that winter, some on their way to or from Florida.
170 Those would have included the Capitol, Supreme Court, but probably not the White House. The Library was the Library of Congress.
171 Quoted from *Republican Party Platforms*: 'Republican Party Platform of 1912,' June 18, 1912. Online by Gerhard Peters and John T. Woolley, *The American Presidency Project*. http://www.presidency.ucsb.edu/ws/?pid 29633.

172 The years covered here are c. 1853-1869. The details often come from a few diaries of her father and from the collection of her daily reminder diaries kept from 1862 until 1914.

173 The Page, Tenney, and Rogers family had long been associated in the establishment and running of the Albany Congregational Church: See *History of Albany*, p.258.

174 The school is shown in 1878 as being in that location: *Atlas of Lamoille and Orleans Counties Vt.* (F. W. Beers & Co., New York, 1878), p.75. It was likely there twenty years earlier when Jabez Page sent his children to the District 7 school near which he also lived.

175 Craftsbury Academy hired college graduates who would have been able to use the Academy's fine collection of scientific instruments to teach physics, astronomy, and chemistry. It also probably had an herbarium. Those things were destroyed in a disastrous fire in 1879 from which the school never really recovered. Unlike Albany Academy, it sometimes taught Greek until c. 1890. This was for those intending to be ministers or headed for arts colleges.

176 An 1869 letter to Mary Abby from her little brother, Fred, thanked her for his Christmas gift, a shovel, and then in labored capitals – he had not yet learned to write a cursive script – said he had 'AN NEW THIRD READER. I AM LEARNING THE MULTIPLICATION TABLE'. This reader would have been (or resembled) the well-known readers of Professor William McGuffey (1836 and after) or Salem Town, LL.D. (1840s). Fred was likely going to her old school.

177 My grandmother, who read this as a child in the 1870s, sometimes quoted this couplet. Mary Abby's copy was not one she had as a child but, as her diary shows, was acquired on 27 December 1869 at a lecture given by a missionary in Lowell, Massachusetts, Later in life, Mary Abby was a supporter of missions. When she went to her first movie in Albany in 1902, 'Mr Edison's pictures' showed Africans in a mission. The show was part of a fund-raising pitch made by a missionary who had come to the town. About the same time she heard her first 'GramaPhone'.

178 *History of Albany Vermont*, p.267. She seems to have learned to play the piano at home.

179 That is where the Tenneys sold bark, apples, oats, grain, and hops. The last crop was worth $50.00 in 1864.

180 In 1865, she again went there to the State Fair.

181 She herself, in 1862, had measles and two years later the family had what she called typhoid fever. A neighbor that year died of small pox and was buried at night with no funeral – so great was the fear of an epidemic.

182 An account of the Catholic Church there can be found in Paul Patrick Daniels, *The Bell Tolls No More to Call the Faithful from Their Chore* (n.p., n.d.).

183 Donation suppers helped pay the minister's salary and sometimes supported other causes such as new school houses as did one held in December 1864.

184 The present November date for Thanksgiving was fixed only in 1941. Before that, its date varied somewhat at the whim of state governors who sometimes ignored the November date set by President Lincoln in 1863.

185 What the 'college' meeting was is uncertain. At a 'concert' she sang 'John Anderson my Jo'.

186 Many of the poets he would have discussed were anthologized by Abby Maria Hemenway in, *Poets and Poetry of Vermont*, (George A. Tuttle & Co., Rutland, 1858) and in *Green Mountain Poets*, edited by A. J. Sanborn (Claremont Manufacturing Co., Claremont, N.H., 1872). That volume mentions fourteen other volumes of poetry by Vermonters and more appear in the notes prefacing many selections. Among the poets given biographical notices, were several from the Northeast Kingdom. Indeed, northeastern and southwestern Vermont contributed disproportionate numbers of poets to that volume. Mary Abby's good friend Delia Darling Honey wrote many verses, some of which were published in local papers and, in her nineties, in a slim volume called *The Honey-Comb: Poems by Delia Darling Honey* (William Bullock, Newport Vt, 1936).

187 This was a sale of some sort.

188 In 1865, she earned about $30.00 and spent some on jewellery, a parasol, a photo album and a 'skeleton' (a dressmaker's-dummy) for which she paid $2.00. Most of her money went on clothing, including $20.00 for 'furs'.

189 All the pieces of this cello were still in her family as late as 1985 when its pieces were sold for $8.00; its whereabouts is now unknown.

190 The Coventry to which she went was not the now lifeless hamlet, overlooked by a mass-produced monument of a Union Soldier on a plinth planted in a small green and set up in 1912. It was one which had created its own Academy in 1858-1860 and supported three music teachers in the village. The Academy is mentioned in Abby Hemenway's *The Vermont Historical Gazeteer*, III:160.

191 Her membership in the Black River Musical Association is likely to have been in 1865 since the back of her ticket has some mathematics calculations on it. What her 1864 diary does not mention is her planned marriage to someone un-named. That is referred to in a letter sent by a friend in Lowell, Massachusetts, Carrie Annis. Nothing came of it. See above, p. 195.

192 On 11 April the bells had rung in the town 'for the capture of Lee's Army school did not keep'. A Fast Day on 15 April commemorated Lincoln's death two days earlier. 'The Meeting house all trimed with black for President Lincoln   he died yesterday morning'. Other towns mourned in a similar fashion.

193 Letters to her from Mary Pine and Carrie Annis suggest that she danced. Molly was one who had stayed out all night – but not in Albany which was too religious for parties such as were held on the New York side of the State.

194 'What-nots' were usually small wooden shelves made to fit into corners. Her's was probably a crocheted thing with pockets meant to be filled and hung on the wall from a hook. Her step-daughter, my grandmother, made them in my childhood.

195 For those non-denominational revivals, attended by as many as 6,500 people, see above, pp. 151, 158.

196 One of her hair wreathes is at the Old Stone House Museum.

197 See the letter from Mary Pine, p. 183.

198 'Seems' because the diary is not well kept in January and is blank from 18 July until the end of the year. The Hamilton Mill and the Merrimack Mill, in which Carrie Annis worked (see above, p. 195), are both shown, as they appeared somewhat later, in *Lowell; The Mill City*, Publications Committee of the Lowell Historical Society (Arcadia Publishing Co., Charleston, S.C., 2005), pp.15 and 16. There were, in the end, over a mile of mills, powered by the falls on the Merrimack River. There were many boarding houses to shelter the hundreds of textile workers. Most of them were women.

199 Payments usually included room, board, and the washing of clothes. Her next recorded pay was received on 11 March – $16.80, probably for fifteen day's of which $6.95 went on board. Board was about half the day's pay. On April 9, she received $25.35 for what appears to have been four weeks work; $11.50 went to board. When compared to the wages Ebe Watson was making in northern Vermont in the 1880s, her pay was better than his. In April, she used her money to buy a fancy black dress for $8.60.

200 The back inside cover of the diary has scrawled the names of animals which seem to have fascinated her: 'Rhinorceros, orang utang, sloth, skelitin muskrat, Guinea pig'. In one corner, she has noted 'skulls' – followed by 'Redman, Indian, Chinese, Black' – an indication of her interest in the racial theories of the times. She also noted the weight of a huge gold nugget on display – 2,166 ounces of which 2,019 3/4 was estimated as pure gold.

201 This was a well-known troupe of both Black and black-faced performers who long entertained Bostonians and were noted for their banjo players.

202 That visit was likely prompted by Delia Darling Honey whose husband had served in the Navy during the Civil War. He may have worked at the Yard.

203 A short letter from her much younger brother suggests she had intended to return home in the spring.

204 One letter, noticed below, shows that she tried to return to working in the Boston area (see p. 195).
205 A successor institution functions today as Vermont College of the Arts.
206 Those meals were not always distinguished as different, which points to the Scots in the area for whom tea and supper were often one and the same.
207 When the candy mixture reached a certain consistency, it could be rolled, cut with shears into lengths, and then pulled with buttered hands to a considerable length. The game was for a couple to pull the longest strand which was cut into small pieces and eaten.
208 These were meetings to raise money and provide supplies for soldiers and for their care. They were sponsored by the Sanitary Commission, a private agency largely run by women to aid the troops.
209 The Fast Day was repeated in 1866 but it was not recorded again in her diaries.
210 Her paragraphing has been changed since she made paragraphs of every sentence. Her prose and spelling is unaltered. Spaces were used by her as punctuation.
211 She may be using an archaic word here. 'Train' sometimes meant, to lay a train of powder to ignite an explosion.
212 Possibly this means, 'you understand me on both matters'.
213 The dances would have been country dances, quadrilles, reels, spathsays, and promenades, not yet risqué waltzes or others in which bodies were embraced and tightly held.
214 'Points' were probably a bit of pricked-in work or embroidery; 'pastillions' are sewn-on decorations.
215 Possibly, a wagon of some sort.
216 Probably what became the Champlain Valley Fair, now the largest in Vermont.
217 Christmas did not yet have a monopoly over the novel decorated trees.
218 Carrie Annis also noted the presence of Thomas [?Pine], writing on 9 December 1866, 'Mary you must not slight Thom so bad for you don't know [what] the poor fellow will feel if you was to giv him the mitten it might brak his heart than you would have some thing to think of all the days of your life   ha ha ha ha ha   Me thinks I hear you say   enough of this I don't know as I can write any thing that will be very interesting to you but if I could see you I would talk // from now untill [next?] winter [? and then] not say half what I want to.' It looks as if Thomas 'got the mitten'.
219 This was the title of a Union song written in 1863 by Charles Carroll Sawyer (1833-?) with music by Henry Tucker (1826?-1882).
220 'You spoke of your being married   I might come to the wedding don't know how long I shall stay if I do that   you can tell beter that I can'. Her work meant less than a friend's wedding.
221 See pages 177-178.

222 Andrew's gun has a whittled stock, a bent metal trigger guard and a stationary trigger. The barrel was a pasteboard tube which had been colored, shellacked and had pins inserted to make its sights. The cannon, was said to be a model of a Confederate cannon but that is unlikely.

223 The yoke is with other objects from this family in the Old Stone House Museum in Brownington, Vermont.

224 *The New American Pronouncing Speller* (Philadelphia, 1872).

225 When I was learning my multiplication table, my grandmother thought I should go beyond 16 times 16 into the 20s times 20s. She still remembered the table to 30 times 30. Rote learning saved her a lot of time in later life and left her never at a loss for words. One could always quote something one had memorized. Her quotes were often Biblical but also came from a range of authors anthologized in her textbooks.

226 My grandmother, until the 1940s, still had a broken slate she had used in that school. Robbie would have had one too.

227 My grandmother had some in my youth but I do not know if they were hers or her children's: they included a Robin Hood, Tom Thumb and Humpty-Dumpty. I wore them out.

228 Jennie was taken, at some time, to New York to have an eye complaint treated but that was probably to Albany or Buffalo, not to New York City. Several poems survive in the same envelope; they may have been school exercises too, but, in that case, they are probably copies for recitations and not her own compositions. I have been unable to trace their sources.

229 This has problems designed to be solved by Vermont students who would then have learned some things about the State's usury and other commercial laws. Robinson, a prolific writer of mathematics and science texts, is noticed above (pp. 191-192, 204).

230 It is not clear when Jennie first enrolled in Craftsbury Academy or if the books noted in this paragraph were used there or in the graded schools she and Robbie had attended.

231 It reads:
And to the boys before me now
    I have a word to say:
Give heed unto my little speech,
    And my advice obey.
Be honest, fair, sincere and square,
    In all you have to do,
And let me tell you, ere I close,
    I neither smoke nor chew.

232 In 1886, she was paid $20.00 for eight weeks and would have had her board as well.

233 Scott was the son of a Professor of Greek at the University of Edinburgh and became an extramural lecturer in Edinburgh where he taught French. He was the author of a French grammar.

234 This was a book likely to have been bought from a traveling book salesman since its title page says it is 'sold only by distributing agents'.
235 The only other 'fact book' which has survived is a portion of M. Young's *New Guide to Horse Owners: A Complete Horse Doctor...* (New York, 1880).
236 The family tended to slaughter 'bossy beef', bull cattle older than calves but not mature. They ate their own mutton, lamb, pork and poultery.
237 Scaling involved estimating the number of board feet a log would yield when milled.
238 Some of that money went to Cornelius's parents who retained title to the farm. Some paid a hired man; some was saved.
239 He used his profits to finance a three and a half week trip to New York City and its environs. He had relatives there with whom he and his wife stayed while they shopped, saw sights, went to the theaters, to concerts, and to a variety of religious meetings.
240 Cornelius's political views seem to have been inherited and probably derived from a family-liking for Jeffersonian democracy, state's rights theory, cheap money, and, later, William Jennings Bryant. Cornelius may have been a 'Northern Copperhead' since he paid a substitute to fight for him in the Civil War. However, he and his second wife admired General Grant, whose tomb they visited on a trip to New York in 1889. His family did not like Southerners. Jennie when she could vote, always did so for Republicans. She took after her step-mother who went to Democratic meetings with her husband but saved the Republican Party campaign ribbon from 1889 which is among her papers (p. 211).
241 The diaries record years in which thirty-six or more adults and children ate dinner at Cornelius's house.
242 In Albany, the singing school was a private venture training singers to sing church music. The ticket shown comes from c. 1890 and was issued by the father or brother of William Sargent, sometime leader of the town's band and a noted Boston musical figure and composer of marches.
243 Some 'sociables' or socials were 'swapping socials' which are described by a clipping which my grandmother nostalgically saved but did not date: 'Each one takes a package to this sociable, of any size he wishes, and containing some article that he is willing to donate, the funnier, the better. At a given signal all begin to "swap" packages. After this has continued ten or fifteen minutes another signal is given, and each one retains the package he then holds. They are then opened, one by one, and exhibited to the company, when the one who brought the package must tell why he wished to give it away and why it is appropriate for the one who has it. Much amusement may be afforded in this way.' Other socials saw picnic lunches being auctioned off or swapped in a similar manner.

244 Arbor Day was inaugurated in 1872. By the time the Rogers children planted their trees, it was, by a State decree, to be observed the first Friday in April.
245 As an old lady, Jennie remembered this as stopping in the 1890s. It was replaced by a parade led by the Albany Band.
246 These lasted into the 1940s; See Jeanette E. Hill, 'Kitchen Junkets', in the *Hazen Road Dispatch 1975-2015*, pp.97.
247 Hulled corn or hominy was regarded as a treat. It was then a northern as well as southern dish and enjoyed throughout the Appalachians. It was still sold in cans in the 1940s. Northerners seldom seem to have ground it into hominy grits.
248 It is not clear what if any medicines were given to him or what other therapies were employed.
249 Funerals at the house were, perhaps, the remains of an old Scottish practice of having none at all in kirks but, sometimes, saying a prayer at the house and then going to the grave-site where there might be a prayer at the committal. That was followed by a gathering of relatives and friends for 'refreshments', more sober in Vermont than in most parts of Scotland.
250 His grandparents both died within the year.
251 On their 1883 western trip, he and his wife managed to stay most of the time with relatives or with people who had once lived in and around Albany. They managed this feat again in 1905-06. They, then, went from Vermont to Iowa, Nebraska, Washington State, then south to San Francisco, Los Angeles, San Diego, Flagstaff in the Arizona Territory, and Enid and Tulsa in the Oklahoma Territory, and finally to St Louis and Joliet, staying almost always with relatives and friends.
252 Side Judges were required to be County J.P.s. Sitting in County Courts, they could not rule on the legal issues raised in trials but they advised the trial judge on matters of fact tried before them and advised on sentences. They had administrative functions in the running of the County. Tenney is not listed in Abby Hemenway's list of such men: *The Vermont Historical Gazeteer*, III, p.34. The family story may be wrong.
253 This incidental information about the family comes from family papers and from the autobiography started, but not finished, by my mother, Doris Sanders Emerson. All of the dated references and quotations are taken from the diaries of Mary Abby Tenney Rogers for 1885, 1886 and 1887.
254 Albany and Craftsbury produced two other musicians of some note, the Bagley brothers, Ezra Mahlon and Edwin Eugene. The older was born in Albany in 1853, the other in Craftsbury in 1857. Both composed marches. Ezra Mahlon, a noted baritone trombone player, wrote 'Independence' in 1874. He died at the age of thirty-three in Liverpool, England, in 1886. Edwin Eugene, a skillful cornet player, played with and directed many bands and orchestras in New England. In later

life, he directed high school bands in and near Keene, N.H. There, he died in 1922. His best known march is the 'National Emblem' but he published others. The Ira Sanders family lived on the Bagley farm c. 1900-1920. It had earlier been owned by Jennie's grandfather Rogers.

255 Earlier, she had had her soft palate clipped, without any anaesthetic, to improve her voice. As she told me, 'The doctor [Dustan], took a snip off its end'.

256 This may have evolved into the present Westfield State University. If it did, then it was founded in 1838 by Horace Mann to be a co-educational normal school, one which eventually admitted Blacks. In 1886-87, it was at a low point in its career. My grandmother never referred to her school as a normal school, never mentioned its boys or any Black students. She may have gone elsewhere but no other likely school has been found.

257 The test she took would have resembled that printed by Dr. Elizabeth Dow in the *Hazen Road Dispatch (2015)*, pp.53-54. I (and perhaps most readers of this book) would not pass it.

258 My grandmother never danced much, if at all, and was not sure dancing was either proper or very moral. That attitude persisted at Craftsbury Academy until well into the 1900s. My mother's school parties at the Academy (1908-1913) allowed no dancing but had lots of promenades. Her family did have a lot of popular music and song books which included dance tunes. My mother loved to dance and thought her mother something of a 'kill joy'.

259 This was the local venue for plays, concerts and lectures. It also had a livery stable. It burned in 1890.

260 In 1946, when she had to sell her home, she still had, packed away in her attic, her elaborate brown silk wedding dress with its bustle. Brown was, then, often the color of wedding dresses; white came later.

261 Dinner would have been at noon; tea meant supper which was often a light meal.

262 This is now at the Shelburne Museum in Shelburne, Vermont.

263 The first of her four children was born in 1888, the last in 1896. My grandparents struggled to make ends meet. Ira mortgaged the farm each year for seed money, and paid off the mortgage after the harvest but he still owed more to his father-in-law. The children needed more than Ira could easily provide. Their youngest child graduated from Craftsbury Academy in 1916. He did not stay at home for long and was gone by 1918. The worst years in this marriage seem to have been c, 1904-1916. After that, life became easier but little happier.

264 I have found evidence of only three trips until 1927 – to Springfield and Westfield, Massachusetts, to visit her friend Clara Reed [III:26]; the other was to Iowa to see her eldest son.

265 Howard Coffin, *Full Duty: Vermonters in the Civil War* (Woodstock, Vt., 1993), p.356.

266 Vermont's 17th Regiment was also in action there.
267 *History of the Town of Glover, Vermont* (Glover Bicentennial Committee, 1983, 3rd printing 1993, Burlington, Vt.), pp.81-82; Joan Alexander, 'Glovers Civil War Places', *Glover History* (Winter, 2007).
268 The service of the Glover men is recounted in Abby Hemenway: *The Vermont Historical Gazeteer*, III, pp.201-205. The neighboring town of Albany is said to have provided 174 men from a population only a bit larger. A figure of 117 is given in the *History of Albany*, p.27.
269 The payment figure is the one my grandmother gave me as a child. She may have confused pay with bounty money. Her father is listed in the *History of Albany* as paying $325.00, which seems about right for the substitute's bounty money. *A History of Albany*, p.27. However, a dollar a day, in addition to Army pay, seems a small enough price not to endure the misery of an enlisted men.
270 The Vermont poets of those years wrote a lot about the War and the services of the Vermont Regiments. See: *e,g., Green Mountain Poets: A Collection of Poems from the Best Talent in the Green Mountain State*, edited by A. J. Sanborn (Claremont, N.H., 1872). There were later editions of this, including an undated one published in Boston, Claremont, and White River Junction, Vermont. See also, Deborah Clifford, *More than Petticoats: Remarkable Vermont Women* (n.p., 2009). Several of them wrote verses.
271 'Sanitary Fairs', such as the one to which Mary Abby went in the summer of 1864, were popular and supported the work of the United States Sanitary Commission (1861-1866) and the Women's Central Relief Association (1861-1865). Both were private groups, formed to raise money and to gather items to be sent to Union soldiers whom some members also nursed and aided in other ways.
272 Alexander, 'Glover's Civil War Places'; some of Captain Mason's letters are held at the Vermont Historical Society in Barre. They are available on line. The Minute Book is now in the Glover Historical Society's Museum. References in this text are to that document.
273 This was a common time for the meetings of eighteenth-century clubs since it offered some moon-light for those riding back over unilluminated roads full of hazards for sleighs, buggies or those on horse-back. This was changed to the second Tuesday of the month on 26 December 1901 (p.83). After 1903, meetings were less frequent as the ranks thinned. On 10 December 1908, it was ordered that they were to occur in January, May, June, and December, and at the call of the Commander (p.118).
274 [Statement of Objectives], *National Roster of the Woman's Relief Corps...1901*, (Bradford Vt.), p.1. The WRC still exists in the form of a national memorial society.
275 Sometimes they met in a local school house as they did in March 1897 when they had a party in West Glover.

276 The first of those in now in the Old Stone House, Brownington, Vermont. In 1908, the ladies of the WRC gave each of the Comrades a small flag (p.115).
277 Those varied objects were carried at a nominal value of $25.00 in their minutes. The badges were worth 30 cents and the buttons 20 cents.
278 These seem to have been to decorate graves on Memorial Day.
279 The one belonging to Benjamin Emerson, Co. X of the 15th Vermont, will be in the Old Stone House [see p.49].
280 This would have been a print issued for the centennial celebrations of Lincoln's birth, an event commemorated by the Lincoln Penny introduced in 1909. Miscellaneous items are listed on pp.27, 34, 46, 52, 71 so on.
281 See pp.238, 241. Those show members wearing their badges and medals.
282 Minutes (pp.27, 42).
283 A much longer and more moving tribute was given to Comrade F. P. Cheney on 18 February 1897, (p.40-41). Cheney had served during the whole conflict.
284 In 1896, they sent men out to seven district schools in Glover and two in Albany (p. 30), a number which seems to have grown to twelve in 1912 (p.132-33). The latter list included a Wheelock school just as earlier ones included a school in Sheffield.
285 That may have been the usual drill but a programme exists for 1896 which is a bit different:
'9 School visits in Glover, South Albany, Albany, Sheffield
Sunday Service 1–3 [Sunday, 24 May]
Veterans meet in the Cemetery at 10:00 AM, Memorial Day [25 May]
Retreat Service in Cemetery at Glover 10-30 AM
[Dinner, either at the Glover Church or the Union House]
Memorial Day "Oration at 1-30 PM"'
Refreshments at the Union House cost more than the music for that occasion (pp.31-33).
286 The GAR commemorated the fiftieth anniversary of the Battle of Gettysburg (1913) with veterans from the South but this did not much reconcile some of the old soldiers in the Northeast Kingdom.
287 A list of the the Glover Campfires is given in Appendix 2; most of featured an outside speaker. See also, Luther B Harris, *A Prison Story: A Vermont Soldier's Memoir of Andersonville and other Rebel Camps*, edited by Denise Brown and Virginia Downs (Vermont Civil War Enterprises and Lyndon Historical Society, 2006).
288 In 1913, dues for associates were remitted, probably in an effort to attract more of them.
289 Margaret Hazen Muller, 'The Strange Tale of George Washington Henderson, '77,' *The University of Vermont Alumni Magazine* (April, 1968), pp.3-7 [a later version appears in the *Hazen Road Dispatch* (1975-2015), pp.142-145; 'Henderson, George Washington (c. 1850-1936)', BlackPast.org .

290 Her account of Mr. Kelly appeared in a somewhat edited version in *Green Mountain Whittlins*, 40 (1989), pp.37-39.
291 Her brother Leslie added several to this list and included the name of _?_Williams, who was imprisoned at Andersonville, but who probably did not live in Albany when he enlisted or was drafted. The names of all the veterans are now on the Town War Memorial – including that of Cornelius Rogers who hired a substitute.
292 Gettysburg had the largest number of casualties over three days but the bloodiest one day battle was Antietam.
293 Dr. John M. Blake was a Barton MD who fitted eyeglasses and practiced there into the 1940s. He was a golfer, a painter of domestic scenes, in oils and watercolors, which sometimes included his wife's "unmentionables". In his youth, he had been a gay blade. Jennie, his wife, was a woman who always gave me a cookie when I mowed their lawn.
294 Kenneth E. McIntyre, 'Tales of an East Hardwick Boyhood', *The Hazen Road Dispatch 1975-2015*, pp.87-89.
295 Those courses are described in pamphlets issued by the Academy in 1910 and 1914.
296 Save for the Latin and a second modern language, that was my curriculum at the Clark School for Boys in Hanover, N.H., 1948-1952. I read more than eight books a year during those years.
297 Several were from Tufts University, which had been founded by Universalists. This sect had many members in Hardwick.
298 I believe this was a temperance society.
299 Part of the farm belonged to Frank's sister, Alice.
300 Dan Swainbank, *Mr Vail is in Town: Theodore N. Vail, and His Lyndon Legacy* (Lyndon Historical Society, Lyndon , Vt., 2010), pp. 78-80, 76 .
301 Harriet Fletcher Fisher, *Lyndon Institute* (Arcadia, Charleston, S.C. , 2000), pp.33-42. This has a picture of his dormitory and shows other Vail School buildings.
302 Swainbank, *Mr. Vail*, p.78.
303 While I do not know his grade, I have the textbook they used: J. Brownlee Davidson, *Agricultural Engineering: A Textbook for Students ... and the General Reader* (Webb Publishing Co, St. Paul, Minn., 1913). This is a basic guide to the construction, functioning and repair of farm machinery, including gasoline and steam engines. It concluded with sections on buildings, ventilation, and sanitation, ending with a bit on knots and the use of ropes.
304 Among his papers is a list of the deportment grades of his classmates.
305 He got a new camera in 1916 and took pictures of boys in the rooms.
306 That was not true of some, like his Aunt Alice Emerson, who knew from her devotional books and hymns what Congregationalists ought to believe. She owned some of the Pilgrim Series books issued by the Congregational Publishing Society of Boston, e. g., *A Hand-Book on the International Lessons for 1882 with Questions*.

307 Those were probably available in his dormitory's reading room, which would also have had papers with more than local news; see Fisher, *Lyndon Institute*, pp.32, 43. Craftsbury Academy in 1899-1900 stocked its reading room with '*The Burlington Free Press, St Johnsbury Caledonian, Vermont Messenger, Century, St Nicholas, Harper's Magazine, Harper's Weekly, Harper's Round Table, Cosmopolitan, McClure's, Youth's Companion, The Outlook, Literary Digest, Ladies' Home Journal, Our Times, Independent* and five teachers' magazines'. *Souvenir Booklet of Craftsbury Academy* (Craftsbury, 1960-1961), p.11.
308 Pickles take away the sweet taste so one can then zestfully eat more sugar.
309 Taft, on his arrival in Lyndonville, had been greeted by the Lyndonville Military Band; a large crowd cheered him through flag-draped streets.
310 This speech was nicely printed on heavy stock, signed by Mr. Vail, and given to each graduate.
311 Arthur's 1916 diary noted their bull had gotten loose and had a fight with a neighbor's bull. Both were pursuing a buck, not a good sign for cattle breeders.
312 Bloat is caused by ill-digested forage which produces gas and prevents the cow from grazing. In severe cases, a hole is made to relieve it with a trochar or cow punch.
313 Jared Van Wagenen (1871-1960) wrote on agricultural topics, a biography of 'Johnny Appleseed', and homey books of reminiscence. George J. Fisher, M.D. (1871-1960) was a noted physical fitness expert and a promoter of volley ball, Scouting, and the vigorous life. Franklin Matthews seems to be unknown to Google.
314 The group, which 'Shorty' had joined earlier, was probably a temperance group.
315 His walk was a pretty complete tour of the Dartmouth College campus and would have involved walking about five or six miles – from the Norwich station to Hanover, sight-seeing and then walking back. Not bad for someone not feeling well.
316 He pitched for the Barton Town Team until sometime in the 1930s; Lee, his brother, was the catcher.
317 This picture is reproduced in *Celebrating Vermont: Myths and Realities*, edited by Nancy Price Graff (Middlebury College, 1991), p.193.
318 Orleans County produced more milk than any other Vermont county. See Darlene Young, *A History of Barton, Vermont*, pp.9-15.
319 Those events drew as many as 500 farmers; *See* Young, *Barton*, p.17.
320 Eva made my birthday cakes and decorated an early one with a little merry-go-round. She was a nice old lady who 'lived in sin' with her man – who amazed me by how accurately, and far, he could spit his tobacco juice. Mr Mossman had owned a grist mill and one of the first car dealerships in Barton.

321 I have been unable to find an obituary for him. One will soon be available when *The Orleans County Monitor* is fully digitized.
322 His sisters gave me his wallet in 1980 but few other personal items were ever given.
323 Elsewhere in the region, there are small specialized farms making cheese, raising sheep and alpacas, or pursuing other types of activities, often subsidized by off-farm work. Some see this as the future; I am not so sure.
324 *See* Catherine Perry Wilkinson, 'A Brief History of Medicine in the Greensboro Area', *The Hazen Road Dispatch* (Greensboro, 2015), pp.44-46.
325 That Reformed Church recently went bankrupt. The church building, designed by Philip Johnson, is the largest glass structure in the world, one seating over 2,700 worshipers. It is now owned by the Roman Catholic Diocese of Orange County, California.

Indices

Selected Names

Annis, Carrie, mill-worker and hop-picker, 180, 181, 195, 367 *ns.191 and 193*, 436 *n.218*.

Bagley, Ezra, G. D., and Mahlon, musicians, xi, 9, 62, 372 *n.254*.
Baxter, Eva, paramour of Orange Mossman, 313.
Bedell, Orpha, fiancée of Bradbury Watson, 152, 162.
Beede, Jack, Nathan, and William, Albany cattle dealers, 23, 124, 210, 351 *n.15*.
Bemis, A., Vermont State functionary, 136.
Bill, Dyer, Albany physician, 335, 355 *n.57*.
Blake, John M., Barton, MD, 252, 376 *n.293*.
Brewer, Mary, friend of Mary Abby Tenney Rogers, 195.
Burke, __?__, physician in West Burke, 165.
Burns, Robert, poet, 41.

Campbell, Flora, wife of Ira Watson, 155.
Carpenter, __?__ , physician in Burke, 140.
Carr, Rosa Emerson, wife of Frank Emerson, 52, 355 *n.47*.
Carson [Casron], Mrs. M., wool dealer, 115.
Coburn, Mary, woolen worker, 116, 117.
Cowdery, Alice, milliner, 195.
Cowles, Roscoe, Albany storekeeper and undertaker, 218.

Dale, Mercie, mother-in-law of William Hayden I, 5, 18, 19.
Dale, Silence, wife of William Hayden I, 5, 18.
Darling, Alden H., Albany farmer and mill owner, 8, 77, 87, 198, 221.
Darling, Delia, later wife of Alden Honey, 175, 176, 177, 217, 367 *n.186*, 368 *n.202*.
Darling, Elizabeth (Lizzie) Rogers, first wife of Cornelius Rogers, 62, 63, 64, 179, 198, 221, 222.
Darling, Elmer, gentleman farmer in Burke, 274.
Darling, Henry, brother of Delia Darling Honey, 217, 218, 219.
Darling, Norris, saw mill owner in Albany, 123.
Debs, Eugene, Socialist, 165.
Dike [Dyke], George and Mondana, 183, 188.
Dike, Nelson, 187, 188.
Dillingham, __?__, physician in Albany, 217, 219.
Dustan, William, MD., 217, 219, 226, 373 *n.259*.
Dustin, [Duston, Dustan], Hannah, *see* Emerson.
Dustin, Thomas, husband of Hannah Emerson Dustin, 35.
Easterbrooks, Abby, wife of Henry, 143
Easterbrooks, Henry, uncle of Leonard Watson, 139, 140, 143, 147, 148, 149, 150.
Emerson, Albert, brother of Alice, 37, 49, 50, 51.
Emerson, Alice, daughter of B. F. Emerson, 49, 50, 51, 169, 279, 296, 300, 303, 304, 310, 376 *n.306*.
Emerson, Amos, colonial soldier, 37.
Emerson, Arthur, second son of Frank and Rosa, xxiii, 52, 102, 254-328 *passim*.

Emerson, Benjamin F., father of Albert, Alice, and Frank, 37-49 *passim*, 51, 71, 76, 100, 290.
Emerson, Dorcas Ball, wife to Lee Emerson, 304.
Emerson, Doris, see Sanders.
Emerson, Dorothy, younger daughter of Frank and Rosa, 52, 284, 355 *n.54*.
Emerson, Elizabeth, hanged 1698, 37.
Emerson, Flora, daughter of Frank and Rosa, xxiii, 34, 35, 37, 52, 384, 300, 303.
Emerson, Hannah Dustin, heroine, 35, 36.
Emerson, Jonathan I, 37.
Emerson, Jonathan II, father of Benjamin, 37, 38, 355 *n.47*.
Emerson, Karl, eldest son of Frank and Rosa, xxiii, 52, 247, 264, 279, 283, 284, 295-98, *passim*, 300, 303.
Emerson, Lee, youngest son of Frank and Rosa, 52, 102, 254, 284, 290, 296, 298, 299, 300, 304, 323, 328, 377 *n.316*.
Emerson, Michael, father of Hannah and Elizabeth, 34, 35, 37.
Emerson, Rosa Carr, see Carr.
Emerson, Russell, third son of Frank and Rosa Carr, 52, 304, 324.
Emerson, Captain Timothy, 37.

Farr, William, 229.
Ferguson, Adam, philosopher, 41.
Fisher, George, MD, lecturer, 298, 377 *n.313*.
French, Lyndon, Craftsbury merchant, 121.
Frost, Robert, poet, 49.

Gates, Hazel ['Spikey'], girlfriend of Arthur Emerson, 284, 286.
Gearhart, G.A., lecturer, 364.
Goldsmith, Oliver, author, 41, 203, 208, 256, 345,

Grant, President Ulysses S., 177, 242, 371 *n.240*.
Gutherie, Flora, girlfriend of Robbie Sanders, 216, 217.

Hanson, Michael and William, Barton cattle dealers, 310, 323.
Harriman, Lottie Rogers, daughter of Jesse Rogers, xxii, xxviii, 3-27 *passim*, 200, 349 *ns.8 and 10*, 350 *ns.13 and 15*, 351 *n.19*.
Harriman, Neil, Lottie's son, 27.
Harrison, President Benjamin, 161, 211.
Hastings, Dr. F. R., Barton physician, 251.
Hayden, Ajubah, wife of William II, 20, 22, 23.
Hayden, Armenia [Mamie], daughter of William Henry and Ajubah, 18, 23, 24, 26.
Hayden, Mary, daughter of William II, 22.
Hayden, William Andrew, son of William Henry and Ajubah, 22.
Hayden, William I, 5, 6, 14, 15, 18, 19, 20, 24.
Hayden, William, II, 6, 14, 20, 22, 25.
Hayden, William Henry, son of William II, 22, 23, 24, 26, 352 *n.29*.
Henderson, Rev. George Washington, Headmaster, Craftsbury Academy, 247.
Hume, David, man of letters, 97, 98, 355 *n.48*, 358 *n.80*.
Hutchinson, Rev. __?__, 323.

Kellogg, Rev. Elias [or Elice], 121, 132, 133, 332.
Kelly, John, Albany, GAR Adjutant, 248-250.
Kimball, Mason or R. M., Barton merchants, 71.

Lee, Gen. Robert E., 102, 182, 367 *n.192*.

Lincoln, President Abraham, 165, 173, 182, 213, 242, 282.
Lutterloh, Col. Henry Emanuel, Albany grantee, 1.

McLellan, John, friend of Robbie Rogers, 219.
McGuire [or MaGuire], Dennis and Patrick, bankers and telephone men, 102, 225, 234, 248, 357 *n.75*.

Mason, Captain John Glover hero, 239, 252.
Mathews, Franklin, lecturer, 298.
Mead, Edward A., lecturer, 298.
Morrill, Lyman, friend of Arthur Emerson, 278, 282, 322.
Morse, Jedidiah, geographer, 207, 208.
Mossman, Orange, Barton mill and garage owner, 313.

Ney, E. H., Glover, GAR member, 246.
Nottage, Carrie, Newell, and Tom, Boston friends of Mary Abby Tenney Rogers, 177, 178.

Page, Anne, third wife of Jabez Page, 128.
Page, Betsy, daughter of Jabez, 129.
Page, Chester, son of Jabez, 121, 123, 127, 237.
Page, Ebenezer, father of Jabez, 115.
Page, Israel, uncle of Jabez, 115, 116.
Page, Jabez, woolman and farmer, 114-34, 135, 351 *ns.17 and 22*.
Page, John, son of Jabez, 132, 133.
Page, Louisa, daughter of Jabez and wife of Lyman Tenney, 117, 129, 131, 166.
Page, Lucy Perkins, 1st wife of Jabez, 117.
Page, Lucyann, factory worker and daughter of Jabez, 114, 117, 129, 130, 131.

Page, Orphenia, Livingston, second wife of Jabez Page, 124, 127, 130, 133.
Perkins, Ezra, 'Uncle' to Lucy Page, 117, 122, 123.
Perkins, Mr. and Mrs. and their son, factory workers, 123, 130.
Pine, John, permissive father of Mary Pine, 172, 180, 183, 187, 189.
Pine, Mary, friend of Mary Abby Tenney Rogers, 182-190 *passim*.
Phillips, Frank and Harry, Glover poets, 252, 344.

Reed, Clara, friend of Jennie Rogers Sanders, 227, 229, 373 *n.264*.
Reed, Dorothy, 'contortionist', 317.
Reynolds, Mike, Barton 'morphadite', 311-12.
Robbins, Fred, hired man, 226, 228, 229.
Robinson, Amos, Barton merchant, 69, 71.
Robinson, Horatio Nelson, mathematics educator, 191, 192, 204.
Rogers, Andrew T., son of Cornelius and Mary Abby Rogers, 72, 179, 201.
Rogers, Cornelius, Albany farmer, 26, 62, 63, 66-69, 72, 75-77, 80, 84, 86, 124, 148, 179, 198, 200, 201, 209-14 *passim*, 216, 218-22 *passim*, 225, 237, 349n.8, 356 *n.66*, 371 *n.240*.
Rogers, James, son of Jesse I, 121, 122.
Rogers, Jennie Lena, wife of Ira Sanders, xxviii, 15, 25, 66, 76, 80, 87, 199, 200-08 *passim*, 212, 213, 219-35 *passim*, 352 *n.30*, 370 *n.228*.
Rogers, Jesse I, 2, 5, 6, 19, 53, 86, 207, 347 *n.8*, 356 *n.58*.
Rogers, Jesse II, 14, 15, 20, 54, 55, 61, 62, 350 *n.11*, 351 *n.15*, 356 *n.58*, 357 *n.69*.
Rogers, Jesse III, 210, 215-220.

Rogers, Mary Abby Tenney, daughter of Lyman and Louisa Page Tenney, xxi-xxii, 62, 63, 66, 69, 75, 84-86, 117, 166-79 *passim*, 180-196 *passim*, 200-201, 213, 214, 217-19, 222, 223, 225, 229, 351 *n.15*, 366 *n.177*.
Rogers, Major Robert, (d. 1795), 1, 2.
Rogers, Robert (d. 1808), 349 *n.8*.
Rogers, Robert ('Robbie', d. 1896), storekeeper, 66, 198-220.
Rogers, Sally Wylie, wife of Jesse I, 15, 18, 19.
Rogers, Sally, teacher, 124.
Roosevelt, President Theodore, 165, 289.
Rowell, Eliphalet, 122.
Rowell, Enoch, 100, 122.
Russell, John, grandfather of Margaret, 41.
Russell, Margaret, mother of Benjamin Emerson, 37, 40, 41.

Sample, Paul, artist, 301, 303.
Sanders, Amanda Sawyer [Courtemanche?], wife of Isaac Levingston Sanders, 29, 31, 32, 33, 222, 223, 230.
Sanders, Doris Emerson, wife of Arthur Emerson, xxii, xxiii, 77, 235, 248-50, 304, 310, 311, 313, 320, 323, 324, 336.
Sanders, Eldon, son of Robert Sanders, xxvii, 2, 349ns.8, 9, and 10.
Sanders, Elwood, 1st son of Ira and Jennie, 75, 235.
Sanders, Elzada, sister of Ira, 29, 135, 307.
Sanders, Ira, son of Isaac and Amanda, 9, 21, 29, 216, 218, 221-35 *passim*, 373 ns. *254 and 263*.
Sanders, Isaac Levingston, husband of Amanda, 8, 29, 128, 221, 222, 223, 356 *n.66*.
Sanders, Leslie, second son of Ira and Jennie, xxii, 235.

Sanders, Lottie, sister of Ira, 29, 98.
Sanders, Robert, 3rd son of Ira and Jennie, 220, 235.
Sargent, A. B., musician, 213, 225.
Sargent, William A., band leader, composer and symphony founder, 223, 225, 248.
Simpson, Jean, 'Laird', 26, 27, 331.
Smith, Peggie ['Dimples'], girlfriend of Arthur Emerson, 284, 286, 296, 301.
Stoughton, Brig. Gen. Edwin W., 43.
Stuart, Gen. J. E. B., Confederate Cavalry commander, 47.
Swan, Timothy, father of Elizabeth Emerson's bastard child, 37.

Taft, President William H., 165, 242, 289.
Tenney, Lyman P., father of Mary Abby, 7, 117, 131, 166, 169, 222, 366 *n.179*.
Tenney, Fred, brother of Mary Abby, 366 *n.176*.
Tenney, Julia, daughter of Lyman P., 166, 174, 182, 190, 229, 231.
Tenney, Mary Abby, *see* Mary Rogers.
Tilton, Louis, Farm Relief and Rehabilitation Administrator, 311, 313, 322.
Twilight, Alexander, Headmaster, Brownington Academy, 247.

Vail, Theodore, founder of the Vail Agricultural School, 264, 273, 274, 289.
Van Wagenen, Jared, lecturer, 298.

Washington, George, 2, 208, 242.
Watson, Bradbury, eldest son of Leonard and Sophia Watson, 137, 150, 152-154, 162.
Watson, Eber, middle son of Leonard and Sophia, 135, 137, 152, 155, 164, 165, 361 *n.124*, 368 *n.199*.

Watson, Ira, youngest son of Leonard and Sophia, 137, 150, 152, 155, 163, 164.
Watson, Leonard, Sutton farmer, xvi, xxiii, 86, 135-65 *passim*, 196.
Watson, Sophia Hunt (or 'Fi'), wife of Leonard Watson, 135-37, 143, 149, 150, 152, 156-59 *passim*, 161-65 *passim*, 362 *n.129*.
Webber, Emma, teacher, 190-194.
Wheeler, Ruby, girlfriend of Arthur Emerson, 281, 284, 286, 299, 301, 303.
Wilson, James, Secretary of Agriculture, 289.
Wilson, President Woodrow, 165, 289.

Selected Subjects [All towns are listed under Towns]

Academies enrolling Northeast Kingdom students, 101, 261-62;
  Albany, 128, 169, 170, 173, 181, 193;
  Barton, 52, 284, 286;
  Brownington, 161, 167, 247;
  Caledonia County Grammar School, *see* Peacham Academy
  Coventry, 101, 173, 182, 190, 191, 367 *n.190*;
  Craftsbury, 4, 9, 192, 203, 204, 207-08, 247, 366 *n.175*, 373 *n.258* 377 *n.307*;
  Danville [Phillips], 39, 40;
  Fairfax, 189, 190;
  Hardwick, 255, 256, 262;
  Johnson Academy and Normal School, 166, 174, 190-92;
  Lyndon Institute, 152, 155, 156, 264, 273, 281-283, 286, 287, 289, 377 *n.307*;
  Montpelier Seminary, 178;
  Newport Institute, 173;
  Peacham Academy, 101, 359 *n.91*;
  St Johnsbury, 190;
  Westfield, Mass., 208, 227;
  Williston, 190.
Automobiles, 21, 68, 86, 105, 313, 320-21.

Bands, see Music.
Banks, 16, 69, 123, 128, 152, 210, 211, 219, 246, 329, 334.
Benevolent Organizations, *see* Societies, 237, 337.
Blacks, 105, 236, 247, 254, 311, 333, 364 *n.158*, 373 *n.256*.
Books owned by the Rogers Family to c.1920, 345-47.
Boston, the regional hub [see also the bibliography for books published there], 37, 55, 65, 69, 77, 104, 135, 136, 143, 152, 162, 164, 177-78, 179, 196, 203, 209, 225, 307, 328, 337, 351 *n.15*, 363 *n.147*.

Campmeetings, see Churches.
Cattle,
  Breeds raised, 22, 24, 26, 209, 274, 363 *n.140*;
Cattle trade, 2, 14, 22, 24, 26, 30, 55, 123, 124, 136, 149, 208, 210, 226, 237.
Churches, 98, 99, 156, 167, 170, 171, 187, 212, 243, 278, 331-33, 338;
  Baptists, 35, 98, 99, 155, 157, 171, 174, 182, 195, 196, 212, 278, 332, 333, 363 *n.151*, 365 *ns.163 and 165*;
  Congregational, 25, 49, 86, 98, 99, 118, 132, 157, 169, 170, 171, 174, 178, 212, 222, 223, 249, 278, 279, 297-99, 322, 332, 333, 376 *n.306*;
  Methodists, 31, 32, 98, 99, 157, 158, 171, 174, 178, 212, 223, 231, 249, 331, 332, 333, 364 *n.158*;
  Presbyterians, 1, 12, 39, 98, 99, 159, 332, 363 *n.151*;
  Roman Catholic, 31, 34, 98, 99, 100, 102, 171, 212, 278, 328, 332-34, 365 *n.166*;

Unitarian and Universalists, 332, 376 *n.297*;
   Others, 98, 99, 132, 178.

Evangelical efforts, 132, 279, 332;
   Campmeetings, 151, 152, 157, 158, 196.
Concerts, *see* Music.
Counties,
   Caledonia, xxiv, xxv, 39, 98, 101, 135, 139, 157, 337;
   Essex, xxiv;
   Orleans, xxiv, xxv, 101, 125, 337, 377 *n.318*.
Crime, 137, 159, 298, 331, 333.

The 'Dale Curse' on the Hayden Family, see Hayden Family and Lottie Rogers Harriman, 15.
Dancing, 26, 137, 140, 150, 156, 173-174, 181, 184, 189, 190, 196, 213, 215, 218, 224, 228, 241, 281, 282, 283, 285, 286, 287, 303, 357 *n.75*, 373 *n.258*.
Diseases, illnesses, and related topics, 22, 25, 31, 47, 52, 126, 130, 150, 160, 174, 180, 183, 217-18, 236, 239, 293, 306, 335, 366 *n.181*.
Donation Suppers, 25, 158, 159, 171, 182, 187, 195, 212, 367 *n.183*.

Education (see also Academies; Universities, Colleges and Institutes), 334, 335.
   Primary Schools, 128, 156, 166, 202, 212, 255, 259-260, 349 *n.3*;
      Curriculum, 101, 167-169, 202-07, 258-60;
   Grammar Schools (**see** Academies), 164, 170, 181, 188, 207-08, 255-63 *passim*;
      Curriculum, 39, 41-2, 66, 167; 255-263 *passim*;
   Other schools, 171, 333, 350 *n.10*.
   Teacher Training and Normal Schools, 155, 166, 174, 178, 190-93.

Texts books, 192-93, 202-07, 255-56, 345-47;
Expenses, 124, 228, 256.
Graduations, see Entertainments.

Entertainments,
   Ball Games, *see* Games;
   Campfires, *see* Grand Army of the Republic;
   Circuses, 137, 156, 182, 214;
   Concerts, see Music;
   Dances, see Dancing;
   Graduation Exercises, 156, 159, 164, 181, 255, 275, 287, 288;
   Lectures, 156, 171, 175, 181, 196, 213, 278, 298, 336, 364 *n.158*;
   Minstrel Shows, 177, 223, 300, 336, 357 *n.72*;
   Plays, Tableaux, and Skits, 41, 156, 171, 213, 256, 279, 281, 299.

Fairs, 86, 137, 156, 159, 196, 237, 355 *n.48*.
Families,
   Bosworth Family, Albany (George and Mary), xxiii, 3, 15, 121, 134, 351 *n.15*.
   Courtemanche Family, 29, 353 *n.34*;
   Emerson Family (c.1650-1914), 34-51;
   Hayden Family, xxiii, 2-26 *passim*, 55-56, 247, 329;
   Rogers Family, xxiii, 1-7, 14-15, 18-19, 53-55, 61-68, 75-80, 86-88, 200, 232, 349 *n.8*, 350 *n.15*;
   Wylie Family, 349 *n.10*.
Farmers Organizations,
   Barton's Farmers' Day, 312, 314-319;
   Cooperatives, 313, 328;
   The Farm Bureau, 303, 320;
   The Grange (National Grange of the Patrons of Husbandry), 156, 252, 297, 300, 303, 336, 363 *n.153*.
Farming,
   Early 19th Century, 53-55;
   Mid-19th Century, 55, 138-149;

Sheep Farming, 104, 117, 128;
  c. 1915-1940, 290-295, 300-03, 328.
'Foreigners' in Vermont, 365 *n.166*;
  The French, 31, 102, 171, 187, 188, 223, 333, 334, 337;
  The Irish, 102, 171, 333, 334;
  The Italians, 263, 267, 297, 333;
  Others, xxiv, 311, 333.
Freemasonry, 219, 279, 286, 300, 301, 312, 320, 322, 323, 336.

Games, 50, 76, 78, 80, 181, 207, 209, 255, 283, 284, 301, 311;
  Baseball, 104, 196, 213, 215, 275-276, 283, 287, 337, 357 *n.74*;
  Basketball, 263, 300;
  Football, track and field, skiing, 275-76.
Grand Army of the Republic, 43, 47, 48, 236-47 *passim*;
  Campfires, 26, 213, 225, 237, 244, 246;
  Women's Relief Corps, 239, 241, 242, 244, 245, 246, 249.

Hayden House, 20, 21, 26, 55-56.
Hazen Road, 5, 6, 14.
Holidays, 140, 166, 363 *n.151*;
  New Year's Day, 171, 189;
  Lincoln and Washington's birthdays, 213;
  Easter, 212, 365 *n.163*;
  Arbor Day, 213;
  Memorial Day, 81, 213, 219, 238, 239, 241-44 *passim*, 251, 286;
  Fourth of July, 150, 189, 213, 337;
  Bennington Battle Day, 160-61;
  Thanksgiving, 63, 71, 146-47, 150, 155, 171, 175, 181, 195, 231, 284;
  Christmas, 70, 71, 72, 140, 150, 155, 158, 174, 181, 182, 189, 212, 226, 254, 255, 284, 310, 336, 365 *n.167*
Horses,
  Races and 'trots', 137, 140, 150, 156, 182, 190, 214, 218, 221, 279;
  Shows, 156, 196, 274.

'Kake Walk', *see* University of Vermont.
Ku Klux Klan, xxv, 89, 223, 225.

Jewellery, 86, 87.

Lakes,
  Caspian (Greensboro), 311;
  Crystal (Barton) 56, 356 *n.65*;
  Memphremagog (Newport), 30, 163;
  Willoughby (Westmore), 49, 149, 155, 164, 255, 295, 296, 301, 303, 323.
Lawyers in Orleans County, 16, 28, 60, 116, 131, 166, 222, 323, 360 *n.113*.
Lectures, *see* Entertainments.

Mills (see Water Power),
  Saw, 118, 123, 143, 156, 221, 291, 320, 324;
  Grist, 14, 122, 128, 291, 378 *n.320*;
  Fulling, xii, 7, 118, 119, 122, 123, 360 *n.110*.
Mill-towns,
  Lowell, Mass., 130, 131, 136, 161, 174, 175-78 *passim*, 195, 214;
  Pittsfield, Mass., 129, 130;
  Springfield, Mass., 81, 129, 210, 214, 307, 337.
Mount Moosilauke [Moosilaukie, Mooselaukee], 296, 297.
Movies, 86, 105, 275, 279, 287, 303, 316.
Music,
  Associations, 173;
  Bands, 81, 82, 212, 213, 223, 224, 225, 244, 248 249, 250, 286, 300, 336, 337;
  Concerts, 158, 171, 174, 175, 177, 178, 181, 196, 212, 218, 223, 226, 228, 279, 336, 357 *n.74*, 371 *n.239*;
  Instruments, 66, 81, 82, 133, 172, 173, 175, 181, 183, 212, 222, 233, 248, 288;
  Instruction, 170, 173, 183, 212, 226, 228, 232;

Sheet Music, 76, 83;
Singing Schools, 171, 173, 181, 212-213, 225, 226;
Venues, see 'Opera Houses', Meeting Halls, and Hotels.

Naming conventions and their implications, 95-105.
Newspapers, 76, 102, 123, 135, 204, 220, 221, 282.
New York City, 2, 65, 66, 81, 179, 199, 200, 202, 203, 209, 214, 221, 222, 232, 307, 350 n.15, 353 n.34.

Old Stone House (Museum of the Orleans County Historical Association), 33, 34, 42, 47, 161, 368 n.196, 370 n.223, 375 ns.276 and 279.
'Opera houses', Halls, etc., 157, 212, 214, 224, 226, 228, 229, 239, 241, 279, 281, 286, 287, 288, 300, 336, 364 n.158.

Paddock & Clark, Craftsbury merchants, 121.
Parties (see also Donation Suppers), By kinds, e.g. card parties, 171, 175, 181, 194, 213, 286, 310, 373 n.258;
Picnics, 171, 196;
Sociables', 158, 164, 212, 371 n.243;
'Socials', 196, 293, 336.
Philadelphia, 2, 200, 222.
Photography and albums, 76, 81, 84, 152, 171, 184, 187, 195-99 passim.

Railroads and their workers, 5, 20, 21, 22, 55, 56, 130, 131, 133, 137, 152, 158, 162, 211, 264, 353 n.37.
Rivers and Water Power, 2, 7, 8, 13, 16, 58, 68, 118, 119, 122, 129, 214, 271, 298, 356 n.65, 368 n.198.

Societies, clubs and benevolent organizations, see also

Freemasons, 330, 336, 337.
Scots and Scots-Irish in Vermont, 1, 3, 39, 53, 98, 135, 348 n.2, 349 ns.8 and 10, 355 n.47, 359 n.91.
Singing schools, see Music.
Spiritualism, 5, 25, 159.
Sunday Schools, 43, 101, 130, 158, 167, 168, 181, 191, 207, 209, 264, 299, 301.

Telephones, 69, 86, 89, 148, 215, 224, 234, 264, 301.
Television, 134, 333, 336, 337.
Temperance and Drink, 150, 158, 181, 196, 213, 225, 336, 377 n.314;
Drink and drunks, 2, 3, 24, 67, 115, 134, 136, 140, 146, 190, 194, 221, 225, 249, 284, 352 n.30;
Good Templars, 171, 174, 181, 190, 215, 228, 352 n.30;
Women's Christian Temperance Union, 24, 263.

Towns in Vermont's Northeast Kingdom (these entries are highly selective),
Albany (formerly Lutterloh), 1, 2, 6, 7, 8, 14, 20, 21, 29, 32, 61, 82, 86, 98, 101, 102, 103, 105, 118, 124, 128, 129, 132, 169-70, 170-74 passim, 182, 194, 195, 207, 210-17 passim, 221, 223, 225, 228, 248-50, 329, 333, 337, 356 n.66;
Barton, Barton Landing and Orleans, viii, xxii, 29, 30, 56, 57, 60, 61, 69, 81, 89, 101, 123, 135, 140, 209, 225, 226, 245, 284, 286, 290, 300, 301, 303, 307, 312, 314-19, 325, 327, 329, 336-37;
Brownington, 51, 101, 161, 247;
Burke and West Burke, 135, 137, 138, 156-57, 164, 245, 274;
Coventry, 101, 119, 128, 173, 367 n.190;
Craftsbury, 9-13, 39, 61, 98, 128, 179, 182, 191, 204, 207, 211, 247,

350 *n.10*, 366 *n.175*, 372 *n.254*, 373 *n.258*, 377 *n.307*;
Danville, 16, 39, 123, 353 *n.42*;
Derby, 101, 137;
Glover, 101, 236, 238- 253, 311;
Greensboro, 6, 39, 55, 61, 135, 245, 251, 312;
Hardwick, 51, 255-62 *passim*, 265-67, 356 *n.66*, 357 *n.75*;
Irasburg, 16, 17, 68, 118, 128, 174, 223, 230, 245, 340, 360 *n.104*;
Lowell, 29, 221;
Lyndon, 52, 81, 101, 137, 145, 151, 152, 156, 158, 264, 270-73, 278-79, 281, 282, 364 *n.158*, 377 *n.309*;
Newport, 69, 81, 101, 126, 137, 162-63, 173, 174, 182, 217, 218, 219, 225, 245;
Peacham, 39, 40, 101;
St. Johnsbury, 55, 81, 86, 101, 137, 156, 164, 214, 245, 292, 301, 335, 364 *n.158*;
Westmore, 49, 135, 162, 284, 300, 301, 327.
Toys, 72, 75-77, 201,
Travels and trips, xxiii, 2, 66, 81, 86, 162, 163, 170, 214, 215, 221, 222, 234, 307, 309-10, 320, 350 *n.15*.

Universities, Colleges, and Seminaries,
Buffalo State College, 155;
Baptist Seminary, Southern Pines, North Carolina, 155;
Dartmouth College, 299;
Montpelier Seminary, 178;
Syracuse University, 52, 300;
University of Vermont, xxiii, 51, 52, 247, 264, 300.

Vail Agricultural School, 264-90 *passim*, 295.

Wars,
Colonial Wars, 1, 35, 36, 37;
Revolutionary War, 1, 2, 5;
War of 1812, 14;
Civil War, xxv, 26, 42, 43-47, 76, 83, 84, 126, 136, 171, 181, 182, 184, 194, 196, 213, 225, 236-53 *passim*, 330, 361 *n.120*, 374 *n.270*;
Indian Wars, 330;
Wars 1898-1950s, xxiv, 58, 105, 250, 263, 297, 298, 300, 337.
Washington, D. C., 43, 52, 164, 252.
'The West', Midwest or Old Northwest, 1, 2, 5, 21, 52, 102, 104, 116, 128, 130, 132, 133, 135, 137, 214, 237, 331.
Women's Relief Corps, see Grand Army of the Republic.
Wool Trade, 2, 104, 115, 116-18, 121-23, 126, 128, 131, 147, 149, 237, 351 *n.22*.

www.ingramcontent.com/pod-product-compliance
Lightning Source LLC
Chambersburg PA
CBHW021847230426
43671CB00006B/299